the
next
stop

the
next
stop

NATURAL GAS AND INDIA'S
JOURNEY TO A
CLEAN ENERGY FUTURE

EDITED BY

VIKRAM SINGH MEHTA

HarperCollins *Publishers* India

First published in hardback in India by
HarperCollins *Publishers* in 2021
A-75, Sector 57, Noida, Uttar Pradesh 201301, India
www.harpercollins.co.in

2 4 6 8 10 9 7 5 3 1

P-ISBN: 978-93-9032-743-0
E-ISBN: 978-93-9032-744-7

Typeset in 11.5/15.2 Linden Hill at
Manipal Technologies Limited, Manipal

Printed and bound at
Thomson Press (India) Ltd

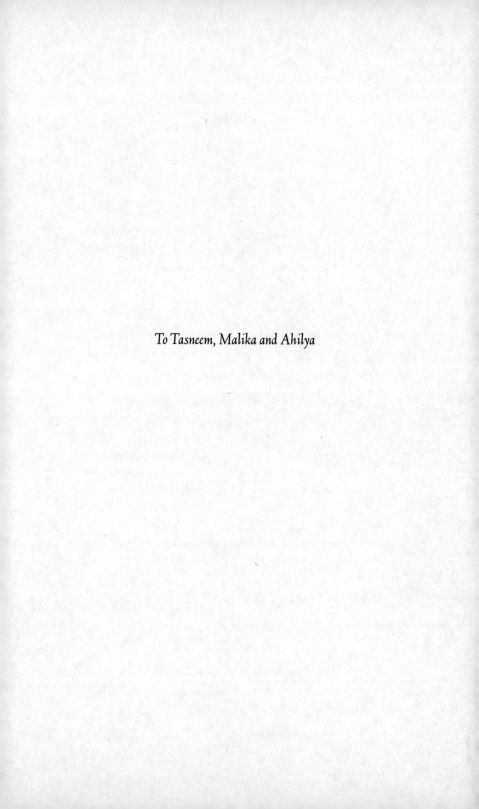

To Tasneem, Malika and Ahilya

CONTENTS

SECTION D: INDIA – THE CURRENT SETTING

FOREWORD

VIJAY KELKAR

*Chairman, India Development Foundation and Vice President, Pune
International Centre*

VIKRAM SINGH MEHTA IS ONE of India's leading, and avant-garde, thinkers on energy and environment policies as well as on governance reforms. I warmly congratulate him for bringing together this outstanding panel of experts and scholars to compile this comprehensive volume on gas and the gas sector, which spans global and national dimensions. This is indeed most timely.

I have been associated with issues related to the hydrocarbons sector since the 1980s and this association intensified in the second half of the 1990s. I have always held, and continue to believe, that natural gas has a positive and pre-eminent role to play now and in the future. The necessity of nurturing this 'peace-building' fuel in our region, and its importance for the energy security of India as well as for broader foreign policy concerns, cannot be overstated.

The contours and evolution of the sector globally, and in India, makes for a tale of two distinct 'cities'—one, where the natural gas sector has flourished and occupies a natural space as a responsible 'bridge' fuel until renewables take centre stage; and the other, where the presence of inconsistent and incomplete policy miasma and market signals have hampered the growth of the gas-based economy. India's tale is clearly the latter, wherein gas today represents a mere 6–7 per cent of total energy consumption vis-à-vis the global average of almost 25 per cent and India's own stated ambitions of 23–25 per cent. Unfortunately, there has been little groundswell to establish the primacy of the following— gas as a key fuel for the economy; the necessity to augment domestic production; and even less, the necessity to create conditions further downstream to allow the sector to blossom.

More than a decade ago, while delivering the inaugural Rajiv Gandhi Lecture at the Rajiv Gandhi Institute of Petroleum Technology, I had pointed out that a key lacuna of India's policy approach to gas emerged from a 'resource shortage' mindset. The consequent policy choices preferred to adopt administrative allocation and under-pricing, which only accentuated the shortage phenomenon, thus landing India in a perennially 'short' position. It needs to be emphasized, even more energetically if necessary, that our world is indeed blessed with an abundant supply of this 'blue gold'.

Indeed, there is a clamouring need for national debate and, more importantly, a resolution regarding the role of the greater supply gas resources in the development of the nation—its role in the economic, social and security spheres. Such a debate will set the tone for developing a more cogent hydrocarbon policy. A cogent policy will go a long way in establishing and 'aligning' and creating comfort in the different constituencies around the economic 'rent' and larger developmental benefits associated with responsible exploitation of our natural resources. I always felt that one of the key themes in the decades ahead would be to complete the transition of the energy base from non-commercial energy to commercial energy. This is a task that is still incomplete.

In India, two policy areas need the most immediate attention to encourage the efficient use of our national resources. These are the creation of a stable fiscal and contractual framework in keeping with the risk and reward paradigm, and the creation of a market-driven pricing mechanism. Attention to these two areas will ensure intergenerational equity and a fair and transparent regulatory regime supported by administrative structures that will evoke confidence among all stakeholders in the policy ecosystem.

The wonderful collection of essays presented in this book encourages me to share some reflections on how to re-energize and foment the growth of the gas sector in India.

First, we must clearly and definitively move to a production-sharing contractual system to replace the current revenue-sharing regime. This is especially urgent given the concerns around materiality and risk associated with most of India's hydrocarbon basins. This is a sine qua non if the sector is to be unfettered and upstreamed, to bring in the much-needed risk capital and expertise to efficiently and effectively explore and develop our hydrocarbon basins, especially for gas. This is the base stack of aspiring for energy security.

Second, one needs to dismantle any and all administered pricing controls on prices for domestic natural gas and bring it in line with import opportunity costs.

Third, it is critical to unbundle the transportation and marketing of the key incumbent (GAIL) in the natural gas sector, create a rules-based 'natural' transportation monopoly with an infrastructure class risk profile and allow the consumers to benefit from a liberalized marketing environment.

Fourth, it is important to ensure the viability of gas-based power through policy reform in the electricity markets through market-based pricing innovations such as 'time-of-day' pricing, non-linear pricing, etc. This will allow markets to absorb the more flexible gas-based power.

Fifth, unleash the power of gas-based micro-grids that are both efficient and responsible from the broader perspective of the climate agenda and simultaneously strengthen the decentralized systems.

Finally, I would also like to resuscitate the discussion on the creation of a sub-sea corridor that connects key gas-producing nations in the Gulf region with India, one of the largest gas markets of the future. In our region, fraught as it is with security risks, this mode will bring much-required symmetric interdependence and contribute significantly to national energy security and regional stability.

The current global context—of a supply glut in the liquefied natural gas (LNG) market and softening demand, with concomitant softening of prices and increased liquidity—against the backdrop of the accelerating juggernaut of renewables, presents a new slot for gas resurgence if provided with the right tailwinds. Given India's promises as part of the Paris Accord, providing these tailwinds is both an economic and a moral imperative.

It is in this context that this book is both timely and pivotal. Vikram Singh Mehta and all the contributors have made a seminal intervention in the debate and discourse on the making of India's policy related to gas, by bringing together a veritable compendium of the who's who of the gas sector, globally and in India. This volume puts together the encyclopaedic anthology of 'everything you wanted to know about gas but were afraid to ask'. I am sure this book will lead our policymakers to make the 'blue gold' achieve our golden goals of greater global peace and prosperity.

SECTION A

INTRODUCTION

EXECUTIVE SUMMARY AND POLICY ROAD MAP

VIKRAM SINGH MEHTA

INTRODUCTION

INDIA IS CAUGHT ON THE horns of an energy and environmental dilemma.

Its economy is driven by fossil fuels and every report on India's energy future forecasts that coal and oil will dominate the energy basket. British Petroleum's 'BP Energy Outlook: 2019 Edition'[1] avers, for instance, that fossil fuels (coal, oil and gas) will account for between 70 and 75 per cent of India's primary energy consumption in 2040. This is down from approximately 90 per cent today. Coal will remain dominant, with a 45 per cent share, and oil will trail in second place, with a 20 per cent share. The share of natural gas will stay stagnant at 7 per cent, whereas renewables will increase from the current levels of 3–4 per cent to 15 per cent.

Reports also highlight the unhealthy nexus between energy demand and the environment. Though India will meet the commitment it made at the Climate Change Summit (Paris, 2015) to reduce greenhouse gas (GHG) emissions by 35 per cent over 2005 levels, it will still be among the largest emitters of GHGs in the world. The World Bank has estimated that the cost of air pollution in 2016/17 was equivalent to 8 per cent of India's gross domestic product (GDP).

The question that has been the subject of much debate and discussion within the policy corridors of governments is: What must be done to resolve this dilemma? How can India pull itself off these horns?

Prima facie, the answer to this is simple and incontrovertible. India must reduce its dependence on fossil fuels. It must accelerate the move towards decarbonization and a clean future by investing in renewables and through demand management, the use of appropriate technology and regulation. This is, however, easier said than done. The challenges are structural, economic, and institutional.

First, the Indian economy is built around fossil fuels. It will take decades to shift it to a different and clean energy base. The United States of America (the US) took more than four decades to shift from steam power to electric power. Thomas Edison illuminated the lower half of New York's Manhattan district in 1885, but it was not until the mid-930s that all the industrial units in the US adopted this revolutionary new technology. The reason for this delay was that industrial units were not configured to use electric power. Most had to be redesigned and some had to be demolished and rebuilt.

In India, the transition to a new energy system could take even longer because, first, the existing grid infrastructure is not robust enough to absorb and manage the intermittency of electricity flows from renewables (the sun does not shine at night and the wind blows erratically). The grid infrastructure will need to be strengthened and expanded, and this will require a massive infusion of capital. Second, despite the sharp drop in the cost of generating power from solar cells and windmills, coal, the dirtiest of fuels, remains the most competitive source of energy. And finally, the institutional mechanisms for driving this shift are not in place. There are many governmental bodies engaged with energy, but they all operate within disaggregated and impermeable silos. Thus, for instance, at the level of the Central government, there are the ministries of petroleum and natural gas, coal, renewables, atomic power, and the NITI Aayog. Each of these is headed by either a member of the Union Cabinet or an official with ministerial rank. Each has a phalanx of bureaucrats and state-owned enterprises to supervise. And each operates within a well-defined framework.

The problem is that there is no formal forum for bringing them together for discussions and debate on the linkages between the different sources of energy (oil, gas, coal, renewables, hydro, and bio) and economic activities (transport, electricity, feedstock, industry and agriculture). There is no platform for bringing together the different layers of government (Centre, state, city, panchayat) to develop a collaborative approach towards energy supply, energy demand, conservation and to meet the challenge of weakening the nexus between economic growth, energy demand and environmental pollution. There are no mechanisms for facilitating partnerships between the public and private sectors, especially regarding technology and innovation, clean energy and ecological balance. There is, in short, no public policy framework within which to develop an integrated, holistic energy policy.

Many papers and articles have been written on different segments of the natural gas industry value chain. Few have, however, looked at the industry through a lens that combines these segments into an integrated whole and offers the decision-maker a seamless overview of the entirety of the gas value-chain. The purpose of this book is to fill this lacuna.

The book has twenty-four chapters, contributed by authors from diverse backgrounds. The authors address specific and separate issues of relevance to the natural gas sector, but the thread running through each chapter is the conviction that as India transits from a predominantly fossil fuel-based energy system, to one built on the pillars of decarbonization and renewables—natural gas should be the 'bridge fuel'. The authors believe that the journey towards a secure, affordable, accessible and clean-energy future will depend crucially on doubling the market share of natural gas in the energy basket and that the next stop in this journey must be this milestone. All of them, therefore, endeavour to answer the question: 'What policy steps must the government take to increase the share of natural gas in the energy consumption basket of the country?'

In editing the work of the authors, I have been guided by the objective to provide readers with a holistic picture of the natural-gas sector. I have not sought uniformity of language, nor have I edited out repetition. My approach has been to maintain the flow so as to respect the 'stand alone' completeness of each chapter and to ensure a clear connect between the analysis of the problem and the suggested solutions. My other objective has been to identify the specific incremental policy steps that must be taken to get to this next stop. It has been to provide decision makers with a clear policy road map.

EXECUTIVE SUMMARY

This Executive Summary is divided into three parts and distils the essential messages contained in each chapter. It does not do so in the order in which these chapters appear in the book, but thematically. There are three parts to this summary. The first part outlines the historical evolution of the international gas market and the developments that have shaped its contemporary contours. The second describes the growth of the Indian gas market and the reasons why natural gas has failed to secure the market-share levels achieved in other countries. And the third pulls together the recommendations contained in each chapter into a policy road map. The summary does not provide the analytical reasoning for such recommendations. Those are provided in the individual chapters.

2(A): GLOBAL CONTEXT

i) Background

The industrial revolution in the nineteenth century ushered in 'the era of coal'. The decision by Winston Churchill, as First Lord of the Admiralty (the British equivalent to the minister of state for the navy), in the early part of the twentieth century, to substitute oil for coal as the fuel for the British navy is regarded by many as the marker defining the start of the 'oil era'. The threat of global warming and the pressure to 'green' the composition of the energy basket is the reason why many have suggested that the first half of the twenty-first century, if not beyond, will be the era of natural gas.

Gurpreet Chugh has in the opening chapter of the book provided a detailed explanation of the logic underpinning this suggestion. I distil three of his messages for this summary.

One: natural gas is the cleanest of all fossil fuels. It emits a fractional amount of GHGs, viz., sulphur oxides (SOx), nitrogen oxides (NOx), carbon dioxide (CO_2) and particulate matter (PM), compared to that emitted by coal or oil. The consequential benefits of substituting combined-cycle gas plants for thermal coal-based plants are significant. Gurpreet estimates the shadow cost of the latter to be ₹13.48/kilowatt hour (kWh) compared to ₹8.22/kWh for the former.

Two: natural gas has the potential to meaningfully contribute to at least four of the seventeen Sustainable Development Goals (SDGs) of the United Nations: viz., Goal 3 'Good health and well-being for all ages' through the reduction of urban air pollution by using piped natural gas (PNG) for residential cooking and heating, and compressed natural gas (CNG) and LNG for transport; Goal 7 by providing access to affordable and clean energy; Goal 9 by helping build and promote resilient and sustainable infrastructure, industry and innovation; and Goal 13 to combat climate change by contributing to decarbonization.

Three: natural gas is 'valuably versatile' and a convenient commodity. It has multiple usages such as feedstock for chemicals, fuel for vehicles, and a source of energy for electricity generation, heating and cooking. Moreover, gas-based power plants are more efficient and flexible than thermal plants. They require less water; they cost less to build; they are easier to site (because natural gas does not require the storage space that coal does); and they are scalable. Gas-based plants (even in combined-cycle mode) can also complement and smoothen the intermittency of electricity generated from solar and wind power. Finally, as technology advances, there is the potential for additional applications such as 'trigeneration', which uses gas to cool, heat, and generate power.

The idea that the twenty-first century would be the era of gas has taken time to develop. This was because petroleum companies were initially focused on the exploration and production of oil. Their relative lack of interest in gas was understandable. Gas was difficult to store; it could not be monetized without the creation of an umbilical pipeline between the producer of gas and the final customer, which required significant upfront capital investment; it was not a convenient or commercially viable alternative fuel for the mobility sector; and it was uncompetitive against oil. For all these reasons, the gas found in 'association' with oil was often flared, and non-associated gas left in the ground. Gas did, of course, have a market, but it was a local market accessed through short-distance pipeline gas networks. This was particularly so in parts of the US, the United Kingdom (the UK), and some countries in Europe.

ii) Evolution of Natural Gas

Post-World War II and following the discovery of large natural gas deposits in Siberia in the former Soviet Union, Europe and the US, the sector moved to a faster growth trajectory. This move was supported by regulation, technology and from the 1970s onwards, the rapid rise in the price of oil.

On 1 June 1968, the Soviet company OMV signed a supply contract to pipe gas from western Siberia to Austria. This was the first international supply contract and it incorporated terms and conditions that subsequently became standard for the gas industry. The duration was sixty years (it has recently been extended by another twelve years); it obligated the Soviets to supply a predetermined quantum of gas and the Austrians to pay irrespective of whether they availed it or not—the 'take or pay' concept, which was rigid and inflexible about sourcing, timing, destination and pricing. These terms and conditions provided the backbone for securing the finance to construct the required 3,000 km-plus trans-Russian pipeline. Gas has flowed uninterrupted from the Soviet Union/Russia into Europe ever since, despite the heightened tensions of the Cold War. In fact, the market broadened beyond Austria, and in 2019, Russian gas accounted for almost 40 per cent of the total gas imports into Europe.

A further marker of growth was the discovery in 1959 of large gas reserves in the Netherlands. The onshore Groningen field was a super-giant discovery. This was supplemented a few years later from the mid-1960s onwards, by the discovery of comparably large offshore reserves in the UK and the Norwegian North Sea. Together, these discoveries altered the face of the natural gas sector in Europe. They brought gas onto the strategic agenda of international petroleum companies and spawned a web of gas pipelines across the length and breadth of Europe. They also compelled a review of the regulatory policies by different governments.

Akshaya Koshy Mason has, in her chapter, traced the evolution of regulatory policy in the US, the UK, the European Union (EU) and the Netherlands. She shows that the common thread linking the regulatory policies of these four countries was the emphasis on creating a competitive and liberalized natural gas market overseen by an independent regulator. The chapter details how, over a period of more than half-a-century, the respective authorities divested pipeline companies of their upstream (production) and downstream (marketing) interests and set them up instead as stand-alone gas transmission entities. The authorities obligated these entities to provide non-discriminatory pipeline access to third parties, on the basis of market-related principles that defined the tariffs, capacity, and terms of payment.

The outcome of these regulatory changes was multifold. It allowed producers and consumers to interact with each other at arm's length and on a transparent basis; it attracted investment into logistics and storage infrastructure; it created liquidity and competition; it led to the development of the spot market, a futures market, and a network of trading hubs; and it enabled the establishment of a single, wholesale reference gas price. Regards the latter, the US reference price is based around the Henry Hub pipeline in Erath, Louisiana. This hub serves as the official delivery location for the futures contract on the New York Mercantile Exchange (NYMEX). The UK reference price is the National Balancing Point (NBP). This is a virtual trading location for the pricing and delivery of futures contract on the Intercontinental Exchange (ICE) in Europe. The Netherlands reference price is also a virtual location for trade within the Dutch network. It is referred to as the Title Transfer Facility (TTF). Henry Hub and NBP attract the widest range of market participants (oil and gas producers, utilities, industry, LNG suppliers and financial traders) and are currently the most widely quoted and best-known benchmark prices for gas in North America and Europe respectively.

In addition to the discovery of substantive reserves of gas and the crafting of the financial and commercial terms to spur investments in pipelines and supply contracts, the development of the LNG value chain has been a major driver of the international gas market. The chain covers the production of gas; its liquefaction; its storage and shipment in specially designed cryogenic ships; and then at the destination port, its regasification. The first shipment of LNG happened in 1959. A cargo was shipped from Louisiana, US, to the Canvey Island, UK, by a converted World War II warship, the *Methane Pioneer*. This triggered the interest of the major petroleum companies and, over the years, it is these companies that have been at the forefront of LNG trade.

The LNG business is highly capital intensive. The establishment of the necessary physical assets across the value chain requires a multibillion-dollar commitment. This is over and above the costs of exploration and production. The upstream investments are typically the largest. The cost of the liquefaction plant varies considerably depending on location, capacity, site conditions and design, but it typically accounts for 50 per cent of the total investment and runs into the billions. The downstream investments account for the next largest slug of expenditure. Here too, the precise costs depend on site and capacity, but as an order-of-magnitude figure, it can be assumed that the investment required to build a 5-million-tonne regasification (regas) terminal would range between $750 and 900 billion. These investments have predominantly been borne by the major gas-consuming entities (power utilities), but petroleum companies and merchant traders have also invested. The midstream shipping costs are also not insignificant. Martin Houston has, in his chapter on LNG shipping, provided details of the various types of cryogenic tankers now on the high seas and their ownership, but for the purposes of comparison, the average cost of one such tanker would range between $175 and 200 million.

Given these large investment numbers and the fact that bankers are looking for long-term assurances, the LNG contracts have historically been set within a standard contract structure. The agreements have been bilateral between one seller and one buyer group: the tenure has been long (typically twenty-five years or more); the terms have been inflexible in that the suppliers are not permitted to sell anywhere other than to the defined buyer and the buyers are not free to source from other suppliers; the prices are indexed to a cocktail of crude oil and petroleum product prices; and both parties are governed by mutually agreed 'take or pay' rights and obligations. This structure has choked the liquidity of the LNG market; it has constrained spot trade and confined LNG trade to a narrow corridor, predominantly between the Middle East producers and the Far East consumers of Japan, South Korea and Taiwan. Some trade, albeit of a lesser quantum, has also taken place between the Middle East, Algeria and Nigeria suppliers and European customers.

iii) Recent Global Developments

In recent years, the natural gas market has undergone major changes along several different fronts. Together, these changes have propelled the rate of increase in the consumption of gas ahead of oil. Thus, whilst the global demand for oil has remained largely stagnant, that of natural gas increased by 3 per cent in 2017, 5 per cent in 2018, and 2 per cent in 2019, driven largely by China and other Asian economies including India. The International Energy Agency's (IEA) *World Energy Outlook*[2] has projected that the consumption of natural gas will grow at an average rate of 1.4 per cent through to 2040, and that it will overtake 'coal by 2030 to become the second-largest source of energy after oil'. The IEA expects the Asia-Pacific Region to account for 25 per cent of global gas consumption by 2024, rising to 28 per cent by 2040.

The most dramatic change in the sector has been driven by technology. Two technologies—hydraulic fracturing and horizontal drilling—have in combination brought about what is now commonly referred to as the 'shale revolution', by enabling the monetization of gas molecules contained within the pores of shale rock.

Prior to the shale revolution, US gas production was in secular decline. In fact, in expectation of rising gas imports, a number of regas terminals for the import of LNG had been built or were under construction. The shale revolution upended these expectations. Gas production increased at a compound annualized rate of 20 per cent from 2007 onwards and the US moved from a position of rising import dependency to the largest producer of gas in the world and an exporter. Construction of regas terminals was halted and those that had been built were converted to LNG export plants.

Covid-19 and the consequential collapse in the price of oil and gas has brought about another dramatic reversal. The drop in demand has led to a slowdown in production rates, and the combined impact of reduced production and lower prices have pushed many relatively higher-cost US shale gas producers into bankruptcy under Chapter 11 of the US Bankruptsy Code. US exports have also crashed. They were averaging

8 billion cubic feet (Bcf)/day in January 2020. But at the time of writing, they had come down to 3.1 Bcf/day. The market conditions will, no doubt, reverse again with economic recovery and increased demand, but the shale industry is not likely to show the gangbuster growth rates of past years again.

This said, like on all previous occasions when the market has gone into a cyclical downturn, the industry has responded with swingeing cost cuts and technology-driven improvements in productivity. Thus, the time taken to drill wells have been sharply reduced, the horizontal reach of each well has been extended, and the application of the fracturing fluids has become more efficient. An argument could be made that if and when the market tightens and oil prices start to rise again, shale companies will be well-positioned to leverage this change and that the current downward trend in production will be seen as no more than a turn (albeit steep) of the cycle and not as a structural shift.

Technology has also lowered the cost-related entry barriers into LNG. Three developments, in particular, are notable. The first is the development of floating liquefied natural gas (FLNG) units. These units allow for liquefaction on board ships and obviate, therefore, the high cost of establishing liquefaction plants on land. The consequential cost reduction can be measured in billions. Such units have capacity and other constraints and, as such, their development does not signal the end of liquefaction plants. What it does signal is the broadening of market participants. The second development is the redesign of the propulsion systems and the increase in the carrying capacity of cryogenic vessels. The *Methane Pioneer* delivered 5000 cubic meters (m³) of LNG in 1959. The carrying capacity of a standard LNG vessel today is 165,000–175,000 m³, and at the highest end, the Qatari owned *Q-Flex* and *Q-Max* have a capacity of 265,000 m³ each. The third notable development is the commercialization of floating regasification and storage units (FSRUs). Like with FLNGs, FSRUs enable regasification on board floating vessels. Given that the costs of an FSRU can be up to 70 per cent lower than an on-land facility, many more entities can now import LNG.

The impact of lowered entry barriers across the LNG value chain is tangibly manifest. LNG is no longer traded within a narrow corridor and under conditions of inflexibility. In 2005, thirteen countries had the capability to export LNG. Qatar dominated the market. By 2020, this number had risen to twenty. Australia had pushed Qatar into second place and the US had joined the exporter club with 70 million tonnes (Mt) of LNG export capacity (15 per cent of global LNG export capacity), and an additional 35 Mt under construction. Similarly, in the downstream, in 2005, there were fifteen countries with regasification facilities, but by 2020, the number had increased to forty-one.

This deepening and fragmentation of the LNG market has changed the nature of the LNG business and triggered major changes in LNG supply contracts. Many of the new players regard LNG as a portfolio play to either balance their energy supplies, optimize their price-driven procurement strategy, or provide a hedge against oil price volatility. These players want shorter-term contracts, flexibility regarding sourcing and destination, and prices based on market forces and gas-on-gas competition. The pricing basis for pipeline gas and LNG has as a result moved away from the conventional and familiar formulaic principles towards market logic.

Mike Fulwood and Tim Boersma (Chapter 4) estimate that 48 per cent of all pipeline and LNG pricing contracts in 2019 were market-based compared to 31 per cent in 2005. There were geographic differences. The percentage in Europe was 68 per cent, whilst in the Asia Pacific, it was only 23 per cent. The trend in both geographies was, however, towards market-based pricing. The explanation for the low numbers in the Asia Pacific is legacy. Most of the customers in this region are still locked into inflexible, long-term and oil-price-indexed contracts. Many of their contracts were signed before the market fragmented and commoditized.

The US companies have become a major driver of the changes in LNG pricing. This is because, as already noted, the US has become a major LNG exporter. At the time of writing, US LNG accounted for almost 15 per cent of the global LNG market of approximately 420 Mt and is the third-largest player after Qatar and Australia. In fact, if all the plants under construction in the US are commissioned, and if Qatar decides to hold off on its expansion plans, the US could become the leading LNG exporter in the world.

The US companies offer their customers four pricing options.

The traditional formulaic price indexed to a cocktail of crude oil and products.

The 'tolling' model wherein the buyer of LNG procures the feed gas, transports it to the liquefaction plant and pays a tolling fee for liquefaction. The buyer has an obligation to off-take the liquefied product.

The standard 'merchant/sale and purchase' where instead of the buyer procuring the feed gas as in the tolling model, the owner of the liquefaction plant procures the feed gas and liquefies it. LNG is then sold to buyers Free on Board (FOB) at a defined price. As of writing, the price being charged by companies that had adopted this model was the aggregate of a fixed fee and 115 per cent of the Henry Hub reference price. The buyer of LNG is unconstrained. They can on-sell their LNG cargo to anyone, to any location and at any price.

And finally, the 'integrated equity' model wherein investors take an equity stake in the gas field, the pipeline network, and the liquefaction plant. This is a hugely capital-intensive model but which gives investors the rights to the LNG (in proportion to their equity) at cost and the freedom to market it without constraint or condition.

Most of the LNG sold out of the US is sold against one or more of the latter three models; the oil-indexed model is hardly used.

It is important to also note the emergence of Australia as a major (in fact, at the time of writing, the leading) LNG exporter, with even greater liquefaction capacity than Qatar. What is interesting is that even as the rest of the market is moving towards market pricing and flexible contracts, 80 per cent of Australian LNG is committed to long-term, oil-indexed contracts with predominantly China and Japan. In time, Australian companies will have to move to a different model, especially if they wish to reduce the risks of dependence on just two markets.

A further manifestation of the changing structure of the natural gas market is the growth of spot trade. In 2014, 60 billion cubic metres (Bcm) of LNG was sold on the spot market. In 2019, this figure was 140 Bcm. The increase was driven in large part by the international trading companies. Wood Mackenzie, the energy consultant, has estimated that in 2018 the three top traders—Gunvor, Trafigura, and Vitol—traded 31 Mt of LNG, or 10 per cent of global LNG trade that year. This trend will continue especially as legacy contracts expire (one-third of all long-term contracts are scheduled to expire by 2024) and as more and more suppliers compete to find new offtakers. Analysts' view is that the futures market for gas will be integrated, competitive and liquid and buyers can expect to enjoy an increasing array of supply and pricing options in the coming years.

2 (B) THE INDIAN GAS MARKET

i) Backdrop

As already noted, natural gas is abundantly available in the Asia-Pacific region. It is also the greenest of fossil fuels. For a country that imports 90 per cent of its oil requirements, and that too predominantly from the geopolitically fragile Middle East, and which has seven of the ten most-polluted cities in the world (which results in millions of premature deaths due to respiratory diseases), natural gas should be the next stop in India's energy journey. There are, therefore, several questions that need to be addressed. Why has this stop not been reached so far? Why has natural gas lagged so far behind other fuels? Why does it account for such a small share in the country's energy basket? And what must be done to increase its share in this basket?

The authors of this book have all endeavoured to answer these questions. Some directly and in full; others indirectly and in part. This summary captures the essence of their explanations, arguments and recommendations. This section sketches the backdrop of the Indian gas market and the challenges and constraints that the industry has faced across the supply chain. The subsequent section provides the policy road map.

ii) Gas Supply

The production of gas has been a major constraint to the development of the Indian gas sector. According to Rajeev Kumar, who has provided a detailed picture of the production profile of domestic gas over the years, the fundamental reason for its flat, and in recent years declining, shape is because the bulk of the gas reserves are found in complex geologies and inhospitable locations. As a result, they are not only difficult to locate, but once located, also difficult to develop on a commercial basis. He does make the point, though, that the country does have sizeable reserves, drawing on the study carried out by IHS Markit for British Petroleum to substantiate this claim. According to this study, India has over 100 trillion cubic feet, or 20 billion barrels of oil equivalent, of gas reserves. But only 41 per cent of these reserves are in conventional geologic basins and accessible. The balance are in complex geologies compounded by inaccessible topography.

The government has taken several steps to attract private capital into the exploration and production of oil and gas. These are detailed in the chapter. The response, however, has not been great. Part of the reason is the still-lingering concern over contract sanctity. There have been too many unforeseen and unpredictable changes in the contract terms. Partly it is related to the administrative pricing mechanism, where the government still decides the price of gas (this is discussed in greater detail in a subsequent section). And part of it has to do with the economic and geological reality that with oil and gas prices in secular decline and the exploration budgets of petroleum companies under pressure, there is little corporate appetite for exploration in high-risk geographies like India.

iii) Pipelines, City Gas Distribution and CNG

The constraint of domestic gas production has been compounded by the inadequacy of the gas pipeline infrastructure linking production to consumption. Ashu Singhal and Rajeev Mathur from GAIL have provided a detailed picture of the evolution of India's gas infrastructure in Chapter 18.

The first interstate gas pipeline was built and commissioned by ONGC in 1987, in the aftermath of the discovery of the giant Bassein gas field in 1976, 80 km offshore Mumbai. The pipeline connected Hazira (in Gujarat) to Vijaipur (in Madhya Pradesh) to Jagdishpur (in Uttar Pradesh). It was accordingly dubbed the HVJ pipeline. Earlier, in 1984, also as a result of this discovery and in the expectation of additional discoveries, the Government of India had set up the Gas Authority of India Ltd (GAIL) as a wholly government-owned public sector enterprise. GAIL was granted monopoly jurisdiction over gas pipelines and gas marketing in 1992 and assumed operating control of the HVJ pipeline.

As of the time of writing, India has 17,000 km of gas pipelines, of which 68 per cent are operated by GAIL, 16 per cent by the Gujarat State Petroleum Company Ltd (GSPL; a Gujarat state government entity), and 11 per cent by Reliance Gas and Transportation Infrastructure (RGTIL)/Pipeline Infrastructure Limited (PIL). The latter own and operate the pipeline from Kakinada in Andhra Pradesh to Bharuch in Gujarat. An additional 15,000 km of pipelines are under various stages of implementation.

GAIL's mandate was to create a national gas grid. But so far, only parts of the southern, western and northern regions of India have been connected. The eastern, central and north-eastern regions still do not have access to natural gas. The question to be asked is: why did GAIL fail to fulfil its mandate? The authors provide four reasons.

Firstly, GAIL had no economic incentive to build pipelines. This was because of the nature of the formula defining pipeline tariffs. This formula was built around the assumption that pipelines would operate at 60–100 per cent of capacity for the first five years of operation. The tariffs were then set to deliver a 12 per cent return on equity. The problem has been because of lower-than-expected domestic production of gas, the pipelines have operated at around 45 per cent of capacity only. GAIL has, therefore, seldom realized this return.

Secondly, and to compound matters, the tariffs were subject to a 'pancaked' tax structure. This meant that the tax rates were increased incrementally as gas flowed from one tariff zone to another. The customers located in distant zones consequently paid a higher tariff than those located in closer zones. This discouraged demand and contributed further to the underutilization of pipelines.

Thirdly, the government has not deemed gas pipelines a priority public good. It has not consequently supported GAIL, as it has the National Highway Authority of India (NHAI) through viability gap funding and/or public-private partnerships and hybrid models.

Finally, bureaucracy, procedure and politics have been a constraint. To commence the laying of pipelines, GAIL has to secure rights of usage (ROU) of land and rights of access (ROA) to land, which are granted by the state governments. The approval of these rights is often delayed by cumbersome bureaucratic procedures, clashes over titles and compensation and the politics of Centre-state relations, especially when the party in power in the state is opposed to the party in power in Delhi. Some approved projects have consequently gathered dust for decades.

The constraint of pipeline infrastructure and the availability of domestic gas supplies are also the reasons for the slow pace of development of City Gas Distribution (CGD) for residential consumption, and CNG for transport. There has been a lack of investment in the creation of city pipelines and CNG retail outlets. In recent years, the government has provided a fillip by, first, allocating a high percentage of the relatively cheaper domestic gas for CGD and CNG and by strengthening the powers of the Petroleum and Natural Gas Regulatory Board (PNGRB) to issue licences for the creation and operation of CGD pipelines.

The CGD business was started by three companies in the mid-1990s: Gujarat Gas Company Ltd (GGCL), Mahanagar Gas Company Ltd (MGL) and Indraprastha Gas Limited (IGL). These companies built up between them a small niche market in Delhi, Mumbai, and a few other cities. This market has now broadened and as of March 2020, and following ten licensing rounds conducted under the supervision of the PNGRB, piped gas and CNG is available to 232 cities/districts, six million households and 3.4 million vehicles. This is commendable, but as Ashu Singhal and Rajeev Mathur have indicated in their chapter, the sector still faces several issues. Two, in particular, are noted here.

The first issue has to do with the reluctance of consumers to switch to piped gas. This is because they are not confident that gas supplies will be provided to them on a regular basis. They are also concerned that the terms of exchange might get altered to their disadvantage once they have incurred the upfront capital costs for the equipment required to shift to piped gas or CNG. They are also sceptical about the assurances given to them about the creation of the pipeline network and the CNG retail outlets. They foresee long delays given the multiple layers of approval required from the central, state and city governments.

The second issue relates to economics. The construction of a CGD pipeline network is highly capital intensive. It is estimated that to meet the demand of around 1.5 million metric standard cubic metres per day (MMscm/d), the capex required would be around ₹3.5 billion. Given the uncertainty of demand and the likelihood of cost overruns, investors are cautious. They want financial guarantees and incentives.

The government will have to address these issues to secure the larger objective of accelerating the pace of development of CGD and CNG.

iv) Regasification terminals

For years, the government had contemplated supplementing domestic gas production with imports of pipeline gas. Three international pipeline projects had been conceptualized. Gas from Iran through Pakistan into India; from Turkmenistan through Afghanistan and Pakistan into India; and from Myanmar through Bangladesh into India. Discussions were held at various levels and MOUs were even signed, but none acquired tangible shape. They all foundered on the rocks of politics, security, economics and finance. Maybe one day they will be resurrected, but in the interim, the focus has shifted to LNG. LNG imports are a supplement to domestic supplies. To support this shift, a number of regas terminals (RLNG) have been built around India's coastline.

The first RLNG facility was set up in 2004 at Dahej (Gujarat) by Petronet LNG, a joint venture promoted by GAIL, ONGC, Indian Oil Corporation Ltd (IOCL) and Bharat Petroleum Corporation Ltd (BPCL). The capacity of this facility was 5 million tonnes per annum (Mtpa). These four companies limited their shareholding to 50 per cent, so that Petronet could operate without the procedural constraints imposed on the public sector. The balance 50 per cent was farmed out to financial institutions, private sector corporations and the general public. Since then, and through a mix of investments by the public sector, Petronet and private companies, an additional 37 Mt of capacity has been added. Furthermore, at the time of writing, an additional 19 Mt of capacity is under varying stages of implementation. Prabhat Singh, has, in Chapter 19, projected that RLNG capacity will increase to 72 Mtpa by the end of this decade. He has, however, indicated that these projections will depend on resolving issues related to access to land, bureaucracy and regulation. Two issues are particularly relevant for RLNG investors.

The first issue is related to 'first-mile' (as distinct from last-mile) connectivity. The problem is the lack of clarity on who has the responsibility for constructing the pipeline that connects the RLNG terminal to the main trunk pipeline—is it the terminal owner, the state government, the main pipeline operator (i.e., GAIL) or the customer? The Kochi and Ennore terminals were delayed because of this blurring of roles and responsibilities.

The second issue relates to finance. The early investors in RLNG were integrated companies. Petronet had upstream (production) and downstream (marketing) interests through its shareholders, as did Shell India, the second investor in RLNG. Banks were ready to finance these companies because of the strength of their integrated balance sheet. The profile of the investors has now changed. An increasing number of traders and merchant terminallers are interested in investing in RLNG to create arbitrage opportunities or to offer 'open access' regas services against fixed toll fees. The Indian government has to decide whether they wish to attract investment from these opportunistic entities. If they do so wish, they will have to provide financial guarantees and other fiscal incentives. This is because banks will not lend for projects that do not have the buffer of integrated balance sheets and are subject to the vagaries of the market.

v) Gas Demand

Arguably the single biggest roadblock to the development of the gas sector in India has been the failure to harness traditional customers—power, fertilizer petrochemicals, and industry. The book analyses each of these demand segments in detail. It provides answers to the following questions: why has gas failed to penetrate these segments?; what is their potential to absorb gas?; and what steps must be taken to realize this potential? The following is a distillation of the messages contained in these chapters.

v) (a) Gas for Power

Gas is the preferred fuel for power generation worldwide. It has, however, hardly made a dent in India. It contributes 6.7 per cent (approximately 25 gigawatts [GW]) of the total electricity generation capacity (370 GW) of the country but provides only 3.5 per cent of the electricity consumed. Further, as of the time of writing, approximately 60 per cent (14 GW) of this gas-based power generating capacity is stranded, and the average plant-load factor (PLF, the utilization capacity) stands at 23 per cent.

Mohit Bhargava and Kishore Kumar Hota of the National Thermal Power Corporation (NTPC) and Rahul Tongia of the Centre for Social and Economic Progress (CSEP) provide, in Chapters 11 and 12 respectively, a comprehensive overview of the reasons for the low penetration of gas in power generation.

The most compelling reason is the lack of competitiveness. Gas-based power is not competitive against coal-based thermal power, especially when it comes to meeting the baseload demand. This is because coal is abundantly available, cheaper to extract, and the variable costs of thermal power are lower than that of gas-based power. Rahul Tongia has analysed the potential of gas for meeting peaking demand and concludes that the potential is marginal (around 3 per cent incremental demand), and that too only if the grid is upgraded and smart meters installed to enable time-of-day, wholesale procurement and time-of-day consumer pricing. The bulk of electricity is currently sold under generalized power purchase agreements (PPA) that do not differentiate between electricity users.

A further reason is the relative uncompetitiveness of RLNG. Aside from price, there are two other contributory factors. RLNG is not eligible for Goods and Services Tax (GST) credit and RLNG suppliers insist that utilities accept 'take or pay' commitments. The Discoms (the state electricity distribution companies) do not have the financial ballast to accept this condition, especially as there is no certainty of demand.

v) (b) Fertilizers, Petrochemicals, and Micro, Small and Medium Enterprises

Ashok Gulati and Pritha Bannerjee have addressed the subject of gas as a feedstock for fertilizers in Chapter 14. They see huge potential, but only if pricing is based on market principles. Currently, the fertilizer industry operates outside the market. Production (in particular, the production of urea) is subsidized and the input costs of gas are reimbursed.

At one time, the fertilizer industry received the largest allocation of subsidized domestic gas. It no longer does so. CGD is now the largest recipient of this gas. As a result, the fertilizer industry has had to resort to imports to meet the gas shortfall. This has led to a sharp rise in the weighted price of feedstock gas and the subsidy burden of the government. The weighted average price of gas in 2018/19 was, for instance, $12.3/million British Thermal Units (MMBtu), up from $9.8/MMBtu in 2015/16.

The potential for gas as a feedstock for fertilizers will depend on the government deciding whether fertilizers should be 'Made in India' or imported. Comparative economics would recommend imports, but 'Atmanirbhar Bharat' (self-reliant India) is a domestic compulsion. Until this decision has been taken, it will be difficult to determine and/or realize this potential.

The petrochemicals sector is another potentially significant market segment for gas. Here too, the potential is difficult to ascertain, in large part because it depends on the availability of 'rich' gas (i.e., gas with a relatively high percentage of ethane and propane). This is currently in short supply because India's domestic gas is 'lean' and LNG exporters generally strip off ethane and propane before shipping the gas to India. On the assumption that the composition of domestic gas will not change, the future of gas in petrochemicals will depend on the government using its negotiating heft to persuade LNG suppliers to sell a larger quantity of rich gas to India.

The micro, small and medium enterprises (MSME) sector is the third potentially important, but underdeveloped, gas market. The energy requirements of this fragmented and disorganized sector are currently met largely by coal. Rajesh Rawat of Reliance Industries Ltd (RIL), in Chapter 15, estimates the upside potential for gas under three scenarios. In a 'high switchover from coal to gas' scenario, gas demand can potentially increase from the current 8 MMscm/d to 193 MMscm/d. In the 'base switchover' scenario, the demand increases to 107 MMscm/d, and in the 'low switchover from coal to gas' scenario, in which only 10 per cent of the current consumers of solid fuels (coal, fuel, wood, etc.) convert to gas, the demand reaches 50 MMscm/d. Whether these numbers are accurate or not is less important than the essential message that there is considerable upside potential for gas among MSMEs.

v) (c) Gas for Transport

Technology has progressed to the extent that gas is now being considered a viable alternative to diesel as a transport fuel. In Chapter 16, Gautham Dasari Babu and Sarah Khoo from Shell have drawn on a study carried out by the Natural and Biogas Vehicle Association Europe, on the 'well-to-wheel' comparative environmental economics of LNG-fuelled, Euro 6 compliant, heavy-duty vehicles (HDVs) compared to diesel-fuelled vehicles. The study had concluded that the former would emit between 6 per cent and 15 per cent lower Greenhouse Gas (GHG) emissions than the latter. Based on this conclusion and further analysis related to the Indian market, the authors have indicated that the SOx and CO_2 emission levels of an LNG-fuelled Indian truck that is BS6 compliant would be three times less than that of a diesel-fuelled HDV. They have also estimated that the costs of converting a diesel-fuelled HDV to LNG would be ₹4 to ₹7.5 lakh (1 lakh = 100,000), assuming no economies of scale. They conclude that a socio-economic case for LNG-fuelled transport can be made for sectors and geographies where HDV traffic is heavy, viz., container terminals, major ports, mining areas, automobile centres, intercity buses and along major intercity corridors such as Mumbai–Delhi or Mumbai–Bengaluru.

vi) Gas Pricing and Taxation

The complex and distortionary pricing and taxation regimes for gas have arguably been the greatest impediment to increasing the share of gas in the energy basket. Anupama Sen from Oxford Institute for Energy Studies has, in Chapter 20, provided a full review of the pricing structure. Neetu Vinayek, Santosh Sonar and Hiten Sutar have done the same for taxation in Chapter 21.

Anupama writes that the gas pricing basis is 'notoriously complicated'. Thus, when exploration and production of petroleum were deemed a strategic activity, and the exclusive preserve of public sector companies (ONGC and OIL), the pricing basis was 'cost-plus'. Thereafter, when this activity was opened up to the private sector, in the late 1980s, the price of gas was indexed to the price of substitute replacement fuels. Later, in 2014, it was linked to the weighted average of four international gas prices—Henry Hub in the US, NBP in the UK, Alberta reference in Canada and the Russian domestic gas price. The choice of these four reference prices raised eyebrows because these countries were surplus in gas and exported it, whereas India was gas deficit and an importer. In 2016, there was a fourth change. This time, the government imposed a price ceiling on gas produced from deep waters under conditions of high temperature and high pressure. They calculated this ceiling as the minimum of the weighted average landed import price of fuel oil (40 per cent), naphtha (30 per cent), and coal (30 per cent), relative to the six-month lagged, landed price of LNG. Here too, the economics were not clear. The six-month lag in the formula resulted in the producers facing an irrelevantly high ceiling in the summer months, when demand for gas was low, and a disincentivizingly low ceiling in winter, when demand was at its peak. It also deterred companies from allocating resources to high risk, high-cost exploration in India.

All these changes in the basis of gas pricing were additive, in that they created a stack, one on top of the other. As a result, at the time of writing, the industry faced an array of pricing regimes. Depending on when the gas was found, the licensing regime prevailing at the time of the discovery and the conditions of the geology, the pricing basis was 'cost-plus', 'replacement value', or formulaic ceiling. There was no single nationally applicable price.

This situation will have to change for India to reach the next stop in its energy journey. The price of gas will have to be based on clear, market-related and economic principles. Else, exploration, production, investment and demand will remain choked and progress will be slow.

The taxation structure is comparably regressive. Chapter 21 explains through simple numerical examples, the nature and extent of the impact on producers, pipeline companies, consumers, and the government of the current taxation structure, including, in particular, the decision to keep gas outside the ambit of the GST.

vii) Regulatory Policy

The petroleum sector was for long deemed strategic and kept within the preserve of the public sector. It was only from the 1980s onwards that the private sector gained a foothold, first in exploration and production, then refining and, finally, LNG and retail. Liberalization necessitated shifts in the role and responsibilities of the petroleum regulator.

The early role of the regulator was to protect the interests of the owner—the government. Later, its mandate broadened to provide the producers with a level playing field; consumers a forum to secure redress against price discrimination and price gouging; and the government the assurance that operators would respect safety standards and environmental norms.

Sudha Mahalingam of the National Institute of Advanced Studies (NIAS) and former member of the PNGRB argues in Chapter 22 that the PNGRB failed to deliver on this mandate—at least during her tenure, because of the disjunction between its formal mandate and the operating reality. The board was set up to create a competitive, efficient and fair operating environment. It was accorded powers to regulate the downstream petroleum sector, unbundle GAIL, approve pipelines and set tariffs and ensure compliance with the 'common carrier' principle of third-party access to pipelines on an arm's length, transparent and non-discriminatory manner. It was assured autonomy in decision-making.

In reality, the powers of the board were heavily circumscribed because it was dependent on the Ministry of Petroleum and Natural Gas for funding and because it did not have its own cadre of employees. The ministry had leveraged this dependence to curtail the authority of the board to impose a financial or operating penalty for breach of regulatory procedure. All they allowed was for the board to signal displeasure. Furthermore, the majority of the employees of the board were on temporary, time-bound assignments from the public sector companies—the very companies that the board had been set up to regulate. It was unrealistic to expect objectivity from these employees in the discharge of their responsibilities as regulators. The board was also understaffed. It did not have the capacity or the capability to cross-check the accuracy of the information received from the companies.

Looking ahead, these issues will have to be sorted out. The need for an independent, knowledgeable, and objective regulator will grow as more players enter the business, and it becomes clear that the market cannot be trusted to self-regulate, on the one hand, and the government should not be the sole arbiter of the business, on the other. What precisely should be done is the subject of the next section, but the first step must be to remove the regulator from the orbit of the Ministry of Petroleum and Natural Gas.

3) THE POLICY ROADMAP

The above summary is a cull of the information contained in the twenty-four chapters in this book. Its purpose is to set the backdrop for the policy recommendations below. These recommendations are presented under broad subject categories. But as has been made clear, a policy change along one subject axis would be ineffective if comparable changes are not made along the other axes. The policy road map for natural gas must be seen through one composite policy lens—the recommendations below should be read and implemented as a package.

(A) RATIONALISE GAS PRICING AND THE TAXATION STRUCTURE

The pricing structure has held back investment, discouraged competition, generated inefficiencies, constrained demand and deepened the environmental imbalance. It has to be rationalized and reframed around clear, market-related principles. The current tiered and differential gas pricing structure should be replaced with a uniform price for gas, based on the principle of 'replacement value' relative to substitute fuels and feedstock and the opportunity cost of production. Subsidies, concessions or premiums should be directly provided without compromising this fundamental principle.

In this context, it should be noted that the digital trading platform, Indian Gas Exchange (ICE), set up in June 2020 in the three trading hubs of Dahej and Hazira in Gujarat, and Kakinada in Andhra Pradesh for spot and forward marketing of imported RLNG, can only be expanded to cover domestic production if the current administrative pricing mechanism is abolished. Were this to happen and were the e-bid RLNG scheme (that was introduced in 2015/16 and then discontinued) restarted, India would be in pole position to set up Asia's first trading hub for natural gas.

Natural gas must be brought into the ambit of GST at the preferential rate of 5 per cent. This will lower its cost. Further, the tax rules must be clarified. There is ambiguity, for instance, on whether pipelines laid within city limits can claim 100 per cent tax deduction on capital expenditure, as is allowed for investment in cross-country pipelines. There has also been much debate and contention on the definition of the income eligible for tax holidays. All these issues must be cleared. In FY 2018–19, natural gas contributed 3 per cent of the tax collected on oil and gas revenues. This percentage would increase substantially if, on account of tax rationalization and clarity, there was a spike in consumption.

Liquefied natural gas should not be charged customs duty and the rate on imported equipment for building regasification terminals should be reduced. The LNG-fuelled trucks that are imported for experimental and pilot purposes should be allowed into the country duty free.

(b) Remove Avoidable Disincentives for Domestic Exploration and Production

- Provide complete freedom to market gas.
- Ensure market-related pricing of gas.
- Remove the price ceiling on gas produced in high temperature/ high-pressure fields.
- Provide/ensure open and transparent access to data.
- Ensure fiscal, contractual, and regulatory stability and predictability.

(c) Leverage LNG to Diversify and Supplement Domestic Gas Supplies

India should take advantage of the liquidity and flexibility of the LNG market to develop a balanced portfolio of spot, short-, medium- and long-term LNG supply contracts. These contracts should allow for sourcing, destination and delivery (FOB or delivery ex-ship [DES]) flexibility, volume swaps, and gas-on-gas market-linked pricing. The price of LNG should not be indexed to oil.

The shipping rates of LNG are cyclical and India has often been caught at the wrong end of the cycle. Global LNG shipping companies are looking for stable, long-term commitments. Indian LNG companies should leverage this fact to secure attractive, flexible, (albeit market-related) chartering terms for LNG supplies into India.

India is currently overly dependent on the geopolitically risky Middle East—the bulk of its oil imports are from this region. Gas offers the possibility of diversifying this risk. India has strong relations with almost every non-Middle East LNG exporter. It should draw on this goodwill to negotiate long-term, but flexible, LNG deals with Australia, Canada, the US and possibly Mozambique. It must also ring fence its LNG relations with Qatar from the intra-regional disputes within the region.

Over several decades, there have been discussions about transnational, overland pipelines. The Iran–Pakistan–India pipeline, the Turkmenistan–Afghanistan–Pakistan pipeline and the Myanmar–Bangladesh–India pipeline are three such projects that have been discussed. All are on hold for geopolitical and economic reasons. In a world where politics does not trump economics, these projects might make sense. They should, therefore, remain on the policy agenda. Another project that has often been discussed is an underwater pipeline connecting the gas fields in Central Asia/Middle East, to India. This should also be on the agenda.

(D) Create Unifying Framework to Expedite Investment in RLNG Terminals

The current institutional and decision-making approach towards investment in RLNG is fragmented. There is no unifying framework. As a result, the roles and responsibilities of various stakeholders (the terminal operator, the pipeline company, state governments and the customers) have become blurred. It is not clear, for instance, who is responsible for investing in the 'first-mile' connectivity from the RLNG terminal to the pipeline; what principles should apply for third-party access to the terminal and, in particular, the tariff policy for such access; or what are the safety and environmental standards to be applied. The government should fill such lacunae and consolidate RLNG-related policies.

Such a policy should balance the interests of all stakeholders while encouraging the coordination and optimization of terminal capacity. This balance should be achieved without abridging the commercial and operational autonomy of individual 'terminallers' and/or companies. The mandate of the regulator under the PNGRB Act should be expanded to regulate the implementation of this policy. The Act should be appropriately amended.

The RLNG merchant terminals—i.e., those which operate on a stand-alone basis without any upstream (LNG supply) or downstream (consumer) commitments and are, therefore, the infrastructure bridge between the supplier and consumer—should be supported with viability gap funding. The government should also provide a buffer against initial cash losses. This is because RLNG has strategic significance and without such support, investor interest would flag. Also, banks are cautious about lending to entities that offer little or no upstream or market collateral.

The delays in acquisition and right of usage of land have been major roadblocks to the timely completion and commissioning of RLNG terminals. The reasons for these delays are many, but they all flow from the differing and/or conflicting priorities of the Central and state governments. The problem is accentuated by the fact that the landowner has no material incentive to permit companies to lay pipelines through his land. Landowners receive little or no rent and have no stake in the resources below the surface. These issues cannot be addressed through any one policy intervention. It requires a deepening of the spirit of cooperative federalism and a realignment of the incentive structures.

(E) UNBUNDLE GAIL (INDIA) LTD

GAIL's upstream (production/regasification) and downstream (petrochemicals/residential) interests should be separated from its pipeline transmission business. The upstream business should be merged into ONGC and the downstream into IOC. This will remove conflicts of interest. It will also facilitate arm's length transactions between suppliers and customers, improve operational efficiency and invigorate competition. The counterargument to this suggestion is that the unbundling should take place only after the market has matured and the existing pipelines are being fully utilized. An early and comprehensive discussion is warranted, especially as the weight of international practice and experience tilts the argument strongly in favour of unbundling. The gas markets in the US, the UK and Europe picked up appreciably after the pipeline companies had been separated from their upstream and downstream interests.

(F) ACCELERATE PIPELINE AND DISTRIBUTION INFRASTRUCTURE

GAIL has made considerable progress towards the creation of a national pipeline grid, but there are still significant gaps. These gaps exist because of a shortfall in gas supplies; the inadequacy of gas demand; the distortionary pricing and taxation structure; the low and uncertain returns on pipeline investment; and land-related and regulatory hassles between the Central and the state governments. Clearly, these issues will have to be resolved before the gaps can be filled.

As already indicated, the calculation of the tariff payable to GAIL is calculated to give it a 12 per cent return on investment. However, it seldom secures this return because the underlying assumption of 60 to 100 per cent capacity utilization is difficult to achieve. Further, tariff rates are subject to a tax structure that depresses demand. The pipeline tariffs should, therefore, be adjusted and framed around market-related principles and there should be one uniform tariff across the country. Further, the current cascading tax structure for pipelines should be replaced by a simpler entry and exit tax system.

Pipelines offer a utility rate of return. To attract private sector capital, therefore, the government will have to offer financial support and fiscal incentives. There is a precedent. The government provided viability gap funding of 40 per cent and a capital grant of $1.85 billion for the Jagdishpur–Haldia–Dhamra pipeline. It also 'created' the gas market en route the pipeline by facilitating investments in fertilizer and power plants. The government has experimented with various financing models to finance the National Highway Authority of India (NHAI) programme. A blended version of these models could be considered for financing gas pipelines. One suggestion is to make viability gap funding the competitive bid parameter with the government committing to mitigate the volume risk by paying the shortfall between the annuity payable by the investor and the revenues generated from the tariffs. The government would keep the surplus in the event the latter exceeded the former.

The CGD investors are currently granted an exclusive marketing licence for eight years. This is not sufficient to recoup their investments in infrastructure, especially from rural and semi-urban geographies, where demand is low and slow to pick up. The exclusivity period should, therefore, be extended. Furthermore, city planners should contemplate the creation of a 'utility corridor' to bring together the multiple agencies involved with utilities (water, sewage, electricity, and gas). Coordination among these agencies would expedite approvals, enable better planning, lower costs through cost-sharing, and hasten implementation. New residential constructions should mandatorily provide for PNG connections. This should be a precondition for approval.

(g) Prioritize Gas-Based Power Generation

As noted, approximately 14 GW of the currently installed 25 GW of gas-based power generation capacity is stranded for want of gas supplies and it has a low rank in the dispatchable 'merit order' (which is based on variable costs) for meeting baseload electricity demand. The variable cost of gas-based power is higher than that of thermal power based on domestic coal. To alter this ranking and stimulate gas-based power demand, the following four policy steps should be taken.

- First, the price of coal should be set to reflect the negative externalities of pollution.
- Two, the old inefficient and high-carbon thermal plants should be closed and no new coal-fired plants should be approved.
- Three, a consortium of 'Indian Power Producers' should be set up to negotiate bulk LNG supplies. Such a consortium would have the bargaining leverage to secure sourcing and destination flexibility, shorter duration contracts, less stringent 'take or pay' conditions, and commercial terms that allow individual plants to adjust for time-of-day and seasonal fluctuations in demand. Such a consortium would also be well-placed to negotiate attractive regasification 'toll rates' with RLNG merchant 'terminallers'.
- Finally, the government should experiment with trigeneration. This is a process that produces electricity, heating and cooling. Trigeneration plants are potentially very efficient. Even at a gas input price of \$8/MMBtu (the delivered price of RLNG at the time of writing), the plants could produce power at a cost of ₹3–4/kWh. This renders them competitive against thermal power plants, albeit only against those located far from the coal mines and, therefore, subject to high rail-transport costs and/or those that rely on imported coal.

Renewable energy capacity is planned to be increased to 175 GW by 2022 and 450 GW by 2030. Renewables are an intermittent source of power. Given that open-cycle gas turbines can be quickly started, ramped up and then stopped, gas-based power could be prioritized for back-up support.

(h) Harness Latent Demand (Fertilizers, Petrochemicals, MSMEs, and Transport)

The latent demand for gas as a feedstock for fertilizers will depend on the government's decision on pricing and subsidies. The authors' recommendation is that the price of gas should be based on market principles and subsidies should be provided directly to the farmer. This would make it possible to ascertain the comparative economics of 'Make in India' versus imports and establish the potential usage of gas in this sector.

The petrochemical sector could absorb up to 100 MMscm/d of gas by 2025, were the price competitive and were there no supply constraint of 'rich' gas (i.e., that is gas containing ethane/propane). As already noted, domestic gas is predominantly 'lean', and LNG suppliers generally strip out the ethane and propane before exporting to India. Therefore, the government should disallow the burning of rich gas as fuel and leverage its buying power to persuade LNG suppliers to supply a richer stream.

The bulk of the energy requirements of MSMEs are met by coal. There is growing pressure to switch to gas. The problem is affordability. Most consumers cannot afford the cost of converting to gas (viz., gas connections, gas-fired equipment and security deposits). Nor can they afford the price of gas. The government should set up a task force to study the measures that must be put in place to evaluate the financing support required to accelerate the conversion from coal to gas. The environmental implications for continuing 'as is' is not sustainable.

Gas as a fuel for transport is a nascent but potentially large business. CNG has already made niche inroads and LNG is now expanding its market share among HDVs in China and the US. The Indian government should initiate an analysis using a team that comprises members from the Central and state governments, automobile manufacturers, petroleum companies and the NHAI to study a) the experiences of the US and China with LNG transport for long-haul journeys; b) the financial support and incentives required by Indian truckers to convert to LNG; c) the cost and other issues related to the establishment of the LNG retail infrastructure; d) the competitive challenge from electric vehicles; and, finally, e) the amendments required to extend the PNGRB Act to cover LNG transport.

(I) REGULATORY AUTONOMY

The PNGRB Act confers extensive powers on the regulator but, as already noted, the regulator does not have the financial resources or the manpower to exercise these powers. The governance structure further shackles its autonomy. These problems have to be addressed. The regulator should be autonomous and financially independent; it must have the powers to plan, monitor and enforce; and it should have an arm's length relationship with the government. The autonomy of the regulator should be safeguarded under the Constitution, à la the Comptroller and Auditor General (CAG).

(J) PRICE EXTERNALITIES

The 'clean' benefits of gas must be recognized through the price mechanism and the regulatory process. In this regard, there are three policy suggestions.

- One: the current renewable power obligations (RPOs)— whereby electricity consumers are obliged to meet part of their demand from renewable energy sources—should be broadened to low-carbon purchase obligations (LCPOs). Purchasers would be given credit for shifting from high-carbon coal to lower-carbon gas.
- Two: the 'perform, achieve and trade' scheme should be broadened to the credit industry for the savings and efficiency

gains achieved by shifting to gas. Industry should be granted energy savings certificates accordingly.

- Three: the public should be educated about the social costs of carbon. This will require a two-pronged approach. The government should calculate the carbon price, based on scientific evidence of the cost of pollutants and in parallel engage in a public awareness campaign to alert the people about the unhealthy linkage between economic growth, energy demand and the environment.

(k) Holistic Decision Making

India will not reach the 'next stop' if gas policy is not seen through the prism of collaborative and integrated decision making. There is a need to establish an institutional forum that brings together the various ministries and regulators that have a direct or indirect impact on the supply and demand of gas. The most important such ministries and regulators are the Ministries of Coal, Petroleum and Natural Gas, Road Transport and Highways, Water Resources, New and Renewable Energy, and Environment, Forest, and Climate Change at the Centre; their counterpart ministries in the states; and the varied regulators (PNGRB, Central Electricity Regulatory Commission [CERC], and the State Electricity Boards [SEBs]). There are linkages between each of these entities and these need to be understood, discussed, and aligned. Demand for gas cannot be doubled if decisions continue to be made within compartmentalized and siloed structures.

NOTES

1   BP, 'BP Energy Outlook 2019.'
2.   International Energy Agency, 'World Energy Outlook 2019.'

SECTION B

WHY GAS?

1

THE 'GREEN FOSSIL'

GURPREET CHUGH

Managing Director, ICF India

A. OVERVIEW

India's Ambitious Economic Growth Targets

INDIA IS WELL ON ITS way towards building the 'New India', envisioned by Prime Minister Narendra Modi. The unprecedented steps being taken in this direction have the potential to redefine growth in India. Modi has set his sights on India becoming a $5 trillion economy in five years (2024–25). A $5 trillion economy has the potential to transform India into a global economic powerhouse, pushing it up the ladder from seventh to third position in terms of the current dollar exchange rate. To achieve this bold and ambitious target, India's GDP needs to grow faster than its current average over the last five years.

Future Energy Demand

A rapidly growing economy, increasing population and rapid urbanization, are set to raise India's energy consumption manifold. In its latest forecast for India, the International Energy Agency (IEA) has predicted, 'Based on current policies, India's energy demand could double by 2040, with electricity demand potentially tripling as a result of increased appliance ownership and cooling needs.'[1] Meeting such rapidly rising energy demand, with its already large base, is not an easy task. It requires strategic planning that is ambitious yet achievable and that keeps the climate agenda on the forefront. This requires a fundamental shift in energy generation and usage technologies.

Meeting energy demand in the context of the Sustainable Development Goals

When India signed the United Nations 2030 Agenda for Sustainable Development in 2015, it committed to the achievement of seventeen SDGs, acknowledging that more equitable and safer societies were critical to creating an inclusive and sustainable future. It was no longer enough to focus solely on economic growth.

This understanding has ushered in a new approach that recognizes that individual goals are not disconnected from each other and that often the way to one involves tackling issues typically connected to another. This fundamental shift in India's approach is being noticed globally. In its 'Energy Policy Review for India' in 2020, IEA noted, 'India has made important progress towards meeting the United Nations SDGs, notably Goal 7 on delivering energy access. Both the energy and emission intensities of India's GDP have decreased by more than 20 per cent over the past decade. This represents commendable progress even as total energy-related carbon dioxide (CO_2) emissions continue to rise.'[2]

Looking at the SDGs in this way highlights their interconnection with India's energy policy in general and natural gas in particular. The greater percentage of natural gas in India's energy mix contributes primarily to Goal 7 (making affordable and clean energy available to all). Other SDGs also rely on a clean and sustainable energy sector featuring natural gas. Natural gas, in the form of PNG, CNG and LNG, has a profound role to play in contributing to SDG 3, in ensuring the good health and well-being of Indian citizens. It has a proven track record of reducing urban air pollution. In addition, SDG 9 defines investments in infrastructure and encourages innovation to drive economic development. The goals of all three SDGs 7, 3 and 9, need to be underpinned by energy sources like natural gas to ensure sustainable progress.

Finally coming to SDG 13, climate action can take many forms but must go hand in hand with an understanding of how different forms of energy can complement each other with the lowest emissions. Natural gas complements the greater expansion of renewable energy, therefore, supporting the transition to a low-carbon future.

INTERCONNECTEDNESS OF ISSUES

As India develops an integrated vision for its future energy supply, the challenge facing policy-makers is primarily to choose an energy mix that supports sustainable development and takes into consideration the key objectives of economic development, energy security and climate security. The World Energy Council describes this as the energy 'trilemma' that policy-makers have to balance. In India's context, there is a fourth vertex of affordability, which is equally important for decision-makers to keep in mind.

To achieve its primary economic objectives, including 7 to 9 per cent sustainable annual growth and a competitive manufacturing sector, India needs to consider how its energy-use patterns will change in the coming years. Taking into account the economy's size and stage of development, anticipated urban and rural population growth and climbing manufacturing output, it has been estimated that India's energy demand will double by 2040. Being able to match supply to demand—through a period when dependence on fossil fuels must decrease to fulfil the country's sustainability ambitions—will require a radical rethink of its primary energy make-up. With fossil fuels still constituting more than

Figure 1: India's energy 'quadrilemma'

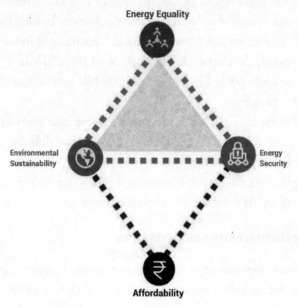

Source: ICF India

90 per cent of the nation's total primary energy consumption,[3] and with dependence on imports continuing to grow, there are increasing concerns about India's energy security. Even the government's commitment to renewable energies cannot alleviate these concerns for the foreseeable future, given the sheer magnitude of the energy needs of a growing Indian economy.

Best case projections envisage a future where fossil fuels will continue to be important in India. Energy diversification, through the use of renewable and fossil fuel sources, is a key aspect of achieving energy security. Globally, natural gas has been accepted as the transition fuel of choice and will provide India with an opportunity to diversify from solid fuels and oil products. India will also have to deal with issues of climate security and sustainability as climate change could affect India particularly hard. Millions of livelihoods depend on climate-sensitive sectors like agriculture. Present urban infrastructure is unprepared to handle extreme weather events. India's rural-to-urban transition is expected to see 200 million more city dwellers by 2030.[4] It must plan for resilient infrastructure. The impact of changing weather patterns is only going to increase. We cannot overstate the implications of SDG 13 and its objectives related to climate action.

Without concerted action, temperature increases alone will threaten the lives and livelihoods of three-quarters of India's population and impact industry. Extreme weather events like the floods of August 2018, which killed thousands, are likely to increase leading to many thousands of more deaths. It is imperative for India's energy policy to address these threats to its people and its economy. The challenges, though daunting, are possible to surmount as scalable solutions are emerging. Significant reductions in the prices of solar and wind energy will no doubt help in creating a clean energy sector, though they may not be enough on their own in the foreseeable future.

The choice, therefore, is not between two extremes—either a renewables-only future, or sole dependence on fossil fuels—but to transition using an integrated approach that balances the two and provides a cleaner mix over time. Natural gas has a definite role to play in this transition.

B. ADVANTAGES OF NATURAL GAS USE

Globally, natural gas has been accepted as the transition fuel of choice. It is expected to take up an increasing share in the energy mix over the next few decades. We are now in an age where it is seen as an indispensable part of a nation's efficient and diversified energy systems. As a key fuel in India's energy mix, it has the potential to meet rapidly growing demand, while supporting the clean energy agenda. Several major reasons highlight the potential of natural gas.

VERSATILITY AND EFFICIENCY OF USE

There is a broad consensus that gas, as the cleanest of hydrocarbons and a highly efficient form of easily storable energy, can be seen as the best-suited bridge to a low-carbon future. Valuably versatile, gas can be used as a chemical feedstock, fuel for vehicles and as a source of energy for electricity generation, heating and cooking. It can also address all kinds of energy demand in four main consuming sectors—electricity, city gas distribution (CGD), refineries and petrochemicals—and in other emerging areas of demand, like transport. Gas also makes for easier handling, better product quality and a cleaner ecosystem (no pilferage) such that once consumers start using gas, they start to think of it as a fuel of choice.

Natural gas is increasingly being used in the automotive industry. More than 28 million vehicles around the world are now running on the so-called 'blue fuel',[5] which is significantly cheaper than diesel and petrol. Emissions from cars powered by CNG or LNG are five times less harmful than those from cars with gasoline engines. Natural gas makes compliance with Euro 6 standards easier and is also perfectly placed to complement renewables. In the power sector too, it is best suited to play a central role in the transition from the fossil fuel era to the solar/hydrogen era.

Natural gas is also used in the bulk chemical industry where it acts as a feedstock, including in the production of organic chemicals (including petrochemicals), inorganic chemicals, resins, agricultural chemicals (fertilizers), and in the production of methanol (and its derivatives, e.g., methyl tert-butyl ether (MTBE), formaldehyde, and acetic acid). According to IEA estimates, the industrial sector will soon take the lead over power-generation, as the main driver of growth in the demand for natural gas globally. Emerging markets, primarily in Asia, are expected to account for the bulk of this increase with uses as fuel for industrial processes, as well as for feedstock for chemicals and fertilizers. Industrial gas demand is also growing in major resource-rich regions, such as North America and the Middle East, to support the expansion of their petrochemical sectors.

Finally, new applications for gas are continually being opened up. These include combined cooling, heat and power (CCHP), also known as trigeneration. This process, using waste heat produced by cogeneration plants to generate chilled water for air conditioning or refrigeration, highlights many of the fundamental benefits of gas. Not only does gas-based cooling have significant financial and efficiency advantages over traditional methods, but it also combines climate protection with economical power generation.

ENVIRONMENTAL BENEFITS

As noted, gas is a much cleaner fuel than other fossil fuels and as such, it meets the newly set emissions standards by India's Ministry of Environment, Forest and Climate Change. These standards cover emissions of sulphur oxides (SOx), nitrogen oxides (NOx), particulate matter (PM) and carbon dioxide (CO_2).

Table 1: Emissions from coal and gas (in power plants)

Pollutants	Units	MOEFCC Norms[6]	Uncontrolled	Existing Controls	Uncontrolled
			Coal	Coal	Gas
SOx	mg/ NM_3	100	1800 to 3000	1800 to 3000	10 to 20
NOx	mg/ NM_3	100	500 to 800	300 to 500	150 to 250
PM	mg/ NM_3	30	2500 to 3500	25 to 70	10 to 20
GHG	gm/ kWh	NA	900 to 980	900 to 980	430 to 460

Source: ICF analysis of publicly available data.

Despite the clear advantage of natural gas with regard to most GHG emissions, one common criticism relates to the fugitive emissions of methane in the gas value chain. It is well understood that methane in the atmosphere is several times more potent than CO_2, in terms of its Global Warming Potential (GWP).[7] One key point to note, however, is that whilst CO_2 remains in the atmosphere forever, methane emitted today lasts for about a decade on average before it decomposes naturally. This means that if we are able to limit and reduce methane emissions over the next few years, then the methane in the atmosphere will also reduce on its own.

Programmes like Natural Gas STAR, Methane Challenge and the Oil and Gas Climate Initiative (OGCI), are aimed at reducing these fugitive emissions of methane from the gas value chain and reducing the carbon footprint of the oil and gas industry. Oil and gas companies are working to reduce methane emissions globally. They are successfully improving their performances by implementing the best practices, information sharing, and technology transfer among partners, thereby increasing the supply of natural gas, saving money and protecting the environment.

Another key advantage of natural gas is the low water requirement of gas-based power plants, compared to coal plants. Studies on water consumption have ascertained that the water consumption of combined-cycle gas plants is half the water needs of a supercritical coal plant per megawatt hour (MWh) of electricity generated.

Finally, while developments in the global gas markets have already brought down the cost of imported LNG to the point where it is cheaper than crude oil products, the tangible, upfront market price of energy is not the only cost with which it is associated. The often overlooked, but harmful, health, social and environmental costs (of energy production, of transport, and of other industries that cause emissions) are real costs to economies and peoples. These are sometimes obvious (such as pollution, flooding and land degradation) and sometimes hidden (such as the costs of asthma and cancer or the impact of the rise in sea levels). They are nonetheless ever present and expensive.

Take, for instance, the burning of coal, traditionally considered a cheap fuel source. In light of the information above, coal is far from the cheapest source of energy in India. The cost of extraction is low but its negative impacts are high. The damage it causes to human health, air quality and water quality increases its real cost. As a result, coal's cost advantage often disappears, and natural gas emerges as a more favourable option.

Table 2: The cost of externalities

FY20 (Rs/KWh)	Coal (imported coal)	Combined cycle (LNG)
Fuel cost	2.97	4.82
Fixed cost	2.30	1.64
Externalities		
SOx	4.50	0.05
NOx	1.10	0.50
PM	0.10	0.01
GHG	2.50	1.20
Total	**13.48**	**8.22**

Source: ICF analysis of International Monetary Fund (IMF) data.

The cost of air pollution in India due to industrial emissions, coal-based power generation, engine fumes, stubble burning, construction and other factors, is astonishingly high. A 2016 World Bank study[8] revealed that in 2013 India lost more than 8.5 per cent of its GDP to air pollution and the associated cost of increased welfare benefits and lost labour. A study by the Indian Institute of Technology (IIT) Mumbai,[9] found that the cost of air pollution to just two major cities, Mumbai and Delhi, was $10.66 billion in 2015. The study also estimated India's pollution-related deaths at 2.5 million in 2015, the highest in the world.

The UN has warned that rising air pollution is also likely to impact rainfall patterns and reduce the duration of the monsoon.[10] This further brings home the unavoidable truth that energy choice and climate change, are inextricably interwoven.

TRANSITION TO A CLEAN FUTURE

The safety and cleanliness of gas offer profound benefits, when compared to the serious health hazards of cooking with biomass fuels. Around 100,000 premature deaths a year in India—related to heart disease, stroke, chronic obstructive pulmonary disease and lung cancer—are attributable to unclean cooking fuels.[11] Indoor air pollution is also responsible for a significant number of acute respiratory illnesses among young children. The launch of the government's Pradhan Mantri Ujjwala Yojana in 2016, to provide fifty million free liquefied petroleum gas (LPG) connections to poor rural households, indicates the seriousness and urgency of this problem. With natural gas available at urban centres through various existing and upcoming CGD networks, the LPG connections are being transferred to rural areas to replace the more harmful cooking fuels used there.

The versatility of natural gas is also the key reason why it complements and balances the integration of different renewables, especially since sources of energy such as wind and solar are variable and difficult to predict. For instance, a sudden cloud cover will reduce solar generation drastically and reduced wind speeds will cut off wind turbines. The impacts can be either long-term or seasonal in nature. For instance, during monsoons in India, wind generation peaks while cooling demand falls at the same time. Solar generation, on the other hand, requires daily balancing for twelve to sixteen hours as the sun goes down.

In order for renewables to supply uninterrupted power, they must be balanced by other sources, such as pumped hydro, coal plants, gas plants or energy storage. Among these, coal plants in India find it difficult to ramp up and down quickly and cannot today go below 40–50 per cent technical minimum. Pumped hydro plants, on the other hand, are limited in capacity and building new plants will have a very long gestation period with high costs. Energy storage solutions are still being tested and are a few years away from becoming cost effective. In such a situation, natural gas provides a very elegant solution as gas plants (even in combined-cycle mode) can be ramped up and down very quickly.

While open cycle (or stand-alone gas plants) can operate in a range of 0–95 per cent generation, combined-cycle gas plants can operate in a range of 20 per cent to 90 per cent generation,[12] without much loss in efficiency. To enable this, power regulators and system operators would need to structure market mechanisms (which can provide appropriate price signals) for plant operators to decide: (i) the level of investments to be made in gas power plants (e.g., reducing the technical minimum for plants); and (ii) mode of operation of the plant (combined cycle or open cycle) as per system requirements. This provides natural gas with a unique ability to support renewables, and thus increases the efficacy of renewable deployment across the country.

AVAILABILITY AND ENERGY SECURITY

As a fuel, natural gas has always been sold at a discount to crude oil in energy content. More recently, with increased LNG supplies and gas prices delinked from crude oil, natural gas has become even more cost effective, compared to crude products. This provides India with a great opportunity to reduce its import dependence on crude and petroleum products, as well as to diversify its energy sources. The recent sanctions on Iran saw India scrambling to find alternative suppliers for crude, as well as alternative options of payment to Iran.

Geopolitically, most countries supplying LNG today have a more stable regime compared to the traditional oil-supplying countries. With newer countries emerging as LNG suppliers, an energy-deficit country dependent on imports now has several options for securing reliable access to affordable natural gas (see Figure 3).

Figure 2: Countries exporting oil vs countries exporting gas (2013–18)

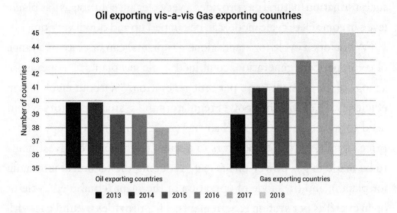

Source: ICF analysis.

Figure 3: Asian LNG prices delivered to terminals

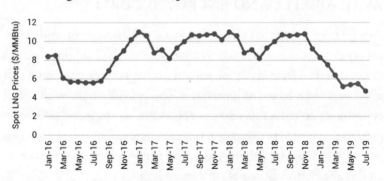

Source: Ministry of Economy, Trade and Industry, Japan.

Figure 4: Share of spot/short-term global LNG trade

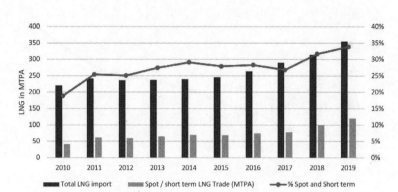

Source: International Group of LNG Importers (GIIGNL) (2020).[13]

C. INTERNATIONAL EXAMPLES

While India's natural gas potential remains largely unfulfilled, other countries have gone ahead and introduced substantial shares of natural gas to their energy mix, showcasing that natural gas is able to perform both as a stable and reliable source of energy as well as a perfect complement to renewable energy.

CHINA: EQUITY ACQUISITIONS PLUS SPIKE IN NATURAL GAS CONSUMPTION

Realizing that natural gas has the potential to meet its rapidly growing demand while also supporting its clean energy agenda, China has achieved a steady increase in natural gas consumption at a 13.5 per cent compound annual growth rate (CAGR) over the last ten years.

Figure 5: China's spike in gas consumption (2009–18)

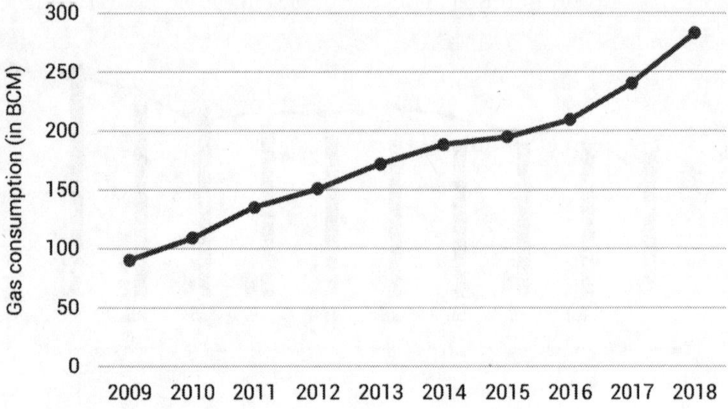

Source: BP Statistics, 2019.

In 2017, China gave natural gas a central role in its fight against air pollution with the introduction of supportive policies like banning the use of coal boilers ('Blue Skies Policy') through which the consumption of natural gas has grown significantly. In just two years, China added 75 Bcm to the global gas demand, the equivalent of the UK gas market, the second-largest European market. Imports of LNG have risen by 50 per cent,[14] thanks to a focus on gradual gas price liberalization and market reforms.

THE US: SPECTACULAR GROWTH SINCE THE EARLY 2000S

Gas consumption in the US has increased significantly in the last few years, particularly due to abundant supplies coming from shale resources at very attractive prices. At the time of writing, gas prices at Henry Hub are at historical lows, which has led to gas-based power generation becoming more cost effective than coal-based power.

This has been made possible by the existence of a robust and competitive gas market in the US, enabled by regulatory frameworks and policies.

From the early 2000s, when Henry Hub was at $8–9/MMBtu and the US was rapidly building import terminals to now—when the Henry Hub stands below $3/MMBtu—this is a success story that is nothing short of spectacular.

Figure 6: US wholesale gas prices, gas production and consumption trends

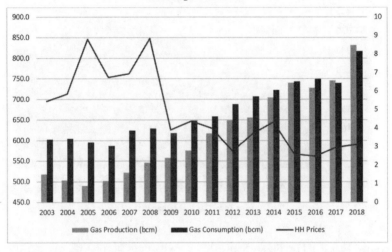

Source: ICF analysis of EIA data.

THE UK: DASH FOR GAS

The now-famous 'Dash for Gas' in the 1990s in the UK was underpinned by a shift in the power-generation landscape through newly privatized electric companies. The key reasons for this shift were: (a) increased availability of gas from the North Sea, which led to reduced wholesale prices for gas in the UK; (b) new technology (the combined-cycle gas turbine plant or CCGT) that was much more efficient and had lower capital costs; and (c) high cost of capital at the time, which provided economic incentives in building power plants quickly (CCGT), over coal and nuclear power stations.

In 1990, gas turbine power stations made up 5 per cent of the UK's generating capacity. By 2002, the new CCGT power stations made up 28 per cent of its generating capacity.

Figure 7: Consumption of gas in the UK (1970–2018)

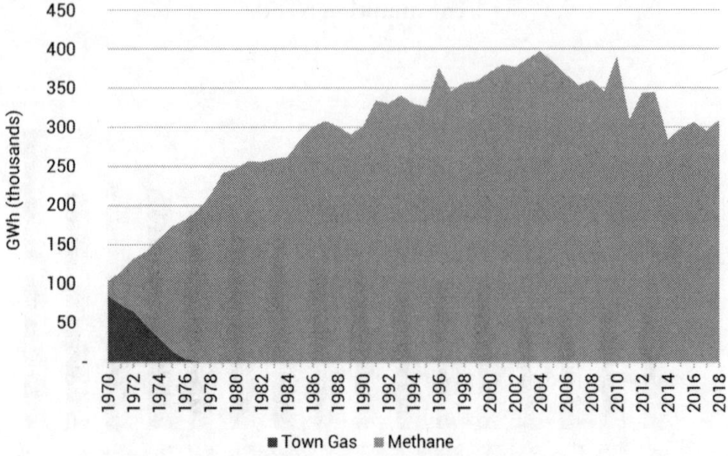

Source: Digest of UK Energy Statistics.[15]

BRAZIL: FOCUSING ON GAS SECTOR DEREGULATION AND PRIORITIZATION

The increase in consumption of natural gas in Brazil has been a recent trend in the last decade. It has been supported by reserves found locally, coupled with the desire to increase gas-based power generation capacity and reduce dependence on hydro-power (which makes Brazil vulnerable, especially during droughts, as seen in 2015).

The share of natural gas in Brazil's energy mix has varied over the years, reaching 13 per cent in 2017. Some key measures that resulted in the increase in the share of natural gas in the energy mix include:

- The privatization of natural gas distribution companies and, consequently, the expansion of the natural gas distribution network
- A gas-based power priority programme resulting in the construction of ten thermal power plants that have added 6,720 MW in power capacity to the country
- Increase in the consumption of natural gas by vehicles
- Investments to expand the pipeline network and setting up of LNG terminals

More recently (2019), Brazil commenced a programme of gas market liberalization with state-run Petrobras announcing divestments. Currently, Petrobras controls 77 per cent of Brazil's gas production, 100 per cent of its imports, 99 per cent of its processing and 69 per cent of its transport, as well as twenty of the twenty-seven state distributors.

The Brazilian government is now in the process of approving a New Gas Law which proposes the following main changes: (a) Implementation of the authorization regime for gas transportation and storage, (b) Replacement of the point-to-point transportation model by the entry-exit model, (c) Third-Party Access to Essential Facilities (evacuation pipelines, processing facilities and LNG terminals) and (d) Gas release programme to bring competition among suppliers.

There are numerous other international examples/case studies where gas has been promoted by national, state or local governments through supportive policy mechanisms:

- Turkey: Under the aegis of the Southern Gas Corridor (SGC) the state gas importer Botas has connected new provinces in Turkey.
- Egypt: Power and industry account for major gas consumption. The government is now focusing on increasing natural gas vehicles (NGVs) with targets for conversion.

- Rwanda: The nation is focusing on biogenic/small-scale gas.
- Mozambique: The country found large world-class gas resources and are moving forward to develop those for both export and to develop a domestic market.

D. WHY HAS GAS NOT ACHIEVED ITS POTENTIAL IN INDIA SO FAR?

The positive international examples, the wide-ranging applications of natural gas and the commensurate advantages, all beg one question. Why—while many countries are embracing all that gas has to offer as a fuel and as a force for climate and air quality protection—is India holding back? There is, after all, a national vision for energy, based on the four pillars of energy access, efficiency, sustainability and security, with which gas naturally aligns. There is also a target for gas to reach 15 per cent of the energy mix, from its current 6.5 per cent, in the next fifteen years.

Part of the answer lies in the fact that some policy issues have undermined the growth of gas including, significantly, no clear policy for increasing the share of gas in the energy mix. There are also some tax-related barriers, like the long-awaited inclusion of natural gas in the ambit of the reformed GST. Part of the answer, however, can also be found in the lack of key initiatives required to support gas to achieve its full potential

No Clear Roadmap for Increasing Natural Gas Share

While the Government of India has set a clear vision for gas to gain a 15 per cent share in India's energy basket, there is no roadmap laid out for reaching this target.

Policies and regulations that support the creation of demand are needed to provide clear direction leading to the increased use of gas. Policies supporting the use of gas in cities (like CNG in Delhi), policies banning the use of polluting fuel, support in establishing infrastructure by providing faster approvals etc., are required to be put in place.

Tax-Related Barriers

One of the biggest challenges facing the gas industry is the exclusion of gas from the GST. This leads to a direct additional cost for gas users, compared to alternate products. The gas industry has been voicing this concern, for a long time without success. Some would argue that for the gas share to reach 15 per cent, perhaps this is the first and most important step that the government should take.

Limited Gas Availability

In considering various reasons why gas has not grown in India as it has elsewhere, the issue of availability is perhaps the most prominent. There is a perception that India does not have enough domestic gas to meet the country's needs and that increasing imports to make up the difference places India at the mercy of international supply chains. This scenario can bring to mind the experience with the Organization of the Petroleum Exporting Countries (OPEC) where a few countries are seen to control supplies and, thus, prices. A decline in domestic production and reliance on imports also brings into play concerns about energy security, which can cause thoughts to turn back to abundantly available domestic coal.

In terms of domestic supply, it can be argued that little gas exploration has taken place in India in recent years, because prices have been tightly regulated. As a result, companies have not been incentivized to invest in speculative endeavours. There may, in fact, be far more gas resources waiting to be found, particularly offshore, where large deposits are more likely to sit.

With changes in the upstream Hydrocarbon Exploration and Licensing Policy (HELP), which allows producers the freedom to market and sell gas at market-determined prices, incentive structures have been set right. This provides the encouragement that industry players need to invest in prospecting, which might lead to hydrocarbon discoveries, thereby further improving the security of supply.

Finally, while ONGC Videsh Ltd (OVL) has been investing in overseas hydrocarbon assets to improve India's energy security; the reserves created through these overseas acquisitions pale when compared to similar activity by Chinese state-owned companies.

Figure 8: Comparative growth in India and China's overseas investments in hydrocarbon assets

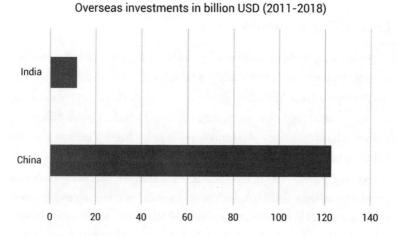

Overseas investments in billion USD (2011-2018)

Source: Reserve Bank of India: 'Data on Overseas Investment'; China's data from: Caixin Global/Sinopec Research Institute of Petroleum Engineering.[16]

Renewables Get All the Attention

Just as worry about the risk of insufficient gas supply has hindered progress in recent years, so has India's intense focus on renewable energies in the same period tended to obscure both challenges and the need for balancing energies. It is not surprising that great store has been set by clean, green energies generated locally (and increasingly cheaply), primarily by the sun and wind. India plans to increase renewable energy capacity to 175 GW by 2022 and the percentage of energy from non-fossil sources from 10 per cent to 40 per cent by 2030.[17] What has been damaging though, is the focused and favourable policies for renewable energies, which has led to their star shining so brightly that it has effectively extinguished the gas flame.

Table 3: Summary of various subsidies provided to renewables

Cost Category	Value (in Rs/kWh)[18]
Capital subsidy (via solar park)	0.15
Accelerated depreciation	0.55
Waiver of Long-Term Open Access Charges	2.40
Total	**3.10**

Source: ICF analysis.

Renewable energies also come with inherent problems, such as silicon pollution resulting from the disposal of solar panels at the end of their usable life, which today seems not to be a concern. Most significant among all the problems with renewables is, of course, their unpredictable nature. Also to be considered is the fact that renewable energies are not going to deliver 100 per cent energy for quite some time. It is unclear exactly when they will become critically important in India, but establishing gas readiness to complement them when they do is the most realistic and helpful strategy.

Infrastructure: The Weak link

Gas will only be able to act expeditiously as a reliable, balancing energy if India prioritizes investment in infrastructure. As of date, the country has only 13,581 km of transmission pipelines delivering gas to limited regions of the country. An additional 15,000 km of pipelines are under

construction.[19] Compared to some other countries, India is woefully
short on the needed pipeline infrastructure to make gas available to the
vast areas of the country. Table 4 provides a comparison of the kilometres
of gas transmission pipelines in various countries.

Table 4: Comparative ranking as per gas pipelines laid out and
functioning (km)

	Country	NG pipeline (km) approx.	Area (km²)
1	United States	1,980,000	9,833,517
2	Russia	177,000	17,098,242
3	Canada	110,000	9,984,670
4	China	76,000	9,596,960
5	Australia	39,000	7,741,220
6	Argentina	30,000	2,780,400
7	United Kingdom	29,000	243,610
8	India	16,000	3,287,263

Source: Databases in the public domain.

Investment in the gas value chain can have a transformative impact
on the opportunities and markets for gas in India. Funding gas pipelines
and storage facilities to enable the movement of gas from the source of
import or production, deep into the market close to the end consumer
has tended to raise the spectre of higher costs and dampen enthusiasm
for gas. Effective progress is, however, on the horizon.

The government is developing an infrastructure investment plan and
exploring economically viable models for its implementation. A start
was made last year with the award of CGD licences, covering over
400 districts for the retail sale of CNG for cars and piped cooking gas
for households. The cross-country pipelines, needed to connect these

areas, need to be developed and discussions have started on the best model to finance them. The Urja Ganga pipeline, for instance, is being financed through the viability gap funding and the government has directly provided 40 per cent capital subsidy to GAIL (India) Ltd to construct the pipeline.

Gas pipeline infrastructure planning may also include provisions to accommodate a blend of natural gas and hydrogen (up to 15 per cent) which, as per studies, may only require some limited modifications to the technical design of the pipeline.

Price Volatility and Lack of Competitiveness

A big concern in India relating to natural gas has been the price of gas and the competitiveness of industries using gas as fuel. Historically, natural gas has had to compete with coal, which is available locally and whose prices have traditionally been set on cost-plus principle, without any volatility. Based on this principle, domestic gas has been set under an administered pricing regime as well. This has kept the prices of domestic gas much below import parity prices. However, limited domestic reserves mean a smaller market share for gas as consumers have found it difficult to buy a higher-priced and more volatile fuel like imported natural gas.

Indian consumers are price-sensitive but require round-the-clock service

Concern about the cost of gas to the consumer has held back the growth of gas to date, in India's primary energy mix. There is certainly no denying the lower cost and higher availability of domestic coal compared to gas. However, a reality check is in order when it comes to the price the consumer is willing to pay for a secure supply of energy. The politics of energy must be separated from the economics of energy.

Figure 9: Approximate cost (in Rs/kWh) of a mini-grid[20]

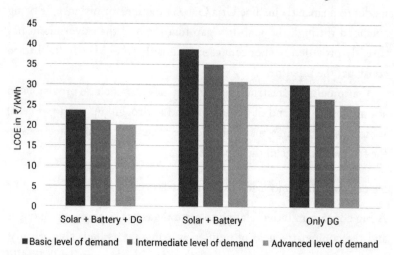

Source: ICF data and analysis.

While policy-makers focus on ensuring low energy prices (especially during elections), without focusing as much on reliable supply, the reality is that consumers are willing to pay the needed price, provided energy is made available as and when needed.

Over the next two decades, as India increases its per capita income and becomes a middle-income country, the low price of energy will cease to be the only issue that will matter. Instead, a reliable, clean and twenty-four-hour supply of energy will become more critical to the economy.

There is also no getting away from the fact that the government will lose tax revenue through a shift away from highly taxed diesel and oil to gas, which isn't currently subject to tax at the same level. The prospect of lower tax revenue has undoubtedly played a part in hindering the take-up of gas.

E. THE WAY FORWARD

Looking at gas through a clear lens, with misunderstandings resolved, progress highlighted and roles and opportunities in focus, it is revealed as a versatile and valuable energy source. It is an energy source on the cusp of realizing its potential as the perfect partner for renewable, and a first-choice fuel for industry and increasingly for transport too, where it can undercut the financial and social costs of old fuels.

As India takes the next steps towards a sustainable energy policy, concerted and focused efforts are needed to ensure that everyone— from policy-makers to consumers and industry players—appreciates the advantages that natural gas can bring and the role it can play in the future. There is also a need for the country's diversification to take a long-term view. There will undoubtedly be twists, turns and uncertainties along the path over the coming years, as older energies jostle for position alongside newer alternatives still finding their place and proving themselves.

For example, viewing gas not as a competitor, but as a partner for renewable energies in a future sustainable energy mix is the most effective way for India to reach its renewable energy goals. The reliability of gas helps balance and stabilize the fluctuating power supply of renewables, enabling them to be more easily integrated into the power grid. There is an opportunity too for gas to partner with the biomass so abundant in India, within novel integrated power plants. Successfully demonstrated in Sweden and Brazil, these highly efficient and environmentally acceptable plants have not yet been replicated in India, despite the strong rationale for this application of gas. Gas could also take on a 'transition fuel' role in relation to batteries, touted as the next big green development. There are still a lot of uncertainties, such as the availability of lithium, in the volume required to support prices. In scenarios like this, gas could step in.

Figure 10 below shows the cost of generation from different options along with the associated cost of firming-up the generation. Since coal, gas and hydro are all dispatchable generation sources, they do not have integration costs associated with them. On the other hand, wind and solar are non-dispatchable generation sources. Hence, they have integration costs, in the form of storage costs or other system integration costs.

Figure 10: Cost of balanced power from various sources (FY2020)

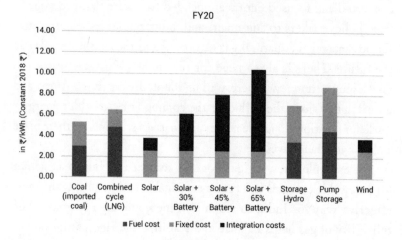

Source: ICF Analysis.

As India picks its way purposefully through these changeable times it will need to look decades ahead, make assumptions about the fate of energy and map out possible scenarios. In this way, it will be able to identify possible roles that gas can usefully perform and gaps that it might fill, to play its part in ensuring the country's long-term energy and climate security. Two hypothetical but realistic pathways open to India on its energy journey from where it is now to where it wants to be in 2047, when it celebrates 100 years of independence, are illustrated in Figure 11.

Figure 11: Alternative Pathways for Role of Gas in Energy Mix

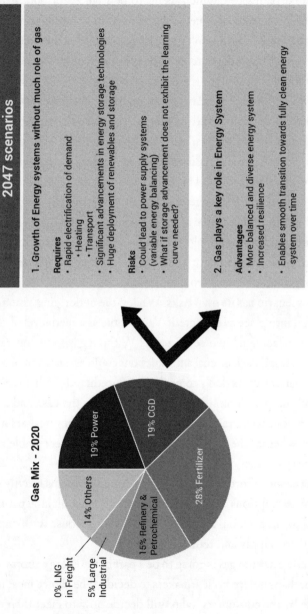

Source: ICF analysis.

The first pathway—which seems to be Plan A for policy-makers today—relies heavily on renewables to meet its emissions targets. It is a scenario where India doesn't grow its gas supply and market between now and 2047, but reduces reliance on coal and renewables become the primary source of supply.

However, for this scenario to be realized, there are two critical assumptions that must fall in place: (i) electrification of energy consumption should happen at a rapid pace and the likes of electric vehicles, electrification of industrial heating, cooling and cooking, should also grow at a massive pace. This in turn will require power distribution companies to get their act together rather quickly; and (ii) energy storage should become highly viable at grid-scale in the immediate future, and renewables and storage deployed at a feverish pace for the foreseeable future to provide the majority of the electricity supply, while also displacing coal somewhat from the mix.

This scenario has its own risks. What if the underlying assumptions do not fall into place as expected? What if the assumed level of climate change is in fact much worse by 2047? Without gas to call on, reliance would likely fall back on coal and emissions could escalate out of control. What if battery costs don't come down as predicted? What would the best back-up plan look like if any of these were the case and nothing had been done to increase the influence of gas? Policy-makers need to consider whether the prospect of this scenario is an acceptable risk for the country to take.

India cannot afford to have only Plan A, which seems heavily reliant on a few assumptions. Plan B, in this context, must include natural gas as a fuel to fall back on. Such a scenario is more robust with improved reliability of supply and reduced emissions.

Whether natural gas is going to be a part of the energy supply mix or not, is perhaps not for policy-makers to decide. The choice must instead be made by the consumers, who will decide how to meet their energy needs today and in future. The only role for policy-makers is to ensure a level playing field for all fuel sources and ensure that all costs (explicit and implicit) are priced into policy decisions. In this context, India must understand the least damaging steps that must be taken today, so that natural gas continues to be an option available to consumers as an energy source in the future.

Figure 12 below illustrates these steps until 2025, which will ensure that natural gas continues to be in the game for the next few years. By then it will be amply clear whether renewables will be able to power energy needs coupled with cost-effective storage options.

ACTION RECOMMENDATIONS: THE NEXT FIVE YEARS

If gas is to be part of the solution in the long-term, keeping it in play in the short term is the most sensible and secure way for India to move forward. It is becoming clearer with time as to how renewables are progressing, what innovations are enabling them and where demand is going. Gas can, therefore, be pulled in, as and when, and how, it is needed. Not only will all options remain open, but India will have established the know-how and framework to choose any one of them with confidence.

By taking action in some key areas (listed below) over the next five years, India can lay the foundations for this future and ensure the sector's prospects are not jeopardized.

Supporting the development of supply infrastructure by building the national gas grid: India first needs to ensure that its commitment to developing an ecosystem for gas, and sufficient infrastructure for its transport, is turned into reality. Its experimentation with different financing models—such as direct government payment to developers (Urja-Ganga pipeline) and interest in European and US exemplars—needs to lead to some consensus about the right combination of financing and business models for its proposed new gas pipelines.

Figure 12: 'Least regret' actions for next five years that will enable gas to remain in the play (ICF estimate of demand)

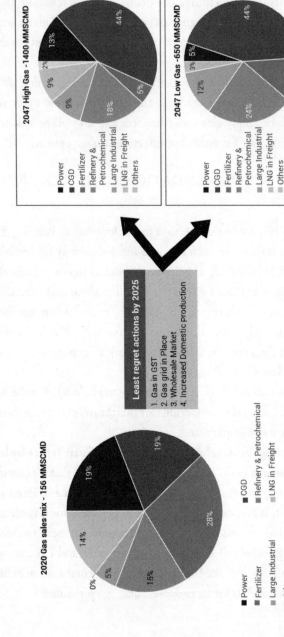

Source: ICF projections based on proprietary data

1. **Ensuring competitive markets for gas by establishing a trading hub:** Attention then needs to turn to creating the required institutional structures, supporting the gas ecosystem and successfully implementing the trading hub. Bringing in a trading hub regime inevitably requires a rethink about various factors—open access, existing allocations of gas to priority customers and harmonization of the rules and processes guiding the operations of different companies—so they all work together as a single entity.

2. **Supporting exploration and production (E&P) policies for unleashing the potential of domestic reserves:** Indian basins still remain poorly explored and there is a need to ensure supportive policies that encourage domestic and international firms to invest risk capital in exploring the regions well. This requires not only marketing or pricing freedom but also supportive arrangements to make operating issues like environmental clearances, defence clearances and various other approvals required from local, state and national bodies, easier.

3. **Equity gas acquisition in resource-rich countries needs to be given more focus:** Increased focus should be on acquiring proven reserves in countries rich in gas, at today's (low) prices. This would help offset India's position as a net consumer and balance exposure to price fluctuations. Buying stakes in very large gas fields abroad and then choosing either to bring the gas back home or selling it on the open market, provides a natural hedge and evens the trade balance.

4. **Bringing mechanisms like an Emissions Trading System (ETS) to put a cost to externalities such as health impacts, resource footprint and other public costs:** Perhaps this will be the most important aspect to ensure various fuels are provided with a level playing field and cleaner fuels get the advantage they deserve. Governments across the world are bringing in market mechanisms to penalize the polluter (the 'polluter pays' principle)

and ETS is one such successful cap and trade mechanism that has the potential to provide natural gas the edge it deserves.

5. **Ensuring that policy decisions provide long-term certainty and a supportive environment**: A policy must provide investors with security for their returns over the long term. Frequent flip-flops and changes in policy dampen the enthusiasm of private investors and can lead to international capital flowing to other lucrative investment destinations.

6. **Engaging in communication with a wide set of stakeholders to showcase the benefits of natural gas**: Although mentioned last, this is certainly not the least effective tool needed to bring natural gas to the forefront. Effective communication is essential to make consumers understand the benefits of natural gas—a fuel that not many know about in India. Even with the best-laid plans, gas will go nowhere in India unless people are open to using it in their everyday lives, and evidence suggests that this is not yet the case. A survey of the beneficiaries of the Ujjwala scheme revealed, for example, that 98 per cent of households provided with a free LPG connection also continued to use traditional stoves powered by solid fuel.[21] With the Indian government seeing a key role for gas in expanding access to energy among the poorest groups in society, it is clear that action to increase 'gas literacy' is critically important to the fuel's future.

If India decides to take the 'no-regret' actions outlined here, it will keep alive the chance of choosing gas in five years' time. This could play a pivotal role in transforming the country's economy, sustainability and quality of life—and enable India to mark energy independence by 2047, alongside celebrating 100 years of independence.

Notes

1. International Energy Agency, 'India 2020: Energy Policy Review', (Paris: OECD/IEA, 2020), https://www.iea.org/reports/india-2020
2. Ibid.
3. British Petroleum, 'BP Statistical Review 2019–India: India's Energy Market in 2018', (London: British Petroleum), https://www.bp.com/content/dam/bp/business-sites/en/global/corporate/pdfs/energy-economics/statistical-review/bp-stats-review-2019-india-insights.pdf
4. As per ICF estimates.
5. NGV Global: Natural Gas Vehicle Knowledge Base, 'Current Natural Gas Vehicle Statistics', accessed September 2019, http://www.iangv.org/current-ngv-stats/
6. For coal power plants set up after 1 January 2017.
7. The United Nations Framework Convention on Climate Change (UNFCCC), for instance, estimates that the warming potential of methane is twenty-one times higher than CO_2 over a century. See: United Nations Climate Change, 'Global Warming Potentials: IPCC Second Assessment Report', (Bonn: UNFCCC), accessed 3 July 2020, https://unfccc.int/process/transparency-and-reporting/greenhouse-gas-data/greenhouse-gas-data-unfccc/global-warming-potentials
8. World Bank; Institute for Health Metrics and Evaluation. 2016. The Cost of Air Pollution: Strengthening the Economic Case for Action. World Bank, Washington, DC. © World Bank. https://openknowledge.worldbank.org/handle/10986/25013 License: CC BY 3.0 IGO, accessed September 2019.
9. 'Economic Impacts of Pollution Growing Too Huge for India', The Weather Channel/ET Online, 31 October 2018, https://weather.com/en-IN/india/pollution/news/2018-10-31-economic-impacts-of-pollution.
10. Ibid.
11. Nitin Sethi and Arun Deep, 'PM's plan for free gas connections is failing its objective – as government had been warned it would', *Scroll.in*, 23

January 2018, https://scroll.in/article/865853/pms-plan-for-free-gas-connections-is-failing-its-objective-as-government-had-been-warned-it-would

12. It is important to note that most of the existing gas capacity in India is combined-cycle capacity with technical minimums of around 40 per cent. However, based on initial discussions with General Electric (GE) and other turbine manufacturers, we understand that the technical minimum of these plants can be brought down to 20 per cent, with small capital investment.

13. International Group of LNG Importers (GIIGNL), 'The LNG Industry: GIIGNL Annual Report 2020', (GIIGNL: Neuilly-sur-Seine, 2020), https://giignl.org/sites/default/files/PUBLIC_AREA/Publications/giignl_-_2020_annual_report_-_04082020.pdf

14. David Sandalow, Akos Losz, Sheng Yan, 'A Natural Gas Giant Awakens: China's Quest for Blue Skies Shapes Global Markets,' New York: Columbia/SIPA Center on Global Energy Policy, 2018.

15. Digest of UK Energy Statistics https://www.gov.uk/government/statistics/digest-of-uk-energy-statistics-dukes-2020, accessed 3 July 2020.

16. Reserve Bank of India, 'Data on Overseas Investment', (Mumbai: RBI), https://www.rbi.org.in/Scripts/Data_Overseas_Investment.aspx, accessed September 2019; China's data from: Caixin Global/Sinopec Research Institute of Petroleum Engineeringhttp://img.caixin.com/2017-11-28/1511864891450319.jpg, accessed September 2019

17. Aman Y. Thakker, 'By the Numbers: India's Progress on its Renewable Energy Target', https://www.cogitasia.com/by-the-numbers-indias-progress-on-its-renewable-energy-target/accessed 7 February 2019.

18. Assuming an average PLF of 20 per cent, for a renewable plant.

19. Press Information Bureau, 'Year-end Review: 2019 of the Ministry of Petroleum & Natural Gas', New Delhi: PIB, Government of India, 2019.

20. Indicates total cost for isolated mini-grids (3 km of public distribution network). Calculated based on ICF assumptions for capital expenditure

(CapEx), operating expenditure (OpEx) of microgrid and different service levels of demand.

21. Arjun Srinivas, 'Ujjwala scheme has limited impact on LPG usage', *livemint.com*, 9 April 2019, https://www.livemint.com/news/india/ujjwala-scheme-has-limited-impact-on-lpg-usage-1554756266457.html

SECTION C
GLOBAL DEVELOPMENTS

2

THE GLOBAL MARKET: AN OVERVIEW

JEAN BAPTISTE DUBREUIL

Senior Natural Gas Analyst, International Energy Agency

AKOS LOSZ

Energy Analyst-Gas, Coal and Power Markets Division, International Energy Agency

NATURAL GAS IS A VERSATILE fuel, which is in growing demand. This is in part because of the air quality and greenhouse gas emission (GHG) benefits it provides relative to other fossil fuels. The strong growth in the global natural gas consumption observed in 2017 (nearly 3 per cent), 2018 (close to 5 per cent) and 2019 (nearly 2 per cent) was driven by both growing energy demand and substitution to cleaner fuels. The People's Republic of China (China), which became the largest gas importer in 2018, has accounted for over a quarter of global gas demand growth since 2016. This is thanks to the Chinese government's strong policy framework in favour of cleaner energy sources (referred to as the 'Blue Skies' policy) and, in particular, to restricting the use of small coal boilers for industrial and residential use—although China's strict coal-to-gas switching rules were somewhat relaxed in 2019.

In the US, abundant and cost-competitive natural gas experienced a 7 per cent growth in the power sector in 2019[1] to meet growing electricity demand while electricity production from coal declined by 15 per cent. Reducing oil burn for power generation with the development of natural gas-fired combined-cycle plants in the Middle Eastern and North African oil and gas producing countries is another component of this global trend in the growth of natural gas.

Natural gas is the fastest-growing fossil fuel in the International Energy Agency's (IEA)[2] World Energy Outlook under the Stated Policies Scenario.[3,4] Natural gas is projected to grow at an average rate of 1.4 per cent through 2040, overtaking coal by 2030 to become the second-largest source of energy after oil. Additionally, gas is the only fossil fuel the consumption of which remains more or less the same in 2040 as in 2018 in the framework of the IEA's Sustainable Development Scenario.[5] Under this scenario, gas consumption decreases only by 0.2 per cent annually, whereas both oil and coal use see much sharper annual declines at 1.8 per cent and 4.2 per cent, respectively. India is expected to further increase its natural gas consumption in the future, with supplies from both domestic production and international imports, thus becoming a key stakeholder in the development of the global natural gas trade.

GOING GLOBAL THROUGH STRUCTURAL MARKET CHANGES

The year 2017 marked a turn in the recent evolution of natural gas markets with the rapid rise of China and other fast-growing Asian economies (including India) as major consumers and importers and the emergence of the US as a major source of gas supply and trade growth. These trends were further reinforced in 2018 and 2019, although 2020 will likely see a sharp but temporary interruption of the rising trajectory of the demand for gas in emerging Asia. The medium- and long-term outlook for gas in Asia will continue to be fuelled by economic development and

policy support to improve air quality, while flexible and hub-indexed
US LNG exports will provide a rising share of global supply growth.

FUEL FOR GROWTH

The Asia-Pacific region is the main source of growth in the demand for
natural gas and it is expected to contribute more than half of the global
consumption increase by 2024.[6] The region, which accounted for 21
per cent of the total natural gas consumption in 2018, will see its share
increase to around 25 per cent by 2024. By 2040, it could reach 28
per cent, according to the IEA's Stated Policies Scenario,[7] in spite of
stagnating demand in some of the most mature markets, such as Japan.
Global natural gas consumption is expected to increase by more than a
third over the next two decades and the Asia-Pacific region accounts
for nearly half of this total demand growth (48 per cent), followed by
the Middle East (20 per cent) and Africa (12 per cent). China and India
alone account for 26 per cent and 10 per cent, respectively, of total natural
gas demand growth to 2040,

Figure 1: Natural gas consumption per main country and region (2000–40)

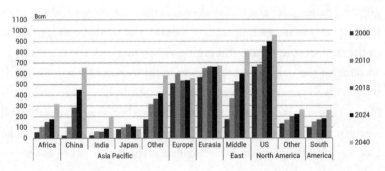

*Sources: International Energy Agency (2019);[8] International Energy Agency
(2019).[9]*

In both countries, natural gas demand is driven by a combination of rising energy consumption on the back of sustained economic development and policy frameworks to curb air pollution. This implies that non-power generation sectors have made a strong contribution to the growth of natural gas consumption in the Asia-Pacific region as well as in other emerging markets. Compared to the previous decade, the industrial sector takes the lead from power generation as the main driver of the global growth in the demand for natural gas.

Emerging markets, primarily in Asia, account for the bulk of this increase with natural gas gaining ground both as a fuel for industrial processes and as feedstock for chemicals and fertilizers. Industrial gas demand is also growing in major producing regions, such as North America and the Middle East, partly to support the expansion of petrochemical industries in these regions. The industrial sector is thus expected to be the main driver of natural gas consumption growth over the medium- and long-term, with the chemical industry being the largest contributor—both to generate heat and steam and as a user of natural gas feedstock to produce ammonia and methanol.

Power generation will retain a strong position in the future natural gas consumption mix, with prospects varying by region. However, the growing demand for electricity as well as the retirement of oil and coal-fired capacity will create expanding room for gas-fired power generation in the foreseeable future. Emerging Asian markets are expected to account for the bulk of future growth in the demand for natural gas. It is difficult to generalize on consumption trends, however, as the role of natural gas varies from one country to another. Gas is already well established for power generation or industrial uses in some markets like Pakistan and Bangladesh, but remains a niche fuel in other countries, including in India.[10]

Figure 2: Share of natural gas* in the energy mix by sector in emerging Asian markets (2018)

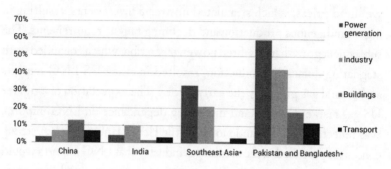

* *Shares in 2017*

Source: International Energy Agency (2020), database.[11]

The future share and expansion rate of natural gas will depend on a range of domestic energy policy and market design decisions related to the security of supply, infrastructure development and fuel prices. The availability, flexibility and competitiveness of natural gas supply is also a major driving force of current and future consumption growth and it has been fuelled by the development of new resources around the world, especially by the rapid rise of US shale gas production.

GAS 2.0: THE SHALE REVOLUTION

The strong growth of US production, thanks to the development of shale gas (both dry gas and associated gas produced from oil wells), has been the most impactful structural change on the supply side of the global gas market in the recent past, with ripple effects on natural gas trading, contracting and pricing.

In the mid-2000s, the US was expected to emerge as a major importer of LNG. Liquefied natural gas was an option used in the 1970s, with the development of several regasification terminals on the

East Coast. Market reforms in the 1980s and 1990s, however, led to the unbundling of natural gas transmission services and the deregulation of wellhead prices, which stimulated upstream investments, resulting in higher indigenous production and declining import requirements. The subsequent growth in gas-fired power generation, which coincided with stagnating domestic production, resulted in rising US LNG imports and natural gas prices by the early 2000s. The expectation of a tighter US gas market balance, and increasing dependence on LNG imports, was reflected in higher and more volatile Henry Hub prices.[12] A strong consensus prevailed in the natural gas industry that LNG imports would continue to increase rapidly. Twenty-one projects competed to increase the regasification capacity by the end of 2003, amidst strong rivalry between the US and Europe to gain access to long-term LNG supplies.

The development of shale gas completely changed the US supply picture, with both direct and indirect impacts on other importers of natural gas. The potential of shale gas was unlocked in the US by the combination and extensive use of horizontal drilling and hydraulic fracturing[13] and further optimized with the development of multi-well ('pad') drilling and mobile drilling rigs. Successive waves of development—from the Barnett and Eagle Ford basins in Texas in the early 2000s, to the Marcellus play in the Appalachian basin in the early 2010s and the tight oil-associated Permian basin in the mid-2010s— enabled shale gas production to increase at a remarkable average annual rate of 21 per cent since 2007.[14] The share of shale gas in US domestic production grew from 13 per cent in 2007 to 75 per cent in 2019. The shale revolution not only stopped the decline of domestic gas production in the US but also opened opportunities for new export projects, both through pipelines and in the form of LNG.

Figure 3: Evolution of US natural gas production (2007–19)

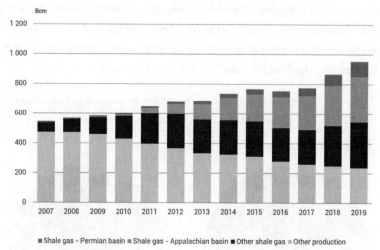

Bcm

■ Shale gas - Permian basin ■ Shale gas - Appalachian basin ■ Other shale gas ▪ Other production

Source: US Energy Information Administration (2020), database.[15]

Shale and other unconventional sources are likely to play an increasing role in the global natural gas supply in the future. While the US is expected to remain the main driver of shale gas production, other suppliers such as Canada, Argentina and China will see their own shale gas industries develop further in the medium- to long-term.

The US is expected to remain the single largest contributor to growth in production of natural gas in the coming years, even after the impact of the Covid-19 crisis, although the 2020 oil price collapse and the ensuing spending cuts and reduced associated gas production have clouded the near-term production prospects in the US shale patch. As a whole, North America will provide the largest contribution to exports, as most of the increase in natural gas output from other major producing areas—such as the Middle East, China or North Africa—will be dedicated to domestic markets.

Other than the US, Australia and the Russian Federation (Russia) will be the main contributors to export growth and most of this additional export capacity will be in the form of LNG. In the long-term, a more diverse range of producer countries could emerge, with the rise of new producing areas in Africa and Latin America as well as the development of new assets in mature producing regions, such as Eurasia and the Middle East.[16]

Figure 4: Medium-term, region-wise share in natural gas production growth in the Stated Policies Scenario

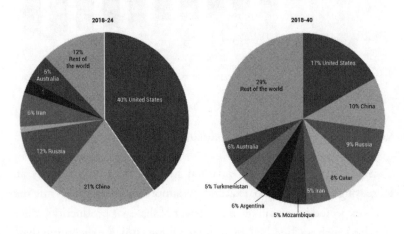

Sources: International Energy Agency (2019);[17] *International Energy Agency (2019).*[18]

LNG RESHAPES THE GLOBAL NATURAL GAS TRADE

Increasing Diversity of Buyers and Sellers

The development of LNG trade has resulted in a strong increase in the number of players involved. From a limited club of mature buyers, the number of countries and territories with LNG import terminals has grown from nine in 2000 to forty-two in 2019. This number is expected to expand further in the next five years, despite demand uncertainty in the aftermath of the Covid-19 crisis.

New buyers have various profiles, from fast-growing economies to mature markets seeking new sources of supply. New technologies, particularly fast-track floating storage and regasification units (FSRUs), are enabling countries to become LNG importers relatively quickly, whether as a bridge during their own domestic production ramp-up or benefiting from favourable arbitrages to supply their price-sensitive markets. The introduction of reloading capabilities in major importing markets, as well as the development of small-scale supply and distribution infrastructures for remote and decentralized uses, further reinforces the technical flexibility offered by LNG. The increasing number of LNG importers is accompanied by greater differentiation among buyers based on their domestic market requirements. A snapshot of the LNG market from 2017 shows that LNG buyers can be clustered in groups based on two primary metrics, namely LNG supply reliance, which can be measured by the share of LNG in total gas supply and LNG buying commitment, which can be quantified by the share of long-term contracts in LNG supply.[19]

The resulting four buyer types can be defined as follows.

- **Buyers dependent on LNG:** These rely almost entirely on LNG supplies due to the lack of alternatives. These buyers tend to have a large share of long-term contracts within their LNG supply mix.

- **Diversified buyers:** These have a more limited exposure to LNG in their gas-supply mix, due to the availability of domestic production, alternative pipeline import sources, or both. Most of these buyers also have a relatively high share of long-term contracts in their respective LNG portfolios.

- **Buyers using LNG as a back-up fuel** (especially in countries with hydro-dominated power sectors): These tend to have a relatively small LNG share in their gas-supply mix and a low proportion of long-term contracts within their LNG supply.

Figure 5: Evolution of LNG buyer types (2016–22)

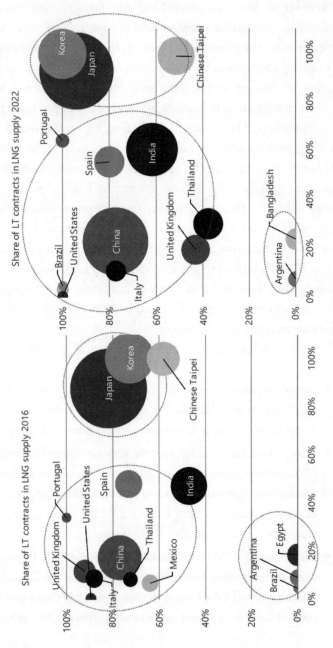

Source: International Energy Agency (2017).[20]

- **Price-driven buyers:** These buyers often use LNG as the main source of natural gas supply, but refrain from making long-term contractual commitments as price competitiveness is the main driver of their procurement strategy.

The LNG buyer landscape that emerges over time is increasingly fragmented yet interconnected and requires greater flexibility from the supply side. Flexibility needs are growing, especially in the power-generation sector, as the growing share of intermittent renewable energy sources increases load volatility. Flexibility requirements are expected to increase further in the future as the rapidly expanding emerging buyer segment gradually transitions from a traditional baseload import model to a semi-flexible or flexible import profile. By 2040, the baseload segment will only account for half of the total LNG demand in emerging Asia.[21]

On the LNG supply side, diversity is also set to increase, not only in terms of the number of sellers but also in terms of commercial approaches to LNG trade. In the upstream part of the LNG chain, the current wave of liquefaction capacity additions will result in a change in the balance of power. Qatar's historically dominant position will be increasingly challenged, even if the country completes its planned expansion project and eventually reclaims the number one spot among the leading LNG exporters later in the decade. The three major suppliers—Australia, Qatar and the US—will together account for more than half of global LNG export capacity by 2024, with similar market shares but rather different commercial models.

- Australia's liquefaction is structured around nine facilities, owned by various international oil companies (IOCs) and Asian LNG buyers. Most of the capacity is covered by long-term contracts with oil-linked pricing and fixed destinations for about two-thirds of volumes. As the majority of these plants are relatively new, contract expiry and renewal is not imminent in most cases.

- Qatar's capacity is controlled by a single player, the state-owned Qatar Petroleum, with minority shares held by IOCs and Asian companies. Its sales portfolio is more diversified, with traditional long-term volumes primarily marketed to Asia, flexible contracted volumes initially assigned to Europe and North America and spare capacity sold on a short-term basis.

- The first wave of US liquefaction infrastructure is largely complete, but a second wave of expansion, which began in 2018, is still under development. Capacity is sold with flexible destination and at hub-based pricing. Whereas most LNG export projects are integrated with upstream investment, US LNG projects are based on commodity supply and thus require only an investment in liquefaction in most cases.

The LNG supply chain is also undergoing structural change midstream, prompted by the emergence of global portfolio players and secondary markets.[22] Traditional contracts between primary LNG sellers and end users are evolving towards greater flexibility, with smaller volumes, shorter durations and the progressive removal of destination clauses.

Portfolio players have played an increasingly prominent role in global LNG trade. These are either major oil and gas companies or large utility companies, which aggregate supplies from a wide range of sources and projects with different maturities and pricing formulae. This process of aggregating supply enables portfolio players to provide LNG supply to various types of final customers according to their requirements. They sell mainly under term contracts but are also active in selling spot cargoes.

The conjunction of more flexible primary sourcing and the intermediation offered by portfolio players led to the emergence of secondary LNG markets, providing access to supply for both traditional end users and new buyers, especially for those without access to primary sourcing through long-term contracts because of duration, volume or financial inadequacy. The more recent arrival of trading houses as intermediary players completes this landscape. Commodity traders have a greater appetite for short-term risk, providing additional flexibility and supply diversification to buyers with lower credit worthiness than those served by traditional suppliers.

Figure 6: The evolution of LNG trade and the emergence of secondary markets

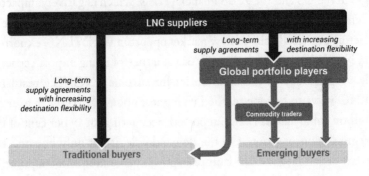

Source: International Energy Agency (2018).[23]

GLOBAL GAS TRADE SHIFTS TOWARDS COMPETITIVE PRICING AND GREATER MARKET FLEXIBILITY

Natural gas pricing is transitioning from a system of netback indexation (usually against oil or oil products) and regulated tariffs to market pricing, based on the fundamentals of supply and demand. The International Gas Union (IGU, 2019) has been reviewing the evolution of gas pricing mechanisms around the world in its annual wholesale gas price survey since 2005.[24]

The evolution of natural gas pricing between 2005 and 2018 shows an overall decrease in regulated tariffs and other forms of administered pricing—which remain dominant in Africa, the Middle East, Eurasia and South America—and a corresponding increase in market pricing (as well as oil-indexed pricing in parts of the Asia-Pacific). Market pricing is progressing in all regions, particularly in Europe where the shift away from oil-indexation has been decisive.[25]

This structural change in European gas pricing was enabled by market liberalization and the development of natural gas hubs but was also triggered by the arrival of market-priced LNG in the European system in the late 2000s. The development of liquefaction capacity (led by Qatar) coincided with the rapid rise of the production of shale gas in the US and the 2008 financial crisis, which negatively impacted demand in key LNG importing economies in Asia. This confluence of factors practically closed new market opportunities for LNG exporters in North America and most of Asia at a time of rising export capacity, leaving Europe as the main outlet for surplus LNG. The resulting LNG wave to Europe reached its highest point in 2011, with over 90 billion cubic meters (Bcm) imported, accounting for 17 per cent of the region's consumption. On the demand side, it not only boosted the share of natural gas in the European power generation mix temporarily, but also displaced non-competitive oil-linked pipeline gas, prompting major European buyers to reduce their offtake to minimum contractual volumes. This LNG surplus to Europe was short lived.

From 2011, Japan's LNG import needs surged to compensate for the shutdown of its nuclear reactors in the aftermath of the Fukushima incident. This triggered a structural change in pricing, as European utilities renegotiated the price indexation formulae of their long-term pipeline gas contracts to increase the share of market pricing at the expense of traditional oil indexation.

Figure 7: Evolution of natural gas pricing per region (2005–18)

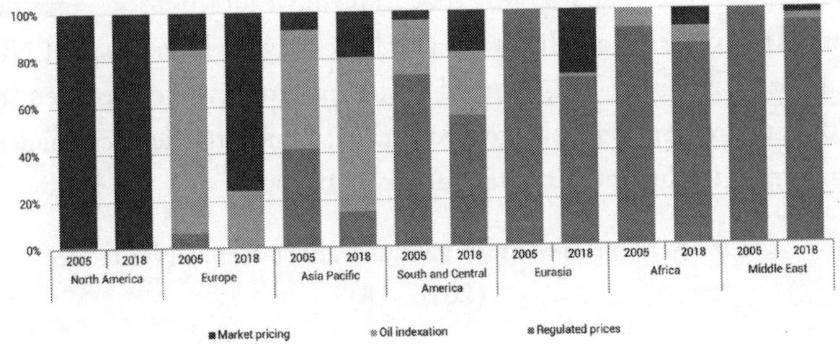

Source: International Gas Union (2019).[26]

The first half of the 2010s saw a rapid development of new LNG export projects. A total of 177 Bcm of capacity received a final investment decision between 2011 and 2015, representing a 50 per cent increase of total liquefaction capacity from 2010 levels. The first projects from this investment wave were commissioned in 2015, in a weakening price environment that was the combined result of decreasing spot procurement from Japan and lower oil prices. This market environment was more favourable to buyers than to sellers and it enabled the development of spot and short-term LNG trade (Figure 8).

The analysis of LNG contracts signed between 2014 and 2017 shows an evolution in the development of flexibility, both in terms of destination flexibility (with more destination-free contracts), and time flexibility (with an increasing share of short-term volumes). Such short-term contracts with durations of up to one year (excluding spot) accounted for almost a quarter of the total contracted volume signed in 2017, although the proportion of short-term contracts declined significantly in subsequent years as the 2018–19 LNG investment wave brought about a revival of long-term LNG contracts.

Spot volumes also expanded from less than 60 Bcm in 2014 to over 100 Bcm in 2018. This near-doubling of spot LNG trade was accompanied by a growing diversity of buyers, with a decreasing role for Japan—the single-largest spot LNG buyer until 2015—and the rapid rise of China and India as major LNG buyers. Korea's spot LNG imports also increased, spurred by the progressive development of 'direct importers' on the Korean market (enabling large-scale consumers to import LNG for their own use).

Figure 8: Development of spot and short-term LNG trade (2015–18)

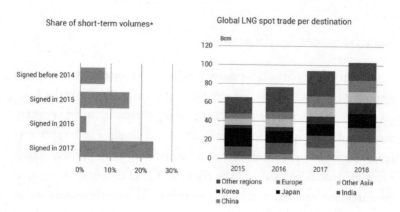

Share of short-term volumes*

Global LNG spot trade per destination

* Up to one year, excluding spot

Source: International Energy Agency (2018).[27]

The expiry of legacy LNG contracts could be an additional catalyst for greater market flexibility over time. Most legacy contracts have destination clauses, but a sizeable part of the contracted volumes will expire in the coming years. If the expiring contracts are not renewed, then the volume of uncontracted supply could surpass 200 Bcm by 2024, representing almost a third of the total export capacity.[28] The expiration of legacy contracts could thus result in a growing share of destination-free, uncontracted LNG on the market, which would increase competition among suppliers and improve supply options for buyers at the same time.

Figure 9: LNG export capacity contracted by destination flexibility (2014–24)

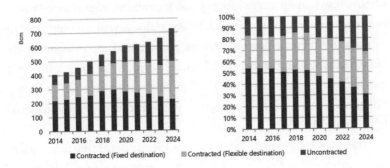

Source: International Energy Agency (2019).[29]

CONCLUSION

The global gas market has undergone significant structural changes in recent years with China, India and other fast-growing Asian economies gaining prominence as major consumers and importers of LNG, and the emergence of the US as the leading source of gas supply and export growth. The growing diversity on both the supply and demand side, in turn, has prompted fundamental shifts in natural gas trading, contracting and pricing, while enhancing competition and market flexibility in the process.

The emergence of global LNG portfolio players and trading houses as intermediaries and the development of secondary LNG markets have greatly contributed to the democratization of LNG trade. At the same time, the shift to market-based pricing, the growing share of spot and short-term LNG trade, the gradual removal of destination restrictions and the expiry of rigid legacy LNG contracts have greatly improved market flexibility and strengthened the hands of buyers vis-à-vis sellers in the global LNG market.

The evolution of LNG trade towards a more competitive market environment is an opportunity for India. To meet the government's target of more than doubling the share of gas in the primary energy mix (from 6 per cent at present, to 15 per cent by 2030), India will not only need to substantially increase domestic production, but also import significantly more natural gas in the form of LNG. By 2040, India's net natural gas imports are projected to reach 115 Bcm according to the IEA's Stated Policies Scenario, which is equivalent to 16 per cent of projected global LNG trade.[30]

There is strong evidence that India is already benefiting from a more competitive global LNG market. In 2019, spot cargoes and deliveries under short-term contracts accounted for more than half of India's LNG imports, and India became the second-largest buyer of spot LNG after China. India now has a more balanced LNG supply mix than it did a decade ago, with LNG imports coming from sixteen different countries in 2019. The buyer's market that prevailed in the last five years enabled Indian companies to renegotiate unfavourable LNG contracts with key suppliers, notably with Rasgas (now Qatargas in 2015, with ExxonMobil in 2017, and with Gazprom in 2018.

However, to take full advantage of a more flexible global natural gas market in the future, India will need to implement a series of gas market and pricing reforms, accelerate its infrastructure roll-out, and provide non-discriminatory third-party access to its infrastructure to ensure that its increasingly competitive and flexible LNG supply can reach end users across the country.

Notes

1. US Energy Information Administration, 'Electric Power Monthly', Washington: EIA, 2020, https://www.eia.gov/electricity/monthly/
2. The IEA is an autonomous organization, which works to ensure reliable, affordable and clean energy. It has thirty member countries and eight association countries including India.

3. The Stated Policies Scenario (STEPS) aims to provide a sense of where today's policy ambitions seem likely to take the energy sector. It incorporates not only the policies and measures that governments around the world have already put in place, but also the likely effects of announced policies, including the Nationally Determined Contributions made under the Paris Agreement.

4. International Energy Agency, 'World Energy Outlook 2019', Paris: OECD/IEA, 2019, https://www.iea.org/reports/world-energy-outlook-2019

5. The Sustainable Development Scenario (SDS) outlines an integrated approach to achieving internationally agreed objectives on climate change, air quality and universal access to modern energy.

6. US Energy Information Administration, 'Electric Power Monthly'.

7. International Energy Agency, 'World Energy Outlook 2019'.

8. Ibid.

9. International Energy Agency, 'Market Report Series: Gas 2019', Paris: OECD/IEA, 2019, https://www.iea.org/reports/market-report-series-gas-2019

10. US Energy Information Administration, 'Dry shale gas production estimates per play', Washington: EIA, 2020, https://www.eia.gov/naturalgas/data.php

11. International Energy Agency, 'World Energy Balances', Paris: OECD/IEA, 2020, http://data.iea.org/payment/products/117-world-energy-balances.aspx

12. These moved from around $3/MMBtu in 2002, to above $8/MMBtu in 2005. (MMBtu is one million Btu.)

13. Both were already mature oil and gas production techniques at the beginning of shale gas exploitation. It is their combination and subsequent intensive and optimized use, which was the main technical innovation.

14. International Energy Agency, 'Global Gas Security Review 2017', Paris: OECD/IEA, 2017, https://webstore.iea.org/global-gas-security-review-2017

15. US Energy Information Administration, 'Dry shale gas production estimates per play'.
16. International Energy Agency, 'Global Gas Security Review 2018', Paris: OECD/IEA, 2018, https://webstore.iea.org/global-gas-security-review-2018
17. International Energy Agency, 'World Energy Outlook 2019'.
18. International Energy Agency, 'Market Report Series: Gas 2019'.
19. International Energy Agency, 'World Energy Outlook 2019'.
20. International Energy Agency, 'Global Gas Security Review 2017'.
21. International Energy Agency, 'Global Gas Security Review 2018'.
22. International Energy Agency, 'Market Report Series: Gas 2019'.
23. International Energy Agency, 'Global Gas Security Review 2018'.
24. International Gas Union, 'Wholesale Gas Price Survey, 2019 Edition: A Global Review of Price Formation Mechanisms 2005 to 2018', Barcelona: IGU, May 2019, https://www.igu.org/app/uploads-wp/2019/05/IGU_Wholesale_Price_Survey_2019.pdf
25. International Energy Agency, 'Global Gas Security Review 2019', Paris: OECD/IEA, 2019, https://www.iea.org/reports/global-gas-security-review-2019
26. International Gas Union, 'Wholesale Gas Price Survey 2019 Edition'.
27. International Energy Agency, 'Global Gas Security Review 2018'.
28. International Gas Union, 'Wholesale Gas Price Survey 2019 Edition'.
29. International Energy Agency, 'Global Gas Security Review 2019'.
30. International Energy Agency, 'World Energy Outlook 2019'.

3

LIQUIFIED NATURAL GAS: PRICING AND EVOLUTION

MIKE FULWOOD

Senior Research Fellow, Oxford Institute for Energy Studies; Fellow, Center on Global Energy Policy, Columbia University

TIM BOERSMA

Fellow, Center on Global Energy Policy, Columbia University

THIS CHAPTER PROVIDES AN OVERVIEW of global trends in LNG pricing. It takes history into consideration while attempting a forward-looking view, especially as the impacts of LNG from the US are just starting to show. The first section provides a brief historical overview of price mechanisms in North America, Europe and Asia, focusing on some of the structural differences in these markets that persist to this day.[1] This section draws heavily on the International Gas Union's (IGU) annual Wholesale Gas Price Survey.[2] The second section specifically considers trends in LNG pricing, for different regions and countries, both levels and linkages. We conclude with a summary of the key messages and our thoughts on what these might constitute for prospective buyers.

A. PRICING DEVELOPMENTS: MECHANISMS

In 2019, there were forty-one countries importing LNG and twenty that exported LNG. In 2005, only fifteen countries imported LNG and thirteen exported LNG, while in 1995, there were just eight importers and eight exporters. It is this rapid growth, especially in importing countries—along with the liberalization of Europe post-2005 and the emergence of the US as an LNG exporter—which has, in part, led to pricing developments.

INTERNATIONAL GAS UNION WHOLESALE PRICE SURVEY: BACKGROUND

The recently published IGU survey, covering the year 2019, was the twelfth survey and began in 2005.[3] The twelve surveys have confirmed significant changes in wholesale price formation mechanisms, during a period of key developments and upheavals in the global gas market.

The surveys incorporate a number of different categories for wholesale prices and these are described in the box below.

Box 1: Types of price formation mechanisms	
Oil Price Escalation (OPE)	The price is linked, usually through a base price and an escalation clause, to competing fuels (typically crude oil, gas oil and/or fuel oil). In some cases, coal prices can be used, as can electricity prices.
Gas-on-Gas Competition (GOG)	The price is determined by the interplay of supply and demand (gas-on-gas competition) and is traded over a variety of different periods (daily, monthly, annually or other periods). Trading takes place at physical hubs (e.g., Henry Hub), or notional hubs (e.g., NBP in the UK).

	There are likely to be developed futures markets (New York Mercantile Exchange (NYMEX) or the Intercontinental Exchange (ICE). Not all gas is bought and sold on a short-term fixed price basis and there will be longer-term contracts, but these will use gas price indices to determine the monthly price, for example, rather than competing fuel indices. Also included in this category are spot LNG cargoes, any pricing which is linked to hub or spot prices and also bilateral agreements in markets where there are multiple buyers and sellers.
Bilateral Monopoly (BIM)	The price is determined by bilateral discussions and agreements between a large seller and a large buyer, with the price being fixed for a period of time, typically one year. There may be a written contract in place but often the arrangement is at the government or state-owned company level. Usually, there would be a single dominant buyer or seller on at least one side of the transaction, to distinguish this category from GOG, where there would be multiple buyers and sellers trading bilaterally.
Netback from Final Product (NET)	The price received by the gas supplier is a function of the price received by the buyer for the final product the buyer produces. This may occur where the gas is used as a feedstock in chemical plants, such as ammonia or methanol and is the major variable cost in producing the product.

Regulation: Cost of Service (RCS)	The price is determined, or approved, formally by a regulatory authority, or possibly a ministry, but the level is set to cover the cost of service, including the recovery of investment and a reasonable rate of return.
Regulation: Social and Political (RSP)	The price is set on an irregular basis (probably by a ministry on a political/ social basis), in response to the need to cover increasing costs, or possibly as a revenue-raising exercise—a hybrid between RCS and RBC.
Regulation: Below Cost (RBC)	The price is *knowingly* set below the average cost of producing and transporting the gas, often as a form of state subsidy to the population.
No Price (NP)	The gas produced is either provided free to the population and industry, possibly as a feedstock for chemical and fertilizer plants, or in refinery processes and enhanced oil recovery. The gas produced may be associated with oil and/or liquids and treated as a by-product.
Not Known (NK)	No data or evidence.

In respect of analysing price formation mechanisms, each country's consumption can be considered to have come from domestic production, pipeline imports and LNG imports. Information was collected for these three categories with additional analysis being done for imports in total and finally, total consumption.

For total world consumption, the GOG share had reached 48 per cent in 2019. The OPE was at 19 per cent, with the regulated categories—RCS, RSP and RBC—in total at around 30 per cent. *Overall, over the 2005 to 2019 period, the share of GOG rose by almost 17 percentage points, while OPE declined by 6 percentage points.* The BIM declined by 2.5 percentage points, while in the regulated categories RCS rose by 9 percentage points, RSP rose by nearly 3 percentage points, while RBC declined by almost 20 percentage points.

Figure 1: World price formation (2005–19)

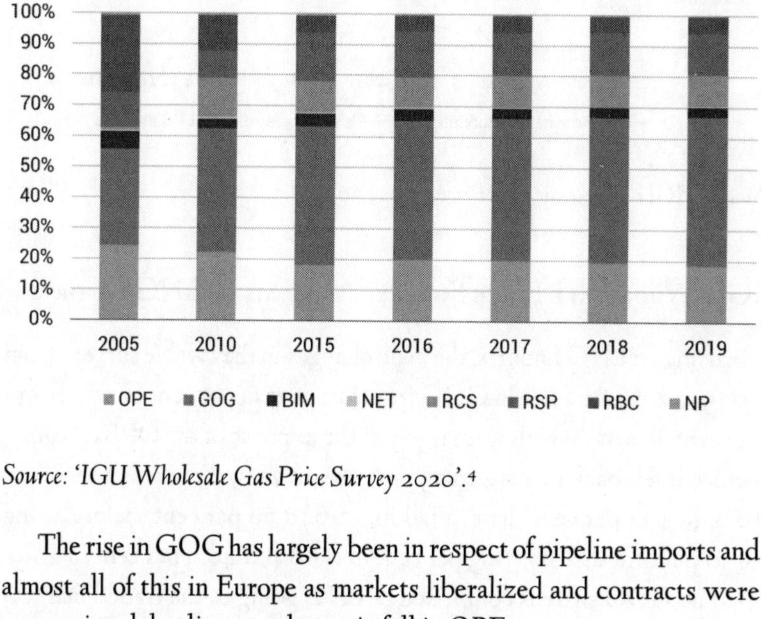

Source: 'IGU Wholesale Gas Price Survey 2020'.[4]

The rise in GOG has largely been in respect of pipeline imports and almost all of this in Europe as markets liberalized and contracts were renegotiated, leading to a dramatic fall in OPE.

There has also been some rise in domestic production, principally as US consumption (all GOG) grew, while the share of LNG imports has moved up and down, although there were sharp increases in 2018 and 2019, discussed further below.

Figure 2: Changes in gas-on-gas by consumption category (2005–19)

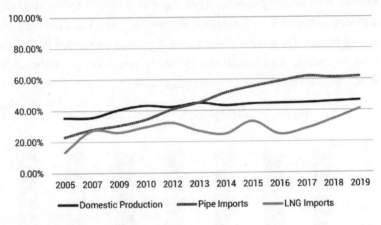

Source: 'IGU Wholesale Gas Price Survey 2020.'[5]

IGU WHOLESALE PRICE SURVEY: ANALYSIS OF LNG IMPORTS

Focusing on LNG imports, the main changes in the twelve surveys from 2005 to 2019 are a rise in GOG from just over 13 per cent in 2005 to 32 per cent in 2012, which was largely at the expense of the OPE category, before it fell back in 2014 to 25 per cent. In 2015 there was a recovery back to a 32 per cent share, a fall in 2016 to 26 per cent, before rising to 30 per cent in 2017, 34.3 per cent in 2018 and 40.9 per cent in 2019.

The GOG share is comprised of LNG going to the traded markets in North America and in Europe (the UK, Belgium and the Netherlands) and spot LNG cargoes to 'traditional' LNG markets in Asia-Pacific and Europe and some newer markets.

There was a significant increase in GOG between 2005 and 2007, principally due to a rise in spot LNG imports in Asia and Asia-Pacific and a smaller rise in North American imports. Since 2007, there have been offsetting changes with North American LNG imports (all GOG) declining, European imports (principally to the UK) increasing in 2009 and 2010 and relative stability in Asia and Asia-Pacific spot LNG imports.

In 2012, as Europe's LNG imports declined, these were more than offset in the GOG category by rising spot LNG imports in Asia and Asia-Pacific. The decline in 2013 reflected the fall in the share of spot LNG imports and a decline in LNG imports into the UK, the US and Canada. The further small decline in 2014 was principally due to lower spot LNG cargoes in Asia and Asia-Pacific, with correspondingly higher OPE under long-term contracts. The rebound in 2015 was largely due to more spot LNG cargoes in all markets but especially in Japan and the new markets, as the fall in spot LNG prices preceded a decline in oil-linked contract prices. In 2016, the decline in GOG was a consequence of LNG trade becoming more contracted, with fewer spot LNG cargoes, which benefitted OPE. In 2017, this was reversed as spot LNG cargoes increased, in part due to the rise in Henry Hub-priced US LNG exports.

The most significant changes in LNG imports of all the surveys came in 2018 and 2019, driven not only by the continued rise in Henry Hub priced US LNG exports, but also by a general rise in spot LNG cargoes[6] plus a sharp increase in LNG imports in 2019 heading to the trading markets of Europe. Thus GOG accounted for 68 per cent of LNG imports into Europe in 2019 as compared to 35 per cent in 2017, while the GOG share in Asia rose from 23 per cent to 40 per cent and in Asia-Pacific from 18 per cent to 23 per cent. Despite the growth in LNG imports between 2017 and 2019 of some 70 billion cubic metres (Bcm) or 17 per cent, the actual volume of OPE imports declined in both 2018 and 2019—the first time this had ever happened.

Figure 3: World price formation (2005–19), LNG imports

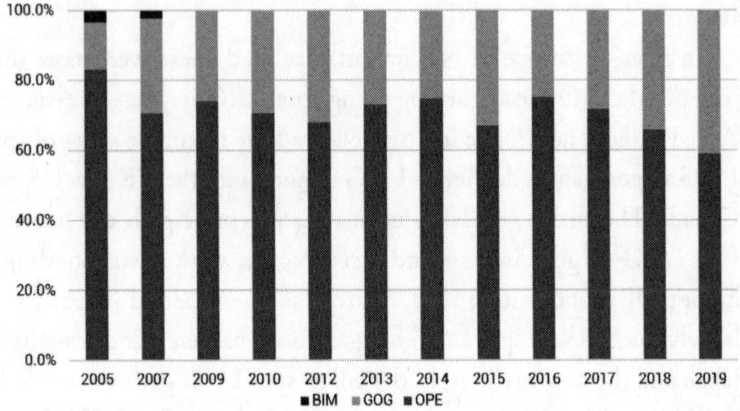

Source: 'IGU Wholesale Gas Price Survey 2020'.[7]

The volume of LNG going to the traded markets was in decline since 2010, reflecting a corresponding decline in US LNG imports, as well as declining imports from the UK between 2014 and 2015. This decline in traded markets, however, was reversed in 2019 as LNG rushed to the European markets. Spot LNG cargoes have increased especially in the last three years, in Asia Pacific, Asia and parts of Europe, plus the newer LNG importing countries. Spot LNG cargoes totalled some 140 Bcm in 2019, compared to 120 Bcm in 2018, 86 Bcm in 2017 and just 63 Bcm in 2016. Figure 4 below breaks down the data from Figure 3, showing spot LNG separately and the percentage of spot LNG in total LNG imports.

It can be seen that in 2005 and, to a smaller extent, in 2010, that out of the GOG share, a significant element was LNG into traded markets and not spot. This was almost all the US in 2005 and then in 2010 the US, Canada and Mexico plus the UK and Belgium.

Figure 4: World price formation 2005 to 2019, spot LNG imports

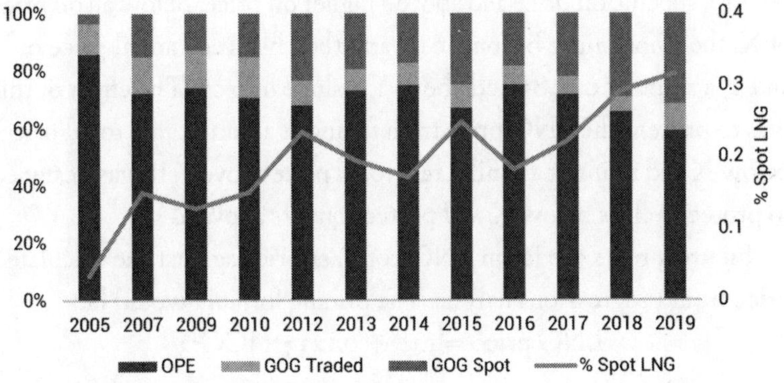

Source: 'IGU Wholesale Gas Price Survey 2020'.[8]

B. PRICING DEVELOPMENTS: LEVELS AND LINKAGES

Asia LNG Pricing

Outside of the US, in 2005 there was little or no GOG in the LNG market with very few spot cargoes, and Europe had yet to liberalize. This was also true of the period before 2005. A good description of early LNG pricing is contained in the Oxford Institute for Energy Studies' book titled *The Pricing of Internationally Traded Gas*.[9] In Asian markets, the early pricing from 1969 to 1973 was on a fixed price basis, but after the 1973 oil shock, parity with crude oil became the norm, up until around 1983. As Japan was by far the biggest buyer, the crude oil benchmark used was normally the Japan Crude Cocktail (JCC) and contract terms would specify a percentage of JCC—which as oil parity would have been 0.172. This percentage was known as the 'slope'. This began to evolve over time to lower slopes, but included a fixed element as well, which was sometime notionally related to the shipping cost.

A commonly used slope was 0.1485 with a fixed cost of 0.61.[10] This would lead to a higher LNG price than crude oil parity below $30 and a lower LNG price than crude oil parity above $30. The next development was the introduction of the 'S' curve, which involved a lower slope both below a specific oil price and above a higher oil price. Below an oil price of X, the slope might become 0.07 and then between an oil price of X and Y, a slope of 0.1485 and above Y, a slope of 0.07. The effect of this was to prevent the LNG price from falling at a similar rate to oil prices below X and rising at a similar rate to oil price above Y. It was designed to protect sellers below X and protect buyers above Y.

Figure 5 plots the Japan LNG contract price against the calculated price from a regression analysis. The pricing formula would be:

$$\text{LNG price} = 1.18 + 0.1233 \times \text{JCC-3}$$

The JCC in dollars per barrel is lagged three months, which is the best fit. The R squared is 96.47 per cent. It is noticeable that the calculated contract price diverges a little from the actual contract prices from 2005 to 2008 and 2012 to 2014. From 2005 to 2008, oil prices jumped sharply, reaching over $100 in 2008. This could have been the effect of some S curves in the contracts. The years 2012 to 2014 were the post-Fukushima period with high oil prices.

Figure 5: Japan LNG contract price (1992–2019)

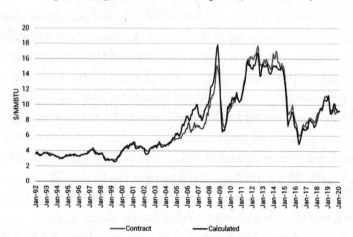

Source: *Argus Media.*[11]

The pre-2005 slope is 0.1131 with an intercept of 1.46, while the 2005 onwards slope is 0.1275 and the intercept is 0.80. This would be consistent with changing contract terms with maybe the removal of S curves. The analysis is little different if the average LNG price (including spot) is used as opposed to the contract LNG price.

Figure 6 below compares the Japan spot price to the contract price. The spot price has been significantly more volatile than the contract price. The spot price is calculated, for the period up to 2012 from the Argus customs data, and from 2012 to early 2014 as the average of the customs data and the Argus ANEA spot benchmark price and thereafter, Japan's Ministry of Economy, Trade and Industry (METI) arrival spot price is also included. Up until 2005, there were probably limited spot volumes.

Figure 6: Japan Contract and Spot Prices (2000–20)

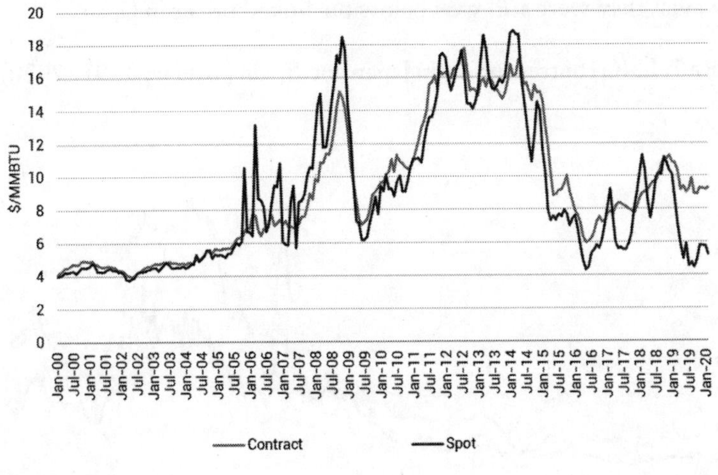

Source: *Argus Media.*

EUROPEAN LNG CONTRACT PRICING

Outside Asia, and until around 2010, the other main LNG importing region was Europe. Spain was the largest LNG importer, followed by France. As for Asia, contracts outside the UK and Belgium markets were largely linked to oil. However, in the case of Europe, the oil linkage was often to gas oil and fuel oil products rather than a crude oil price, although there was some linkage to Brent in some contracts. This tended to follow the oil linkage in the pipeline import contracts from Russia, Norway and Algeria, until markets liberalized, combined with the 2009 recession, and oil linkage began to disappear (as noted in the IGU surveys).

However, European LNG prices linked to oil were generally lower than Japanese prices, as shown in Figure 7 below, when compared to Spanish contract prices. Spain had some lower-priced contracts from Algeria, but prices in France were a little higher than Spanish prices. However, they were still well below oil-linked prices in Japan.

Figure 7: LNG contract prices in Japan and Spain (January, 1991–2020)

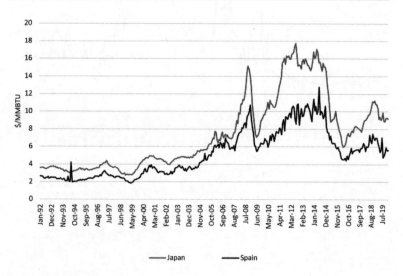

Source: Argus Media.

US LNG Export Contract Pricing

The development of US LNG projects helped lead a fundamental change in contracting and pricing in the LNG market. The traditional contract structure of a delivered price to the buyer's facilities at a single bundled price was already under threat from new portfolio players in the market led by British Gas (BG), which was subsequently bought by Shell. Cheniere, as the developer of the first US LNG export project in the Lower 48,[12] took this one step further by effectively unbundling the LNG contract and pricing elements. Cheniere offered to sell on a free on board (FOB) basis at the export loading point at its Sabine Pass facility, with a price based on 115 per cent of Henry Hub,[13] plus a liquefaction fee. The standard liquefaction fee was $3 per Metric Million British Thermal Units (MMBtu), but early buyers such as BG and Gas Natural received a discount on that.

In contrast to oil price linkage (which incorporates the concept of a market value for the LNG), based on alternative fuels, the Cheniere contract price is effectively a cost-plus contract and once delivered to the market, may be different from a concept of market value. In Asian markets where for the most part the cost of the LNG can be passed through and the FOB buyer is the Asian utility, then the recorded price might well be the cost of the cargo (including shipping). However, in trading markets in north-west Europe, the LNG can in reality only be sold at the hub price. Similarly, if a portfolio player is the offtaker from Sabine Pass and then sells the LNG on a spot basis to Japan, for instance, the most likely delivered price would be the spot price (i.e., market value not cost-plus).

With US LNG exports from the Lower 48 being a fairly recent occurrence, comprehensive data on the delivered prices is only just becoming available, largely in Asian markets. Only sporadic data is available for European markets. Table 1 below shows the US-delivered LNG price to the main Asian markets in 2018 and calculates the margin—or profitability—by deducting the shipping costs, tolling fee and 115 per cent of Henry Hub.

Table 1: Delivered US LNG prices, 2018[14]

$/ MMBtu	US LNG Delivered Price	Shipping Cost	Tolling Fee	115% of Henry Hub	Margin
China	9.92	2.20	3.00	3.50	1.22
Japan	10.60	2.00	3.00	3.50	2.10
Korea	9.11	2.15	3.00	3.50	0.46
India	8.45	2.15	3.00	3.50	0.20

Source: Argus; Author calculations.

The delivered US LNG prices are simple monthly averages for 2018 and could be from different suppliers under different contractual terms (2019 wasn't used although data was available, since there were very few US LNG cargoes to China because of the tariffs imposed). Table 2 below compares the delivered US LNG price for each market with average contract prices and average spot prices in those markets.

Table 2: Asia–comparative LNG prices

$/MMBtu	US LNG Delivered Price	Contract Price	Spot price
China	9.92	9.26	10.20
Japan	10.60	9.85	9.88
Korea	9.11	9.86	9.97
India	8.45	9.07	8.81

Source: Argus Media.

Apart from Japan, the delivered US LNG price has been lower than the spot price and also the contract price in India and Korea. Only in India has the delivered price apparently been less than the full cost of US LNG.

It should be noted that LNG prices in Asia were high in 2018 and in 2019 prices dropped significantly. As we proceed with much lower prices, it will be interesting to see how the delivered US LNG prices are recorded. With high prices in 2018, the recorded prices are broadly consistent with the contract and spot prices and also largely more than cover the full costs.

Spot LNG Pricing

Asian spot LNG pricing remains largely based on benchmark prices provided by reporting agencies such as Platts, Argus and Independent Commodity Intelligence Services (ICIS). The Asian markets are as yet far removed from the liquid trading markets of North America and north-west Europe. A report published in April 2018 by the Centre on Global Energy Policy included an extensive discussion on the prospects for the development of an Asian LNG trading hub.[15] This report concluded that there was still a long way to go before there would be a trading hub in Asia, although it noted the strong growth in the Japan–Korea Market (JKM) futures contract.

The lack of a trading hub notwithstanding, there are a number of benchmark prices as noted above. Figure 8 below compares the Japan spot price to the Notional Balancing Point (NBP) of the UK hub, going back to 2000. The Title Transfer Facility (TTF) in the Netherlands is the largest hub now, but price data on that only started in 2006. Prior to 2012, the Japan spot price was calculated from Argus data for uncontracted LNG prices.

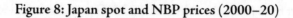

Figure 8: Japan spot and NBP prices (2000–20)

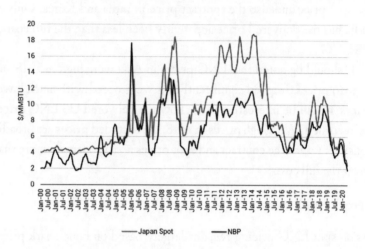

Source: Argus Media.

For the most part, the Japan spot price has been above the NBP price, significantly so between 2010 and 2015. Figure 6 suggests that the Japan spot price closely tracked the oil-linked contract price but was more volatile. Since oil linkage dominated the LNG market in this period, the spot price was heavily influenced by the contract price. The situation in Europe was very different with market liberalization driving contract renegotiations and, as shown by the IGU Wholesale Price Survey, a continued switch away from oil linkage. The NBP price, therefore, was more reflective of the underlying supply and demand situation. This process may just be beginning in the Asian markets and in 2019, we saw the first real delinking between spot and contract prices.

INDIA's LNG PRICES

India began importing LNG from Qatar in 2004, first under a fixed price and then linked to oil prices, but with a long five-year average lag. This was renegotiated in 2015. Since then, contracts with Australia and the US have been added, as well as portfolio contracts with a continuous supply from Nigeria. Figure 9 below shows prices from Qatar, Australia and Nigeria.

Figure 9: India's LNG contract prices (2004–20)

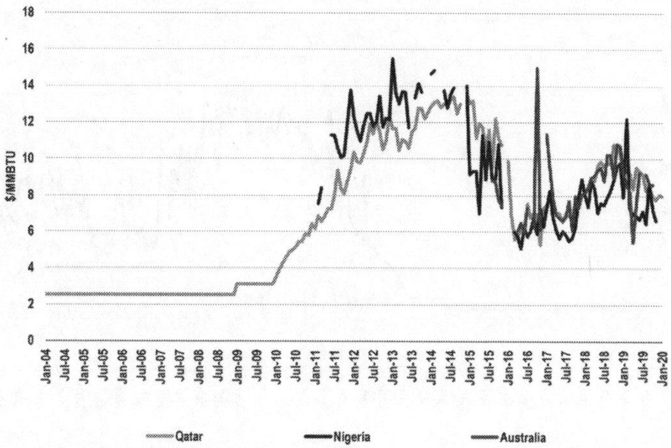

Source: Argus Media.

All these contracts are linked to oil prices, although the Nigerian volumes may be from different suppliers under different pricing arrangements, hence the volatility. These prices have been significantly higher than domestic prices.

Figure 10 below compares the average contract price with other prices, which will largely be spot and short-term contracts plus the US volumes. Also shown is the Dubai–Kuwait–India (DKI) price from SGX and Tullet Prebon[16]. In the early years, the other (spot) series was very volatile, reflecting limited volumes. However, the series is now less volatile and is much closer to the average contract price. The series is also reasonably close to the DKI price.

It should be noted that the DKI price has declined to well below the prices under the oil-linked contracts, in early 2019. The DKI series has now been discontinued but was fairly close to Japan spot prices so this differential between Indian spot prices and contract prices is likely to have continued.

Figure 10: India contract and spot prices (2004–20)

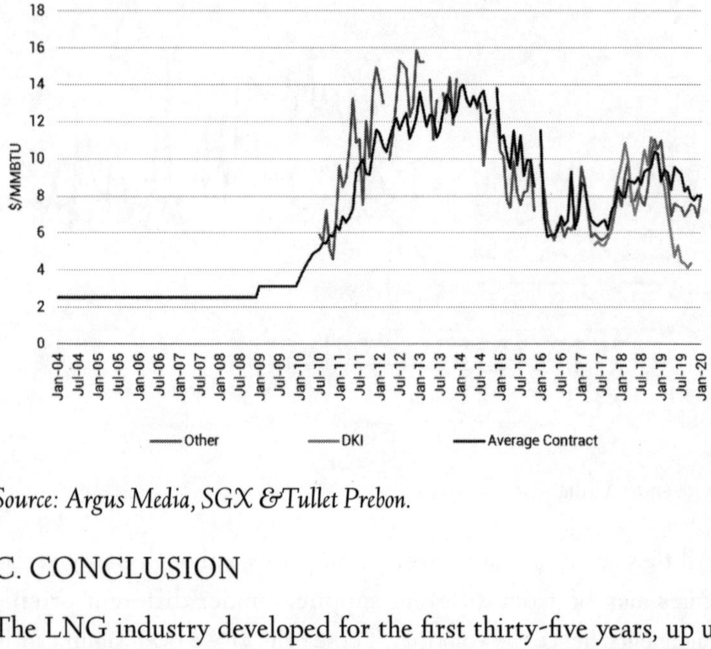

Source: Argus Media, SGX &Tullet Prebon.

C. CONCLUSION

The LNG industry developed for the first thirty-five years, up until 2005, on the back of long-term contracts—first with prices fixed, then with linkage to oil prices in 1973 after the oil price hike. This started as crude oil parity up until the mid-1980s, when the now-familiar formulae of a percentage (slope) of JCC plus a fixed element became the norm. At oil prices below $30 a barrel, this led to LNG prices being higher than parity but lower than parity above $30 a barrel. The S curves were also introduced in some contracts, which further reduced the response to oil prices.

In the 1990s and 2000s, first the US and North America and then Europe, led by the UK, began liberalizing their gas markets, creating liquid trading hubs. The LNG imports into these markets were priced against hubs and spot LNG cargoes also began to grow. Even then the average share of OPE in LNG imports between 2005 and 2016 was 73 per cent. During this same period, there was a sharp decline in OPE in Europe, as trading hubs spread to most parts of Europe. It is only in the last two years, 2018 especially, that spot LNG has grown significantly, helped by growing US LNG exports.

Liberalization has not yet taken hold in the Asian markets. Prices have remained mostly linked to oil in the absence of a truly liquid trading market and have been higher than in the trading markets of North America and Europe. Even with oil linkage, prices in Europe have been lower than in Japan and other markets. The experience in Europe—when hub prices, reflecting supply and demand, were much lower than oil-linked contracts and led to widespread price renegotiations—has not been repeated in Asian LNG contracts. The spot prices in Asian markets have for the most part been close to the oil-linked contract prices, so the decoupling seen in the European markets has yet to emerge. However, in 2019, Asian spot prices were consistently below oil-linked contract prices, which may well change the market dynamics.

With the supply of LNG outstripping demand since late 2018, Asian and European spot prices have converged. While it might be expected that the Asian premium would re-emerge as the LNG market moved back into balance in the coming two to three years, the markets are becoming increasingly interconnected, with US LNG adding to Qatari LNG and both acting as market balancers.

The large markets in Europe and in Asia, the traditional LNG markets of Japan, Korea and Taiwan plus China and potentially India, are likely to be the key demand centres that drive prices. In Europe and potentially China, competition between LNG and pipeline imports, principally from Russia in both markets, is increasingly important. Much of European pricing is already dominated by supply and demand fundamentals. With the changes in contracting practices, as will be seen in the next chapter of this volume, notably in respect of destination flexibility, the importance of portfolio players and shorter duration contracts, it seems likely that supply and demand will increasingly be setting prices in the Asian markets.

If the current divergence between spot prices and oil-indexed prices persists, which given the current supply overhang seems likely, then this could prompt buyers to put pressure on sellers to renegotiate existing contracts. In any event, for new contracts, it might be expected that there would be little incentive to agree to oil-indexed pricing, even as the search for a reliable pricing benchmark (particularly in Asia) to incorporate into long-term contracts goes on. The Platts JKM benchmark is being used as a hedging tool, in the futures market, but there is little or no use in long-term contracts.

Another pricing option is to use Henry Hub pricing, as is used in the US LNG contracts. That introduces an element of spot or hub pricing into the contracts. However, Henry Hub pricing only reflects the market conditions in the supply area, not in the end-user market and is essentially a cost-plus approach. As those looking to export US LNG to Europe are finding out, the cost-plus pricing model does not survive first contact with the reality of market forces. In liquid trading markets where market fundamentals rule, we are all price takers, whether buyers or sellers.

Notes

1. A complete and more detailed review of LNG pricing, including the history and issues, can be found in a joint publication by the Oxford Institute for Energy Studies (OIES) and the Riyadh-based King Abdullah Petroleum Studies and Research Center (KAPSARC): Anne-Sophie Corbeau and David Ledesma (eds), *LNG Markets in Transition: The Great Reconfiguration*, London: Oxford University Press,

2016; and an earlier OIES publication: Jonathan P. Stern (ed.), *Pricing of Internationally Traded Gas*, London: Oxford University Press, 2012.

2. International Gas Union, 'Wholesale Gas Price Survey 2020 Edition: A Global Review of Price Formation Mechanisms 2005 to 2019', Barcelona: IGU, June 2020, https://www.igu.org/app/uploads-wp/2020/07/IGU_WholesalePriceSurveyReport2020_01_07_20.pdf

3. International Gas Union, 'Wholesale Gas Price Survey 2019 Edition: A Global Review of Price Formation Mechanisms 2005 to 2018', Barcelona: IGU, May 2019, https://www.igu.org/app/uploads-wp/2019/05/IGU_Wholesale_Price_Survey_2019.pdf

4. International Gas Union, 'Wholesale Gas Price Survey 2020 Edition'.

5. Ibid.

6. The definition of Spot LNG in the IGU survey is not the same as the definition of spot and short-term contracts by the International Group of Liquefied Natural Gas Importers (GIIGNL). In this survey, spot LNG excludes the short-term contracts element (i.e., contracts over one year but less than four years) of the GIIGNL reports. In addition, since LNG imported by the trading markets of North America and northwest Europe is classified in the 'Trading' category, there may be significant volumes, of what might be regarded as spot, not included in the 'Spot LNG' category.

7. International Gas Union, 'Wholesale Gas Price Survey 2020 Edition'.

8. Ibid.

9. Stern (ed.), *The Pricing of Internationally Traded Gas*, pp. 68–73.

10. Ibid., p. 71.

11. All data for LNG contract and spot prices sourced from Argus Media, an online data service, www.argusmedia.com, accessed March 2020.

12. The forty-eight contiguous states of the continental US, thus excluding Alaska and Hawaii.

13. The 15 per cent uplift on Henry Hub covers the cost of gas used in the liquefaction process and any pipeline transport costs to deliver the gas to the plant plus a margin for Cheniere.

14. Shipping costs assumed $80,000 a day charter costs and $70 a barrel crude oil. Henry Hub average for 2018 was $212.55 (NYMEX settlement price).

15. Mike Fulwood, 'Asian LNG Trading Hubs: Myth or Reality?', Working Paper, New York: Centre on Global Energy Policy, Columbia SIPA, 2018.

16. The DKI Sling was created by SGX in collaboration with Tullet Prebon, a leading LNG broker, and is part of a series of indices created to reflect the price of spot LNG cargoes at selected locations.

4

LIQUIFIED NATURAL GAS CONTRACTS: THE SHIFTING CONTOURS

MIKE FULWOOD

Senior Research Fellow, Oxford Institute for Energy Studies; Fellow, Center on Global Energy Policy, Columbia University

TIM BOERSMA

Fellow, Center on Global Energy Policy, Columbia University

HISTORY: TRADITIONAL LNG CONTRACTS

TRADITIONALLY, LNG ASSETS HAVE TYPICALLY been long-lived, highly specialized, site-specific projects with substantial economies of scale and major sunk investment costs. These features warranted long-term offtake agreements with take-or-pay conditions (typically covering 90 per cent of the nameplate capacity of a liquefaction project) between buyer and seller, usually with limited flexibility, in order to cover the risks associated with these investments.[1] In the absence of a global market for natural gas, or one based on competition for that matter, linking the price of LNG to oil (Brent or Japan Crude Cocktail [JCC]) was an imperfect alternative. However, a reliable price reference was necessary to raise capital to secure project finance.

121

Because buyers and sellers realized that natural gas and oil prices did not always move in sync, price review clauses were introduced to help address that problem.[2] Essentially, these review clauses contained criteria against which the agreed base price could be adjusted.[3] The contract price could be analysed in relation to the cost of other natural gas imported into the same country or region, as was typically done in Asia. Other price reviews could also take a broader regional look and include other fuels, as was historically done in European countries.

Price review clauses were widely used in European markets, but less so in Asia. In the latter markets traditional offtakers (like major utilities) were mostly monopolies at home and price fluctuations could, therefore, easily be passed on to their captive consumer base.[4] Now that (some of) these markets are slowly opening up for competition, incumbents are increasingly interested in review clauses, because otherwise they are at risk of being exposed at some point and may then lose market share.

This is just one example of the changing structure of global LNG markets and contracts. In this chapter, we first discuss several structural changes in the market, including the entrance of various new players. We then reflect on how this growing diversity in the market is illustrated in the diversity of LNG contracts that have been signed. We conclude with some implications of these changes for companies in India.

STRUCTURAL CHANGES WITH MAJOR IMPLICATIONS

As discussed in the previous chapter, the most obvious structural change in the market has been the rise of unconventional gas. Whereas it was relatively recent that analysts were wondering when we were going to run out of natural gas resources, today discussions centre around keeping resources in the ground because of concerns about climate change.[5] This has also brought more diverse sources of supply from countries like Australia and the US to the market. It is worth noting that industry also continues to discover major conventional natural gas deposits in places as diverse as South Africa, Egypt, Indonesia, Nigeria, and the Shetland Islands in the UK.

On the demand side, the application of floating storage and regasification units (FSRUs) specifically deserves attention, as these smaller-scale import facilities have given lower credit requirements and allowed offtakers in smaller countries to tap into the LNG market. In effect, FSRUs have helped with the 'democratization' of LNG, as scholars have noted based on the observation that this technology has helped lower the entry base into the market for LNG. On the supply side, floating LNG (FLNG) facilities are increasingly used to monetize resources in locations—e.g., in Mozambique, Cameroon and Mauritania/Senegal—where this has been historically challenging for a variety of reasons.

The next structural change has been the advent of more competitive models in key LNG importing countries that facilitate trade. In the EU, in particular, market liberalization, the build-out of infrastructure to connect markets, introduction of antitrust measures (such as declaring destination clauses illegal), and the creation of a strong legal system to uphold fair competition have all helped to create a competitive landscape.[6]

In East Asian countries, where roughly 75 per cent of global LNG demand is centred, market reform has typically taken more time. To this day, markets are still heavily regulated with price controls and limited access to infrastructure (or so-called third-party access, TPA). It will likely take quite some time for countries like Japan, Korea and China to open their markets for competition, but they seem to be slowly moving in that direction.[7]

The next major structural change will be the expiration of existing LNG-offtake agreements in the years ahead. Historically almost all LNG has been tied into long-term offtake agreements. By our accounts, global annual contracted volumes in 2019 mounted up to 435 Mtpa.

However, with legacy contracts expiring, by 2025 this number will have declined to an estimated 350 Mtpa, the largest suppliers for which contracts are coming to an end being Qatar, Malaysia, Algeria, and Nigeria. This will have profound market impacts that have not been broadly discussed.

- It will leave suppliers with liquefaction capacity that has been fully depreciated, searching for new offtakers—only now they do not need to lock that demand into long-term contracts like new projects mostly do (more about this later).
- Given that their loans have been paid off, these suppliers will likely be able to sell their product competitively in the market.
- On the demand side, it will leave major LNG importing countries that had historically often over-contracted (for reasons of security of supply), short of contracted supply to cover all domestic demand and thus in search of additional cargoes of LNG.

This process will likely be reinforced by phases in which supply exceeds demand for LNG as witnessed in 2019 and the first half of 2020 and may possibly again witness around 2025 (depending on supply and demand assumptions). When markets are over-supplied, buyers can be more selective in what they want and dictate preferred terms. Traditional sellers looking to renew their contracts would probably be quite pleased to continue with business as usual, but buyers may not necessarily agree.

Entrance of New Players

Next to these structural market changes, new players have been entering the market with implications for LNG contracting. First, starting in 2018 with the final investment decision on LNG Canada, several projects that have now moved forward are financed off balance sheets, contrary to traditional project-based financing. These projects have so far included major international oil companies, and in some cases equity offtakers. These in turn will sell cargoes of LNG on different duration contracts and presumably will use their home market, be it Japan, Korea or elsewhere, as a possible market of last resort. In other words, the buyers are still committed for the long term but are likely selling these volumes for shorter terms. A brief overview of balance-sheet financed projects to date can be found in Table 1 below, but this is a model that we anticipate being used more frequently going forward.

Table 1: Balance-sheet financed projects

Project	Project participants and shares	Nameplate capacity
LNG Canada phase 1	Shell (40 per cent), Petronas (25 per cent), PetroChina (15 per cent), Mitsubishi (15 per cent), Kogas (5 per cent)	14 MTPA (2 trains)
Greater Tortue Ahmeyim FLNG phase 1	British Petroleum (BP Gas Marketing being the sole buyer for LNG offtake)	2.5 MTPA
Golden Pass LNG	Exxon Mobil (30 per cent) and Qatar Petroleum (70 per cent)	16 MTPA

Source: Authors' analysis.

Second, it is important to note that these balance-sheet financed projects in the coming years will be competing with written-off legacy projects in Qatar, Malaysia, Algeria, Australia and Nigeria, among others. As legacy contracts expire, operators of these plants may seek to renegotiate them, but they do not have to. In addition, it remains to be

seen how interested offtakers are to renew long-term offtake agreements
in a market that seems well supplied in the years ahead.

However, major offtakers such as utilities and industrial consumers
will want to maintain a degree of certainty and predictability, which can
translate into new contracts. In the context of a market in flux, one way
to manage risk is to sign shorter-term contracts, something that we have
witnessed increasingly in recent years. One good recent example of an
expiring long-term contract involved Abu Dhabi LNG. Its twenty-five-
year supply contract with Japanese utility TEPCO expired in March
2018 and soon thereafter new and shorter-term offtake agreements with
various trading houses kicked in. These trading houses made money in
the subsequent months, selling the majority of UAE cargoes to Indian
buyers.[8]

Figure 1: Current contracted volumes in decline

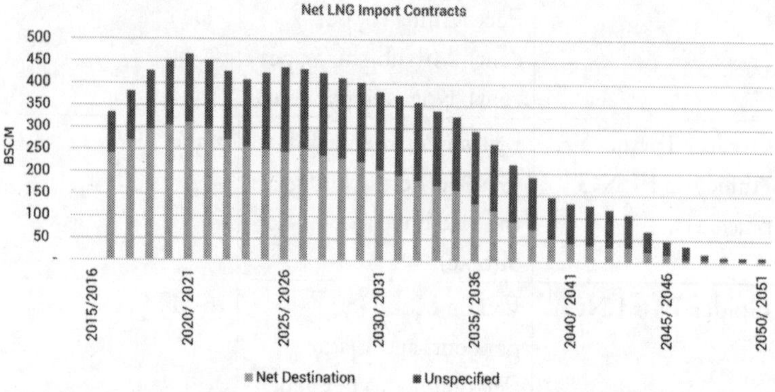

Net LNG Import Contracts

■ Net Destination   ■ Unspecified

Source: Nexant World Gas Model and authors' analysis.

As Figure 1 shows, the volume of LNG under contract will
decline post 2020/21 and then more sharply post 2025/26. The LNG
contracts can be broadly divided into three categories—those with a
specific export terminal for lifting and a specific offtake in an importing
country; those with a specific export terminal for lifting but no specific

destination (unspecified destination); and those with no specific export terminal (unspecified offtake), but with a specific destination. The contracts with no fixed destination can be used to supply contracts with no fixed offtake, so aggregating them all together leads to double counting. The figure above nets these out.

We also witnessed an important reminder in 2018 and 2019 that long-term contracts are by no means a relic of the past. Even though contract duration had been trending down for a few years, several long-term offtake agreements were signed in 2018. The US company Cheniere alone was able to ink four major offtake agreements with CPC Taiwan (2 Mtpa, twenty-five years, delivered ex-ship or DES), trading house Vitol (0.7 Mtpa, fifteen years, free-on-board or FOB), Polish PGNiG (1.45 Mtpa, twenty-four years, DES), and Petronas of Malaysia (1.1 Mtpa, twenty years, FOB) respectively. As PGNiG CEO Wozniak indicated when signing one of the company's recent LNG offtake agreements, the company enters into these agreements not only to build an LNG portfolio for the Polish market, but also to trade LNG in the global market.[9]

Figure 2: Average contract length and total LNG contract volumes by seller type

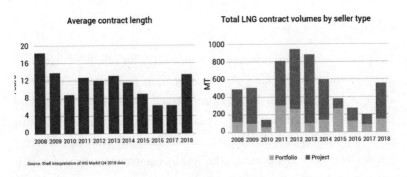

Source: Shell interpretation of IHS Markit Q4 2018 data.[10]

Purchases of spot cargoes have been on the rise in both emerging and mature markets. This illustrates the growth of the amount of cargo that is available to end users at any given time, the growth of market participants, investors and traders that are not end users. By our account, in a non-Covid world, seventy cargoes of LNG would have hit the water on a monthly basis in 2020 from the US alone—almost all of them effectively without a firm end user. Main players in the short-term market at the moment are portfolio sellers like Shell and Total; sellers with liquefaction capacity that has depreciated like QP and Petronas; large importers who optimize their portfolio; commodity traders; and offtakers in emerging markets that have to deal with substantial credit risks (and can thus not sign long-term offtake agreements).[11]

GROWING DIVERSITY OF INTERESTS AMONGST OFFTAKERS

DIVERSITY OF CONTRACTS SIGNED

The previous section touched on some of the structural changes that LNG markets have been undergoing, a process which we can safely say is not remotely finished. What impacts can that have on contracts being signed?

Contract Duration

Long-term offtake agreements are here to stay for offtakers that want stability and predictability. At the same time, shorter-term contracts and spot trade are both on the rise—a trend that is likely to continue (and to be sure, both can easily coexist in a market that continues to grow at the pace at which the LNG market has been growing). Diverse portfolios in our view portray attempts by companies to spread risk in a changing world.

Flexibility in Deliveries

Next to contract duration, we may also anticipate that a growing amount of cargoes will be delivered FOB, contrary to the traditional DES. Contrary to the latter, where a port of delivery is contractually agreed, buyers are increasingly interested in having more flexibility to do what they please with their purchase. They may wish to do so because demand in their home market is difficult to predict. For example, a Japanese utility may contract LNG to generate power for its customers but find that the Japanese government and regulatory authorities bring back more nuclear-generation capacity in the years ahead, consequently dampening demand for gas-fired electricity. Having LNG contracted on a FOB basis—as the Japanese companies buying LNG from the US have done—subsequently allows that utility to sell the possible excess LNG somewhere else in the (global) market.

In addition to these well-defined end users, a growing amount of LNG is contracted by non-end users. According to consultancy firm Wood Mackenzie, the top three trading houses in the world—Gunvor, Vitol and Trafigura—delivered more than thirty-one Mt of LNG in 2018 (roughly 10 per cent of the market), a number that in 2019 was almost matched by Gunvor and Trafigura alone, as they reported traded volumes of sixteen and 12.6 Mt, respectively.[12] These companies need as much flexibility in their contracts as possible, to allow them to find end users wherever market prices dictate, so they can make a profit of arbitrage.

We are likely to see less use of destination restrictions because buyers are in a position currently to not only ask for more flexibility, but also as a consequence of a regulatory push in various parts of the world. Law in the EU does not allow for such restrictions in contracts anymore and the Japan Fair Trade Commission (JFTC) ruled in 2017 that such restrictions may be anti-competitive as well. To be precise,

JFTC found that destination restrictions in combination with FOB contracts for LNG may be anti-competitive. For DES contracts this is not necessarily the case, if requests to resell are not ignored.[13] The JFTC also found that destination restrictions prohibit the development of a spot market in Japan. In turn, various Japanese offtakers have indicated that they wish to get rid of destination restrictions and so, in addition to expiring long-term contracts, the expectation is that in the years ahead significant volumes without destination restrictions will be available in the market.

In this context, it is also worth noting that international cooperation among major buyers in various parts of the world, to support the development of a more liquid LNG market, has emerged—as shown by partnerships between British Centrica and Japanese JERA as well as Tokyo Gas and French EDF. Importantly, destination restrictions are not likely to disappear soon for two reasons. First, obviously, changing existing contracts take time and effort and in many cases still require legal changes (regardless of buyers' preferences). Second, sellers may find ways to accommodate buyers' concerns without offering full destination flexibility. In September 2018, for example, Qatar Petroleum and PetroChina signed a twenty-two-year deal to supply the offtaker with approximately 3.4 Mtpa of LNG, to be delivered at receiving terminals across China.[14]

Pricing

Japan, where industry ministry METI announced a push for market reform in 2016 (that has moved along only gradually, with important elements still on the drawing board), may thus be offering us a glimpse of what can come next for various key LNG importing countries. Next to the shunning of destination restrictions in new contracts, buyers are also less interested in crude oil indexation, and instead more interested in diverse LNG pricing structures (even though it is important to note that a clearly preferred alternative is still lacking). To be sure, as we described in detail earlier, market reform is required to create the ecosystem within which competition can take place, as a precondition for an LNG price that better reflects supply and demand for natural gas.[15] Japanese offtakers currently seem to be sourcing their long-term volumes from various sources, e.g., Australia, Qatar, the US and Malaysia, and supplementing with spot cargoes that are increasingly available globally. Transportation costs for the latter cargoes can, therefore, typically also be slightly higher, depending on market conditions.

The public discourse around changes in LNG contracts tends to focus on duration, flexibility and pricing. We believe that it is helpful to distinguish between changes related to price and non-price modifications and that there is a fair amount of nuance that tends to get lost. The table below gives an overview of some of the non-price changes that we may increasingly see in LNG contracts going forward and what used to be more common practice previously. We also include our (speculative) suggestions of what changes there may be in the future of LNG contracting. It is important to note that there are various non-price elements in contracts that we do not discuss here, chiefly because they do not stand out as being subject to major change, although as the LNG world becomes more complicated, contracts tend to include more details on these matters as well. These include provisions regarding force majeure, default, choice of dispute resolution and termination rights. We have not included contract changes in pricing here, since these are covered in the earlier chapter, but evidently, there are major changes taking place on that front as well.

Box 1: 'Non-price' change potential in LNG contracts (historically, at present, and in future)

CHANGES IN LNG CONTRACTS (NON-PRICE)			
	Past	Present	Future
Contract period	Historically 20–30 years.	Today, more mixed bag, with growing amount of spot, short-term (<2 years) and medium-term (<7 years) contracts.	A mixed bag, since some offtakers will continue to focus on long-term predictability, but as the market matures, more buyers will be comfortable with shorter-term contracts.
Flexibility on the start date of LNG contract	Limited flexibility as the number of alternative buyers was very limited, there was dedicated shipping, and buyers' focus was on the security of supply.	Risk lies more with the seller, who may need to sell cargoes in the first six months on the spot market, possibly at a loss. Start-up phase often governed by reasonable efforts to deliver and take LNG on both sides.	Sellers' risk will diminish as market liquidity grows: more players, more trade, more options to divert risks.

CHANGES IN LNG CONTRACTS (NON-PRICE)

	Past	Present	Future
Flexibility on annual volumes (as specified mostly in annual contract quantity, or ACQ)	Risk resided with the buyer as the pool of alternative customers was limited, though ACQ subject to a variety of adjustments, e.g., round-up/round-down provisions, excess quantities, and (limited) volume flexibility.	More risk for the seller, since the buyer may, on the provision of agreed written notice, opt for flexible annual delivered volumes. Seasonal bias of delivery may also include seasonal bias to meet peak demand in certain parts of the year.	As the market matures, sellers will have more options to sell their cargoes elsewhere if necessary due to demand fluctuations.
Take-or-pay	Historically provided a guaranteed level of income for the seller. If buyer did not take the cargo, he had to settle the difference, as agreed per contract.	Take-and-pay is increasingly common, so the buyer will receive cargo regardless and will need to find a home for it.	Increasingly, volumes will be seen in the market that are not tied to an end user, but are either contracted by a middleman or purposed for spot trade.

CHANGES IN LNG CONTRACTS (NON-PRICE)			
	Past	Present	Future
Right to divert	Destination restrictions were the norm, and cargoes could be sent to another destination after reloading them at the original port of sale.	The point above is made possible by increased flexibility to divert cargoes. There may still be geographical constraints, but in general, there is more flexibility.	Flexibility of cargoes will only grow going forward, supported by both legal provisions in key Asian countries and buyers' desires to have more flexibility as they manage their portfolio, and uncertainty of demand grows.
Credit security	Risk of default used to be very low, since offtakers were all major companies in mature markets.	Risk exposure is changing as more offtakers join the market, including some with more credit challenges. Sellers, therefore, like guarantees, e.g., from host government or development banks, that they will be paid.	With demand for LNG mostly growing in emerging economies, risk exposure for sellers will continue to grow as well. Key role for host governments and development banks to support.

CHANGES IN LNG CONTRACTS (NON-PRICE)			
	Past	Present	Future
Transportation and title transfer	Historically, mostly DES, with seller carrying risk of shipping and ownership transfers after destination or after reloading.	Increasingly, cargoes also sold free-on-board, where the buyer is responsible for arranging shipping, and takes ownership of the natural gas after loading.	
Natural gas quality	Traditionally mostly a formality, since Pacific buyers were after heavier blends of LNG (with a higher proportion of liquids).	With the advent of LNG of leaner quality, mostly from eastern Australia and the US, interchangeability has become more of an issue, resulting in price-adjustment provisions to compensate buyers if treatment is required.	As more advanced gas turbines are constructed and emission standards tighten, gas quality specifications are more precisely reflected in contracts.

Source: Author's compilation based in part on Niall Trimble (2018; see endnote 4), Ann Sophie Corbeau and Davis Ledesma (eds) (2016),[16] and Michael D. Tusiani and Gordon Shearer (2016).[17]

In short, as the LNG world expands and LNG trade becomes more complicated, it is reflected in the various non-price components of LNG contracts.

Notes

1   Craig Pirrong, 'Liquefying a Market: The Transition of LNG to a Traded Commodity', *Journal of Applied Corporate Finance*, Vol. 29, No. 1 (2017), pp. 86–92.

2. Lisa G. Henneberry and Gorge M. von Mehren, 'Considerations in Natural Gas and LNG Price Review Claim Quantification', *Journal of World Energy Law & Business*, Vol. 8, No. 2 (2015), pp. 103–15.

3. Carol Mulcahy, 'The changing face of disputes in the liquefied natural gas market', *Journal of Energy & Natural Resources LawI*, Vol. 33, No. 3 (2015), pp. 271–87.

4. Niall Trimble, 'Changing LNG Markets and Contracts', *Journal of World Energy Law & Business*, Vol. 11, No. 5 (2018), pp. 427–39.

5. Tim Boersma and Akos Losz, 'The New International Political Economy of Natural Gas', in Andreas Goldthau, Michael F. Keating, and Caroline Kuzemko (eds), *Handbook of the International Political Economy of Energy*, New York: Edward Elgar Publishing, 2018.

6. Andreas Goldthau and Nick Sitter, 'A Liberal Actor in a Realist World? The Commission and The External Dimension of the Single Market for Energy', *Journal of European Public Policy*, Vol. 21, No. 10 (2014), pp. 1452–72.

7. Mike Fulwood, 'Asian LNG Trading Hubs: Myth or Reality?', Working Paper, New York: Centre on Global Energy Policy, Columbia|SIPA, 2018.

8. Patrick Sykes, 'Trading Houses Soak Up UAE LNG Cargoes as Japan Contracts Ends', London: Independent Commodity Intelligence Services, 17 July 2019, https://www.icis.com/explore/resources/news/2019/07/17/10393092/trading-houses-soak-up-uae-lng-cargoes-as-japan-contract-ends

9.   'Port Arthur LNG and PGNiG sign Definitive Agreement for US LNG', Sempra Energy, 19 December 2018, https://www.sempra.com/newsroom/spotlight-articles/port-arthur-lng-and-pgnig-sign-definitive-agreement-us-lng

10. Shell Global, 'Shell LNG Outlook 2019', (The Hague: Royal Dutch Shell plc, 2019), https://www.shell.com/promos/overview-shell-lng-2019/_jcr_content.stream/1551087443922/1f9dc66cfc0e3083b3fe3d07864b2d0703a25fc4/lng-outlook-feb25.pdf

11. Ruchdi Maalouf, 'The Essential Evolution of LNG Trading: Moving to GTCs', *Journal of World Energy Law & Business*, Vol. 11, No. 5 (2018), pp. 410–26.

12. 'Commodity Traders Sharply Increase LNG Presence', Financial Times, London, *ft.com*, https://www.ft.com/content/4923077c-039f-11e9-99df-6183d3002ee1; see also James Cocklin, 'Global LNG Traders Report Sharp Increase in 2019 Volumes', Washington DC: NGI, 31 December 2019, https://www.naturalgasintel.com/articles/120626-global-lng-traders-report-sharp-increase-in-2019-lng-volumes

13. Chantal Carriere, 'The Effects of Japan's Push for Greater LNG Market Flexibility on LNG Pricing and Destination Restrictions', *Journal of World Energy Law & Business*, Vol. 11, No. 2 (2018), pp. 136–44.

14. 'Qatar Gas Agrees on 22 Year LNG Supply Deal with China', *Reuters*, 10 September 2018, https://www.reuters.com/article/us-qatar-petrochina/qatargas-agrees-on-22-year-lng-supply-deal-with-china-idUSKCN1LQ0DM

15. Fulwood, 'Asian LNG Trading Hubs: Myth or Reality?', 2018.

16. Anne-Sophie Corbeau and David Ledesma (eds), *LNG Markets in Transition: The Great Reconfiguration*, London: Oxford University Press, 2016.

17. Michael D. Tusiani and Gordon Shearer, *LNG: A Fuel for a Changing World: A Non-technical Guide*, Tulsa, OK: PennWell Publishing, 2016.

5

REGULATORY LIBERALIZATION

AKSHAYA KOSHY MASON[1]

Commercial Manager, ExxonMobil, Angola

THE LIBERALIZATION PROCESS OF THE natural gas marketplace has been unique for each market and several regulatory steps have ensured success. This chapter examines the regulatory evolution of three markets—the US, the UK, and the Netherlands—which took place largely during the second half of the twentieth century. These markets have successfully transitioned from monopolies to efficient, well-functioning, competitive markets. While the Indian context may differ, the aim is to provide key outcomes from each, which could be used as guidelines for Indian policy-makers as they continue making changes to the domestic gas market.

THE US: AN ACT IN FOUR STAGES

The natural gas market in the US went through four stages of transformation on its path to market liberalization. The Acts and Orders listed below encompass the key stages of evolution:

- The 1938 Natural Gas Act
- 1978 Natural Gas Policy Act

- 1985 FERC Order 436 and 500
- 1992 FERC Order 636

The details of these Acts and the nature of these changes are briefly described in the paragraphs below.

THE 1938 NATURAL GAS ACT: THE FIRST STEP OF INTERSTATE PIPELINE REGULATION

The natural gas industry in the US began in the mid-1800s to early 1900s. Private companies, which developed as natural monopolies, built distribution networks within municipalities to connect producing areas with consumers nearby. Pipelines that crossed state boundaries (interstate pipelines) were beyond the regulatory oversight of the state-level government and remained unregulated.[2] By 1935, a quarter of the interstate natural gas pipelines were owned by only eleven holding companies. Concerned over higher prices being charged by these entities, the US Congress passed the Natural Gas Act (NGA) in 1938 to fill the regulatory gap with regard to interstate pipelines.

The NGA gave authority to the Federal Power Commission (FPC), to regulate interstate pipeline rates and to issue certificates for the construction of new interstate pipelines. This eased the challenges of obtaining pipeline right of way and helped to attract investment in pipeline infrastructure in subsequent years for investing companies (termed 'natural gas companies' in the NGA). The framework for the development of interstate pipelines established by the NGA encouraged the construction of a number of major long-distance pipelines connecting the Gulf Coast with the upper Midwest (Chicago) and North-east (New York) US over the course of the 1940s. World War II and the ensuing demand for gas as an alternative to oil spurred the boom in pipeline construction. Approximately half the currently existing mainline natural gas transmission network and a large portion of the local distribution network was installed in the 1950s and 1960s as consumer demand had more than doubled after World War II.

Wellhead prices were set at rates that allowed producers to cover the actual costs of producing natural gas, plus a fair (FPC judgement) profit. Since much of the gas sold to the pipelines was associated with oil production, it was assumed that producers had recovered most of their costs through oil sales and wellhead prices were regulated at very low levels (compared to the alternative). The FPC tried setting rates based on each producer's cost of service, then tried setting ceiling prices for wells based on geographic regions. However, all these measures were administratively unfeasible as there were a great number of different producers and producing wells. The low level of regulated wellhead prices caused demand to grow almost three-and-a-half times from 1950 to the early 1970s. Concurrently, it provided little incentive for new gas reserve exploration—which remained predominantly associated with oil production—and gas supply shortages started in the 1970s.

Since intrastate and interstate markets were totally separate, states like Texas, where wellhead prices were unregulated if sold within the state, experienced no shortages. Producers preferred to sell new gas supplies into the segregated intrastate gas market (unregulated by the FPC) when possible, which further exacerbated the supply shortfall in consuming regions such as the Midwest and North-east during the winter of 1976–77. The FPC and state utility regulators advocated curtailment policies that set a schedule of priority, directing distributors and transporters to curtail supplies to certain customers who were deemed 'low priority'. However, these policies resulted in numerous litigation suits and FPC proceedings that turned out to be extremely complicated and time consuming.

1978 Natural Gas Policy Act: The Deregulation of Wellhead Prices

In 1978, the second Arab oil shock reinforced the need to bolster the domestic supply of natural gas across the US. To address producer concerns over low wellhead prices, the Congress enacted the Natural Gas Policy Act (NGPA) in 1978, as part of the broader National Energy Act (NEA). The FPC was abolished and replaced by the Federal Energy Regulatory Commission (FERC), an independent agency under the Department of Energy Organization Act of 1977. Jurisdiction over the import and export of natural gas was given to the FERC. The secretary of energy could recommend, but not dictate, actions to the FERC.

To provide economic incentives for producers, the NGPA dictated the following:

- Gas brought into production before the passage of the Act would forever be subject to pre-NGPA regulations and price limits.
- Wellhead price ceilings for new production were increased and mechanisms for raising these prices, with a design to phase out wellhead gas price regulation completely by 1985, were established.

Section 311 helped break down barriers between interstate and intrastate markets. It mandated a FERC compliance of intrastate services if an intrastate pipeline sold or transported gas to an interstate pipeline, or to a local distribution companies (LDC) that was serviced from an interstate pipeline. This ruling caused an increase in connections between interstate and intrastate pipelines.

Average wellhead gas prices rose dramatically to reflect market value in the years following the NGPA. Pipeline companies, accustomed to gas shortages in the past years, signed up for many long-term take-or-pay natural gas contracts with producers, to ensure the security of supply. Producers expanded exploration and production (E&P), drilling new wells and using these long-term sales contracts with pipeline companies to recover their investment. Prices for consumers increased but were partially mitigated by pipeline companies—which blended the cost of gas under new contracts with regulated gas under old contracts—when selling their bundled product to their customers.

The increasing prices caused many consumers to switch from natural gas to other fuels, resulting in a 20 per cent decline in the overall gas demand. The resulting over-supply scenario left pipeline companies with excess take-or-pay obligations to producers. Customers purchasing a bundled gas-plus-transportation product from pipeline companies lobbied for reduced natural gas prices. In addition, pipeline customers sought the right to purchase their own gas from producers and transport it over interstate pipelines, instead of purchasing the bundled product from pipeline companies.

Despite the decline in demand, producers continued drilling for new gas and a supply overhang of some 5–6 trillion cubic feet (Tcf) of productive capacity was created.

1985 FERC Orders 436 and 500: A Move towards Open Transportation and Competitive Markets

With FERC Orders 436 and 500, Congress set up the foundation for more competitive gas markets, with the unbundling of services and open access to pipeline programmes.

- The Orders allowed interstate pipeline companies to provide open access to transportation services on a first-come-first-serve basis (previously each instance of third-party access required FERC approval).
- They enabled consumers to negotiate gas prices directly with producers and contract separately for transportation.

They barred pipeline companies from discriminating against transportation requests, based on protecting their own merchant services.

Transportation rate minimums and maximums were set and pipeline companies were free to offer competitive rates to their shippers,[3] within these boundaries.

Eventually, all major pipeline companies participated in this voluntary open third-party access programme. Pipeline companies were also allowed to continue to provide bundled (gas-plus-transportation) merchant services. The spot market prices of natural gas-plus-transportation tariffs were much lower than the bundled prices offered by pipeline companies. This was because the latter bundled prices included a combination of spot market prices and the high prices of long-term take-or-pay contracts between pipeline companies and producers. Consumers realized cost savings by directly purchasing from producers.

The pipeline companies' take-or-pay obligations to producers became a burden, as few customers were willing to purchase higher-priced gas directly from pipeline companies. This forced most pipeline companies into litigation with producers over take-or-pay contracts.

Order 500, issued in 1987, encouraged the following.

Interstate pipeline companies could buy out costly take-or-pay contracts and pass a portion of the costs of doing so, to their sales customers.

Distribution companies, to whom these costs were passed on, were allowed by state regulatory bodies to further pass them on to retail customers.

Producers were encouraged to grant take-or-pay credits to pipeline companies when they transported gas volumes that were resold by the producer directly to a customer, against the volumes the pipeline companies were not taking under its take-or-pay contract.

The FERC never ordered the formal abrogation of any of the traditional take-or-pay contracts, but the effect of Orders 436 and 500 incentivized most producers to initiate settlement talks with pipelines so that they could regain possession of gas that had previously been locked up in long-term supply contracts. Thus, the US effectively achieved virtually complete gas release, without ever actually mandating a specific gas release programme.

The Natural Gas Wellhead Decontrol Act (NGWDA) passed in 1989 amended the NGPA to repeal and eliminate all remaining wellhead price regulations over a four-year period. The spot market started thriving and by 1991 over 80 per cent of all interstate pipeline deliveries were no longer from pipeline company merchant sales.

1992 FERC ORDER 636: THE GREATEST STEP IN THE DEREGULATION OF THE US GAS MARKET

The greatest step in the deregulation of the US industry came in 1992-93 with FERC Order 636, which resulted in the major restructuring of interstate pipeline operations.

- It mandated complete separation of sales activities from pipeline transportation, or 'unbundling.'
- Pipeline companies were restricted to providing transparent, non-discriminatory transportation and storage services only.
- It allowed pipeline operators to form legally separate, independent, marketing affiliates to handle gas sales activities.
- These affiliates were required to compete equally for available transportation and storage services, with standards-of-conduct firewalls separating activities between marketing employees and pipeline-transmission employees.

Order 636 also required interstate pipeline companies to offer 'no-notice' transportation services, 'capacity release' programmes and to set up interactive websites called 'Electronic Bulletin Boards' (EBBs).

No-notice transportation service allowed local distribution companies (LDCs) and utilities to receive natural gas from pipelines on demand to meet peak service needs for their customers, without incurring any penalties. These services were provided, based on LDC and utility concerns, that the restructuring of the industry might decrease the reliability needed to meet their own customers' needs.

The capacity release programmes allowed the resale of unwanted pipeline capacity between pipeline shippers. These programmes provided a mechanism for shippers to recoup some of their firm reservation fees during times when they did not require all their reserved capacity for their own needs.

The EBBs made pipeline information accessible to all shippers on an equal basis. They showed the available and released capacity on any particular pipeline and allowed shippers to purchase or lease unused capacity from one another.

Order 636 made it possible for customers to select gas supply, transportation and storage services from any provider in any quantity. The LDCs that previously bought gas plus transportation from pipelines at their city gates, converted their contracts to transportation-only contracts (that is, they only became shippers) and entered into separate gas purchase contracts with suppliers of their choice. They used the same delivery points and quantity reservations and picked supply points for their transportation contracts. This conversion of contract type was less burdensome than terminating and redoing all contracts. Hence, most interstate pipelines have had LDCs as the primary shippers.

In this radically changed, unbundled market environment, many producers and consumers did not want to incur the expenses of staff to directly sell or procure supply and transportation services. Thus, a niche was developed for new market players called 'gas marketers'. These were companies that neither owned equity production nor pipelines, nor were LDCs or consumers. Marketers, even today, aggregate natural gas purchases from producers into quantities that fit the needs of different types of buyers (commercial, industrial, utilities or LDCs) and their varying demand profiles. They may either acquire transportation and

storage services from pipeline companies or manage the transportation
or storage contracts of their buyers to meet needs.

IMPACT OF THE REGULATORY FRAMEWORK: A LIQUID AND WELL-ESTABLISHED COMPETITIVE MARKET

In the 1990s, electronic trading and transportation capacity release
programmes continued to evolve to support a fully competitive spot
market with sophisticated physical and financial transactions.

Competitive Prices

Price competition led to the development of an extensive network of
trading hubs or market centres across the US, in line with the FERC's
stated goal of facilitating the meeting of gas purchasers and sellers in a
national market. While the FERC did not mandate the establishment
of either market centres or hubs, it did encourage their development by
prohibiting anything in pipeline tariffs that would inhibit hub formation.

Creation of Market Centres

Order 636 defined market centres as places where gas from one pipeline
and one producing area intersected with gas from other pipelines and
other producing areas. Market-centre development drove additional
pipeline interconnections. Pipeline companies, offering transportation
services, connected with other pipelines to increase the value of their
services by reaching more markets. The costs of interconnecting
were shared by connecting pipelines, based on the benefits of the
interconnection to each pipeline. A number of pipeline companies
consolidated and merged to gain scale and to combine complementary
segments.

Transparent Pricing Information

As sales at these market centres increased, both buyers and sellers called
for a transparent means of referencing their sales. Accordingly, a number

of publications began to follow each of these markets and, through a series of phone calls to industry members, reported aggregate prices. Price transparency and a large number of buyers and sellers at multiple market centres (liquidity) are clear indications of the development of a liquid market.

Another aspect that has aided the development of liquidity in the US market has been the evolution of paper trading and natural gas futures. In 1990, the New York Mercantile Exchange (NYMEX) established a natural gas futures market modelled after its crude oil and petroleum products futures markets. The NYMEX selected Henry Hub as its delivery point for natural gas and started trading futures. Henry Hub was chosen not only because it had many interconnects to other pipelines—with plenty of available capacity due to declining production volumes in that area—but also because of the innovative hub services promoted by the infrastructure (Sabine Pipeline) owners.

Among other services, Henry Hub offered its users 'imbalance services' that simplified the physical delivery process and intra-hub transfers (IHT). The IHT is a non-jurisdictional accounting service used to track multiple title transfers of natural gas at market centres. Today, Henry Hub is the most well-known benchmark in North American natural gas markets. However, relatively little physical gas actually flows through it.

The basic regulatory framework for the interstate gas market has been fairly constant since the FERC Order 636. The FERC has been continually monitoring market effectiveness and making changes as needed. The continuing growth in the size of the natural gas market, the growing number of producers, and increasing consumer demand, along with very competitive gas prices that benefit consumers, reflect the success of the regulatory framework.

THE UK: PATH TO MARKET LIBERALIZATION

The UK gas market which began in the early 1900s, with synthetic gas made from coal gas, was developed by many small, privately owned and provincial gas companies. Significant natural gas reserves were discovered in the North Sea in the late 1960s. The gas production sector was open to competition and the government licensed large privately owned E&P companies to develop these reserves.

Gas Act 1972: Centralization to Improve Market Efficiency

In 1973, on the basis of the Gas Act of 1972, the British Gas Council was dissolved and the twelve area gas boards[4] were merged to create the British Gas Corporation (BGC) as one central entity and monopoly to improve market connectivity and efficiency.

The larger E&P companies built offshore pipelines to bring natural gas to terminals onshore (interconnects between the offshore pipelines and the BGC's network was termed 'beach'). The BGC held the monopoly of supply from beach terminals to consumers and had long-term exclusive take-or-pay gas purchase contracts with all offshore producers. The BGC was responsible for transportation, distribution and sales to consumers across virtually the entire market. Residential and small consumers accounted for roughly 65 per cent of total demand, while the remainder consisted of large industrial end users. All gas prices, wholesale and retail, were set by the government. Gas demand almost doubled under this new market structure—until the oil price shocks of 1979.

Gas Act 1986: Privatization of British Gas and First Attempts to Create Competition

In the 1980s, faced with an economic downturn, the government saw the need to remove inefficient government control of the energy sector and pursue a competitive market-based policy. The Oil and Gas Act, adopted in 1982, began the transition of public utilities to private companies. The BGC's privilege of first access to North Sea gas was withdrawn, and it was privatized and rechristened British Gas Plc based on the Gas Act, 1986. It remained a single, vertically integrated company to speed the transaction and maximize the sale proceeds to the government. British Gas Plc (BG) was now obliged to offer its competitors regulated third-party access (TPA) to its pipelines.

Some features of the Gas Act, 1986 included:

- The gas market was separated into three major segments, based on annual consumption:
- Large industrial customers (>25,000 therms/year consumption), could choose their supplier (including producers and independent gas marketers)
- Small industrial and commercial customers (between 2500 therms/year and 25,000 therms/year), exclusively supplied by BG
- Domestic (household) consumers (<2500 therms/year), exclusively supplied by BG[5]
- Established the Office of Gas Supply (OFGAS), an independent regulator, to safeguard end-user interests and maintain a level playing field for all private gas sector companies.
- OFGAS regulated the price that BG charged customers with <25,000 therms/year consumption and transportation tariffs charged to third parties.
- Wellhead gas prices, for the large industrial customers, were deregulated.

However, all these measures did not do much to break up BG's market dominance, owing to the long-term contracts it had with producers of existing (larger) fields and their control of the gas infrastructure. Competition evolved very slowly.

1990S: REGULATORY INTERVENTIONS TO SPUR COMPETITION

In 1988, the British Monopolies and Mergers Commission (MMC) issued a report, which recommended that BG increase transparency and grant fair access to third parties on its networks by publishing their terms and prices for supply. Based on its recommendations, OFGAS introduced the '90:10' rule in 1989 to limit BG from contracting more than 90 per cent of its supplies, effectively forcing producers to market some of their gas to independent suppliers. This promoted the development of wholesale gas trading (spot market) at the beach, where independent suppliers had unrestricted and flexible access to gas deliveries from more than forty producers and access to BG's transportation capacity.

The Office of Fair Trading (OFT), tasked in 1991 to monitor BG's compliance, reported that the gas market share held by BG's competitors had only grown from 0.4 per cent in 1990 to 5.2 per cent in 1991. The OFT proposed that BG release some of the gas it had contracted, to help accelerate the growth of its competitors' market share. After intensive negotiations, BG agreed to a market share ceiling of 40 per cent to be achieved by 1995. In 1992, BG's supply exclusivity threshold was lowered from 25,000 therms/year to 2500 therms/year, to increase the number of customers available to its competitors.

Further, it was announced that smaller markets (<2500 therms/year) would open in phases between 1996 and 1998. The 1995 Gas Act provided for the separation of gas supply, shipping and public gas transport and set the end of 1998 as a clear deadline to achieve full competition in the gas market. The 1995 Act required BG to develop a Network Code for regulated TPA, cost-of-service tariffs and system balancing.

1996: ESTABLISHMENT OF A CENTRALIZED SPOT MARKET

Based on the 1993 MMC report, British Gas Plc unbundled its gas merchant and transmission activities and restructured into two separate affiliated companies in 1994. The trading arm owned offshore production and all supply contracts, and the transmission arm owned and operated transportation and storage systems.

Despite the increasing volume of gas traded at the beach spot markets, trading remained relatively illiquid (not more than 10 per cent of the total daily supplies at each). Thus, BG introduced a single central market location to aggregate trading within its pipeline system—the 'National Balancing Point' (NBP)—in 1996. Transactions on the NBP (a notional hub) were facilitated by BG, which kept track of traded volumes and provided transportation services. This created one gas price for the wholesale gas market in the UK, irrespective of where the gas came from.

The NBP became increasingly popular among shippers because of its central location, accessibility, and low transaction costs. In January 1997, the International Petroleum Exchange (IPE, which later became the Intercontinental Exchange or ICE), adopted the NBP as the delivery and pricing point for its first natural gas futures contract. The IPE offered buyers and sellers of its contract the right to settle their purchases and sales, either by cash settlement or by effecting physical delivery at the NBP.

EUROPEAN UNION DIRECTIVES AND REGULATIONS

Beginning in the late 1990s, the EU issued a series of directives affecting the gas market. It is important to note that each gas directive was a progressive improvement to further the original goals for market liberalization.

1998 GAS DIRECTIVE

In June 1998, the council adopted the first Gas Directive (Directive 98/30/EC) to improve the functioning of the internal natural gas market.

- It set rules for third-party access (TPA) to the gas infrastructure.
- Owners/operators of infrastructure were not to discriminate between shippers, particularly in favour of related undertakings.
- Member states could choose between a system of negotiated access or regulated access.
- Negotiated access: Third parties were to negotiate access terms and conditions with the infrastructure owner.
- Regulated access: Third parties had a right of access on the basis of terms and conditions determined by a regulator and published by the infrastructure owners.
- Access could be refused under both systems on the basis of lack of capacity or system security.
- Integrated natural gas companies were to keep separate accounts for their natural gas infrastructure, production/import and gas retail sale activities.

Member states were required to implement the directive into national laws within two years after its entry came into force. Countries with immature gas industries or using minimal quantities of natural gas produced in the EU were allowed to derogate from some of the provisions of the directive.

Impact of the Directive

The gas directive took a gradual approach to the opening of the gas markets, to enable industry to adjust to its new environment in a flexible and orderly manner. Member states were obliged to open at least 20 per cent (annual gas consumption basis) of their natural gas market immediately. This was to be increased to 28 per cent within five years and to 33 per cent within twenty years after the directive entered into force.

Many countries achieved the immediate 20 per cent requirement by opening the market for gas-fired power generators and large industrial consumers. Six years after the directive was passed, still only the very largest consumers were allowed their choice of supplier.

Although a step in the right direction, some of the first directive's provisions (such as the accounting separation and negotiated TPA option with the right to refuse access) provided integrated companies too many ways to avoid opening their networks and were not sufficient to ensure non-discriminatory access. In addition, the directive did not establish a requirement for a regulatory agency to monitor the industry and enforce rules, leaving competition vulnerable to market abuses.

2003: Second Gas Directive

The European Council (EC) considered issues of access to the network, access to storage, tariff issues, interoperability between systems and the different degrees of market opening between member states, among other things, the main obstacles in achieving a fully operational and competitive internal market. Thus the Second Gas Directive (Directive 2003/55/EC) adopted in June 2003, removed some of the less liberal options in the 1998 directive and required establishing regulatory oversight.

- The negotiated TPA option was withdrawn except for gas storage facilities, where the member states could still choose between negotiated or regulated TPA.

- Access to the transmission and distribution system and to LNG facilities was to be based on published tariffs and applied objectively and without discrimination between system shippers.

- The applicable tariffs, or the tariff method, were to be approved by a regulatory authority (regulated TPA).

Article 22 of the 2003 directive did provide for the possibility of requesting an exemption from the regulated TPA rules for major new gas infrastructures (interconnectors, LNG, and storage facilities), so as not to impede its development. Unbundling requirements were significantly strengthened with integrated companies required to legally separate their transmission activities from gas production and retail.

Member states were required to designate independent national regulatory authorities who would be responsible for ensuring non-discrimination, effective competition, and efficient functioning of the market by cooperating with each other and the commission in a transparent manner. The directive required the member states to provide an annual report to the commission and the commission to provide one to the European parliament which included the status of market dominance, predatory and anti-competitive behaviour. National Regulatory Authorities (NRAs) had the authority to modify terms and conditions for access to the system and to decide on complaints against system operators.

The Second Gas Directive was much more aggressive on the phased market opening and introduced the following requirements:

- By 1 July 2004, all final customers consuming more than 25 million m^3 of gas per year on a consumption site were designated eligible customers, meaning they could choose their suppliers.

- From 1 July 2004, all non-household customers were designated eligible customers.

- From 1 July 2007, all gas customers (including households) were free to purchase gas from suppliers of their choice.

The directive was, however, criticized for not doing enough to break up dominant companies. It was argued that the provisions required the commission and national regulatory authorities to merely take measures that mitigated the effects of dominance; it did not require them to break up dominant companies to ensure a competitive field.

Impact of the Directive

Member states were slow to implement the terms of this directive. A little over a year after the adoption, the commission had to send formal warnings to more than 50 per cent of the member states about their failure to comply. A number of gas hubs developed in central and western Europe but the liquidity at these hubs was very low and the price signals were not reliable.[6] Most EU member states achieved minimal to no competition, due to the continued dominance of a single large company, within their country.

2009: THIRD PACKAGE

Continued dominance of a few large vertically integrated companies impeded non-discriminatory network access across the EU. Further, the European Commission (EC) and parliament wanted to accelerate investments in energy infrastructure to enhance cross-border trade and to further open the markets. For these reasons, the Third Energy Package was adopted in September 2009.

With respect to natural gas markets, the package consisted of one directive,[7] and two regulations.[8] The Third Gas Directive repealed the Second Gas Directive.

- Mandatory ownership-unbundling of transmission system operators (TSOs) was sought. They could no longer be owned by an integrated company with production or gas marketing interests.
- Member states were given a choice between ownership unbundling,[9] setting up an independent system operator (ISO), or independent transmission operator (ITO) that would be independent of sales and production interests.
- Specific additional rules applied to ISOs and ITOs to ensure the full effectiveness of this unbundling solution.

- The independence of NRAs was enhanced by mandating that the regulatory authority be legally distinct and functionally independent of any other public or private entity.

- Each member state had to designate a single NRA but could designate other regulatory authorities for regions within the member state, as long as there was a senior representative at the national level.

- Regulatory staff was required to act independently from any market interests and not seek or take instructions from any government or other public or private entity while carrying out regulatory tasks.

- Conditions were added for requests for an exemption from the regulated TPA regime for new major gas infrastructures to ensure fair, non-discriminatory access. The minimum requirements for the exemption included open season and congestion management rules. For storage system operators (SSOs), the obligation for legal and functional unbundling was introduced where SSOs were part of an integrated natural gas undertaking (i.e., company or group of companies or affiliated companies).

- Regulation (EC) No 713/2009 established an Agency for the Cooperation of Energy Regulators (ACER) to assist NRAs and, where necessary, coordinate their actions. Today, the ACER has approximately sixty-eight full-time equivalent staff and their activities include the following:

- To issue opinions and recommendations to TSOs, NRAs, and EU institutions (European parliament, the Council, and the Commission).

- To submit non-binding framework guidelines to the Commission for the development of EU-wide network codes.

- To decide cross-border issues where competent NRAs have not been able to reach an agreement or upon joint requests thereto from competent NRAs.

Regulation (EC) No 715/2009 established the European Network of Transmission System Operators for Gas (ENTSOG) to ensure cooperation among TSOs, to promote the completion and functioning of the internal market in natural gas and cross-border trade, and to ensure optimal management of the natural gas transmission network.

The ENTSOG develops and monitors the implementation of EU-wide network codes. Different national network codes were seen as one of the main remaining barriers for cross-border trade and market integration after the implementation of the third package. The harmonization of network codes has made it easier for new entrants into the market because they can better understand the applicable rules. In addition, national rules may not always facilitate cross-border trade because of inconsistencies at cross-border interconnection points. The objective of EU-wide network codes was to identify and resolve these inconsistencies and thus facilitate market integration. The EU-wide network codes have been developed: for congestion management,[10] capacity allocation,[11] gas balancing,[12] interoperability and data exchange,[13] and tariffs.[14]

The ENTSOG is also responsible for developing a forecast of required actions to ensure sufficient interconnectivity within an EU-wide network and to indicate and prioritize where investments are required. However, the ENTSOG's development plan is not a requirement for the TSOs to invest but rather an input for individual member states and their TSOs' development plans.

Gas Regulation 715/2009 also required TSOs to adopt an entry-exit tariff system to ensure a uniform market design across the EU. In an entry-exit system, physical gas may be shipped anywhere within the transmission network with purchases of just two capacity contracts (one entry contract purchased by the pipeline customer adding gas to the network, and one exit contract purchased by the pipeline customer removing gas from the network).

In 2011, the Council of European Energy Regulators developed the Gas Target Model (GTM) to facilitate the implementation of the EU directives. The GTM vision consists of a limited number of liquid hubs in the EU, connected by entry-exit gas zones. EU legislation does not mandate the number of hubs per member state. However, GTM provides guidance on the metrics for virtual trading hubs to have liquidity potential. This includes physical demand (volume) and is used to support the merger of virtual hubs in adjacent member states with a small gas market (such as the Czech Republic, Slovakia and Austria).

THE NETHERLANDS

The Netherlands adopted more aggressive measures than those mandated by the EU directives and regulations. In addition, its domestic production and infrastructure development at the beginning of the reforms allowed the Netherlands to achieve a highly competitive market ahead of some other EU member states which liberalized to different degrees.

2000 Gas Act: Move towards Market Opening

The gas industry in the Netherlands started with the discovery of the giant Groningen gas field (L-gas),[15] which triggered the creation of Gasunie (an integrated network and supply company) in 1963. This entity was a public-private partnership with the state holding 50 per cent of the shares and Shell and ExxonMobil each owning 25 per cent. Gasunie built the transmission system in the country, for the transportation of gas from Groningen and other gas fields in the Netherlands and held a monopoly position in the Netherlands gas market. About 50 per cent of the production was exported to Germany, Belgium, France and Italy. The domestic gas price was set by the minister who also had approval rights on gas export contracts.

The monopoly structure lasted for four decades, but the situation started to change in 2000 when the Netherlands developed the Gas

Act to implement the EU 1998 Gas Directive. The Netherlands put a more aggressive time schedule towards market opening than the EU directive, aiming to be fully open by July 2004. The Netherlands Gas Act appointed an independent energy regulator and implemented negotiated third party access rules for infrastructure.

2003: Establishment of a Spot Gas Market

The Title Transfer Facility was created in January 2003 by Gasunie, when it adopted an entry-exit regime. The TTF was set up to promote gas trading at one central market place, similar to the NBP in the UK. Using the TTF, gas that is brought into the national system via an entry point can change owners before it leaves the national network at an exit point.

Before the TTF became the most liquid gas trading hub in Europe, a number of barriers had to be removed. The key actions that have facilitated market competition and impacted the development of liquidity at the TTF will be discussed in this section.

Despite the Netherlands achieving full retail competition in July 2004, there was no significant increase in gas trading at the TTF since Gasunie did not offer its main customers the choice of the TTF as a delivery point for its supplies and continued to supply its customers with all-in contracts (gas, transport and volume flexibility) at its customer facilities or at the borders. The retail market was mainly consuming low-calorific gas (L-gas) of which Gasunie was the main supplier. Quality conversion from high-calorific gas (H-gas) to L-gas was limited and controlled by Gasunie.

2005 Unbundling: First Step to Breaking up the Market Dominance

In 2005 Gasunie was broken up ahead of European rules on ownership unbundling, to boost competition in the gas market. A separate network company (keeping the name Gasunie) and a merchant company (GasTerra) were created. The state became 100 per cent owner of Gasunie. GasTerra ownership remained 50 per cent state, 25 per cent Shell and 25 per cent ExxonMobil. The regulated transmission system operator, named Gasunie Transport Services (GTS), became a subsidiary of Gasunie. The GTS managed the TTF so the TTF was operated by a neutral player. The infrastructure network became Gasunie's sole priority and Gasunie had an interest in seeing the transport business grow.

2009: Adjustments to Quality Conversion Service Model

By 2009, the total gas consumption in the Netherlands was split roughly 50/50 between L-gas and H-gas, and these gases were transported on separate systems. The TTF trades had to specify if they were either TTF-H or TTF-L. It did have nitrogen injection facilities to blend H-gas into L-gas, but the capacity at these quality conversion facilities was committed to incumbent shippers under long-term contracts. The unavailability of quality conversion contractual capacity was seen as an entry barrier for new H-gas shippers to supply L-gas consumers. See illustration of service model prior to 2009, below.

Figure 1: Management of different gas qualities prior to 2009

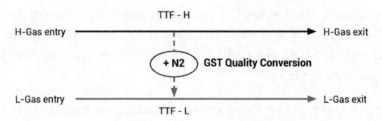

Source: © 2019 Exxon Mobil Corporation.

In 2009, this quality issue was resolved by GTS as illustrated in Figure 2 below. Instead of contracting the quality conversion capacity out to shippers, GTS now actively managed gas quality differences without restricting shippers. Shippers could now trade gas on the TTF without quality restrictions and as energy-only. GTS could manage gas quality using the existing conversion facilities on their network. The total quality conversion costs were socialized and added to the transmission tariffs. This change caused an increase in volumes traded at the TTF.

Figure 2: Management of different gas qualities from 2009 onwards

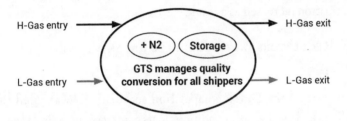

Source: © 2019 *Exxon Mobil Corporation.*

2010: Adjustments to System Balancing Model

In a market survey, GTS identified that its high penalties to shippers for being out of balance was deterring market players from participating in the market. In the then existing balancing regime, GTS applied tolerances or margins for hourly imbalances, cumulative hourly imbalances and daily imbalances. The balancing position of each individual shipper was continuously monitored. The shipper would be charged 10–15 per cent of the gas price for volumes in excess of the hourly imbalance tolerance, and 100 per cent of the gas price in case of a cumulative hourly excess or a daily excess.

In 2010, the TTF changed to a market-based balancing regime. Under this new regime, although the shippers were subject to within-day balancing obligations, they were not subject to penalties unless the whole system balance signal (SBS) exceeded specific tolerances. The TSO monitored the SBS continuously (compared to each shipper's imbalance), and if it was outside the toleration zone, the TSO took balancing actions. The costs of GTS balancing actions were allocated only to the shippers that caused an imbalance. Shippers with an opposite imbalance, which helped the overall system balance, did not incur these costs. The TSO took more immediate action for more significant imbalances. This was a significant improvement for shippers and market participation increased as a result.

2011: Regulatory Intervention to Break Market Dominance

In early 2011, the Dutch competition authority (NMa) ruled that GasTerra had used supply conditions in its contracts, including a refusal to deliver gas at the TTF, which impeded the creation of competition in the gas market. The NMa considered this behaviour the abuse of a dominant position and therefore fined GasTerra. However, after an objective review process, NMa concluded that there was insufficient certainty that GasTerra had abused its dominant position. In the meantime, GasTerra also put an end to the identified behaviour and started taking measures to demonstrate the facilitation of competition, giving NMa no cause to investigate further.

In the first half of 2011, GasTerra started the delivery of gas products at the TTF and increased its within-day and day-ahead product offerings at the TTF. These short-term products improved access to flexibility and enabled market players to better adjust their gas purchases to the fluctuating gas demand in the short term. In addition, GasTerra started to offer year products with a flexible component, allowing market parties to contract a seasonal profile on the hub. Furthermore, GasTerra introduced virtual gas storage (system-wide storage services without customers having to contract capacity at specific storage facilities) to provide market players seasonal flexibility to meet their seasonal demand profile.

Today, traded volumes and the number of market participants have significantly risen, and bid-offer spreads have fallen both in within-day, day-ahead as well as future trades, showing that traders have started to use the TTF for balancing as well as for hedging purposes. The increase in liquidity for spot, as well as future products, has been self-reinforcing and increased the attractiveness and reliability of the TTF as a means to manage gas portfolio hedging and optimization. It has reinforced the focus on TTF as the hub of choice for forward trading. The TTF has become the clear continental (euro) price benchmark, and the TTF is used extensively as a contractual price reference for long-term contracts indexation and for other EU hubs.

The strong development of the TTF can be partly attributed to the underlying physical characteristics of the Dutch market, with its large domestic production volumes, particularly from the Groningen field, gas storage facilities, and high levels of interconnection to surrounding markets including an interconnector to the UK and an LNG terminal. The TTF also benefits from a commitment by authorities to competitive markets and a stable, predictable regulatory regime.

CONCLUSION

The US, the UK and the Netherlands have followed different journeys to gas market liberalization but share some common success factors.

Establishment of an independent regulator: The 1938 US NGA established the FPC and the 1978 NGPA replaced the FPC with the independent FERC. The UK Gas Act of 1986 established OFGAS, which later merged with the electricity regulator to form OFGEM. The EU's Second Gas Directive in 2003 mandated member states to designate an NRA for their countries and its Third Gas Directive in

2009 enhanced the NRA's independence. These regulatory bodies have enacted regulations to create and sustain a fair playing field and protect emerging competitors from incumbent market dominance. They continue to be responsible for enforcing regulations, market monitoring and interventions if necessary.

Third-party access (TPA) to gas transportation infrastructure: The US FERC Order 436, the 1986 UK Gas Act and the EU 2003 Gas Directive introduced TPA in their respective jurisdictions. The TPA—offered without discrimination and with transparent regulated tariffs—has enabled competition in these markets by allowing new market entrants both access and efficient use of infrastructure.

Unbundling: The ownership unbundling of gas transportation services from gas marketing and production services as required by FERC Oder 636 in the US, and accomplished by British Gas in the UK in 1997 and Gasunie in the Netherlands in 2005, was necessary to preclude the ability of vertically integrated companies to control infrastructure access to their advantage and to break market dominance.

Market opening: This refers to both allowing suppliers to sell to customers of choice, and customers buying from the supplier of choice. The US FERC Order 636, UK's 1992 Utilities Act and the Netherlands 2000 Gas Act aimed for full opening in a phased approach, which helped reduce market dominance and attract additional market participants.

Continued identification and removal of barriers to facilitate market competition: The three countries discussed took a number of measures to remove barriers or correct previous missteps to achieve their market liberalization goals. Some were driven by regulators (e.g., TPA, unbundling, market opening, 2011 Dutch NMa ruling, 1978 NGPA section 311) and some were initiated by industry players (e.g., introduction of NBP, adjustments to quality conversion and balancing models).

By studying the liberalization paths of these successful markets, countries beginning their own path to liberalization can identify commonalities with their markets and success factors needed as well as missteps to avoid in their journey. The transitions to a competitive gas market have not followed a straight path and have had many challenges. The will to initiate and make adjustments to sustain market reforms over a number of years has played a key role in ensuring that market goals were achieved.

Notes

1. With contributions from Kees Bouwens, John Poe and Shelley Ruszkowski.
2. The discussion in the rest of this section on the US is focused on interstate pipelines and not intrastate pipelines. Retail-level unbundling is a decision that has been left up to each state's regulatory authority and varies across the US.
3. Customers with transportation-only contracts.
4. Created in 1949 on the basis of the Gas Act of 1948.
5. The government believed that competition in gas supply to small consumers at this time was not economically feasible.
6. Steve Thomas, *The European Union Gas and Electricity Directives*, London: Public Services International Research Institute, University of Greenwich, 2005, p. 32.
7. Directive 2009/73/EC, https://eur-lex.europa.eu/legal-content/EN/TXT/PDF/?uri=CELEX:32009L0073&from=EN
8. Regulation (EC) No 713/2009, https://eur-lex.europa.eu/legal-content/EN/TXT/PDF/?uri=CELEX:32009R0713&from=EN and Regulation (EC) No 715/2009, https://eur-lex.europa.eu/legal-content/EN/TXT/PDF/?uri=CELEX:32009R0715&from=EN
9. Where a TSO was part of a vertically integrated company on 3 September 2009.

10. Congestion Management (Commission Decision 2012/490/EU amended by Commission Decision 2015/715), http://eur-lex.europa. eu/LexUriServ/LexUriServ.do?uri=OJ:L:2012:231:0016:0020:en :PDF and http://eur-lex.europa.eu/legal-content/EN/TXT/PDF/? uri=OJ:JOL_2015_114_R_0004&from=EN

11. Capacity Allocation (Commission Regulation 2017/459), https://eur-lex.europa.eu/legal-content/EN/TXT/PDF/?uri=CELEX:32017R 0459&qid=1541407394653&from=EN

12. Gas Balancing (Commission Regulation 312/2014), https://eur-lex. europa.eu/legal-content/EN/TXT/PDF/?uri=OJ:JOL_2014_091_ R_0015_01&from=EN

13. Interoperability and Data Exchange (Commission Regulation 2015/703), http://eur-lex.europa.eu/legal-content/EN/TXT/PDF/ ?uri=OJ:JOL_2015_113_R_0003&rid=1

14. Tariffs (Commission Regulation 2017/460), https://eur-lex.europa.eu/ legal-content/EN/TXT/PDF/?uri=CELEX:32017R0460&qid=1 541407394653&from=EN

15. Gas from Groningen has low heating value (L-gas) and gas from the North Sea has high heating value (H-gas).

6

TECHNOLOGY AND ITS IMPACT

SAMANTHA GROSS

Director, Energy Security and Climate Initiative, Brookings Fellow

DAVID VICTOR

*Professor, School of Global Policy and Strategy, University of California,
San Diego and Non-resident Senior Fellow, Brookings*

TECHNOLOGY IS BRINGING ABOUT SIGNIFICANT changes in global natural gas markets. A revolution in the production of gas from tight formations has opened vast new reserves at low prices, beginning in the US, but with the potential to move to other areas as well. Technologies that focus on the efficiency of operations and environmental performance will contribute to a growing gas supply. At the same time, improvements in the efficiency of the use of gas in power-generation are making gas an even more attractive choice for reducing carbon emissions and partnering with renewables. Finally, gas is becoming a practical and affordable fuel in more markets, as the supply of LNG grows and floating regasification units reduce the capital investment needed to tap into LNG.

Greater use of gas could bring many advantages to India, including more flexibility for the expansion of renewable energy (RE) in the power sector. Infrastructure and pricing are the primary impediments to greater natural gas use in India. Pipeline constraints prevent gas from reaching many potential customers. Additionally, the gas market is bifurcated, with much lower prices for domestically produced gas, than for imported LNG.

Domestically produced gas is rationed for specific industries, especially fertilizer, leaving less gas available for other sectors. Gas-fired power plants in India operate at low utilization rates, in part because gas is expensive relative to coal. The greater use of gas in the power and transportation sectors would require building pipeline infrastructure and making gas competitive with other fuel sources, perhaps by pricing the externalities of coal in the power sector.

SUPPLY

The International Energy Agency (IEA) forecasts that natural gas will be the fastest-growing fossil fuel in the coming decades. As shown in Figure 1, the Middle East, North America and Asia-Pacific are leading in the growth of gas production.

Figure 1: Global natural gas predictions

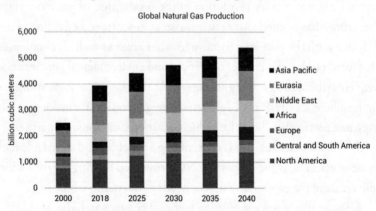

Global Natural Gas Production

Source: International Energy Agency, 'World Energy Outlook 2019'.[1]

The development of unconventional natural gas resources in the US is a key driver in today's markets and future gas supply. The combination of horizontal drilling and hydraulic fracturing has unlocked gas resources in shale and tight formations that had previously been uneconomical to produce. These technologies have come to dominate oil and gas production and shale gas today makes up 63 per cent of natural gas production in the US. Within five years, this share is forecast to reach 80 per cent.[2]

At the outset of the shale revolution in 2005, dry gas production in the US was 513 billion cubic meters (Bcm).[3] By 2019, it had touched 960 Bcm and is predicted to grow to 1,270 Bcm by 2050 as per the US Energy Information Administration (EIA).[4] The US, which made up 22 per cent of the global gas supply in 2018,[5] is expected to continue as the world's largest gas producer.[6] Even with the extensive US gas pipeline infrastructure, some associated gas produced along with oil is being flared in the Permian basin today. The construction of the pipelines needed to move this gas to market will bring in additional supply at a very low cost.

Technical progress continues to increase natural gas production in the US, while decreasing costs. Consistently low prices have forced operators to become more efficient to remain profitable. The time needed to drill, fracture and complete a well has been cut in half in recent years. Better delineation and targeting of 'sweet spots' in gas-bearing formations, more efficient fracturing fluids and longer lateral reach of wells are making each well more productive, thus decreasing costs.

Unconventional natural gas resources, similar to those in the US, exist in other countries as well. Canada has seen extensive development. Countries with similar resources include China, Argentina, Mexico and even Saudi Arabia. Production in these countries is likely to increase as they develop the knowledge and commercial infrastructure needed for successful shale gas development. The Vaca Muerta formation in Argentina is the current global front-runner in new shale gas development and Argentina could become a gas exporter over time. China has significant shale and tight gas resources, but they are challenging to develop. However, China is likely to overcome these challenges over time as its domestic gas demand grows rapidly.

Conventional gas production is also set to grow with Russia, Iran, Iraq and Qatar leading the way. Construction of infrastructure to capture gas produced along with oil is an important development in Iraq, while the lifting of the moratorium on additional production from the North Field in offshore Qatar will add to global LNG volumes.

Environmental concerns and local opposition raise challenges to onshore natural gas production. This is especially true in areas outside the US, where these are subsurface resources generally owned by the government. This leaves the owner of the (surface) land with little incentive to cooperate with development. Several countries have banned hydraulic fracturing, including Germany, France and Uruguay. Technologies that lessen the environmental and community impacts of unconventional natural gas development could increase support for such development and increase supply.

Lower impact drilling and hydraulic fracturing technologies are one option to increase the social acceptability of gas development. Drilling slimmer holes with smaller rigs and drilling many wells with long laterals from a single location reduce the surface impact of drilling activities. Reducing or eliminating water-use in the hydraulic fracturing process can be another important aspect of limiting the impact of drilling. A large volume of water is used for a short time during the drilling and fracturing process, so reducing water-use can significantly decrease the surface impact and vehicle traffic involved during the drilling process. Fracturing with propane gel or liquid carbon dioxide can reduce water-use, wastewater and the chemicals that must be disposed of during production.

Reducing methane emissions is another important step toward increasing acceptability and decreasing the environmental impact of natural gas production. Methane is the primary component of natural gas, but is also a potent greenhouse gas (GHG), with thirty-six times the global warming potential of carbon dioxide over 100 years.[7] Therefore, detecting and minimizing methane releases throughout the value chain is essential to preserving the role of natural gas as a lower-carbon fuel. Methane emissions are not a primary driver of objections to gas production today—opponents generally focus on local issues—but they could become more important over time as citizens and laws focus more on GHG emissions.

Finally, ongoing advances in reservoir-imaging can make the process of identifying natural gas resources less expensive and more accurate. Such technologies can also reduce the environmental impact of development, by getting the maximum production out of each well and keeping dry holes to a minimum. Seismic imaging uses sound waves to generate images of the subsurface. Supercomputers now allow the analysis of the full waveform generated by 3-D seismic studies, generating more accurate models of the subsurface, while 4-D seismic studies add the dimension of time, modelling how a reservoir changes while it is under production and also increasing potential recovery from existing wells.

DEMAND

Natural gas is the cleanest fossil fuel, making it a natural choice to reduce local air pollution and GHG emissions when replacing coal or petroleum. Natural gas turbines for power generation are becoming more efficient and flexible. Combined-cycle turbines are more efficient than simple cycle, with the most efficient models now reaching a maximum efficiency of 64 per cent.[8] However, gas-fired generation often is used to respond to variations in the production of power from wind and solar energy. The cycling and ramping required in this application tend to reduce efficiency. Nonetheless, the operating efficiency of gas-fired plants is improving over time in the US. From 2006 to 2015, the heat rate (the amount of energy used to generate a unit of electricity) of US gas plants improved by 7 per cent, as the share of more efficient combined-cycle systems in gas-fired generation grew from 75 per cent in 2006 to 85 per cent in 2015.[9]

Natural gas-fired power generation has other advantages in new construction. Gas turbines are scalable, with efficient models in sizes from hundreds of kilowatts to hundreds of megawatts. Gas-fired generation requires lower upfront investment than other forms of dispatchable power and can generally be built more quickly than a coal-fired power plant. Because gas-fired generation does not require space to store fuel on site and produces fewer local pollutants such as sulphur oxides and particulate matter, gas plants need less land and can be easier to site than coal-fired generation.

Although natural gas power plants emit half the GHGs per unit of power compared to coal-fired plants, coal-to-gas switching cannot achieve the level of deep decarbonization that will be required to meet the goals of the Paris Agreement. Carbon capture and storage (CCS) combined with gas-fired generation is likely to be one solution to decarbonizing the power sector. Carbon capture and storage is more challenging when combined with the varying generation of natural gas power plants that provide backup to intermittent renewable sources of power. However, in some areas and applications, load-following gas-fired generation with CCS may prove cost effective. Additionally, a new type of gas-fired power plant that uses the Allam cycle may make CCS much more energy efficient and cost effective. These power plants burn natural gas with pure oxygen and use supercritical carbon dioxide as the working fluid in the system. Thus, a pure stream of carbon dioxide is a natural output, rather than requiring an energy-consuming system to separate and concentrate carbon dioxide at the back end of the power plant. All carbon-capture systems require either a site to geologically sequester the carbon dioxide or a use for the captured gas.

Transportation has the potential to be another growth area for natural gas, but this market is not as developed as that for power. In the light vehicle fleet, CNG can be a good fuel for vehicles that regularly return to a central station, to overcome the lack of refuelling stations. India is currently a leader in CNG vehicles globally and the Government of India is calling for up to 10,000 CNG stations to be built over the next ten years, up from 1,424 stations currently. More than 80 per cent of these existing stations are in the cities of Delhi and Mumbai and in the state of Gujarat.[10] The total cost of ownership for a CNG vehicle is roughly 20 per cent lower than a comparable gasoline or diesel vehicle, so increased refuelling infrastructure could be a game-changer in the market penetration of CNG vehicles.

Liquified natural gas is a potential fuel for heavy transportation, such as long-distance trucking and shipping, although it is not yet in wide use. It is more attractive for long-distance transport because it has greater energy density than CNG, allowing greater vehicle range. However, LNG must be stored at very low temperatures and faces the challenge of methane boiling off the fuel over time. Nevertheless, LNG is a potential way to comply with the International Marine Organization's low-sulphur bunker fuel regulation that came into force at the beginning of 2020.

GAS INFRASTRUCTURE AND MARKETS

Trade in natural gas is inextricably linked to infrastructure. Gas requires more specialized infrastructure to transport (either pipelines or LNG liquefaction and regasification facilities), than does oil. As shown in Figure 2, LNG volumes have grown substantially since 2000 and are expected to continue their rapid growth, compared to relatively slow growth in pipeline gas trade. Growth in LNG trade has brought more flexibility to gas markets. Pipelines directly connect a buyer and seller, but LNG allows cargoes of gas to go to markets where they can fetch the highest price or where they are most needed; LNG is thus allowing a global market in natural gas to develop.

Figure 2: Global gas trade

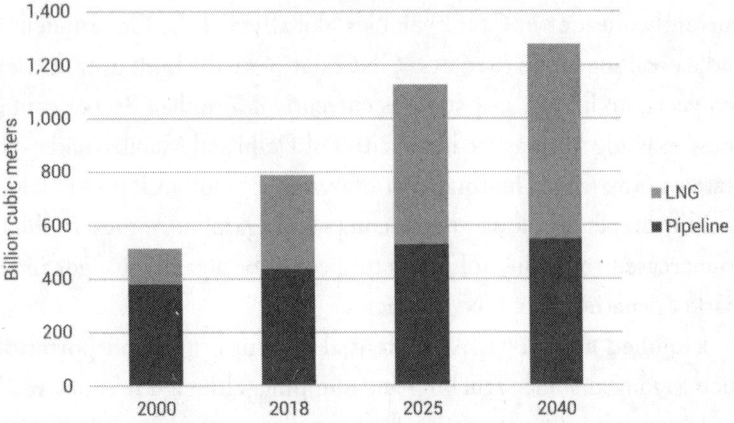

Source: *International Energy Agency, 'World Energy Outlook 2019'.*[11]

Long-term contracts have long dominated the gas trade, either because of the pipeline connections between producers and markets or because long commitments were needed to finance LNG infrastructure. Since LNG is a very capital-intensive business, liquefaction, transportation and regasification add $4 to $7/MMBtu (Metric Million British thermal unit) to break-even prices.[12]

In the past, LNG was often sold through twenty-five-year contracts that typically contained restrictions on diverting the gas to different destinations and take-or-pay provisions that required the purchase of minimum volumes. Additionally, gas prices in Europe and Asia were typically indexed to oil prices, rather than based on supply and demand fundamentals in the gas market. This situation is changing as more gas is traded on a spot or short-term basis and new gas-trading hubs develop, with enough depth and liquidity to allow price discovery. Such hubs generally need to be located at the centre of gas-infrastructure networks, such as pipelines and LNG terminals, and serve the needs of a diverse customer base.

Henry Hub in the US was the first gas-trading hub, at the centre of vast gas production in the south-east region of the US. The UK National Balancing Point (NBP) is a virtual trading hub rather than a physical location, but serves the same purpose by providing market liquidity and price discovery. Even though Asia is the largest global market for LNG, it does not have a significant trading hub or a gas-based pricing benchmark. China, Japan and Singapore are all attempting to develop gas-trading hubs and price benchmarks.

An oversupply of LNG came about when expected shortages in natural-gas supply in the US turned into an overwhelming surplus. Qatar, in particular, took final investment decisions on LNG projects intended for the US market in the early- to mid-2000s, before the natural gas revolution took hold. Natural gas production skyrocketed in the US as these new Qatari facilities came online, meaning that this gas was available to be sold in other markets. The surge of supply made LNG more of a buyers' market and encouraged the loosening of contract conditions.

Additionally, advances in floating storage and regasification units (FSRUs) have made LNG-supply more widely available and with less capital investment. The FSRUs contain all the equipment of an onshore regasification facility and use the same technology, but they are built on a vessel similar to an LNG tanker. Such vessels can be constructed at roughly half the cost and in half the time as a permanent onshore facility.[13] They also do not require a long-term commitment to a market; the unit can be moved if demand or supply conditions change. Egypt, Jordan and Pakistan have been important markets where FSRUs have led LNG growth. Egypt, in particular, demonstrates the flexibility of the technology. Egypt was an LNG exporter, but gas production there fell sharply after the Arab Spring and the end of the Mubarak regime.

Importing gas using FSRUs has helped fill the gap until new projects come on line.[14]

Changing technology and market conditions have revolutionized how LNG is sold. The Oxford Institute for Energy Studies (OIES) estimates that as much as 43 per cent of LNG volumes in 2020 may be traded through spot sales and short-term contracts.[15] These contract terms make it easier for new buyers to enter the market and buy only the gas that they need, without the encumbrance of long-term contracts or required volume provisions.

HOW INDIA CAN TAKE ADVANTAGE OF THE NATURAL GAS REVOLUTION

The energy system in India is changing fast, opening up opportunities for natural gas. India's urban population is expected to grow from roughly 400 million to more than 600 million by 2030 and half the infrastructure that will be needed by 2030 has not yet been built.[16] Natural gas makes up only 5 per cent of India's energy supply, compared to a global average of 22 per cent.[17]

Other gas markets provide lessons that India can learn from, as it moves to include more natural gas in its energy system. One crucial lesson is that price regulation has clear downsides. In the US, natural gas prices were regulated until the late 1970s. The resulting low prices increased demand for gas and decreased supply; prices were too low to encourage additional production. A policy intended to protect consumers from high monopoly prices ended up hurting them instead through gas shortages.

India faces a similar situation today. Regulated prices and industrial policy largely determine how natural gas is used. The Indian market for gas is bifurcated, with much higher prices for imported LNG than for domestically produced gas. Prices for domestic gas are set based on a basket of international gas prices, including those in the US, the UK and

Canada. This scheme results in prices that are acceptable to users, but not high enough to incentivize exploration and production of additional gas supply.[18] Higher gas prices and a stable price environment could bring additional investment in supply.

Lower-priced domestic gas is allocated to fertilizer plants, city gas distribution (CGD), CNG vehicles and some gas-fired power plants. Fertilizer production dominates the use of natural gas in India, taking up more than 30 per cent of the supply.[19] Deregulation of gas prices is unlikely to be successful without deregulation of fertilizer and power prices. These industries must be able to pass changes in gas price to their final consumers to remain competitive.

Much discussion focuses on the potential for natural gas to displace coal in the Indian power sector, but the existing base of gas-fired power plants is vastly underutilized, largely because of the lack of affordable gas supply. Policies and incentives that encourage the use of gas in the power sector are key to allowing India to enjoy the advantages of natural gas. The challenges of meeting coal demand and increasing concerns about air pollution and GHG emissions open the door to greater gas use. Pricing the externalities of the use of coal (such as a carbon price) could help move more gas into the power sector.

The lack of infrastructure is currently an important impediment to greater natural gas use in India. Even as India builds more LNG import terminals, they are operating well below capacity because pipeline constraints within the country prevent gas from reaching more customers. Capital investments are needed, both in a long-distance gas transport grid and in local gas distribution networks.

A number of factors need to be in place for India to attract the patient capital required for infrastructure investments. Clear indicators of long-term demand are important, through government policy encouraging the use of gas or long-term contracts. The use of gas in power generation can serve as an 'anchor' to support infrastructure development and support the spread of other uses of gas, such as in cities and in CNG vehicles.

City gas use and CNG today are concentrated in the largest cities and in Gujarat, where gas production and state support have brought extensive infrastructure investment.

Gujarat provides an example for other states to follow. It is the centre of India's oil and gas and refining industries and has the most developed gas pipeline network. As a result of the incentives for the construction of pipelines, gas-fired power plants and fertilizer production, gas now makes up 25 per cent of Gujarat's energy mix. Gujarat has three of India's five LNG terminals to meet local demand.

Notes

1. International Energy Agency, 'World Energy Outlook 2019', Paris: OECD/IEA, 2019, https://www.iea.org/reports/world-energy-outlook-2019

2. International Energy Agency, 'World Energy Outlook 2018', Paris: OECD/IEA, 2018, https://www.iea.org/reports/world-energy-outlook-2018

3. US Energy Information Administration, 'U.S. Dry Natural Gas Production', Database, Washington: EIA, accessed 19 May 2020, https://www.eia.gov/dnav/ng/hist/n9070us2A.htm

4. US Energy Information Administration, 'EIA expects natural gas production and exports to continue increasing in most scenarios', Washington: EIA, 19 February 2020, https://www.eia.gov/todayinenergy/detail.php?id=42875

5. British Petroleum (2019), 'Statistical Review of World Energy 2019, 68th Edition', London: British Petroleum, 2019, https://www.bp.com/content/dam/bp/business-sites/en/global/corporate/pdfs/energy-economics/statistical-review/bp-stats-review-2019-full-report.pdf

6. International Energy Agency, 'World Energy Outlook 2019', Paris: OECD/IEA, 2019, https://www.iea.org/reports/world-energy-outlook-2019

7. US Environmental Protection Agency, 'Understanding Global Warming Potentials', Washington: EPA, accessed 19 May 2020, https://www.epa.gov/ghgemissions/understanding-global-warming-potentials

8. Darrell Proctor, 'Efficiency Improvements Mark Advances in Gas Turbines', *Power Magazine*, 3 January 2018, https://www.powermag.com/efficiency-improvements-mark-advances-in-gas-turbines/?printmode=1

9. US Energy Information Administration, 'Natural gas-fired electricity conversion efficiency grows as coal remains stable', Washington: EIA, 21 August 2017, https://www.eia.gov/todayinenergy/detail.php?id=32572

10. S. Ronendra Singh, '10,000 CNG Stations to be set up in 10 years: Pradhan', *Hindu Business Line*, 6 September 2018, https://www.thehindubusinessline.com/companies/10000-cng-stations-to-be-set-up-in-10-years-pradhan/article24884980.ece

11. International Energy Agency, 'World Energy Outlook 2019'.

12. Howard Rogers, 'Does the Portfolio Model spell the end of long-term oil-indexed LNG contracts?', Working Paper, Oxford: Oxford Institute for Energy Studies, April 2017, https://www.oxfordenergy.org/wpcms/wp-content/uploads/2017/04/Does-the-Portfolio-Business-Model-Spell-the-End-of-Long-Term-Oil-Indexed-LNG-Contracts-OIES-Energy-Insight.pdf

13. Brian Songhurst, 'The Outlook for Floating Storage and Regasification Units (FSRUs)', OIES Paper: NG 123, Oxford: Oxford Institute for Energy Studies: Oxford, July 2017, https://www.oxfordenergy.org/wpcms/wp-content/uploads/2017/07/The-Outlook-for-Floating-Storage-and-Regasification-Units-FSRUs-NG-123.pdf

14. Teddy Kott and Akos Losz, 'They Might be Giants: Emerging LNG Importers are Reshaping the Waterborne Gas Market', *Columbia Academic Commons*, 16 November 2017, https://academiccommons.columbia.edu/doi/10.7916/D81C28HX, accessed 20 May 2020.

15. Howard Rogers, 'Does the Portfolio Model Spell the End of Long-term Oil-indexed LNG Contracts?', 2017.
16. 'India's Intended Nationally Determined Contribution: Working Towards Climate Justice', https://www4.unfccc.int/sites/ndcstaging/PublishedDocuments/India%20First/INDIA%20INDC%20TO%20UNFCCC.pdf, accessed 20 May 2020.
17. International Energy Agency, 'World Energy Outlook 2018'.
18. Michael Ratner, 'India's Natural Gas: A Small Part of the Energy Mix', Congressional Research Service Report, Washington DC: Congressional Research Service, 13 February 2017, https://fas.org/sgp/crs/row/R44765.pdf
19. Ratner, 'India's Natural Gas', 2017.

7

SHIPPING LIQUEFIED NATURAL GAS

Independent Non-Executive Director, Euronav; Chief Commercial Officer Tellurian Inc.

MARTIN J. HOUSTON

Vice Chairman and co-founder, Tellurian Inc.; Chairman, EnQuest PLC; and Non-Executive Director of BUPA Arabia and CC Energy

INTRODUCTION

IN JANUARY 1959, A GLOBAL industry was born when a converted World War II Liberty-class ship, the *Methane Pioneer*, set sail from Lake Charles in the US, for Canvey Island in the UK. Carrying approximately 5,000 cubic metres (m^3) of LNG and travelling at an average speed of 9.4 knots, the vessel transited the Atlantic in twenty-three days; the first-ever transatlantic crossing of LNG. This successful voyage paved the way for the world's first LNG export scheme, a fifteen-year contract for one Mtpa from Algeria to the UK.[1]

Image 1: The *Methane Pioneer* in the Foreground at Canvey Island

Image courtesy of SIGGTO and GIIGNL

In the years since, a true sea change has occurred in the LNG industry. The LNG trade has been facilitated by significant advances in LNG shipping, with carriers becoming larger and more energy efficient, and more numerous (546 vessels sail the world's oceans today). Appendix 1 shows a fleet-breakdown analysis.

This chapter will focus on a range of issues that shape the LNG shipping industry:

- Technical advances in LNG vessel design
- Impact on shipping due to the changing nature of the LNG business
- Charter rates
- Impact of new trade routes

TECHNOLOGICAL ADVANCES IN LNG VESSEL DESIGN

Prior to the last decade, LNG vessels saw few major advances in vessel design and their operations since the first ships came into service fifty years ago. However, during the last decade, there have been major changes regarding propulsion options, vessel size and boil-off management. These changes have come at no expense to safety. Due to well-designed safety systems and high international standards, there has never been a loss of cargo tank containment or onboard fatalities directly attributable to cargo and this has contributed to an excellent LNG shipping industry safety record.

Vessels to ship LNG were traditionally built with a very reliable, but not very efficient, steam-turbine (ST) propulsion system. Boilers were the only means of consuming boil-off gas (then viewed as waste gas), which could be substituted for heavy fuel oil (HFO). As these steam ships consumed large amounts of HFO, there was no significant impetus to reduce boil-off.

By 2010, more fuel-efficient Dual/Tri-Fuel Diesel Electric (D/TFDE) engines (ships able to burn HFO, diesel oil and gas) were introduced, alongside increased ship sizes of approximately 160,000 m^3 to 174,000 m^3. These TFDE ships delivered fuel-efficiency improvements of 25–30 per cent over previous generation steam ships.

Increasing the size of the ship counterbalanced improvements in the efficiency of propulsion systems, since these ships now had more boil-off than necessary for operations.

Therefore, the design of containment systems also had to evolve in order to prevent excess boil-off (no longer required for propulsion) from being sent to onboard gas combustion units, since this was now viewed as 'lost' cargo that could have been sold. Newly designed membrane containment systems for the TFDE vessels, with more effective insulation, reduced the amount of boil-off from approximately 0.15 per cent to 0.10 per cent. Some vessels also included re-liquefaction plants, since there was still more boil-off than needed for propulsion, even with improved containment systems.

After the very large Qatari ships (Q-Flex and Q-Max) started utilizing slow-speed diesel engines for propulsion, re-liquefaction plants were added to handle the boil-off gas. This prompted a renewed interest in finding a solution enabling slow-speed engines to run on gas. The inability to utilize boil-off in the Qatari ship engines is a major limitation for fuel arbitrage purposes, and at least one vessel has since been retrofitted to enable gas burning.

Over the last few years, propulsion technology has continued to improve, with vessels being delivered from shipyards with the latest slow-speed diesel engine designs. These include gas injection from manufacturers MAN and Wärtsilä, the high-pressure M-Type Electronically Controlled Gas Injection (MEGI) and the low-pressure 'Generation X' Dual Fuel (X-DF). Compared to TFDE, slow-speed diesel engines with gas injection offer approximately 15–20 per cent better fuel efficiency when the ships run at higher operating speeds. Ultra-steam and reheat-steam are improved steam turbine technologies, generally proposed by the Japanese yards, but still suffer from lower efficiency than the medium-speed TFDE and slow-speed X-DF/MEGI diesel-electric solutions.

The breakdown of the existing fleet plus the current order book, in terms of propulsion, is shown below.

In addition to advances in propulsion technology, the standard average vessel size has grown to 174,000m³–180,000m³, and the membrane containment systems boil-off rate has dropped to 0.08 per cent. The impact on charterers has been significant. The operational costs of shipping have dropped by up to 45 per cent through the changes in propulsion and boil-off described above

An example of the savings across various propulsion types and ship sizes at a speed of 16.5 knots, using various shipping routes to India, is shown below. The Yamal route, discussed later in this chapter, assumes

Figure 1: Existing fleet composition

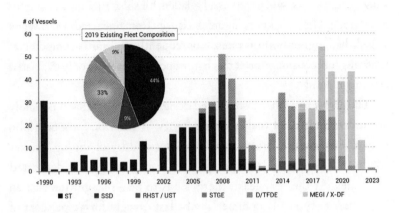

Source: Poten (2020)

the same vessel is performing the entire voyage and does not include trans-shipments from ice-class vessels onto conventional vessels, which would substantially increase the overall cost.

Figure 2: LNG carrier voyage details

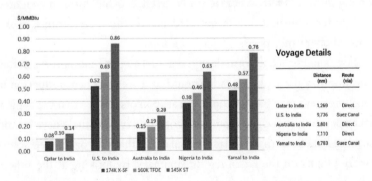

Source: Poten (2020).

Another evolution in ship design centres on the relationship between efficiency and speed. In designing ships, shipyards traditionally optimized the hull form around the ship-build contractual guarantee value at 19.5 knots, when the vessel is laden, for ships running a point-to-point trade. The '19.5 knots' figure is a legacy from liner trades and when vessels had higher boil-off rates. Consequently, the yards competed at lowering fuel consumption at this figure and designs were only evaluated at a single point.

The problem with the one-speed design approach is that it is simply not representative of real trading activity. A solution for a portfolio player may include multiple routes dictated by changing market conditions, versus project-specific liner trade that follows dedicated schedules. At the very least, there needs to be a recognition that an LNG carrier typically operates at a ballast draught for 50 per cent of its time, not always in calm weather conditions and at varying speeds. The bulbous bow, as one obvious example, which is optimized for a fully loaded vessel at 19.5 knots, will not necessarily be the best for 16 knots in ballast.

As portfolio players started becoming the dominant charterers, they pushed for lower operating costs to support their trading activities, forcing shipyards and owners to study the effect of hull form on weighted average fuel consumption in both laden and ballast conditions, over a range of operating speeds (12 to 19.5 knots).

For example, a hull form design that had a 1 per cent increase in fuel consumption at 19.5 knots laden could have a 15 per cent reduction in consumption in the ballast condition at 16 knots. Given that the typical fleet operating speed is around 16 knots, this type of fuel curve would be more beneficial than the traditional curve that was optimized solely for 19.5 knots on the laden leg. In summary, by looking at the whole operating profile of the ship, there was potential to significantly reduce the weighted average fuel oil consumption of a ship, considering the typical operating profile at each speed.

Figure 3: Hull form design and fuel consumption

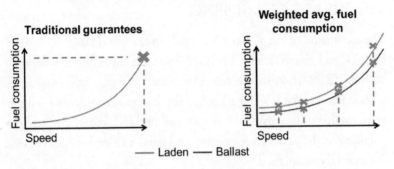

Laden ———— Ballast

Source: Author analysis.

Propulsion, size and containment system changes over the last decade have had a significant impact on reducing operating costs by around 50 per cent, while absolute Capex costs for ships have remained fairly static. This has been one of the largest positive cost changes within the entire LNG supply chain, not to mention the improvement in emissions.

This begs the question: has the technological evolution ended? The next step—change in propulsion plant efficiency, while maintaining fuel and speed flexibility—is not clear. A possibility is a hybrid system that would combine boil-off gas with less carbon-intensive solutions. However, the marine industry has traditionally not favoured high complexity systems, as these must be reliable since vessels are out of touch of shore-support for most of the time.

Fortunately, there are many other aspects of LNG carriers that can be made more efficient, such as hull form and wake flow into the main propulsor and rudder. These may not lead to the big changes we have seen over the last decade, but every improvement helps reduce fuel consumption and, ultimately, is more environmentally friendly.

CHANGING NATURE OF THE LNG BUSINESS AND THE IMPACT ON SHIPPING

The expansion of the global LNG trade in the last decade, influenced by local and global factors, has had a dramatic impact on the shipping market. In addition to shorter-term weather events and exogenous market shocks, the LNG market has also had to accommodate longer-term (multi-season) cycles in supply and demand, partly because the planning lead-time between supply and demand elements has become increasingly misaligned.

According to Poten & Partners, in 2010, short- to medium-term charters represented 27 per cent of all fixtures, up from 12 per cent in 2009. By 2011, medium-term charters represented 45 per cent of all fixture activity whilst spot charter activity (defined as a charter less than 180 days) was generally limited to sub-charters. The few vessels available for fixture reached a post-Fukushima peak rate of approximately $140,000 per day.

Growth in freight liquidity started in 2013 as a wave of new-build LNG carriers began to enter service following a period of tightness that occurred after the Fukushima crisis. High oil prices created a material arbitrage, pulling Atlantic volumes to the Pacific. Prior to 2013, steam-turbine vessels dominated the spot market. Since then, a wave of TFDE new builds have hit the water, some of them ordered on a speculative basis following Fukushima, increasing the availability of the TFDEs in the spot market. In the meantime, the inter-basin arbitrage collapsed when new Pacific basin supplies hit the market (e.g., Australia, Papua New Guinea, etc.), thereby reducing shipping tonne-miles and placing an increased focus on shipping costs. In the fourth quarter of 2016, most spot and short-term fixtures were performed by TFDE vessels, pushing steam-turbine vessel utilization to very low levels and even leading to lay-ups.

Analysis done by Poten & Partners for this paper shows that LNG shipping spot market fixture activity continued its approximately 35 per cent compounded annual growth rate (CAGR) trajectory in 2016, with 285 spot fixtures reported. However, the rate of growth for spot fixtures has recently slowed with 357 fixtures in 2017 and 368 in 2018. As spot rates wavered briefly around the record-high $200,000/day range in the winter of 2018, mainly owing to the pull of spot volumes during a cold winter spell in China and other parts of Asia, charterers flocked back to the shipping market seeking the stability of medium- and long-term rates. A similar spike occurred in the winter of 2019.

The lesson here is clear. The LNG shipping market is not yet liquid or fungible enough to be relied upon by any buyer or seller who is responsible for delivering long-term supply or sales commitments. Simply put, it would be unwise to underestimate the ability of the LNG shipping market to turn quickly from long shipping to short shipping, in a matter of a few days.

CHARTER RATES

Understanding the cost structure of charter rates is crucial for LNG market participants. Headline rates do not provide the full picture on ship-owner earnings since they do not include additional attainable revenue and ignore repositioning costs and idle time. Adding utilization and ballast bonus to the headline spot rate returns, an estimate of the time charter equivalent (TCE) rate, is a more accurate representation of ship-owner earnings over a given period.

Ballast bonus and repositioning fees are lump-sum cash payments made by the charterer to the ship owner to compensate for repositioning costs at the conclusion of the charter; these are paid regardless of the actual movements of the vessel. These fees are heavily negotiated and owners are generally able to push for them when the global fleet utilization is very high (during tight periods) and they are generally not paid during long periods.

Comparing TCE rates on a quarterly basis with the headline spot charter rate, as shown in Figure 4, demonstrates that the TCE rate will often be lower than the spot rate. However, during periods of tight shipping supply, when utilization rates are extremely high, such as in 2018, TCE rates more closely approach and even surpass headline rates.

Figure 4: A comparison of TCE rates and headline spot charter rates across different time periods

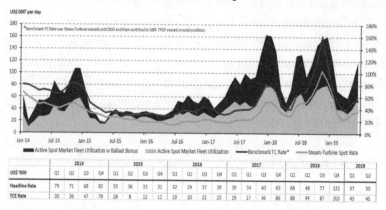

US$ '000	2014				2015				2016				2017				2018				2019	
	Q1	Q2	Q3	Q4	Q1	Q2	Q3	Q4	Q1	Q2	Q3	Q4	Q1	Q2	Q3	Q4	Q1	Q2	Q3	Q4	Q1	Q2
Headline Rate	79	71	68	82	55	36	33	31	32	29	37	39	39	34	40	63	68	48	77	132	57	50
TCE Rate	30	36	47	79	28	8	12	11	10	10	22	23	19	27	36	86	88	44	87	203	43	45

Source: Poten (2020).

The most interesting thing about looking at these historical spot rates is that, on average, they do not allow the ship owner to make a return on investment. Given that the price of a new-build LNG vessel is around $200 million and the average operating cost is approximately $17,500/day, a charter rate of approximately $60,000 would allow a ship owner to make a sustained return, provided there was a high utilization rate as well. As the chart above shows, the last five years (some short-lived winter highs notwithstanding) would not have allowed returns on investment. Until this is remedied, rational ship owners will not order speculatively in bulk, thereby always limiting the liquidity of the spot market.

Despite shipyards and ship owners being in the vanguard of improvements in LNG supply-chain costs, the reality is that over the last decade, charterers have pushed an inordinate amount of risk onto ship owners by demanding lower rates and shorter charter periods. This has forced residual value onto owners in an imbalanced way, particularly given the long-term nature of the actual LNG contracts the ships support. At the same time, charterers have pushed a plethora of reporting needs, standards and auditing onto ship owners, unique to each company, without uniform consistency, despite owners already meeting stringent industry guidelines and regulations.

Until there is a more thoughtful sharing of risk and reward, based on the understanding of the very difficult task of running a shipping company, the cyclicity, volatility and uncertainty will continue unabated. As charterers push ship owners to reduce terms and rates, ship owners have pushed shipyards for better terms in order to preserve margins. In turn, the shipyards have suffered their own woes owing to downturns in the non-LNG sectors, particularly offshore vessels. Downward pressure on LNG new-build pricing has led to consolidation in both Korea and China and restructuring in Japan. Financiers have left the shipping industry in droves in the last decade, citing higher risks and smaller profits. All these factors indicate that LNG shipping costs will go up in the near-term.

IMPACT OF NEW TRADE ROUTES

The Panama Canal

Since the *Maran Gas Apollonia* became the first large LNG vessel to pass through the expanded Panama Canal in July 2016, traffic has increased steadily. Beginning in 2018, the canal changed its transit reservation system to offer two slots per day to LNG vessels. The largest amount of LNG traffic to date occurred on a single day in October 2018, when four LNG vessels passed through the Neo-Panamax locks. Earlier that year, the Panama Canal Authority had announced it would accommodate vessels up to 51.25 metres wide, effectively opening up the canal to the wide-beam Q-Flex fleet. The 210,000 m³ *Al Safliya*, which has a length of 315 metres and a 50-metre beam, made the 82-kilometre (km) transit on 12 May 2019, becoming the first LNG carrier of this size to navigate the expanded waterway.

The LNG tariffs are based on a vessel's cubic metre capacity. Today, according to the Panama Canal's published tariffs, a one-way transit costs $360,000 to $390,000, with a reduction on the round-trip return leg if it is taken within sixty days.

The canal offers significant cost and schedule savings. For example, a round trip voyage from Sabine Pass to Tokyo Bay reduces shipping costs by 29 per cent and voyage time by 35 per cent, over the most efficient alternative routes. A round trip voyage from the Sabine Pass to Chile, via the Panama Canal, reduces costs by 25 per cent and voyage time by 48 per cent, over the alternative Cape Horn route.

Image 2: The *Maran Gas Apollonia* navigating the Panama Canal

Image courtesy of Maran Gas Maritime

The Northern Sea Route

In August 2017, LNG shipping reached another milestone. The *Christophe de Margerie* became the first of fifteen Arc7 ice-breaking vessels built to service Yamal LNG, to deliver a cargo for Total from Norway to South Korea—a journey via the Northern Sea Route (NSR). In 2020, the same ship was able to make the transit as early as May. The voyage demonstrated the new opportunity available for inter-basin trading through a short, but difficult, route.

The 12,200-mile voyage from Hammerfest, Norway, to South Korea via the Suez Canal would have been long with a relatively high cost. Because of the new Arc7 technology, the distance was almost halved.

Between July and November, when ice patterns allow, some ice-breaking vessels will navigate from Yamal, through the East NSR to Asia. When the ice is severe, the vessels will travel via the West NSR to Zeebrugge, after which the cargoes destined for Asia can be trans-shipped to conventional carriers and delivered via the Suez Canal. In July 2019, the *Vladimir Rusanov* transited the ice-laden route in only six days, setting a new record for independent passage via the NSR without ice-breaking support, with a cargo on board. The net voyage time from Yamal to China was completed in another record of sixteen days, half the time it would have taken via the Suez Canal.

The Yamal trade creates an optimization challenge. In the summer months, fewer ships are needed than in the winter months, leading to underutilization in the summer. These idle ships will compound an already traditionally weak summer market for spot rates.

FUEL REGULATION: IMO 2020

According to the International Maritime Organization (IMO) over 90 per cent of global trade happens on our oceans. A major side effect from the shipping industry is the release of sulphur oxide (SOx), a greenhouse gas, into the atmosphere.

The shipping industry has been significantly impacted by the introduction of new regulations called IMO 2020, which enforced a 0.5 per cent sulphur emissions cap worldwide from 1 January 2020; a dramatic decrease from the prior emissions cap of 3.5 per cent. It is one of the most sweeping fuel regulations to have ever been implemented in the marine sector.

Since LNG vessels can burn LNG and indeed, even force boil-off to fully supplant high-sulphur fuel oil (HSFO), they can also use low-sulphur fuel oil (LSFO), or marine gas oil (MGO) and therefore, no modifications are required for them to meet the IMO 2020 requirements. Only operational decisions need to be made as to whether to force boil-off or use liquid fuel.

In non-LNG shipping sectors, approximately 20 per cent of the crude tanker fleet has planned to employ scrubbers. Scrubbers remove the sulphur content from the emission stream, so vessels can continue to use HSFO. Since the cost of HSFO is less than that of LSFO, the price difference can pay for the Capex of the scrubber, within one year. However, the use of open-loop scrubbers is being heavily scrutinized as detractors view the pollution as simply being transferred from the air into the water. Several ports and states have banned open-loop scrubbers and their long-term viability is under question.

Some players are looking to retrofit or build LNG-fuelled vessels, even though the cost versus scrubbers is more expensive, because of the backlash on the use of open-loop scrubbers, as well as concerns over the efficacy of the scrubber technology and potential operational impacts. However, LNG as a fuel is still an embryonic industry, with significant fuelling infrastructure required to make it more accessible. In addition, the 2020 International Council on Clean Transportation has suggested there is no climate benefit (in terms of GHG emissions) from using LNG over a twenty-year life cycle, but there is a 15 per cent benefit over a 100-year cycle (compared to using MGO), although they do not argue that

LNG is a much cleaner fuel from a carbon perspective. This analysis is being actively challenged by the LNG industry.

More environmental regulations are on the way; IMO 2050 aims to reduce CO_2 emissions by 50 per cent by 2050. Furthermore, the 'Poseidon Principles' have been developed by eleven major banks with significant holdings in the global shipping industry to provide an extensive set of guidelines designed to accelerate decarbonization efforts across the shipping industry, in order to align with IMO 2050.

LESSONS FROM THE CHINESE SHIPPING INDUSTRY

India has previously attempted to build LNG ships through joint ventures with Korean shipyards and ship owners. Ultimately, these attempts were premature, since it was unclear what the exact demand was in terms of numbers of ships and tenor of charters. Combined with a lack of experience in Indian shipyards, these uncertainties led to difficulties in obtaining financing for the vessels, owing to asymmetric risk profiles.

Lessons may be learned from the Chinese shipping industry's successful entry into LNG, which has now resulted in the delivery of 20 LNG vessels since 2008.

Investment in LNG vessel construction in China used the same governmental approach as taken by Japan back in the 1980s and early 1990s, i.e., LNG sales into China required the vessels to be built in China. Early Japanese LNG import projects had to rely on vessels built in Europe and the US (Brunei/Shell, Malaysia/ETC), but with the expansion of LNG imports from projects such as the Australian Northwest Shelf, Japan later insisted that LNG vessels be built and maintained (dry-docked) in domestic shipyards.

Mitsubishi Heavy Industries (MHI), Kawasaki Heavy Industries (KHI) and Mitsui all took part in this domestic programme, building vessels based on the Kvaerner Moss-type containment system. This requirement allowed Japanese shipyards to gain experience in LNG construction and enter into non-Japanese LNG vessel projects, although often Japanese trading houses also got involved as part of the deal. Japanese yards also gained considerable experience in ship repair and maintenance of these vessels, as all were required to dry-dock in Japan every two-and-a-half years. The repair of LNG vessels continued until the early 2000s, but by then it became too expensive to continue maintenance in Japan and this work then shifted to Singapore. The main issue was the lack of volume necessary to keep the skill-set employed full time, as no other ship repair business was going to these Japanese repair yards.

During the 2000s, China saw a need for alternative energy supply and looked to follow the same approach as Japan by keeping some of the initial investment costs for the project with Chinese companies. After negotiating LNG sales and purchase agreements for Chinese imports, both Shell and British Petroleum (BP) helped China shortlist two competing shipyards, Hudong Zhonghua (HZ) and DSIC. Ultimately, they selected HZ. Shell was selected to become the owner's technical manager and worked with HZ on the skills and tools needed to build a successful LNG vessel; BP was selected as the vessel operator and formed a joined venture with China Merchants to operate the vessels. BP was responsible for initially manning the vessels, then transitioning them to Chinese crews once suitable training time had elapsed.

The first LNG design that HZ purchased was from the French Shipyard Chantier D'Atlantique (which later became part of the STX Group), which was then building LNG vessels in Europe and had relative up-to-date designs available. At the same time, Korea and Japan were in fierce competition for LNG orders and were not interested in any form of technology transfer.

Chantier had built a successful project for the Malaysia International Shipping Corporation (MISC) using the Gaztransport & Technigaz (GTT) No. 96 containment membrane containment system; this was selected by HZ as the containment system of choice. To ensure a successful technology transfer during the project, the owner's technical managers required a tripartite agreement to be signed between HZ, Chantiers and GTT to cover items such as design, construction and commissioning. For the first vessels, Chantiers De Atantique was responsible for undertaking gas trials using its own teams that had experience in this specialized area. The five vessels delivered under this agreement were successfully built and commissioned and have delivered cargoes for their project. Lessons learnt have been subsequently acted upon to remedy some of the early issues around quality control, responsibility for commissioning and obsolescence of design considering the project duration. These learnings include the following:

- Though HZ was unfamiliar with the higher quality control needed during construction and initially resisted these measures, it then realized that if they were adopted, re-work could be reduced, and construction time could be shortened.
- Responsibility for commissioning and trials should reside with the shipyard, although experts familiar with the needs of LNG vessels are required and must be part of the shipyard team.
- The time taken for the initial project was longer than planned. As such, the delivered vessels were not comparable in performance, size and technology to those delivered in the same time from Japan and Korea. Subsequent vessels designed in China would be more forward looking. This was a balance between the risk of adopting new technology versus using proven technology. Although these initial vessels were not as modern as possible, the construction risk was reduced.

Recent Chinese LNG import projects also require vessels to be built in domestic Chinese shipyards, and three subsequent projects have been built by HZ. These latest vessels have benefitted from early lessons learnt and future vessels will be more comparable to those being offered by the Korean shipyards.

Like Japan, the knowledge gained in these first projects has allowed orders to be taken for non-Chinese import projects. Today we see vessels on order and being delivered by HZ, as well as other Chinese shipyards, utilizing novel technology, containment systems and a range of sizes.

CONCLUSION

The LNG trade, and the shipping industry upon which it is reliant, have experienced significant changes in the last decade. It is expected that the pace of change will continue as the world continues to rely upon natural gas, owing to its abundance, affordability and low carbon characteristics.

Beyond the utilization of LNG as a fuel, India is opportunistically placed in the LNG seascape: as a charterer of the latest-generation LNG carriers, as a provider of talented employees to captain, crew and design these vessels and as a potential future shipbuilder to ensure that India, and the world, have ample shipping resources to meet the growth demands of the LNG industry.

APPENDIX 1: FLEET ANALYSIS

Table 1: Existing Fleet

Size	# of Vessels	Capacity (m³)	Fleet %	Age
185–266,000 m³	46	10,585,300	12 per cent	10
167–185,000 m³	144	25,012,550	29 per cent	2
150–167,500 m³	132	20,839,789	24 per cent	6
130–150,000 m³	184	25,977,414	30 per cent	15
100–130,000 m³	33	4,177,062	5 per cent	34
65–100,000 m³	7	534,090	1 per cent	18
Total	546	87,126,205		9.44
Laid-up	19	2,439,973		36

Table 2: Orderbook

Size	# of Vessels	Capacity (m³)
167-185,000 m³	112	19,556,600
150-167,500 m³	2	320,000
Total	114	19,876,600

Table 3: Fleet Composition

	Existing	New Build
Conventional	503	107
FSRU	35	7
FSU	8	
FLNG	4	3
Includes FLNG numbers		

Table 4: Propulsion

	Existing	Orderbook
DFDE	33	1
MEGI	42	25
RHST	5	-
SSD	48	-
ST	240	-
STGE	7	1
TFDE	145	18
UST	14	-
X-DF	12	69

Table 5: Containment type

	Existing	Orderbook
CS1	3	-
GT82	1	-
GT88	3	-
KC-1	2	-
Mark III	137	4
Mark III Flex	65	55
Mark III Flex+	-	11
Moss	114	2
Moss (Sayaendo)	8	-
Moss (Sayaringo)	7	1
NO85	1	-
NO88	3	-
NO96	136	22

	Existing	Orderbook
NO96 GW	47	14
NO96 Lo3	14	-
NO96 Lo3+	-	4
SPB	5	1

Table 6: Age

	# of Vessels
0-5 years	179
5-10 years	87
10-15 years	159
15-20 years	55
20-25 years	26
25-30 years	13
30-35 years	2
35 years +	25

Table 7: Ice Class

	Existing	New Build
Ice Class 1A/Arc4	1	-
Ice Class 1A/Winterised	6	-
Ice Class 1B/Winterized	3	-
Ice Class 1C	11	-
Ice Class 1C/Winterized	14	-
Ice Class 1D	1	-

	Existing	New Build
Ice Class ARC4	4	-
Ice Class ARC7	11	5
Winterized	5	-

Table 8: Owner Type

	Existing	Orderbook
Independent Ship-owner	375	108
Major	28	-
Project	138	2
Trader	1	2
Utility	3	1
Unconfirmed	1	1

Table 9: Charterer Type (>1 yr)

	Existing	New-build
Independent Ship-owner	17	-
Major	127	18
Project	204	11
Trader	26	24
Utility	109	12
Length of charterers		
>1 year	483	65
<1 year/Available	63	49

(All data provided by Poten & Partners Ltd, 2019. The above analysis excludes vessels < 65,000 m³ and FLNG, unless explicitly stated in any of the tables.)

Notes

1. These historic endeavours are described in more detail in the 2014 commemorative joint publication by the Society of International Gas Tankers and Terminals Operators (SIGGTO) and the International Group of LNG Importers (GIIGNL) to celebrate 50 years of LNG shipping.

8

LIQUEFIED NATURAL GAS: FROM THE UNITED STATES TO THE INDIAN MARKET

MARTIN HOUSTON

Vice Chairman and co-founder, Tellurian Inc.; Chairman, EnQuest PLC; and Non-Executive Director of BUPA Arabia and CC Energy

RENEE PIRRONG

Director, Research and Analytics, Tellurian Inc.

OVERVIEW

THE US, WITH AN EXPORT capacity of 9.4 billion cubic feet per day (Bcf/d) in 2020 and 13 Bcf/d capacity by 2025, is emerging as one of the world's largest exporters of LNG. Along with this, US suppliers also have a variety of new business models and contracting terms from which Indian buyers can choose. In this section, we will discuss the opportunities available to Indian buyers seeking to initiate or expand their LNG supply.

Natural gas production has accelerated dramatically in the US, due to drilling productivity and technological improvements in shale development. Since the time GAIL (India) Ltd secured its first US LNG volumes in December 2011, dry natural gas production has grown over 40 per cent to around 94 Bcf/d as of early 2020, according to data from the Energy Information Agency (EIA).

Costs of production have declined correspondingly. Henry Hub natural gas prices have averaged $3.07 per Metric Million British thermal units (MMBtu) since 2012, but for the majority of producers, the costs of production are frequently well below Henry Hub prices. Since prices are set at the margin, Henry Hub prices reflect the highest breakeven price of wells at the margin of US production. Furthermore, Henry Hub prices reflect the full-cycle breakeven including a rate of return for the producer. Actual costs of production are lower on a cash cost basis, as shown in Figure 1.

Figure 1: Plentiful, low-cost US natural gas

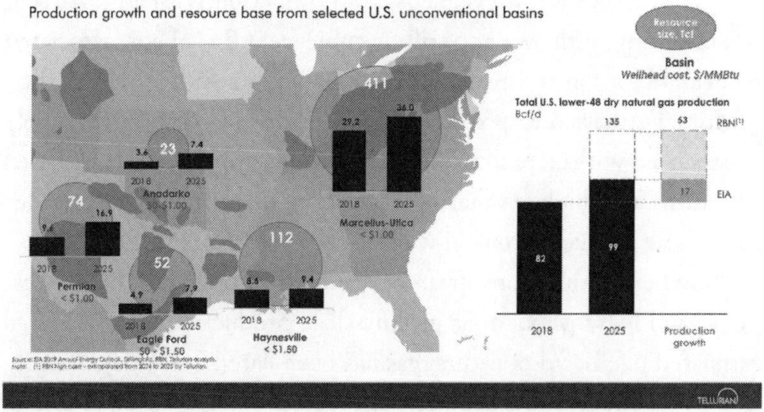

Note: RBN high case, extrapolated from 2024 to 2025 by Tellurian

Source: US Energy Information Administration, '2019 Annual Energy Outlook',[1] Drilling information data, RBN, Tellurian analysis.

Figure 2: Break-evens of US dry gas shale plays

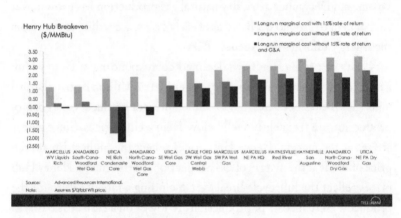

Note: Assumes $70/Bbl WTI price

Source: Advanced Resources International.

Figure 2 shows full-cycle costs of production with a 15 per cent rate of return, with over 550 trillion cubic feet (Tcf) of non-associated recoverable resources available at a breakeven cost less than $3.00/ MMBtu. Furthermore, approximately one-third of US natural gas supply is associated with oil production. The economics of such wells are based on returns from higher-value oil production, so the breakeven price for natural gas produced from oil wells may be *below* $0/MMBtu.

Nowhere is this more apparent than in the Permian Basin of West Texas and New Mexico—a prolific shale production area where an estimated one Bcf/d of natural gas has been flared every day in 2019, as a by-product of oil production—based on Rystad data. On an LNG-equivalent basis, flared gas in the Permian Basin alone represents ~5Mtpa of LNG-equivalent. Pipelines have been proposed to link stranded gas supply to US LNG export projects. For example, in 2019, Tellurian made strong regulatory and commercial progress in developing a pipeline that will link the Permian Basin to southwest Louisiana, where multiple proposed LNG export facilities represent substantial demand pull for natural gas supply.

The size of the US natural gas resource, the country's oil and gas infrastructure, workforce availability and its stable fiscal regime and political institutions represent competitive advantages for the US LNG export industry. At the same time, global buyers are provided with a low-cost option that provides diversification from conventional supply sources.

LIQUEFACTION BUSINESS MODELS AVAILABLE TO BUYERS

The US LNG export projects offer a range of options to fit buyer needs, making commercial flexibility a feature of US-sourced LNG. Another advantage is cost transparency, since gas production, transportation and liquefaction costs in the US are generally disclosed to the public.

Conversely, LNG sourced in other parts of the world is generally contracted on market terms where the buyer may not have full visibility of the costs associated with the various components of the LNG supply chain. These projects typically sell LNG at prices pegged to an oil index, thereby preventing LNG buyers from realizing the benefits of low-cost natural gas. Qatar, for example, has abundant gas reserves and low production costs, but its LNG contracts are generally oil indexed. In Australia, the LNG supply is generally higher in cost and has been marked by project cost over-runs and feed-gas shortages for some east coast projects as they compete with domestic markets for gas volumes.

In both the first and second waves of US LNG export projects, buyers could choose among several business models, depending on their desired risk profile and pricing preferences. In this section, we explain the costs and benefits of each business model and the potential impact on buyers in the Indian gas market. There are four major project models offered in the United States as described below.

TOLLING PROJECTS

Main features:

- The LNG developer is responsible for building and operating the LNG facility.
- Feed-gas procurement is the offtaker's responsibility.
- The customer enters into a Liquefaction Tolling Agreement (LTA), agreeing on a fixed fee for the right to use the LNG plant.
- The take-or-pay fixed fee covers the operating, capital and financing costs of liquefaction over the life of the contract. The fixed fee also includes a return on capital to the project developer.
- The customer of a liquefaction project takes on 'basis risk', which means that the cost of feed gas may be much higher or lower than the benchmark price of gas at Henry Hub.
- The customer must also arrange pipeline agreements to transport natural gas to the liquefaction facility, adding additional costs.

Tolling projects include Dominion Cove Point LNG, Freeport LNG, Cameron LNG and Elba Island LNG. Since the responsibility for gas procurement falls on the buyer, tolling arrangements are well-suited to customers that have substantial US natural gas supply portfolios, or want to build a gas trading and/or upstream production presence in the US for strategic reasons. For example, Shell's Elba Island facility in Georgia requires 350 MMcf/d of feedstock, a small fraction of Shell's overall upstream natural gas portfolio in the US. As all tolling projects except Elba Island LNG have multiple customers, offtakers competing for finite pipeline transportation capacity and gas feedstock can experience higher than anticipated gas sourcing costs.

In summary, the benefit of the tolling model is that the buyer has full control over sourcing the gas, which may result in lower upfront costs and fees. However, there are a number of potentially negating factors:

- Competition between customers for pipeline access can lead to hidden costs and a higher cost of LNG on the water.
- The buyer must pay a fixed fee every month, regardless of a decision to lift gas or not.
- The buyer is responsible for gas sourcing and transportation to the terminal, requiring substantial investment and presence in the US. Without experience in the US market, there is a risk that the buyer could incur higher costs due to commercial or operational error.

THE MERCHANT/SALE-AND-PURCHASE AGREEMENT MODEL

This merchant/SPA business model was created by Charif Souki, the founder of Cheniere Energy and co-founder of Tellurian, whose projects include Sabine Pass LNG and Corpus Christi LNG. Some features of this model include the following.

- The developer in the merchant/SPA model is responsible for procuring feed gas for customers.
- Gas is liquefied and sold free-on-board (FOB) for a fixed fee plus 115 per cent of the New York Mercantile Exchange (NYMEX) Henry Hub futures settlement price in the first month of the cargo's delivery window.
- The customer pays a fixed fee regardless of whether it lifts a cargo. This fixed fee pays for the capital, operating and financing costs of the plant plus a return to the promoter.
- The customer takes Henry Hub price risk rather than basis risk.
- The developer arranges gas supply and transportation agreements and takes the risk between the sales price (Henry Hub) and the cost to source feed gas.

The streamlined delivery process for the customer mitigates the requirement for a gas procurement strategy, but the offtaker may still wish to take an upstream position as a physical hedge to its Henry Hub price risk. Alternatively, a customer can financially hedge (at least some of) its position given the liquidity of the NYMEX Henry Hub.

In summary, the benefits of the merchant/SPA model are that the buyer does not bear the responsibilities and risks associated with feed-gas sourcing, and can hedge commodity risk in financial markets.

Conversely:

- The buyer must pay a fixed fee or contractual cargo price every month, regardless of a decision to lift.

- The developer charges a premium over the market price of gas, to pay for transportation services.

- The buyer pays for LNG at market price, or a premium over the actual cost of production.

Traditional Oil-Indexed SPAs

These have not been signed for existing or under construction projects in the US, but NextDecade is marketing volumes from its Rio Grande LNG project in Texas at an index to Brent oil prices, in addition to US natural gas prices. There has been limited public information on the structure and terms of NextDecade's Brent-linked US LNG contract with Shell, but the developer would presumably bear responsibility for natural gas procurement from the Permian Basin.

INTEGRATED EQUITY

Prevalent globally, integrated equity projects offer the LNG customer the ability to lift volumes at cost rather than at a negotiated price. In addition, buyers are able to take advantage of sub-market prices for gas supply and transportation.

Traditionally, integrated equity project models served to monetize stranded natural gas reserves, requiring the offtaker/developer to invest substantial capital upfront in exchange for lifting LNG on the water at operating costs. Only two US project developers have chosen this model: Golden Pass LNG and Driftwood LNG. In the case of Golden Pass, the 15.6 Mtpa project was developed by ExxonMobil and Qatar Petroleum by leveraging Exxon's substantial existing upstream production position in the US and their joint ownership in the existing regas terminal infrastructure in Texas. From the perspective of a buyer in India or an end user in general, there has been no opportunity for equity participation in the Golden Pass project, as capacity was split between the two developers.

The Tellurian merchant/SPA model discussed earlier also offers customers equity in interconnected components of the LNG development chain. This includes proven production in the Haynesville Shale of Louisiana and Texas, a pipeline infrastructure that will transport gas from mega-shale plays in Texas and a site-advantaged 27.6 Mtpa liquefaction facility with deep-water access located near Lake Charles, Louisiana.

The Tellurian approach provides both developers and customers with true transparency and control of costs. Because the customer is an owner in the complete LNG development chain, a layer of development and gas production costs are removed.

In summary, the integrated equity model is the lowest volatility option for buyers and offers true cost transparency. By owning equity in a project, the buyer is able to lift LNG at cost, undercutting the market price for gas supply while avoiding rate-stacked transportation fees.

Participation in an integrated equity project requires an equity investment during the construction period. The buyer also shares operational risks with the other partners in the project.

Figure 3: US LNG Models

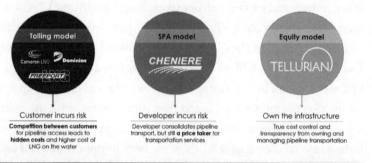

Source: *Tellurian analysis.*

DESTINATION FLEXIBILITY

The first US liquefaction contracts were commercially very innovative at the time. Destination flexibility was not unheard of, but including the contractual term in LNG SPAs, it certainly was not the prevailing practice when most LNG was traded on an inflexible, point-to-point basis.

After the first US contract was signed between Martin Houston of BG Group and Charif Souki of Cheniere Energy in 2011, every subsequent contract signed with a US project developer included destination flexibility. The contractual term is useful for aggregators and end users alike. Portfolio players favour flexibility as an optimization tool, while end users with uncertain or variable downstream gas demand find it valuable to redirect volumes outside their home markets.

GAIL (India) Ltd's experience with Sabine Pass and Cove Point demonstrates the importance of flexible LNG supplies to buyers in India. GAIL sells a portion of LNG contracted from the US in the international market due to a mismatch between domestic demand and supply availability. Further, GAIL undertakes destination swaps to ship

LNG to India. Without destination flexibility, arranging such a swap agreement would be far more complex contractually. Additionally, swap arrangements facilitate shipping optimization and, therefore, can reduce the delivered cost of LNG.

COMPARISON OF US LNG SUPPLY WITH ALTERNATIVES IN INDIA

TRADITIONAL OIL-LINKED SPAs

Indian companies have purchased LNG under traditional oil-linked long-term contracts from a variety of sellers since 2006. Though the prices of those contracts are not necessarily disclosed, it is understood that they are priced as a percentage of Brent or Japan Crude Cocktail (JCC) oil prices, ranging from 11.80 to 14.85 per cent, depending on the delivery terms and year signed.

Figure 4 shows the implied landed price of LNG in India, based on reported prices of two oil-indexed long-term LNG contracts, which, in turn, are based on historical Brent prices and the Brent forward curve as of 2 January 2020. For comparison, GAIL's Henry Hub-linked SPA with Cheniere Energy is shown at 115 per cent of Henry Hub plus $3.00/MMBtu fixed fee plus $2.00/MMBtu of shipping costs delivered to the west coast of India Additionally, we show Tellurian's lifting cost between $3.00 and $4.00/MMBtu, plus ~$2.00/MMBtu of shipping costs delivered to the west coast of India under its equity model.

Before the oil price crash in late 2014, there was a wide spread between global oil prices and US natural gas prices. Though annual average Henry Hub prices have declined by 40 per cent from 2014 to 2019, oil prices fell by 35 per cent over the same period, narrowing the spread between Brent and Henry Hub-linked LNG contracts. At the same time, a partner—lifting from Tellurian's equity model at cost and delivering offtake to India—is not as reliant on volatile commodity prices.

Figure 4: Implied landed price of LNG in India

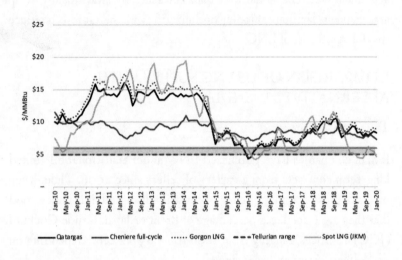

Sources: IHS Markit, Platts, Tellurian analysis and market view[2]

Alternative Liquid Fuels

India's energy mix includes liquid fuels such as LPG, fuel oil, diesel and naphtha. In most cases, natural gas is already competing with these liquid fuels in India's markets, including in the residential heating and cooking, industrial and refining, transportation and fertilizer sectors. These liquid fuels, particularly fuel oil, diesel and naphtha are linked to the global price of oil and are often a more expensive and carbon-intensive form of energy relative to natural gas.

Natural gas and LNG have already begun to displace these liquid fuels in India and the demand for natural gas in these sectors appears to be poised for further growth. For example, in the fertilizer sector, the landed price of US LNG is competitive as compared to the landed price of C3 and naphtha.

Figure 5: Landed price of competing fuels in India

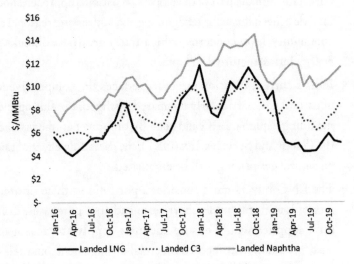

Sources: IHS Markit, NYMEX and market view (Assumes $1/MMBtu transportation costs for both Naphtha and C3).

CONCLUSION

The US market offers a great opportunity for India to source cheaper LNG. Indian consumers can choose from a range of business models to suit their needs, which are often cheaper than traditional oil-linked contracts. Further, the destination flexibility offered by US suppliers provides consumers with options when there is a mismatch between domestic demand and supply, something which GAIL (India) Ltd has already taken advantage of. However, the Indian domestic market needs to undergo some changes as well to eventually benefit from cheap LNG.

- We believe that India should develop a national policy to encourage the development of LNG and pipeline infrastructure. Without addressing pipeline connections that serve end users, any terminal development plans (currently under way in India) would result in reduced usage, creating a potential financial burden and uncertainty on the part of developers. A national approach should include a mechanism for recognizing and addressing regional and community-level concerns, which today create roadblocks for energy infrastructure development.

- India's current taxation structure reduces the competitiveness of natural gas, particularly compared with more polluting fuels, including naphtha, LPG and coal. By bringing natural gas under the Goods and Services Tax (GST), the cascading effect of taxes on natural gas pricing will be eliminated.

- The LNG buyers must consider a portfolio with an optimum mix of long-term, mid-, short-term and spot purchases. Long-term supplies would ensure adequate supply at a reasonable cost, preferably through commercial arrangements marked by transparency and backed by strong production and transportation resources. Mid-, short-term and spot purchases would ensure control over the sourcing portfolio while providing exposure to the spot prices which may be favourable, as is the case in the current over-supplied market.

India and the rest of the world face a challenging balancing act—to meet the demands of a growing population with strategies that lessen environmental impacts. We believe there are great opportunities for India as the country expands its natural gas usage, as well as opportunities for Indian LNG buyers tapping into the US shale-resource and the next generation of US liquefaction projects.

Notes

1. US Energy Information Administration, '2019 Annual Energy Outlook: with projections to 2050', Washington: EIA, 24 January 2019, https://www.eia.gov/outlooks/aeo/pdf/aeo2019.pdf

2. 'LNG Contract Database', 2018; S&P Platts data. 'Japan Korea Marker historical prices', 2018.

9

AUSTRALIA LNG

IAN CRONSHAW

Consultant; Former Division Head, International Energy Agency
(2005 to 2011)

INTRODUCTION

AUSTRALIAN GAS RESERVES ARE ESTIMATED at around 3,000 billion cubic metres (Bcm), with around two-thirds located offshore in an arc from Barrow Island in northwest Western Australia to Darwin in the Northern Territory. Most of the balance is located onshore to the east in Queensland, with significant, but depleted, reserves in offshore Victoria, which supply the domestic gas market. Actual resources are at least double these numbers. While these reserves are not large by global standards, their location offshore, far from any major domestic markets, has made them the basis for an important export industry in the form of liquefied natural gas (LNG).

While discoveries were made in the 1960s and 1970s, serious development of the North West Shelf (NWS) project did not commence until 1980—when a group of eight Japanese power and utility buyers committed to long-term contracts. These were based initially on oil indexation, with protection for both sellers and buyers at low and high oil prices respectively. At the time, Japan was making a serious effort to diversify its energy imports away from very high oil dependence, using gas, coal and uranium in the context of the two major oil shocks of the 1970s.

The offshore location of Australian gas—requiring a large platform, undersea pipelines and construction of onshore treatment and liquefaction in a very remote location—meant the project was very capital intensive. Hence the need for long-term contracts priced to reduce buyer's risk and a large consortium of international oil companies to provide investment in production and shipping. A key factor in reducing risk was the high-level assurance from the then Federal Government that the project would not be subject to future changes in pricing, export rules or taxation for its life. This policy was reaffirmed by subsequent governments, notably in the mid-1980s and again in the early 1990s, when offshore taxation arrangements were changed. First gas from this North West Shelf project was shipped to Japan in 1989, some twenty years after gas was discovered.

Subsequent expansions of this first project and other projects in Darwin and one close to the NWS, followed this development model, with long-term contracts with mostly Japanese buyers as well as with buyers from Korea and China. The contract with China enabled the expansion of the North West Shelf project, with first gas (from the expanded project) shipped in 2006, and marked the first imports of gas by China, where imports now total over 120 Bcm annually. By 2010, Australia was exporting around 24 Bcm of gas, a little less than 1 per cent of the global gas supply. Almost all of it went to Japan, which was sourcing about a quarter of its demand from Australia.

This relatively modest contribution to global gas use began to change sharply in the years 2009 to 2012, as seven major new projects were committed for development. While four were in the northwest of Australia—following the established development pattern, based on the large remote offshore resources generally discovered decades earlier—three were based near Gladstone in Queensland, relying on gas resources of the inland Surat Basin. These resources were developed using unconventional technology from gas contained in coal formations. Such gas is generally higher-cost, requiring more or less continual drilling to release the gas, with wells having higher depletion rates than the more conventional offshore, stranded gas.

Again, all of the developments in this second wave were very capital intensive, with long lead times and, hence, high commercial risk—especially given the locations of the gas and the relatively new technology deployed. And again, long-term contracts with consortia of Asian buyers, including Japan, Korea, China and Taiwan, were the key to managing this risk and obtaining the necessary finance, mostly involving large international energy companies, such as Chevron, ExxonMobil, Total and BP, plus some buyer equity, notably China's CNOOC and, more recently, Japan's INPEX.

In total, over AUS $200 billion was invested in these new gas projects, with cost overruns experienced, especially where multiple projects were constructed almost simultaneously and in one location, such as in Gladstone. The massive Gorgon project in Western Australia saw costs increase by 50 per cent over the initially budgeted amount, putting a severe strain on the project operator Chevron, notwithstanding that company's size.

AUSTRALIAN LNG PRODUCTION AT THE END OF 2019

By 2019, Australian exports of LNG totalled over 100 Bcm, making it the world's largest LNG exporter, supplying more than a quarter of global LNG and around 2.5 per cent of global gas demand. The NWS development has expanded from its initial capacity of 6 Bcm per annum to 23 Bcm, through additional production of trains and careful productivity improvements. Japanese buyers continue to be the backbone of the development, although as noted above, expansion in 2003–06 was driven by Chinese demand.

At the end of 2019, Woodside, the NWS project's operator, proposed to develop the Browse gas deposit, some 900 km by pipeline from the existing project, to underpin output from the five trains of the NWS development. The field contains a massive 400 Bcm of gas, and would entail investments from Shell, BP, Petrochina and Japanese interests.

Australia's second LNG project, at Darwin, was initially developed by ConocoPhillips, drawing on gas from the Timor Sea Joint Petroleum Development Area, jointly administered by Australia and Timor Leste. First LNG shipments from the 5 Bcm capacity project took place in 2006. In 2018, ConocoPhillips announced the development of the Barossa gas field in Australian waters by way of a floating facility and tie-in to the existing gas pipeline, thus underpinning Darwin LNG output. SANTOS now controls two-thirds of the Darwin project.

Woodside was the major developer of Australia's third LNG project also located near the NWS. This was the almost 7 Bcm per annum Pluto project, underpinned by Japanese utility buyers (Tokyo Gas and Kansai Electric). By the end of 2019, Woodside had completed front-end engineering and design for a second train at Pluto, which doubled the facility's capacity and also provided a possible link with the nearby NWS project to optimize the use of the liquefaction capacity of both projects. Gas for the expansion was to be sourced from the Scarborough gas development, some 375 km offshore from Pluto.

The second wave of Australian LNG projects featured a number of marked differences from these earlier projects. Three projects built near Gladstone in Queensland, use coal-bed methane from the Surat Basin, some 400 km to the southwest. The projects, totalling some 35 Bcm of annual capacity, feature relatively high shares of buyer equity, notably CNOOC and Sinopec, reflecting China's share of output; in 2018, China purchased nearly 70 per cent of the production of 30 Bcm. Late in 2019, the Arrow development received final approvals from both state and national government. The project is a 50:50 joint venture between Shell and Petrochina. It is designed to tap the 140 Bcm of reserves held by the joint venture, initially producing around 3 Bcm annually, split between local and LNG plant sales. Shell acquired the Queensland-based Curtis LNG plant (QCLNG), when it took over the BG Group. The Arrow development will underpin capacity utilization at the QCLNG plant.

The year 2009 saw a final investment decision taken on the Gorgon project, on an island off Western Australia. This project was a more classical LNG project, based on large offshore gas resources discovered nearly thirty years earlier, totalling over 1,000 Bcm. Because of the high carbon dioxide content of the source gas, the development of one of the world's largest carbon capture and storage (CCS) projects was a condition of government approvals. The final cost of the project at $60 billion, made it among the most expensive hydrocarbon projects on the planet.

Production is from three trains that progressively entered service over 2016 and 2017. Almost half the project is owned by project operator Chevron, with Shell and Exxon Mobil splitting half. Modest shares are held by key Japanese buyers. In 2018, Chevron announced a gas supply expansion programme, costing $4 billion over four years, designed to maintain a long-term gas supply to the plant. Drilling started in 2019 and in June 2020, Chevron filed a detailed environmental plan for the installation of subsea infrastructure for this gas supply programme.

Again, as in earlier Australian LNG plants, the Gorgon project was underpinned by long-term sales agreements with Asian buyers. Chevron sold its gas to mainly Japanese and Korean buyers, while ExxonMobil signed long-term sales agreements with Petronet LNG Limited of India for 2 Bcm annually over twenty years and with PetroChina for 3 Bcm annually over the same term. The Petronet contract (deliveries started in 2017) was renegotiated later in that year, with lower prices agreed in return for additional annual volumes of 2 Bcm over fifteen years.

In 2011, Chevron took a final investment decision on the Wheatstone project in Western Australia. First shipments from the $34-billion project took place late in 2017. The project is majority-owned by Chevron, with smaller interests from Woodside and Kuwait, plus small Japanese buyer equity shares.

The Ichthys LNG project draws on a large gas and condensate field, which was discovered in 2000 in offshore north-western Australia. The gas is piped some 900 km to Darwin for liquefaction and liquids from the field are processed by onsite floating facilities. The LNG output started late in 2018 and stands at 12 Bcm annually, while liquid production is expected to peak at 100,000 barrels per day (Bpd). The development is almost two-thirds owned by INPEX, a Japanese company, representing one of the largest Japanese investments outside Japan; Total holds 26 per cent; with smaller holdings mostly with Japanese buyers.

INPEX also has a holding in the Shell-operated Prelude project, based on gas reserves off the coast of northwest Australia. This floating production and processing facility is the second of its type in the world, designed to produce some 5 Bcm annually, plus 1.7 million tonnes of liquids. First LNG was shipped to Asian customers in June 2019. Production ramped up to half-capacity in the second half of 2019 but has been halted since February 2020, following a number of technical problems. The Crux gas field, located 160 km from Prelude, is designed to be developed as an unmanned platform, to provide additional or backfill gas to the Prelude floating-gas processing facility, beginning in about 2025.

Thus by late 2019, Australian LNG exports had almost quadrupled over the decade, based on ten major facilities, seven of which had started in the last five years. However, with no major greenfield plants in the offing, new developments would be based mainly on new gas field developments to ensure gas supply to existing plants. These projects included Arrow (onshore Queensland), Scarborough, Barossa, Crux, and Browse—all offshore in northwest Australia.

AUSTRALIAN LNG EXPORTS

Australia's LNG exports have been based on sales to major utility buyers in countries such as Japan, Korea and China. Growth in the Japanese and Korean markets has slowed substantially, whereas China's gas demand has grown sixfold in the last fifteen years. In 2005, China's energy supply was dominated by cheap domestic coal. Gas, (let alone costly, imported LNG) was not seen as competitive. Subsequently, China's LNG imports exceeded 60 Bcm in 2018 and are likely to rise further, approaching 90 Bcm in 2020, potentially exceeding Japan's imports as early as 2022. China is clearly the key to global LNG markets.

In the first months of 2020, Asian-traded spot LNG prices fell below \$4/MMBtu, and by April 2020, even lower, to below \$2/MMBtu, allowing price-conscious buyers—notably by China and India—to ramp up spot purchases. Subsequently, from the beginning of April 2020, Indian gas demand has fallen sharply. The current spot price weakness is a reflection of both sharply weakening demand, and the nearly 60 Bcm increase in global LNG supply in 2019, 14 per cent above 2018.[1]

However, more than two-thirds of Asian LNG sales are under long-term contracts, where the LNG price is linked to the oil price, averaged over several months, with several months delay, thus smoothing out much of the oil market's volatility. Asian LNG prices ranged between \$8 and \$10/MMBtu in 2019. Given oil prices in 2020 contracted, LNG prices can be expected to fall further in 2021.

With around three-quarters of Australian LNG exports oil-indexed, at an FOB price of around \$8/MMBtu in 2019, sales yielded an export income of almost AUS \$50 billion, second only to iron ore in Australia's commodity exports. Given oil price movements, export revenues look set to fall markedly in 2020 and into 2021, by at least a quarter.[2] The development of the three Queensland LNG export projects has connected the hitherto insulated Australian East Coast gas market to the relatively high-priced Asian gas markets, causing in some cases a fourfold increase in domestic wholesale gas prices, with policy consequences (see below).

Given the current high degree of oil indexation, should crude oil prices stay in or around $25/barrel for an extended period in 2020, oil-indexed prices could fall below $6/MMBtu, putting pressure on higher-cost suppliers such as those using onshore coal bed methane in Queensland. However, oil prices have recently recovered to around $40/barrel, although further significant price rises would likely be capped by increased US output. Additional pricing pressure will likely come initially from producers in the US, pricing off Henry Hub, currently below $2/MMBtu, (implying a delivered price to western India of $7/MMBtu) and in the medium term, from additional Qatari supplies. Established Australian producers in the northwest have shown some flexibility in pricing, both in methodology and quantum, and can anticipate lower costs from brown-field expansions. This suggests the most likely source for additional Australian supply to India would come from those regions.

In summary, by end-2019, Australian LNG exports had expanded from 24 Bcm in 2010 to 105 Bcm, with shipments surpassing those of Qatar, hitherto the largest global LNG exporter. Around 90 per cent of exports were sold to Japan, China and Korea, with smaller amounts to Taiwan, Singapore and India. Australia has become the largest supplier of LNG to both Japan and China, although both countries have a diverse gas supply mix, so their dependence on Australian LNG as a proportion of their total gas use is around a third and a seventh respectively.

THE GLOBAL LNG MARKET AT END OF 2019

China has dramatically expanded gas use, from 50 Bcm in 2005 (barely 2 per cent of its energy needs) to an estimated 300 Bcm in 2019 (over 7 per cent). China has moved to diversify its energy mix and improve air quality, with gas as one component of that policy approach. It has rapidly increased gas imports from nothing fifteen years ago, to become the world's largest gas importer (120 Bcm), more than half coming from LNG. India has also rapidly emerged as a gas importer (30 Bcm), in its case all from LNG, making it the fourth-largest LNG importer. Gas use in India is driven mainly by industry, with the power sector taking a lesser role, as domestic coal is generally much cheaper.

On the supply side, the rise of the US as a major oil and gas exporter has been a pivotal development based on the rapid deployment of cost-effective unconventional hydrocarbon technologies. Given that the US government only granted permission for the construction of the first LNG export plant in 2011, the speed at which LNG export-capacity increased has been phenomenal, certainly compared to that of Australia. Furthermore, as noted earlier, the expansion is based on a totally different business model to that of the traditional long-term, oil-indexed contracts of the last forty or so years.

Gas is sourced mainly from the thick network of gas suppliers around the Gulf of Mexico, the Henry Hub, at prices recently below $2/MMBtu. Liquefaction facilities can be built relatively quickly and cheaply in this location, reducing risk, so contractual terms are much shorter and priced off Henry Hub, with an allowance for liquefaction and transport (typically adding around $4–5/MMBtu). Buyers are being serviced by consortia of intermediary traders, sharply increasing the flexibility and responsiveness of supply, including destination flexibility. This is one key reason giving the LNG market some semblance of the oil market. Between 2016 and 2019, US gas output rose by almost 30 per cent and LNG exports from nothing to 50 Bcm, with projects under construction likely to double the capacity in the next few years.

New large-scale Russian projects have also entered the market and Qatar has lifted its more-than-a-decade-old moratorium on LNG expansions. Hence, recent years have seen a sharp increase in global LNG supply, (14 per cent in 2019 alone) with the promise of more to come depending, of course, on market conditions. Unsurprisingly, given the relatively weak global economic and energy growth, plus the rise of dramatically cheaper renewable power technologies, LNG spot prices have weakened in mid-2020 to as low as $2/MMBtu, certainly in Europe and the US and even in the generally higher-priced north-east Asian markets. Pressure has mounted on long-term oil-indexed contracts, even as the slope of newer contracts (the ratio of gas to oil prices) has declined.

As noted earlier in this chapter, the rise of North American LNG, in particular, is changing the way LNG projects are financed, away from the traditional model seen in Asian LNG markets. There, projects proceed when 80 per cent of output is covered by long-term take-or-pay contracts (often twenty years) from large, creditworthy buyers on some transparent price index. This index is usually based on oil, with little or no destination flexibility. Large industry players, with diverse portfolios of gas sources and markets, are buying gas from US terminals and are becoming increasingly confident on the spot market, which is accounting for a growing share of global sales (about a quarter at the moment). Contracts are being written for shorter periods, often, say, four years, (in 2019, around one-third of contracts globally were for four years or less), with more innovative pricing terms and indices, such as off electricity prices.

Many more companies and intermediaries are entering LNG markets, increasing diversity and flexibility in marketing. Seasonal demand needs (for example, winter heating or summer power) are traditionally difficult to handle in the long-term contract model but can be managed by portfolio players more readily. Contracted volumes are also getting smaller; contracts for less than 3 Bcm/annum accounted for around two-thirds of the new market in the second half of this decade, compared with well under half in the first half of the decade.

New technologies have also had an influence. In particular, floating storage and regasification units have meant buyers can quickly take up import opportunities. These units have relatively low capital cost and are flexible, in that they can be leased for short or even seasonal periods, to cover declining production or shortfalls in domestic gas output. Bangladesh provides an illustrative example of their deployment. Floating production facilities (including the ground-breaking Prelude development offshore in Australia) offer the potential for reduced costs and projects on a smaller scale, with production facilities potentially moving to newer fields. However, capital costs still need to be kept under control and high levels of operational performance demonstrated.

In addition, globally, around half of all long-term contracts are set to expire in the next decade (around 200 Bcm), with a higher proportion in Asian markets. Existing and new buyers of un-contracted capacity may seek differing price terms, given that much of the high initial capital cost has been written off and risk is now much lower. Against that, extending supplies to existing plants will frequently involve investment in new gas supplies. Given all these factors, the predominance of oil-indexation can be expected to decline markedly over time even in Asian markets, with perhaps only legacy contracts seen by mid-century.

By the end of 2019, global gas-use looked set to grow over the next twenty years by around one-third. Even where much more stringent sustainability objectives are enacted, and coal and oil use fall sharply, gas is expected to maintain or even increase its share in the global energy mix.[3]In almost any scenario, gas trade is set to grow led by LNG, which is anticipated to double by 2040 to over 700 Bcm. Demand will be led by China, Japan and Korea, plus India and other developing Asian countries. This latter group can be expected to double LNG imports over the next five years.

LNG IN A POST COVID WORLD

The impact of COVID 19 on global economies and the energy scene has been unprecedented in terms of the rapid fall in energy demand and prices. Gas demand had already been falling in the first quarter of 2020, probably by around 3 per cent, as warm winters in many regions and growing renewable power-generation, drove gas use down. This further pressured an already over-supplied gas and especially the LNG market, where prices tend to be higher than pipeline gas. Spot LNG prices in Asia fell to $2/MMBtu. Henry Hub prices fell below this level, prices not seen for two decades. April 2020 saw the use of gas, in power generation, in particular, fall by between 20 per cent and nearly 40 per cent, while industrial demand was a little more resilient. India saw a 25 per cent fall in power production and gas use fell by 30 per cent, although gas use in fertilizer production is expected to drive a rebound quickly.[4]

Continuing uncertainty seems certain to drive declines in energy investment, with the possible exception of renewables in the power sector, where ambitious global policies are driving investment. The duration of these cuts will depend largely on the rate of recovery of global economies and seems certain to postpone what had been anticipated for 2021–22, namely energy and gas demand growth and consequent rebalancing of the current over-supply in global gas and LNG markets.

Most international energy companies have cut capital expenditure (CapEx) commitments with dramatic speed, typically by 20 to 30 per cent in 2020, with deeper cuts in 2021 (Saudi Aramco, Shell, BP, ENI are typical). In the US, the oil drilling rig count fell from around 700 to less than 300 over six weeks by mid-May. The gas rig count fell less dramatically but is still down by 40 per cent. Both presage falls in unconventional oil and gas output relatively soon, although the industry is extremely flexible and price-responsive in both directions.

In Australia, all major companies have moved quickly to reduce capital expenditure. Woodside cut its commitments by over AUS $2 billion in March 2020 (down to AUS $1.7 to 1.9 billion), delaying Scarborough, Pluto train 2 and Browse developments (and any gas output), well into the second half of this decade, since any final investment decisions are unlikely before late 2021 at the earliest. While

Woodside has said that it will maintain LNG output and honour long-term contracts, these postponements mean that as existing gas supplies inevitably decline, the ability of Woodside to maintain high output levels may be compromised in the medium term.

Oil Search has similarly reduced capex by AUS $675 million. Santos has indicated that a decision on Barossa will be deferred and CapEx cut by 38 per cent for 2020, or almost AUS $1 billion. Shell has deferred a final investment decision on Crux until well into next year. Note this list of delays covers all the projects which have been listed in the section above as necessary for sustaining and potentially increasing Australian LNG output, with the exceptions of the Gorgon gas supply expansion and the Arrow project. In April 2020, Shell—in a joint venture with PetroChina—gave the go-ahead for the Arrow gas development project in the Surat Basin in Queensland, to eventually supply up to 7 Bcm per annum to customers in the domestic market and the Gladstone LNG plants. This is an especially positive development, given the global economic background. In addition, most of these companies also hold equity shares in US LNG plants. In the current price environment, the output of these plants, generally not covered by long-term contracts, must be questioned, even as Henry Hub prices plumb historic lows.

FUTURE SUPPLIERS OF LNG TO INDIA

To date, Qatar has been the dominant supplier of LNG to India. Its massive export capacity was built to supply markets in the US, Europe (including the UK) and Asia. Only some of these markets were available when capacity came on line, allowing Qatar to divert supplies to emerging markets (such as India), as well as meet the increasing needs of a post-Fukushima Japan. The developments were based on a massive offshore North Field gas deposit, offering exceptionally low extraction costs and low construction costs. Qatar has proved a very reliable supplier, despite its constrained location, with almost all shipments passing through the Straits of Hormuz and ongoing political difficulties with Saudi Arabia. Currently, Indian imports from Qatar are under long-term contracts for 12 Bcm at around $8/MBtu.

The more merchant model of the US producers has seen gas from that source recently enter the Indian market, at around 8 Bcm per annum, despite the US's distance from this market. Supplies have also been sourced from Russia's remote Yamal project, through swap arrangements, at prices less than Qatar's. As noted earlier, the Gorgon development supplies around 2 Bcm per annum, via ExxonMobil. All recent shipments have seen renegotiated prices, as the market over-supply has grown. Purchases have also been made from spot markets, where prices are well below contracted prices.

For the future, both Qatar and the US are likely to expand production. Qatar recently ended its decade-old moratorium on new developments and is planning to rapidly expand capacity by almost half to 150 Bcm, based on very cheap gas from its offshore field. The US also has a number of plants under construction, with a likely doubling of capacity in the next five years. Both countries are estimated to have liquefaction plant costs in the range of $500–$1000 per annual tonne of capacity (Qatar at the lower end of that range), which are among the lowest globally, yielding long-run marginal costs of around $4/MMBtu and $6/MMBtu respectively. Russia, the world's largest gas exporter, is also keen to expand LNG production, with costs a little above these two countries.

Relatively few major new gas projects were underway at end-2019 in Australia, so that LNG export capacity is likely to remain at around current levels to 2025, during which time Australia's LNG output is likely to be surpassed by Qatar and the US. Construction costs for new greenfield LNG projects in Australia are in the range of $800–$1500 per tonne annual capacity and gas production is more expensive, giving long-run costs of over $9/MMBtu. Potential projects in Australia, as of end-2019, would likely have a post-2025 time frame for delivery and would mainly provide additional, or replacement, gas at existing projects (Barossa, Crux, Browse, providing sustaining gas to Darwin, Prelude floating facility and the NWS respectively). Brownfield projects—such as additional trains at existing projects (e.g., train 4 at Gorgon, an extra train at Pluto) with lower costs than greenfield projects—are possible depending on market conditions. As observed above, most of these projects are being delayed.

From the viewpoint of output of Australia's eastern states, further expansions of LNG export capacity seem unlikely, given the relatively high production costs, continuing social and political opposition to expanded coal-bed methane production and concerns generally over high domestic gas prices. The Arrow development should ease these pressures, if not eliminate them. The Australian government introduced the Australian Domestic Gas Security Mechanism (ADGSM) in 2017. The ADGSM provides the government with the ability to restrict LNG exports to secure domestic supply and is scheduled to cease in 2023. Since the ADGSM's introduction, supply pressures in the eastern gas market have moderated markedly. An industry-led initiative has resulted in a Heads of Agreement between the Australian government and LNG companies to ensure gas is available in the domestic market.

CONCLUSIONS

India has a relatively low share of gas in its energy mix, as its own production has disappointed and coal has remained cheap, available and particularly important in the power sector. Nonetheless, Indian gas use looks set to rise—notably in the industrial sector and potentially in the power sector—if strong GHG reduction policies are implemented as a complement to rapid rises in renewable power. Imports by pipeline have proved impossible; hence LNG imports look set to rise. However, LNG in the Asian region has remained expensive, being based on oil indexation and relatively inflexible until recently. The Indian market remains extremely price sensitive, a situation unlikely to change over the medium term. Nonetheless, imported gas offers important environmental, security and efficiency benefits.

In recent years, the global LNG industry has begun to change, with shorter contract periods, more flexible pricing terms, the breakdown of destination clauses—all of which have made for a more flexible price-sensitive market, although far from that of the oil market.

Recent months have seen unprecedented collapses in the price of oil and gas, with spot gas prices falling to historic lows. India has been able to profit from these prices with increased spot purchases. However, gas remains a marginal fuel in the Indian energy mix, gas-fired capacity remains underutilized and more widespread pipe-distribution systems, essential for increased gas penetration, remain in future plans.

India can be expected to continue to seek to diversify its energy mix away from coal, towards renewables in the power sector and gas in industry. It should be encouraged along this path, along with internal policy reforms for more cost-reflective pricing in electricity, coal, coal transport and gas. Efforts to expand gas infrastructure will be a key component of any expanded gas sector.

Australia has significant gas resources, mostly offshore in northern and western Australia, but in the current environment, it may struggle to maintain or expand LNG exports. While the industry has been nimble in coping with an expanding spot and short-term market, the investment environment over the next few years looks very tough, unless economies rebound rapidly. New investments are needed to cope with declines from existing fields, but capital and gas production costs for greenfield developments appear uncompetitive with newer supplies from Qatar, the US and probably Russia.

As noted above, new export supplies are most likely to come from northern and western developments, rather than those on Australia's east coast. More competitive pricing and more flexibility (including timing and destination flexibility) will likely be essential in the emerging competitive supply environment, if new markets are to be developed or expanded. The example of China, where Australian producers secured an early foothold in the country's LNG imports, provides a strong example of the benefits of entering rapidly emerging markets. China is now close to Australia's largest LNG customer and its recent purchases may exceed those from Japan. But these two markets account for around 80 per cent of Australian LNG exports. Diversity of markets is important to suppliers too.

Mature LNG projects in Australia have been remarkably reliable over three decades, even as Category 5 cyclones have hit production facilities. Additional security benefits undoubtedly accrue to Indian gas supply, from having such a reliable supplier located close to their demand centres. Other suppliers are more distant, or located in unstable regions, or subject to major weather disruptions (Gulf of Mexico hurricanes, for example). The Indian government's efforts to diversify both energy sources (away from coal) and import sources are a perfectly normal and rational response to security and environmental concerns. These approaches have been used successfully in other Asian countries, such as Japan, Korea and China, to improve energy security. New buyers may seek equity in new or expanded projects and Australian ventures have been prepared to accommodate appropriate involvement noting, of course, that any equity investments are commercial decisions for both producer and consumer.

Again, the example of China—which is successfully diversifying away from coal, using renewables, gas and nuclear power—provides a powerful illustration of the benefits of this approach. It yields significant air quality and efficiency benefits, while maintaining secure, reliable and affordable energy. China initially found LNG imports to be expensive, but rolled gas in from a number of sources, both domestic and imported, to provide a reliable, clean fuel for industry, household use, and peak power generation.

Notes

1. International Energy Agency (IEA), 'Global Energy Review 2020: Impacts of COVID 19 on global energy demand', April 2020.
2. Institute of Energy Economics Japan (IEEJ), 'COVID 19 and the outlook for oil, natural gas and LNG Demand', April 2020.
3. IEA World Energy Outlook 2019.
4. IEA World Energy Outlook 2020.

10

MIDDLE EAST LNG

TALMIZ AHMAD

Former Indian ambassador to Saudi Arabia, Oman and the
United Arab Emirates

OVERVIEW

IT IS USEFUL TO EXAMINE the outlook for West Asian gas in the context of the ongoing Covid-19 pandemic. In a recent study, energy analyst Robin Mills noted that the total growth of annual demand for consumption *within* West Asia would, after two decades of rapid expansion, begin to decrease through to 2035.[1] He identified four reasons for this: improved efficiency, higher gas prices, slower economic growth and alternative sources for power generation. Mills points out that with domestic demand slowing alongside major plans for expansion of production by some countries, there will be a strong incentive for West Asian producers, particularly low-cost producers, to go in for increased LNG exports.[2]

Qatar will play a lead role in this planned expansion: it is expected to produce an additional 33 million tonnes per year (45 Bcm) by 2024. In Iran, the further development of the South Pars field should provide an additional 50 Bcm of gas, though there could be constraints on both production and storage due to sanctions. Saudi Arabia and the

United Arab Emirates (UAE) are also pursuing new gas development projects. Saudi Arabia plans to produce shale gas and export 30 Bcm by 2030, while the UAE, presently obtaining piped gas from Qatar, plans to become self-sufficient by 2030. Mills' conclusion is that 'only Qatar appears to have the abundance of low-cost resources required to build new plants'. He estimates that West Asian producers will have an exportable surplus of 127 Bcm in 2025 and 189 Bcm in 2030. The Oxford Institute for Energy Studies (OIES) has forecast an exportable surplus of 228 Bcm in 2030 only for Gulf producers.[3] Taking account of the impact of the pandemic on gas exports, Vincent Lauerman projects Qatar's exports at about 129–133 Bcm in 2024.[4]

While Qatar has been the traditional bedrock of India's gas imports, over the last few years, India has imported liquefied natural gas (LNG) from almost all the major global exporters—Qatar, Nigeria, Australia, Angola, Indonesia, Malaysia, Equatorial Guinea and the US. The only exception was Russia, but this was made up in June 2018 when India obtained an LNG shipment from Russia, which flowed from a supply contract that was re-negotiated by the Indian government-owned company, GAIL (India) Ltd, with Gazprom.[5]

India has thus become fully familiar with the working of the global gas economy and the principal suppliers and can benefit from the diverse sources of supply and the contract terms that the market offers at present. Though the global LNG market is far better integrated than before and hosts a number of suppliers in different parts of the globe, a review of the post-pandemic market scenario, with all its attendant uncertainties, still suggests that India's principal needs are likely to be anchored in supplies from West Asian producers, primarily Qatar, usually on the basis of long-term supply contracts.

In keeping with competitive market trends, India's contracts with its West Asian suppliers will include considerable flexibility regarding prices and supplies delivered annually, usually without take-or-pay provisions. These medium/long-term contracts will be supplemented by spot purchases and short-term contracts to benefit from market conditions and to meet urgent needs. While Australia, Russia and the US are likely to emerge as major LNG producers in coming years, each of them could experience constraints that will restrict their becoming major suppliers to India. Given this, as well as the fact that the bulk of global LNG trade is intra-regional, it is very likely that contracts with producers outside West Asia will only be of a supplementary character, usually spot purchases, and India's principal source of LNG will continue to be West Asia.

INDIA'S ENGAGEMENTS WITH WEST ASIA

Energy Needs

India's ties with West Asia are firmly anchored in its energy-security interests since this region meets the bulk of its import needs. This scenario should continue at least over the next two decades, when fossil fuels are expected to dominate the global energy mix. India is viewed as a major market for hydrocarbons produced in the Gulf.

India has officially committed itself to increasing the share of gas in its energy mix from 6.2 per cent to 15 per cent by 2030. This means that the average growth rate of natural gas consumption has to increase from 6.3 per cent in 2008–09 to 12.4 per cent during the period from 2018–19 to 2029–30.[6] Most of India's gas needs will have to be met through the import of LNG. As its demand soars, Qatar, with its plans to expand production, will remain well-placed to meet India's needs; if sanctions ease, Iran could also enter the export market and supply to India.

Further, a number of investments have been planned in the oil and gas sector in India by West Asian producers, based on bilateral ties.

- In October 2018, DP World of Dubai won a $78 million concession to develop a warehousing zone at Mumbai port.

- A joint investment by the Abu Dhabi and Saudi national oil companies, ADNOC and Aramco, of $22 billion each, in the $60 billion refinery and petrochemicals complex in Maharashtra—originally to be located at Ratnagiri, but is now likely to be located at Raigad, near Mumbai.

- ADNOC has also agreed on a seven-year contract to store nearly six million barrels of crude in storage tanks in Mangalore.

- The Saudi petrochemicals company, SABIC, is looking at a 50 per cent stake in a $4.6 billion petrochemicals plant in Gujarat.

- The Indian upstream company, ONGC Videsh (OVL), has acquired a 10 per cent stake in an offshore oil concession in Abu Dhabi for $600 million.

- Aramco is expected to purchase a 20 per cent stake in Reliance Industries for $15 billion. Under this deal, Reliance will buy half-a-million barrels per day of crude (25 million tonnes) from Aramco on long-term basis for its refinery at Jamnagar, doubling the quantity it is already buying from Aramco; this oil will meet 40 per cent of its refining capacity.[7] According to reports in March 2020, Aramco said it was still conducting due diligence on the proposed investment. According to Aramco's annual report, it is seeking downstream investments in high-growth nations that are major oil importers.[8]

BILATERAL TIES

Given the importance of India's energy-based ties with West Asia, India and major West Asian producers have maintained steady high-level engagements, making every effort to imbue the relationship with long-term value by moving from transactional buyer-seller links to engagements based on investments and joint ventures and, more significantly, going from energy-related and economic ties towards strategic partnerships.

Prime Minister Narendra Modi has surpassed all his predecessors in the frequency of his personal interactions with West Asian leaders. In his first term as prime minister (2014–19), he visited the UAE, Saudi Arabia, Iran and Qatar and hosted Abu Dhabi Crown Prince Sheikh Mohammed bin Zayed Al-Nahyan, the Iranian president, Hassan Rouhani and the Saudi Crown Prince Mohammed bin Salman, in Delhi. Again, within the first three months of his second term as prime minister from May 2019, he visited the UAE and Bahrain and later, in October 2019, was in Riyadh for Saudi Arabia's annual financial conference. Modi's focus on West Asia has yielded a series of investments by producer-countries in India, leading energy commentator Robin Mills to note that Gulf exporters seem to prefer 'exciting India' to 'reliable Japan and lucrative China'.[9]

The joint statements concluded during these interactions have highlighted the central importance of energy ties, while seeking to build on them and move to new 'strategic' areas.

United Arab Emirates

The joint statement of August 2015 with the UAE saw the two countries committing to promote their 'strategic partnership' in the energy sector and identified the development of strategic petroleum reserves, cooperation in upstream and downstream sectors, and collaboration in third countries as new initiatives to be pursued. The statement also noted that the UAE proposed to invest $75 billion to support the next generation of infrastructure in India.[10]

Saudi Arabia

The Indo-Saudi joint statement of 2015 saw energy security as, 'a key pillar of the strategic partnership' and spoke of pursuing a 'deeper partnership' through investments, joint ventures and joint exploration in third countries.[11] The statement of February 2019 hailed the kingdom as the, 'world's most reliable supplier of oil and gas and key supplier to India'. The Saudi side affirmed that it was looking at investments in India worth $100 billion in energy, refining, petrochemicals and other infrastructure projects.[12]

Qatar

The agreement with Qatar, in 2016, noted the country's contribution to India's energy security as the largest supplier of LNG and LPG to India and sought to move forward to the joint exploration and development of new fields in Qatar and India.[13]

Iran

The agreement with Iran, in 2016, highlighted the importance of the development of Chabahar port and multimodal connectivity links from the port to Afghanistan, Central Asia and Russia, while encouraging an Indian role in Iran's hydrocarbon development projects.[14]

DEFENDING INDIA'S ENERGY SECURITY IN WEST ASIA

Scholars have recently noted that the Gulf, 'represents a natural economic, political and strategic hinterland for India',[15] shaped by India's historic ties with the region, its energy and economic links and the presence of the eight million-strong Indian community that remits over $35 billion annually to India.

These 'strategic partnerships', however, have been jeopardized by the region's ongoing confrontations. Peace and stability are central to India's energy security interests. However, ongoing competitions and confrontations (see box items) threaten to engulf the entire region in conflict. This would put the long-term interests of India and several other countries, mainly in Asia—that crucially depend on this region for their energy requirements—at serious risk.

Box 1: The 'Siege' of Qatar

In June 2017, Saudi Arabia, in association with the UAE, Bahrain and Egypt, initiated a comprehensive land, sea and air blockade of Qatar to protest its ties with the Muslim Brotherhood and links with Iran and imposed very stringent conditions for lifting the 'siege'.

The Saudi-Qatar divide brought both Turkey and Iran to Qatar's aid. Turkey has deployed 5,000 troops at its base in Qatar, ensuring that Qatar will not be attacked nor an internal *coup d'etat* engineered against the ruling family. Iran opened its ports to meet Qatar's requirements and also rushed urgently needed supplies. Other GCC countries—Oman and Kuwait—did not join the blockade and continued to maintain normal links with Qatar.

Nearly four years after the initiation of the blockade, it is clear that Qatar has effectively weathered the challenges posed by its neighbours by organizing new sources for its essential needs, with access to other port facilities in the region and alternative over-flight routes for its national carrier. It also remains active in the foreign affairs field, maintaining strong ties with the US, building relations with Iran and Russia and diversifying investments into Germany, Turkey and China. On 5 January 2021, the GCC summit in Al Ula in Saudi Arabia agreed to do away with the restrictions on Qatar, taking the first steps to normalize ties with their GCC partner and obtain some modicum of unity within the deeply divided regional grouping in the face of a more accommodative approach that the Biden administration is expected to adopt towards Iran.

Box 2: The Saudi-Iran confrontation

Another source of concern for regional security in West Asia is the ten-year-old confrontation between the two Gulf neighbours—Saudi Arabia and Iran. Its roots lie in the Saudi sense of strategic vulnerability vis-à-vis Iran as it saw Iran expanding its regional influence across West Asia on the basis of its affiliation with Shia communities in the region and the Shia militia it had sponsored in different countries—Lebanon, Iraq and Yemen. Saudi Arabia believes Iran is seeking regional hegemony, which it views as an 'existential threat'.

Their proxy conflict began in Syria in early 2011, when the kingdom initiated an effort to effect regime change in Damascus with the help of Salafi militia. The confrontation has been complicated by Saudi Arabia opening another proxy military front against Iran in Yemen from March 2015. In many instances, the fighting has blocked food and medical supplies and targeted health facilities, creating 'the world's greatest man-made humanitarian crisis' of modern times.

The Syrian and Yemeni conflicts have caused widespread death and destruction, without, however, yielding the prospect of a military solution. These conflicts have pulled in several other neighbouring countries, which are backing local militia structured on a sectarian basis.

Israel, with its concerns about the presence of Iranian forces at its border with Syria, has also launched several air attacks on Iranian targets in Syria and even in Iraq. In Syria, Turkey and Russia have set up a strong military presence, with the former attacking the Kurds and the latter supporting the Al Assad government in Damascus. The US also has a small military force in the north-east to back the Kurds and curb Iranian influence in the region. Though the conflict is now a decade old, there is no credible peace process in place.

Box 3: The US-Iran confrontation

The greatest source of anxiety relating to regional peace was the Trump administration's policy of applying 'maximum pressure' on Iran. After unilaterally withdrawing from the nuclear agreement with Iran in May 2018, the US administration's public position was that the sanctions were intended to persuade Iran to return to the negotiating table to finalize a fresh agreement. This new agreement would cover not only nuclear issues, but also significantly dilute Iran's role in regional affairs—a role that the US and its allies, Israel and Saudi Arabia, view as 'malign' and a threat to West Asian security and their interests.

The US reinstated sanctions in November 2018 that were directed at Iran's oil and gas exports. They restrict its financial transactions by denying it access to the US financial system, preventing investments and technology transfers to the energy sector and imposing 'secondary sanctions' on companies that trade with Iran in the hydrocarbon sector. From May 2019, the US ended its 'waivers' on selected countries (including India), that had been permitted to buy Iranian oil over the previous six-month period.

Since the lifting of these waivers, the security situation has deteriorated, with attacks on oil tankers in the Gulf waters and, in September 2019, a major missile and rocket attack on Saudi oil facilities at Khurais and Abqaiq, in the Eastern Province, allegedly by the Houthis in Yemen. The US continued to impose fresh sanctions on Iran, practically by the week, so that almost every aspect of Iranian political and economic life is now affected by sanctions. It also became clear that the Trump administration had little interest in a fresh agreement and the sanctions were merely an instrument to inflict the maximum pain on Iran so that its disgruntled populace would seek regime change. However, while the people are experiencing extraordinary economic privation, the government has responded with 'maximum resistance'.

To provoke Iran into a military confrontation, in January 2020, US drones assassinated the head of Iran's Al Quds Force, General Qasem Soleimani, outside Baghdad airport. This led to several relatively lowkey tit-for-tat attacks being exchanged between US and Iran-backed militia in Iraq, but both sides ensured that the situation would not deteriorate into a major conflict. Iran showed similar restraint after the killing of its prominent nuclear scientist in November 2020, most probably by elements linked with Israel.

These escalating tensions have raised concerns about the safe movement of energy supplies in the event of conflict. One-fifth of the world's oil supplies (21 million barrels, 20 per cent of globally traded oil) passes through the Straits of Hormuz daily, carried by thirty-five super tankers. In addition, 4.1 trillion cubic feet of LNG, a quarter of global supply, also traverses the Hormuz daily. A region-wide conflagration would, of course, totally disrupt the region's energy production and devastate the economies of most countries, particularly those in Asia.

The Biden victory in the presidential elections raises the possibility of a US return to the nuclear agreement and the easing of sanctions. But domestic opposition from the Republicans and other influential political groups (the Israel lobby, the Christian evangelists, etc.) and the hostility of Israel and Saudi Arabia to the revival of the nuclear agreement suggest that Biden will face serious difficulties in reducing regional tensions and rebuilding ties with Iran.

THE IMPACT OF COVID-19

The global pandemic has further escalated regional tensions. West Asia, described by a commentator as 'the world's most volatile region for more than seven decades',[16] has been hard-hit by the twin impacts of the pandemic and the unprecedented collapse of global oil prices. These dual disasters have wreaked havoc on the economic, social and even political orders of West Asian nations.

In several instances, they have exacerbated existing economic and governance issues that had remained unaddressed, largely due to the availability of oil revenues. Iran, Iraq, Lebanon and Algeria have been witnessing widespread street demonstrations, with young protestors demanding changes that would root out corruption, end sectarian and ethnic-based spoils systems that inform their political order, and make governance both transparent and responsive to their aspirations. Most West Asian states are crucially dependent on oil revenues for their welfare programmes and economic development. With the depletion of these revenues, they are facing catastrophe.

Above all, the pandemic is expected to be a 'conflict-multiplier'. Antagonists in ongoing conflicts are seeking to maximize their advantages against vulnerable foes. This is aggravating the health effects of the pandemic in states that are experiencing civil conflict, such as Syria and Yemen, that are barely coping with the health challenges, amidst displacement of millions of people who are in urgent need of humanitarian assistance.[17]

Iran—already experiencing the adverse impact of US sanctions—was the epicentre of the pandemic in the early stages in West Asia. By end-December 2020, it had suffered nearly 1.22 million infections and over 55,000 deaths, amidst an inadequate and non-transparent government response, complicated by very limited supplies of medicines and healthcare equipment due to sanctions. During this period of considerable pandemic-related stress in both the US and Iran, hostile rhetoric and low-key provocations continued between the two countries. As US Senator Diane Feinstein noted: 'The [Trump] administration is at times threatening and at times conciliatory, giving Iran little sense of what actions the president will take. This could inadvertently lead us to war, and neither the US nor Iran can afford to engage in hostilities that distract us from the pandemic.'[18]

PROPOSED PEACE INITIATIVE TO DEFEND INDIA'S ENERGY SECURITY

As West Asia teeters on the brink of a region-wide conflict, it is proposed that India shape and promote a diplomatic initiative that will encourage mutual confidence and dialogue in the region. Once this has been achieved, India, in association with appropriate partners, should pursue the realization of a regional cooperative security arrangement.

It makes sense for India to lead the peace initiative: it has the longest, most substantial and multi-faceted ties with all the Gulf countries. It has a well-established regional standing for its political, economic and technological achievements. Its conduct in international engagements has consistently been non-hegemonic, non-intrusive and non-prescriptive. Above all, it has a resident community of over eight million in the Gulf region, whose welfare is of paramount importance to all governments in Delhi and to several state governments.

The first part of the peace initiative will need to focus on building mutual trust and confidence between the two estranged neighbours, Saudi Arabia and Iran. This will be a daunting challenge, given the very divergent perceptions the two countries have of the current regional instability and the architecture of regional security. During this stage of confidence-building, antagonists should be encouraged to focus on issues on which they have shared interests and see if some modicum of cooperation on these matters is possible. These include:

- Energy, including coordination of policies relating to production and pricing of oil and gas, renewable energy and nuclear energy
- Promotion of intra-regional economic cooperation
- Regional logistical connectivity projects
- Initiatives relating to promotion of water conservation, food security, renewable energy and digital technology
- Cross-sectarian dialogue; promotion of pilgrimages

- Combating extremism through promotion of moderate and accommodative religious discourse
- In the political area, working closely on combating extremist groups, promoting the peace process in Afghanistan, etc.

REGIONAL SECURITY COOPERATION

The successful outcome of the confidence-building effort will set the stage to address the more serious issue of shaping a regional security architecture that will include all the regional entities and external powers with a stake in regional security. This peace process will have long-term value only if it is institutionalized within the framework of a broad vision of regional cooperation that gives all participants a stake in stability, peace and prosperity.

This can best be achieved through integrating the Gulf states with two major regional organizations—the Indian Ocean Rim Association (IORA) and the Shanghai Cooperation Organization (SCO).

The Indian Ocean Rim Association

The Indian Ocean Region (IOR) is at the centre of global commerce: nearly 100,000 ships transit the ocean annually, with 30 per cent of global containerized cargo, while 42 per cent of global crude oil, product and distillate is lifted from and within the region. The IOR has over 50 per cent each of global oil reserves and global proven gas reserves. India is at the centre of the ocean: it has a coastline of 7,500 km, 1,200 islands, 13 major ports and an exclusive economic zone of 6.2 million sq. km; 90 per cent of its exports are sea borne as are all its energy imports from the Gulf and Africa. Today, out of about $800 billion of India's total annual foreign trade, 95 per cent of trade by volume and 68 per cent by value moves through the Indian Ocean.

This region is today in the throes of competition and conflict, where failed and failing states have bred dangerous forces of discord and destruction.

The absence of a comprehensive security management system has meant that no effective platforms are available for dialogue and conflict-amelioration. Hence, as a first step towards shaping regional security, India will have to lead a diplomatic initiative to put in place government-to-government dialogue and policy coordination mechanisms that would embrace the Indian Ocean community. The principal responsibilities of the restructured IORA will be preserving freedom of navigation for commercial shipping, countering piracy, terrorism and human and weapons trafficking, and, above all, managing international naval competition.

This is only a part of a larger vision, which calls for the linking of the Indian Ocean with Eurasia through institutionalised connections between IORA and the SCO.

Shanghai Cooperation Organization

Engagement with the SCO will bring several advantages to the Gulf countries. In the energy sector, they will be able to engage with major global oil and gas producers and consumers. They will, thus, not only be able to coordinate policies with producers, but also be able to participate in the various pipeline projects that will link Eurasian producers with consumers. In the trade and investment area, the SCO countries are already among the Gulf's most important global trading partners and offer attractive opportunities for investments.

Through links with the SCO, the Gulf countries will become partners in ambitious logistical connectivity projects that are today under consideration and from which the Gulf countries are largely excluded. These projects need a stable West Asia for them to go forward. Participation with the SCO will make the Gulf countries active partners in projects as financiers, consultants and contractors and beneficiaries of the trade bonanza that will be available to the region when they are completed.

New Regional Strategic Architecture

From the Indian perspective, the IORA-SCO combine will yield enormous benefits for its energy security and strategic interests. It will link India with the energy resources of Central Asia and successfully pursue the connectivity projects from Chabahar port to Afghanistan and Central Asia and facilitate the International North-South Transport Corridor (INSTC) to Russia and Central Asia. This will also enable India to reach Afghanistan and participate in the development of its mineral potential.

Beyond these specific achievements, this reshaping of the regional strategic architecture will help address India's concerns regarding the West Asian security scenario and its implications for India's energy, economic and political interests. The integration of the Gulf nations into the larger strategic space provided by the IORA-SCO combine will reduce their mutual concerns and enable them to focus on cooperative projects in energy and connectivity areas. This benign environment will ensure that India's energy security interests are protected.

This will set the stage for convening of a regional conclave under UN auspices to achieve a regional cooperative security arrangement. The process will have three attributes:

- One, it will be a *diplomatic* initiative: military force will not be brought into the picture in an effort to replace US hegemony with that of another nation or a group of nations.

- Two, the process will be *incremental*: regional states will be required to dilute or withdraw from their existing security agreements only when there is real progress in achieving mutual accord on matters of security.

- Three, it will be *inclusive* in that all countries, regional and extra-regional, with a stake in West Asian security will be invited to participate in the conference. In order to ensure that the agreements are binding and effectively enforceable, all participants will become co-guarantors of the treaty, which will have clear provisions setting out the steps to be taken to enforce the concord and deal with recalcitrant conduct, within the framework of the UN Security Council or any other arrangement acceptable to the participants.[19]

CONCLUSION

West Asia will remain India's principal gas supplier due to the following factors:

1. The region has been and will remain the key global source of energy.
2. Geographical proximity makes supplies to India from the Gulf countries very economical; this is particularly important as India might not be able to obtain its needs through trans-national pipelines due to political considerations.
3. Given global and regional competitiveness, these suppliers will be most accommodative of India's needs as they will be anxious to retain their premier status in the Indian market.
4. These countries are best placed to invest the billions of dollars required to develop India's energy and related infrastructure, such as ports, roads and railway lines.
5. India has excellent political and economic ties with the principal West Asian countries; their differences among themselves have not negatively impacted their relations with India.
6. Over the last fifty years, the Gulf has witnessed major conflicts, but India's energy supplies have not been disrupted; India has been able to source its needs from different countries in the region.

In July 2019, Prime Minister Modi declared his vision to achieve a GDP of $5 trillion by 2024. This will require very heavy investments from external sources, particularly West Asia. The UAE and Saudi Arabia have already announced their interest in investing $75 billion and $100 billion, respectively, in India. Thus, India's long-term energy security and economic interests, particularly its transition to gas through LNG imports, are closely tied to a stable West Asia.

India has both the ability and the credibility to pursue a peace initiative for the region; an initiative that will boost confidence between estranged neighbours and promote dialogue between them. Over time, as mutual trust increases, the stage would be set to shape a new regional security architecture that will integrate the Gulf nations in a cooperation framework that embraces the Indian Ocean countries with those of Eurasia through the SCO. While competition between the major neighbouring countries will not be eliminated, the cooperative security arrangements will ensure that channels for interaction and dialogue remain open and competitions do not escalate into full-fledged conflict.

These initiatives for peace and cooperation will involve the active participation of regional states as key role-players in determining their own destiny. They will also, for the first time in several decades, provide a non-militarized framework for regional stability.

Notes

1. Robin Mills, 'Under a Cloud: The Future of Middle East gas Demand', New York: Center on Global Energy Policy, Columbia |SIPA, April 2020, https://energypolicy.columbia.edu/sites/default/files/file-uploads/MiddleEastGas_CGEP-Report_042920.pdf

2. Ibid.

3. Ibid.

4. Vincent Lauerman, 'Gas & LNG brace for tougher times', *Petroleum Economist*, 1 May 2020, https://www.petroleum-economist.com/

articles/midstream-downstream/lng/2020/gas-and-lng-brace-for-tougher-times

5. 'India begins importing LNG from Russia', *The Economic Times*, Dahej, Gujarat, 4 June 2018, https://economictimes.indiatimes.com/industry/energy/oil-gas/india-begins-importing-lng-from-russia/articleshow/64449583.cms?from=mdr

6. Lydia Powell and Akhilesh Sati, 'Natural gas in India: From Cinderella to Goldilocks', New Delhi: Observer Research Foundation, 20 May 2020, https://www.orfonline.org/expert-speak/natural-gas-india-cinderella-goldilocks-66385/

7. Wam, 'India strengthens energy tie-up with Gulf region', *Emirates 24x7*, 14 August 2019, https://www.emirates247.com/business/energy/india-strengthens-energy-tie-up-with-gulf-region-2019-08-14-1.688363

8. Press Trust of India, 'Amid talks with Reliance, Saudi Aramco says focusing investments in high-growth India market', *The Times of India*, 22 March 2020, https://timesofindia.indiatimes.com/business/india-business/amid-talks-with-reliance-saudi-aramco-says-focusing-investments-in-high-growth-india-market/articleshowprint/74757993.cms

9. Robin Mills, 'Why India is a front-runner as the Gulf's main energy partner', *The National*, 25 August 2019, https://www.thenational.ae/business/comment/why-india-is-a-front-runner-as-the-gulf-s-main-energy-partner-1.902217

10. Ministry of External Affairs, 'Joint Statement between the United Arab Emirates and India', New Delhi: MEA, Government of India, 17 August 2015, https://www.mea.gov.in/bilateral-documents.htm?dtl/25733/Joint_Statement_between_the_United_Arab_Emirates_and_the_Republic_of_India

11. Ministry of External Affairs, 'India-Saudi Arabia Joint Statement during the visit of Prime Minister to Saudi Arabia', New Delhi: MEA, Government of India, 3 April 2016, https://www.mea.gov.in/bilateral-

documents.htm?dtl/26595/IndiaSaudi+Arabia+Joint+Statement+ during+the+visit+of+Prime+Minister+to+Saudi+Arabia+Apr il+03+2016

12. Ministry of External Affairs, 'India-Saudi Arabia Joint Statement during the State Visit of His Royal Highness the Crown Prince of Saudi Arabia to India', New Delhi: MEA, Government of India, 20 February 2019, https://www.mea.gov.in/bilateral-documents.htm?dtl/31072/ IndiaSaudi_Arabia_Joint_Statement_during_the_State_Visit_of_His_ Royal_Highness_the_Crown_Prince_of_Saudi_Arabia_to_India

13. Ministry of External Affairs, 'India-Qatar Joint Statement during the visit of Prime Minister to Qatar', New Delhi, MEA, Government of India, 5 June 2016, https://www.mea.gov.in/bilateral-documents. htm?dtl/26870/IndiaQatar_Joint_Statement_during_the_visit_of_Prime_ Minister_to_Qatar

14. Ministry of External Affairs, 'India-Iran Joint Statement "Civilisational Connect, Contemporary Context" during the visit of Prime Minister to Iran', New Delhi: MEA, Government of India, 23 May 2016, https://www.mea.gov.in/bilateral-documents.htm?dtl/26843/India_ Iran_Joint_Statement_quot_Civilisational_Connect_Contemporary_ Contextquot_during_the_visit_of_Prime_Minister_to_Iran

15. Jonathan Fulton and Kadira Pethiyagoda, 'India and the Gulf', in Jonathan Fulton and Sim Li-Chen (eds), *External Powers and the Gulf Monarchies*, London: Routledge, 2019, 122.

16. Robin Wright, 'Can the Middle East Recover from the Coronavirus and Collapsing Oil Prices?', *The New Yorker*, 8 May 2020, https:// www.newyorker.com/news/our-columnists/can-the-middle-east- recover-from-the-coronavirus-and-collapsing-oil-prices

17. Ranj Alaalddin, 'COVID-19 will prolong conflict in the Middle East', New Delhi: Brookings India, 4 April 2020, https://www.brookings. edu/blog/order-from-chaos/2020/04/24/covid-19-will-prolong- conflict-in-the-middle-east/

18. Diane Feinstein, 'In times of the coronavirus pandemic, US and Iran need a peace plan', The Print, 15 May 2020, https://theprint.in/opinion/in-times-of-the-coronavirus-pandemic-us-and-iran-need-a-peace-plan/422196/

19. In an earlier paper, this author has explained how peace-makers could use lessons from the Peace of Westphalia to shape a peace process in West Asia: Talmiz Ahmad, 'Shaping a peace process for the Gulf: An Indian Initiative to realise the Ideas of Westphalia', *Asian Journal for Middle Eastern and Islamic Studies*, Vol. 13, issue 4, 25 October 2019.

SECTION D

INDIA – THE CURRENT SETTING

DEMAND

11

POWER: LAGGARD PENETRATION?

MOHIT BHARGAVA

Executive Director, NTPC Ltd

KISHORE KUMAR HOTA

Additional General Manager, NTPC Ltd

INTRODUCTION

NATURAL GAS HAS BEEN THE preferred fuel for power generation worldwide. Gas-based power plants emit lower carbon dioxide (CO_2) and nitrogen oxides (NOx), are more efficient and require significantly less land and water in comparison to coal-based power plants. In addition, gas-based plants with quick ramping can support peaking and balancing power requirements.

The first gas turbine for power generation in India was installed at Namrup in Assam in 1965. Following Oil and Natural Gas Corporation's (ONGC's) big oil and gas discoveries in Bombay High (now Mumbai High) in 1974 and in western offshore (Cambay basin), gas turbines for power generation came up at Uran in 1982. The first cross-country Hazira–Vijaipur–Jagdishpur (HVJ) gas pipeline, commissioned by the GAIL (India) Ltd between 1986 and 1997, gave a further impetus to gas-based generation and led to the development of a number of gas-based combined-cycle gas turbines (CCGTs),[1] including CCGTs by NTPC Ltd.

However, constraints in upstream gas production meant that most gas plants used naphtha/high-speed diesel (HSD) as backup secondary fuels. In 2009, as production from Reliance India Limited's (RIL) KG-D6 basin increased to about 60 million metric standard cubic metres per day (MMscm/d), the Government of India allocated top priority to existing gas-based power plants, after fertilizer plants and LPG extraction units. Projections of additional domestic gas by the Ministry of Petroleum and Natural Gas and the Directorate of Hydrocarbons encouraged promoters to plan new gas-based projects.

The Government of India stated that there was no reservation of gas and, subject to availability, the allocation of KG-D6 gas would be made to power projects as and when they were ready to commence production. In all, 6,880.5 MW of new gas-based capacity was commissioned during the Twelfth Five-Year Plan (2012–17),[2] mostly by independent power producers, without any firm allocation of gas.

At the height of its production, gas-based power plants received 26.4 MMscm/d,[3] or 47 per cent of the total supply from KG-D6. But the decline in production from KG-D6 (42.33 MMscm/d in 2011–12 and 16 MMscm/d in March 2013) had a major effect on gas-based power plants and supplies were reduced to 'nil' in March 2013. At that time, around 14,305 MW of gas-based capacity was stranded, thus running the risk of transforming investments into non-performing assets (NPAs). In March 2012, the Ministry of Power was compelled to issue an advisory, asking that all new gas-based power projects be postponed due to the non-availability of gas.[4] After this, no planning document on electricity supply has projected an increase in gas-based capacity.

CURRENT STATUS

Out of a total installed capacity of 3,70,106 MW as of 31 March 2020, gas-based power capacity was 24,955 MW (6.7 per cent), which includes a liquid fuel capacity of 1,054 MW (Figure 1).

The contribution of gas-based generation is only around 3.5 per cent (Figure 2)—20,922 MW is connected with the main pipeline/ gas grid, and 2,978 MW is connected to isolated gas fields out of the Central Electricity Authority (CEA)-monitored gas-based capacity of 23,901 MW (except liquid fuel-based gas).

Figure 1: Gas-based installed capacity in India's electricity mix

Figure 2: Generation from gas-based power plants

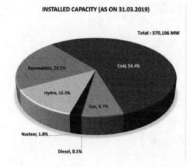

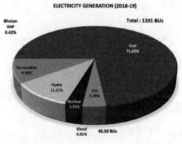

Source: CEA website; Installed capacity/National Power Portal website-Generation.

Despite a requirement of 115 MMscm/d at 90 per cent PLF[5], actual supplies to gas plants have always fallen short of the required/allocated quantity due to low availability (see Annexure III). The PLF was ~50 per cent till 2009–10, when the Government of India allocated substantial volumes of KG–D6 gas with the objective of running the gas plants at 70 per cent PLF.[6] Thereafter, the average PLF peaked at 67 per cent in 2009–10 and then started to decline as supplies from KG-D6 gas dwindled. Since 2013, the PLF of gas plants has been ~23 per cent. In 2019–20, of the allocated quantity of 86.66 MMscm/d, plants received only 19.2 MMscm/d of domestic gas and also consumed 10.3 MMscm/d of regasified liquefied natural gas (RLNG). The gas grid connected capacity received total gas of 20.39 MMscm/d (19.4 per cent PLF) and gas-based capacity, connected with isolated gas fields, received 9.12 MMscm/d of domestic gas (48.9 per cent PLF).

Figure 3: Decline in plant load factor of gas-based plants over 20 years

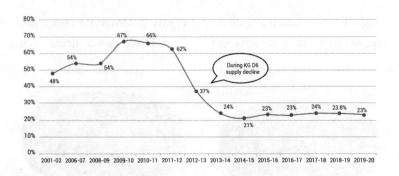

Source: CEA Annual Reports.[7]

DOMESTIC GAS PRICE FOR POWER

Domestic gas prices for the power sector have seen several revisions over the years. These prices were regulated as per Administered Price Mechanism (APM),[8] initially on a cost-plus basis.

- Based on the recommendations of the Kelkar Committee in 1992, APM gas prices were revised to ₹1,550/Mscm ($22.16/Mscm) and then to ₹1,850/Mscm ($26.45/Mscm) by 1997. The Shankar Committee recommended linking prices to the fuel oil basket and APM prices were revised to ₹2,850/Mscm ($40.76/Mscm). In July 2005, APM prices were revised to ₹3,200/Mscm ($45.76/Mscm).[9]

- Gas prices from the pre-New Exploration Licence Policy (pre-NELP) fields like Panna-Mukta and Tapti (PMT) and Ravva were based on production-sharing contracts. The price of gas from PMT was raised from $3.25 MMscm/d to $4.75 million British thermal units (MMBtu) and then to around $5.7/MMBtu. The PMT gas was supplied to gas power plants at APM prices by GAIL, which was adjusted against the Gas Pool Account. In 2008–09, gas from KG-D6 was priced at $4.2/MMBtu through a price formula.

- In 2010, APM gas prices were revised from ₹3,200/Mscm ($45.76/Mscm) to $4.2/MMBtu,[10] even though investments made in these depleting fields had been largely recovered. It was also the first time APM gas was denominated in US dollars, thereby opening the gas power tariff to the variation of foreign exchange.

- As per the Gas Price Guidelines 2014,[11] the price of existing gas was fixed every six months according to a combination of global market determined indices. Under the new Hydrocarbon Licensing Exploration Policy (HELP), gas producers are allowed 'marketing and pricing freedom' for new gas supplies. A price ceiling is declared every six months for gas produced from deep/ ultra-deep water, high-pressure/high-temperature (HP/HT) fields. The ceiling prices are linked to LNG, naphtha, fuel oil and imported coal, etc. The price ceiling for April–September 2020 was $5.61/MMBtu,[12] which is unaffordable for gas-based power plants.

The Kelkar Committee, in its report titled 'Roadmap for Reduction in Import Dependency in the Hydrocarbon Sector by 2030',[13] stated that natural resources should be priced at the highest market price possible. However, the report also advised that the government must ensure adequate support and subsidies to key sectors that use gas as an input, and it should be routed directly to the sector and end consumers.

CHALLENGES TO GENERATION FROM GAS-BASED POWER PLANTS

The share of gas-based power in India has been only around 3.5 per cent against the world average of around 22 per cent. Issues hampering gas-based generation include unavailability of allocated domestic gas, and the competitiveness of gas-based power plants in the 'merit order' vis-à-vis other sources.

Accordingly, the CEA in its draft report, 'Optimum Generation Capacity Mix' for 2029–30,[14] envisages no gas-based capacity addition in India, beyond the existing capacity (Figure 4).

Figure 4: Expected installed capacity and generation from different sources in 2030

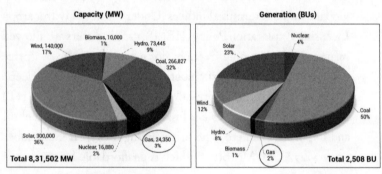

plus Battery Storage of 34,000 MW/136,000 MWh

Source: CEA draft report 'Optimum Generation Capacity Mix' for 2029–30 (see, endnote 13).

COMBINED-CYCLE GAS TURBINES AS BASE-LOAD PLANTS

A large capacity of CCGTs was established in line with the prevailing policy as base-load stations to meet power requirements. There were significant investments, due to dependence on foreign original equipment manufacturers (OEM) like Alstom, Mitsubishi, Asea Brown Boveri

(ABB), Siemens and General Electric. The cost of maintenance, repairs and life extension has also been substantial.

Despite the investments and costs, a number of factors in the intervening years have resulted in the sub-optimal utilization of the CCGTs.

Diversion of Domestic Gas Allocations

Until 2013, gas-based power plants (as 'anchor customers') were accorded top priority after the fertilizer sector and LPG extraction plants. However, as the city gas distribution (CGD) sector expanded, the government accorded it the highest priority. Domestic gas earlier allocated to the power sector was diverted to the CGD sector (CNG and PNG).

Energy Deficit

India's power situation earlier maintained a huge deficit, with energy shortages of over 10 per cent and peak shortages at around 13 per cent, until 2009–10. This deficit was almost wholly eliminated in 2018–19, because of a large coal-based capacity addition (Annexure IV).

Scheduling Issues

Gas plants used for power generation have to compete in the 'merit order' (based on variable cost or fuel cost) for scheduling against coal. While the variable cost of power with existing domestic gas is quite competitive (from ₹2.03 to 2.65/kWh), supplies have dwindled sharply. New domestic gas and RLNG are not competitive in the merit order for base-load operations. Further, despite significant taxations on domestic coal (including environmental compliance costs), pit-head coal-based power is cheaper than RLNG-based power (Table 1). Moreover, given lower PLFs of coal-based stations, due to large capacity addition and less demand growth, any increase in demand will focus on increasing coal generation because of the significant base. Thus, the role of gas plants has changed to meet peaking/balancing requirements. However, CCGTs have inherent challenges in meeting this role, which is discussed later.

Table 1: Cost of gas-based power, versus alternatives

Gas/RLNG	Basic Price (US$/ MMBtu)	Delivered Price (US$/MMBtu)	Variable Cost (₹/unit)
Domestic Gas	2.39*	3.16 to 5.5	2.03 to 2.65
New Domestic Gas	5.56**	7.5 to 8.5	4.5 to 5.5
PLL LT RLNG	8.08***	9.8 to 11.2	6.3 to 7.4
Spot RLNG	4****	4.97 to 5.23	3.18 to 3.45

* Fixed by the Government of India for April–September 2020
**Assumed with ceiling price fixed by the Government of India for April–September 2020
*** Ex-Terminal Price in April 2020
**** Ex-Terminal price

Source: Author analysis.

Table 2: Cost of power from different sources

Source	Average rate of power from different sources (₹/unit)
Coal	3.35
Hydro	2.41
Solar	2.5 to 3.00
Wind	3 to 3.50
Power Exchange Price (Max)	3.25

Source: Author analysis.

Figure 5: Competitiveness of gas plants in the 'merit order'

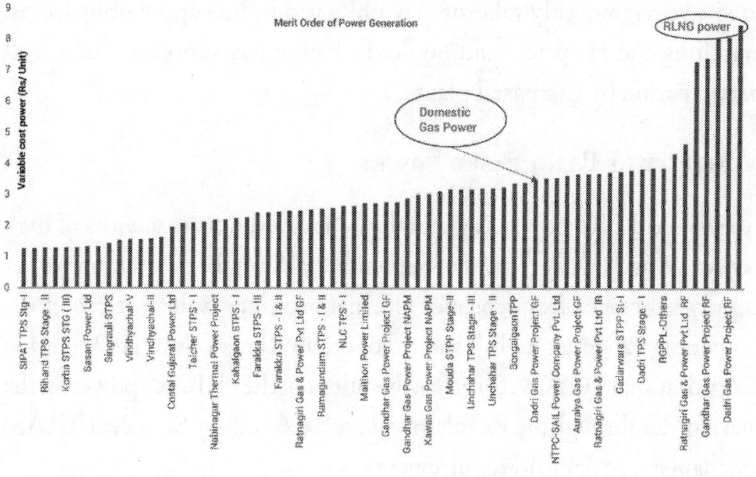

RRAS: Regulatory Reserve Ancillary Services

Source: Power System Operation Corporation, 'POSOCO RRAS Merit Order Stack 16 June to 15 July, 2019'.[15]

COMPETING FOR NEW DOMESTIC GAS

The policy of marketing and pricing freedom for new domestic gas by the Ministry of Petroleum and Natural Gas has arrested the declining trend in domestic gas to some extent. Further, production is expected to increase significantly to 49.5 Bcm in 2020–21 and 60.5 Bcm in 2021–22.[16] However, the gas market in India is still a sellers' market until such time as a demand–supply balance is established. Also, considering 'merit order' power scheduling, the price appetite of the power sector is the lowest as compared to other buyers (Figure 5).

Domestic producers such as ONGC and RIL came out with tenders for the sale of new domestic gas. Gas pricing in these tenders were close to RLNG prices, because of which power generators could not participate in the bidding. Further, high liabilities on account of onerous terms and conditions of the contract—including a fixed term of two to six years, monthly take-or-pay obligations, no supply obligations, matching the H1 price, and no flexibility in gas supplies—deterred participation by gas-based plants.

VIABILITY OF RLNG-BASED POWER

Regasified LNG power is generally scheduled during months of high power demand (May–June and September–November) or during power supply shortages from cheaper alternate sources, when prices in the power exchange are high. The grid operator, Power System Operation Corporation (POSOCO) also schedules costlier RLNG power in the merit order through the Regulatory Reserve Ancillary Services (RRAS) mechanism, as per grid requirements.

Figure 6: Trend showing when gas-based power from RLNG is scheduled (in 2018–19)

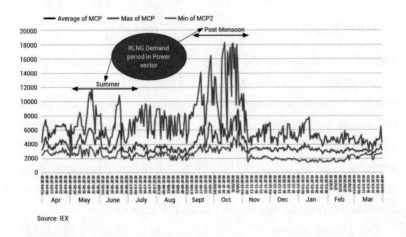

Source: IEX

MCP: Market Clearing Price

This type of scheduling comes into conflict with long-term LNG/RLNG agreements between the power sector and gas suppliers. Some contractual issues are highlighted below.

- Uniform offtake obligations throughout the year, along with take-or-pay commitments, is not feasible for the power sector, given the way RLNG power is scheduled, as discussed above.

- Spot RLNG suppliers require an upfront commitment of thirty to forty-five days and do not supply under 'best effort or reasonable endeavour' agreements. But distribution companies (Discoms) do not agree upfront to consume a designated quantity of RLNG-based power.

- In addition to the take-or-pay stipulation, power plants face the liability of 'ship-or-pay'/imbalance penalties for booked transportation capacity in the event of non-scheduling of RLNG-based power in the grid.

Hence, most power producers are not able to take advantage of the customs duty waiver on LNG for power generation, as it is difficult to commit a designated quantity of LNG to be consumed.

In 2015–16, the Government of India introduced an 'e-Bid RLNG' scheme, with an objective to make RLNG affordable for power generation. The scheme envisaged waivers by all stakeholders—generators, suppliers, Central and state governments, pipeline operators, regasification terminal operators—and financial support from the government. The scheme was valid for two years (2015–16 and 2016–17), but was not extended further as it did not receive the support of all stakeholders and was unsustainable.

Following the Covid-19 lockdown, spot LNG prices fell in the international market in the fourth quarter of 2019–20 due to oversupply and a crash in demand.[17] At delivery ex-ship (DES) prices of around

$3/MMBtu and delivered prices around $5.4/MMBtu, the variable cost is ₹~3.40/kWh ($0.04/kWh) at a gas power plant (Figure 7) in the northern regions (say, Uttar Pradesh). Despite low spot prices in Asian markets ($2/MMBtu), very little sale-purchase happened in India in April–May 2020, as storage tanks at the regasification terminals were full, with earlier inventory as per suppliers.

Figure 7: Variable cost of RLNG power at different prices

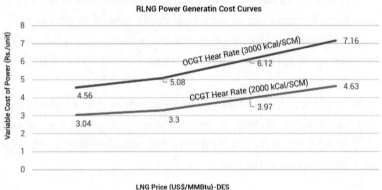

Source: Author analysis.

STRESSED/NON-PERFORMING GAS POWER PLANTS

In its January 2019 report, the Standing Committee on Energy,[18] was critical about the Central government's role in the stress on gas-based power plants. The committee stated that the financial stress occurred largely because the government had did not fulfil its obligation to supply domestic gas. Further, change in the gas-allocation policy rendered these plants unviable and jeopardized public investments. The gist of the recommendations of the committee is as under:

- The government should explore possibilities to revive stranded gas-based plants—which may include gas allocation from ONGC deep-water fields, diversion of domestic gas from non-core sectors and moderate RLNG costs—till sufficient domestic gas is available. For the next two to three years, the Government of India will hand-hold these stranded assets and provide requisite support with schemes such as 'e-bid RLNG', with desired exemptions/modifications and financial support.

- Free-market pricing of domestic gas may be beneficial to gas producers, but it is detrimental for gas-based power plants, which operate in a regulated sector.

- The RLNG may be pooled with domestic gas through an aggregator like GAIL, to achieve a reasonable price.

- Natural gas should be taxed under the Goods and Services Tax (GST).

- Gas plants can be operated as peaking plants, given the increasing renewable energy capacity.

OPPORTUNITIES FOR GAS-BASED GENERATION

PEAKING AND BALANCING

India plans to increase its renewable capacity to 175 GW by 2022, and to 450 GW by 2030. The CEA's National Electricity Plan of 2018,[19] estimates that the net demand curve is likely to be very steep and will require generation from conventional sources, which can be ramped up quickly. Further, adequate balancing power will be needed to take care of the variability and uncertainty associated with renewable generation.

A net load ramp of the order of 500 MW/minute (min), will be required during the months of November to February (Annexure V). The balancing and ramping requirements of the grid can be sourced in order of priority from hydro plants, pumped-storage plants and open-cycle gas turbine plants, CCGTs, and flexible coal-based plants. Grid-scale battery storage could also be an option for grid-balancing, as costs come down gradually.

Coal plants are being encouraged to increase their ramping capability from below 1 per cent to 3 per cent. Gas-based power plants are also expected to contribute around 80–90 MW/min (one-and-a-half to three hours). As per CEA projections, gas-based power plants will increase their present utilization from 22 per cent to 37 per cent PLF in 2021–22. This implies a gas requirement of $\sim$45 MMscmd. Ideally, open-cycle gas turbines or gas engines are suitable for balancing and ramping requirements of the grid because of their quick start and stop times.

DISADVANTAGES OF CCGT FOR PEAKING

While CCGTs are flexible to a limited extent, it is best run as base-load plants or intermediary-load plants. However, CCGTs may not be ideal as peaking plants in 'cold start-up' mode, since the Heat Recovery Steam Generators (HRSG) and the steam turbine take time to load.

Case Study at NTPC Dadri

The CEA has conducted full-load peaking operations at NTPC Dadri. When the machine starts-up after around sixteen-hours, in the 'warm-start mode', it takes four hours to reach full-load operation. It takes one hour to stop, in an evening peak operation of three hours.

NTPC Dadri (830 MW) has two modules. Both modules are operated by POSCO. During the day (off peak), it runs 1 GT + 1 ST, where GT stands for gas turbine and ST for steam turbine. A second GT is started two hours before the evening peak hour. This is done to avoid the challenge of a 'cold start-up'.

During high renewal-energy penetration in future, when the net load requirement is lower during the day, continuing the operation of 1 GT +

1 ST during the day will be an issue. It may be advisable to run the GTs of both modules in 'open-cycle' mode if the plant is required to generate only during peak hours. The GTs can ramp-up within fifteen to twenty minutes. However, the cost of the 'open cycle' operation will be around one-and-a-half times the cost of 'closed-cycle' operations, and would need to be paid for. Further, for a 3 GTs + 1 ST module configuration, it is not advisable to operate 1 GT + 1 ST as it causes lower loading of the ST: going below 20 per cent loading ST will cause damage to the Low Pressure (LP) Turbine last-stage blades due to condensation of steam.

Requirements for peaking

- Frequent starting and stopping of gas plants decreases the life of the machine by ten to twenty hours per start.

- Frequent maintenance is required and will increase operations and maintenance (O&M) costs.

- As loading decreases below 85 per cent, the heat rate increases exponentially. Accordingly, factors such as suitable operating norms for O&M costs, start-up costs, heat-rate compensation and auxiliary power consumption (APC) need to be established by the regulator for peaking/balancing operations.

- Suitable changes in regulations and grid management, with respect to the declaration of availability and scheduling mechanism, must be carried out.

- Consent of the gas supplier/pipeline operator is required to allow modifications in the gas supply contracts, providing flexibility in the gas delivery rate and in intra-gas day-renomination and carrying forward gas in the pipeline

Table 3: Technical capacity across different technologies to meet peaking and balancing needs

Meeting Peaking and Balancing Requirements At A Glance[20]				
	Installed Capacity	Ramp Rate (MW/min)	Variable Cost (₹/unit)	O&M (Cr/ MW)
CCGT	23 GW	5 per cent	2.2‑7	0.15‑0.20
Open Cycle	‑	40‑50 per cent	3.5‑8	0.15‑0.20
Hydro	45 GW	50 per cent	1.0 ‑ 3.5	0.10‑0.12
Pumped Storage	5GW	50 per cent	5.5 ‑ 7	0.10‑0.12
Flexible coal	‑	1 per cent	1.5‑3.5	0.18‑0.25

FLEXIBLE COGENERATION AND TRIGENERATION

Rapid development of manufacturing hubs, smart cities, LNG terminals, trunk gas pipelines and CGD networks throws up significant opportunities for flexible and efficient gas‑based power generation at competitive prices, along with the production of heat and cooling. Gas turbines in open‑cycle operation mode have a low efficiency of ~30–35 per cent, while combined‑cycle operation efficiency is generally ~40–50 per cent. The latest machines can reach 55–60 per cent operation efficiency. However, efficiency deteriorates substantially as the load is reduced below the rated loading of 85 per cent.

In a flexible operation regime, with high renewables, part‑load efficiency is more important than full‑load efficiency. In such scenarios, flexible gas‑based cogeneration and trigeneration throw up opportunities of more efficient operations. The waste heat of such a power plant is utilized to produce heat/cooling for productive use in cogeneration. Trigeneration plants thus produce power, heat and cooling. If the waste heat of the power plant is gainfully utilized, the overall efficiency of trigeneration can be 80–85 per cent or even more. The modular gas-engine power plant in a trigeneration system is quite flexible and highly efficient in part-load operation as compared to gas turbines.

Some advantages of trigeneration include:

- Cost saving, high-operating efficiency; buffer against increase in electricity cost; reduced electricity consumption; reliable and good quality uninterrupted power; environment-friendly and less dependent on grid power.

- As per Energy Efficiency Services Limited (EESL), it can reduce the end user's primary energy demand by 60–70 per cent and cut GHG emissions by up to 30 per cent.

- Can provide 300 tonnes of refrigeration for every megawatt of power the system generates, saving up to 195 kW of electricity and eliminating the need for investments in centralized cooling equipment and hot-water boilers.

- Protects consumers against surging tariffs by creating a parallel source of electricity.

Figure 8: Schematics of trigeneration

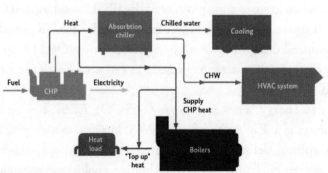

CHP: Combined Heat & Power; CHW: Chilled Water; HVAC: Heating, Ventilation, Air Conditioning

Source: EESL.

The EESL estimates the potential of trigeneration at around 15 GW, which can be scaled to 30 GW over the next five years. This will require an investment of ₹9 trillion ($120 billion) across the building and industry sectors, resulting in an annual emission reduction of 32.2 million tonnes. Some potential consumers of this technology are commercial establishments such as hospitals, hotels, shopping malls and technology parks; industries such as dairy, food and beverage, and pharmaceuticals; and large engineering manufacturing facilities.

Currently, most of these facilities/industries rely on grid power supply and have stand-alone systems for heating and cooling applications. Switching to trigeneration can help in environmentally friendly power generation, cooling/heating solutions. The affordability of gas/RLNG will be much higher at around $8/MMBtu,[21] and because of the increased system efficiency, the cost of power generation will reduce substantially to ₹3–4/unit ($0.04–0.05/unit) vis-à-vis the high industrial/commercial tariffs of Discoms of around ₹7–8/unit ($0.10–0.12/unit).

Case Study at Energy Efficiency Services Ltd

The company signed a memorandum of understanding (MoU) with GAIL for the supply of gas/RLNG at competitive prices for cogeneration/trigeneration projects run by EESL, in authorized CGD areas. It also acquired Edina Power Services Ltd in the UK, which has the required design/engineering/implementation/O&M expertise in cogeneration/trigeneration projects in various countries across the world.

As an energy services company (ESCO), EESL ties up with consumers in a 'Pay As You Save' (PAYS) business model, which is a zero CapEx model, providing integrated turnkey solutions and services for trigeneration. It provides metered heating, cooling and power under ten- to fifteen-year cooling, heating and power purchase agreements. It bears the upfront capital costs and risks, while providing turnkey product installations for gas engines and vapour absorption machines, along with annual operations and maintenance services. Thus, EESL recovers the costs through savings in consumers' operating expenses.

THE WAY FORWARD

Efficient and environment-friendly coal-based power will continue to be the mainstay fuel for India for a couple of decades at least, though its contribution is going to reduce gradually with the increasing penetration of renewables in the capacity mix. Thus, while transitioning to a low-carbon footprint regime, natural gas will be a transition fuel for power generation to complement/supplement renewables. At the same time, natural gas in India is gradually evolving towards market-based mechanisms. Hence, it is vital for the government to formulate policies conducive to encourage the production of enough domestic gas, development of gas infrastructure (pipelines, regasification terminals, CGD networks) to ensure connectivity to consumers, regulatory frameworks and appropriate taxation.

EARLY IMPLEMENTATION OF GST

Domestic gas/RLNG has so far been kept out of the purview of GST. At present, the Value Added Tax (VAT) on domestic gas/RLNG for power generation varies across states (0 per cent in Delhi to 15 per cent in Gujarat/Andhra Pradesh). This has a significant impact on the cost of power and deters the use of gas/RLNG for power generation. In addition, purchase tax in Gujarat was increased from 4 per cent to 15 per cent in November 2016. This created double taxation for domestic gas/RLNG, bought by GAIL in Gujarat and sold in other states. Uttar Pradesh used to have a VAT of 26 per cent, which was reduced to 10 per cent in November 2018.

Taxation constitutes as high as around 20 per cent[22] of the total landed cost of gas in certain states (APM gas in Rajasthan). Considering the prevailing cost of domestic coal, which is already taxed significantly, the cost of gas-based power should be made competitive. There have been deliberations to bring domestic gas/RLNG under the purview of GST. Cleaner fuels like gas should be taxed at the minimum. The GST on domestic gas/RLNG needs to be implemented at reasonable rates (maximum 5 per cent, as in the case of coal) without any further delay. This will eliminate the market anomaly and make gas-based power competitive. In case the GST on gas/RLNG is decided at 5 per cent, the variable cost of power will come down substantially. The variable cost of power of Petronet LNG Limited (PLL) LT RLNG (say at Dadri station) will reduce by around ₹1.00/kWh.

FLEXIBILITY IN GAS SUPPLY CONTRACTS

Gas Supply Agreements (GSAs) and Gas Transportation Agreements (GTAs) should reflect adequate flexibility with respect to variable gas-flow rates to meet the requirement of gas-based power plants in peaking/balancing operations. There is also a need to align/synergize regulations of the Petroleum and Natural Gas Regulatory Board (PNGRB) and the Central Electricity Regulatory Commission (CERC), as far as scheduling and revisions of gas transportation are concerned.

Gas producers need to provide flexibility in take-or-pay liability on an annual basis, have short tenures for contracts and provide flexibility in gas supply during peak demand season/peak hours. These are key enablers to encourage gas-based power producers to bid in tenders to tie up new domestic gas. Further, reasonable transportation tariffs and transparency in 'open access' for pipeline capacity booking will be important. The creation of a gas exchange/hub, along with the establishment of a system operator in line with the electricity market, will help evolve a 'model gas supply agreement/gas transportation agreement' with the required flexibility.

COGENERATION AND TRIGENERATION OPPORTUNITIES

Apart from providing efficient, flexible, distributed and captive power generation, cogeneration/trigeneration can also be used to meet the ever-increasing cooling requirement. Consumers can benefit from reliable power round the clock, with cooling and heating supplied at a nominal cost compared to prevalent electricity tariffs.

While the technology of cogeneration/trigeneration has not been the challenge in India, institutional issues need to be addressed with appropriate business models. The important issue here is to address technical and financial risks and the right sizing is important to derive a viable economy of scale. Dubai is a good example of cooling scale economics. The ESCOs can tie up with potential customers in India to offer innovative business models, like bearing upfront capital costs of turnkey installation for gas engines and vapour absorption machines, annual O&M, services, etc. An ESCO can recover these costs out of the savings in the operating expenses of the consumer through a long-term agreement. Collaborative business tie-ups by the ESCOM with technology implementation partners and gas/RLNG suppliers, could help in the successful working of such business models.

It is important to ensure that gas/RLNG is made available at the consumer's doorstep at predictable and viable prices, together with last-mile connectivity. With the rapid expansion of LNG terminals, gas pipelines and CGD networks being taken up in India, the availability of gas/RLNG across geographies will improve substantially. This will encourage group captive solutions for multiple clients in a geographical area, which will improve the economy of scale and thus bring down costs to make it techno-commercially viable. Institutional issues can thus be addressed with appropriate business models. This will also facilitate fund-raising by ESCOs to implement such projects for various clients.

Business Models for RLNG Supply to the Power Sectors

As discussed above, going forward with the increasing penetration of renewables in the system, gas-based power plants have the opportunity to improve their utilization (PLF) levels primarily to meet the peaking/balancing power requirements of the grid. The challenge that needs to be addressed here is how gas plants can tie up costlier gas/RLNG and compete in the 'merit order'.

One way to address this issue could be entering into collaborative business partnerships between major LNG/RLNG suppliers and gas-based power producers in India. This will ensure competitive and predictable RLNG prices in the short to medium term, on flexible supply terms to meet the requirements of the grid. Further, spot LNG sale on 'high sea' basis could result in reduced costs of RLNG for the gas-based power plant on account of savings in taxes/duties. This will engender confidence in the Discoms/market for scheduling competitive RLNG-based power.

The prevailing regime of spot RLNG now in the market has also thrown open opportunities for suppliers, power producers and bulk consumers to take advantage of competitive RLNG-based power in a collaborative manner. For example, bulk power consumers can tie up with gas-based power plants on a 'tolling model', wherein LNG/RLNG will be tied up by the bulk consumer, and the power plant will generate competitive and reliable power based on such RLNG to meet their requirement against a pre-agreed conversion cost of RLNG power.

The government is also constantly focusing on reforms in the power sector, and the 'open access' in the grid is likely to gradually get relaxed further, with minimum cross-subsidy surcharge. While taking advantage of such open access, bulk power consumers can collaborate/tie up with gas-based power plants for the direct supply of competitive and reliable power for their establishments.

Further, round-the-clock power procurement proposals are being initiated by various procurement agencies/aggregators to address issues of uncertainty and intermittency associated with renewable power. With a competitive/predictable RLNG price, gas-based power may be appropriately combined with renewable power to offer the market a competitive price on an RTC basis. Moreover, the introduction of Real Time Market (RTM) by CERC will throw up an opportunity for gas-based power plants to trade competitive RLNG power in the exchange. Thus, gas-based power generation can be maximized within the prevailing policy/regulatory framework and market environment.

ANNEXURE I

Plan-wise growth of installed generation capacity in India of gas/liquid fuel-based power plants

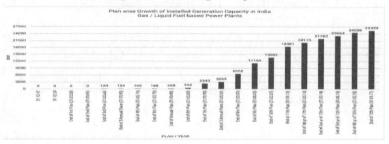

Source: CEA.

ANNEXURE II

Gas-based power plants connected to main pipeline grid

S. No	Name of Power Station	Installed Capacity (MW)	State
1	NTPC, FARIDABAD CCPP	431.59	HARYANA
2	NTPC, ANTA CCPP	419.33	RAJASTHAN
3	NTPC, AURAIYA CCPP	663.36	UTTAR PRADESH
4	NTPC, DADRI CCPP	829.78	UTTAR PRADESH
5	NTPC, GANDHAR (JHANORE) CCPP	657.39	GUJARAT
6	NTPC, KAWAS CCPP	656.20	GUJARAT
7	RATNAGIRI (RGPPL-DHABHOL)	1967.00	MAHARASHTRA
8	I.P.CCPP	270.00	DELHI
9	PRAGATI CCGT-III	1500.00	DELHI
10	PRAGATI CCPP	330.40	DELHI
11	DHUVARAN CCPP(GSECL)	594.72	GUJARAT
12	HAZIRA CCPP(GSEG)	156.10	GUJARAT
13	HAZIRA CCPP EXT	351.00	GUJARAT
14	PIPAVAV CCPP	702.00	GUJARAT
15	UTRAN CCPP(GSECL)	374.00	GUJARAT

S. No	Name of Power Station	Installed Capacity (MW)	State
16	URAN CCPP (MAHAGENCO)	672.00	MAHARASHTRA
17	GODAVARI (JEGURUPADU)	235.40	ANDHRA PRADESH
18	RITHALA CCPP (NDPL)	108.00	DELHI
19	GAMA CCPP	225.00	UTTARAKHAND
20	KASHIPUR CCPP(Sravanthi)	225.00	UTTARAKHAND
21	BARODA CCPP (GIPCL)	160.00	GUJARAT
22	ESSAR CCPP	300.00	GUJARAT
23	PAGUTHAN CCPP (CLP)	655.00	GUJARAT
24	SUGEN CCPP (TORRENT)	1147.50	GUJARAT
25	UNOSUGEN CCPP	382.50	GUJARAT
26	DGEN Mega CCPP	1200.00	GUJARAT
27	TROMBAY CCPP (TPC)	180.00	MAHARASHTRA
28	MANGAON CCPP	388.00	MAHARASHTRA
29	GAUTAMI CCPP	464.00	ANDHRA PRADESH
30	GMR-KAKINADA (Tanirvavi)	220.00	ANDHRA PRADESH

S. No	Name of Power Station	Installed Capacity (MW)	State
31	GMR-Rajamundry Energy Ltd	768.00	ANDHRA PRADESH
32	GODAVARI (SPECTRUM)	208.00	ANDHRA PRADESH
33	JEGURUPADU CCPP (GVK) PHASE-II	220.00	ANDHRA PRADESH
34	KONASEEMA CCPP	445.00	ANDHRA PRADESH
35	KONDAPALLI EXTN CCPP.	366.00	ANDHRA PRADESH
36	KONDAPALLI ST-3 CCPP (LANCO)	742.00	ANDHRA PRADESH
37	KONDAPALLI CCPP (LANCO)	368.14	ANDHRA PRADESH
38	PEDDAPURAM (BSES)	220.00	ANDHRA PRADESH
39	VEMAGIRI CCPP	370.00	ANDHRA PRADESH
40	VIJESWARAN CCPP	272.00	ANDHRA PRADESH
41	PCIL POWER AND HOLDINGS Ltd	30.00	ANDHRA PRADESH
42	RVK ENERGY	28.00	ANDHRA PRADESH
43	SILK ROAD SUGAR	35.00	ANDHRA PRADESH

S. No	Name of Power Station	Installed Capacity (MW)	State
44	LVS POWER	55.00	ANDHRA PRADESH

Source: CEA.

Gas-based power plants in the isolated grid

S. No	Name of Power Station	Installed Capacity (MW)	State
1	KATHALGURI (NEEPCO)	291.00	ASSAM
2	AGARTALA GT+ST (NEEPCO)	135.00	TRIPURA
3	MONARCHAK(NEEPCO)	101.00	TRIPURA
4	TRIPURA CCPP (ONGC)	726.60	TRIPURA
5	RAMGARH (RRVUNL, Jaisalmer)	273.80	RAJASTHAN
6	KARAIKAL CCPP (PPCL)	32.50	PUDUCHERRY
7	KOVIKALPAL (THIRUMAKOTTAI)	107.00	TAMIL NADU
8	KUTTALAM (TANGEDCO)	100.00	TAMIL NADU
9	VALUTHUR CCPP	186.20	TAMIL NADU
10	LAKWA GT (ASEB, Maibella)	97.20	ASSAM

11	LAKWA Replacement CCPP	69.76	ASSAM
12	NAMRUP CCPP + ST (APGCL)	161.25	ASSAM
13	BARAMURA GT (TSECL)	58.50	TRIPURA
14	ROKHIA GT (TSECL)	111.00	TRIPURA
15	KARUPPUR CCPP (LANCO TANJORE)	119.80	TAMIL NADU
16	P.NALLUR CCPP (PPN)	330.50	TAMIL NADU
17	VALANTARVY CCPP	52.80	TAMIL NADU
18	DLF ASSAM GT	24.50	ASSAM

Source: CEA.

ANNEXURE III

Domestic gas supply detail versus requirement/allocation

Financial Year	Gas-based Capacity-CEA Monitored (MW)	Gas Required (MMsc-md)	Average Gas/ RLNG Supplied (MMscmd)	Shortfall (MMsc-md)	PLF per cent
2000–01	9029	44.45	24.4	20.05	48
2001–02	9433	46.31	24.33	21.98	48
2002–03	9949	48.26	25.12	23.14	#
2003–04	10155	49.25	25.62	23.63	#
2004–05	10225	49.73	30.7	19.03	#
2005–06	10920	53.38	35.37	18.01	#

Financial Year	Gas-based Capacity-CEA Monitored (MW)	Gas Required (MMsc-md)	Average Gas/RLNG Supplied (MMscmd)	Shortfall (MMsc-md)	PLF per cent
2006–07	12444	61.18	35.1	26.08	54
2007–08	13409	65.67	38.14	27.53	#
2008–09	13600	66.61	37.45	29.16	#
2009–10	15769	78.09	55.45	22.64	#
2010–11	16640	81.42	59.31	22.11	67
2011–12	16926	81.78	55.98	25.8	62
2012–13	18362	90.7	40	50.7	37
2013–14	20385	97.9	27.13	70.77	24
2014–15	21666	104	25.2	78.8	21
2015–16	23076	113.6	28.26	85.34	23
2016–17	24037	118.2	30.32	87.88	23
2017–18	23842	116	30.72	85.28	24
2018–19	23883	115	30.99	84.01	23.7
2019–20	23901	116	29.51	87.49	23

– Data not available

Source: CEA Annual reports, Gas reports.

ANNEXURE IV

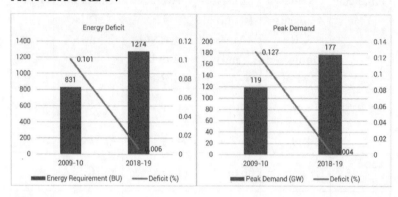

Source: CEA

ANNEXURE V

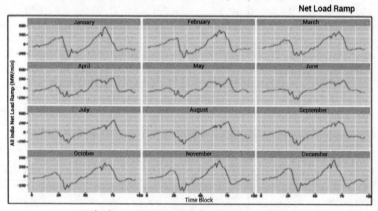

Net load ramp - 500 MW/min during November to February
Gas power expected to contribute 80-90 MW/min (1.5 to 3 hours)
Source: POSOCO report

Source: Discussion Paper on Flexible Operation of Gas Based Generation, submitted by Power System Operation Corporation (POSOCO) to the Ministry of Power.

Notes

1. Including Anta (419 MW), Auraiya (663 MW), Dadri (830 MW), Kawas (656 MW), Gandhar (657 MW) and Faridabad (432 MW).

2. Central Electricity Authority and the Ministry of Power, 'National Electricity Plan, Volume 1: Generation', a Joint Project Report, New Delhi: CEA and MOP, Government of India, January 2018, http://www.cea.nic.in/reports/committee/nep/nep_jan_2018.pdf

3. Standing Committee on Energy (2018–19), 'Stressed/Non-Performing Assets in Gas-based Power Plants', Forty-Second Report, New Delhi: Ministry of Power, Government of India, January 2019, http://www.indiaenvironmentportal.org.in/files/file/16_Energy_42.pdf

4. Plan-wise capacity addition in Annexure 1.

5. CEA Annual Report- 2019, https://cea.nic.in/annual-report/?lang=en

6. RGPPL, Ratnagiri plant at 90 per cent; plants in Andhra Pradesh at 75 per cent.

7. CEA Annual Reports-2019, https://cea.nic.in/annual-report/?lang=en

8. http://petroleum.nic.in/sites/default/files/Pricing%20and%20commercial%20utilization%20of%20non-APM%20gas%20produced%20by%20NOC%27s%20from%20their%20nominated%20blocks%20dt%2023.12.2011%20%26%2028.06.2010_0.pdf

9. Notification L-12015/5/04-GP(I), New Delhi: Ministry of Petroleum and Natural Gas, Government of India, 20 June 2005.

10. 'Price of APM natural gas produced by National Oil Companies', Notification L-12015/8/10-GP, New Delhi: Ministry of Petroleum and Natural Gas, Government of India, 31 May 2019, http://petroleum.nic.in/sites/default/files/PriceAPMGas1.pdf

11. 'New Domestic Natural Gas Pricing Guidelines', Notification 22013/27/2012-ON DV, New Delhi: Ministry of Petroleum and Natural Gas, Government of India, 10 January 2014, http://petroleum.nic.in/sites/default/files/1NewNaturalGasPricingGuidelines.pdf

12. Petroleum Planning and Analysis Cell, 'Gas Price Ceiling for the Period April–September 2020', New Delhi: Ministry of Petroleum and Natural Gas, Government of India, 31 March 2020, https://www.ppac.gov.in/WriteReadData/CMS/202003310533454733935GasPriceCeilingfortheperiodApril-September2020.pdf

13. Vijay Kelkar, 'Report of the [Kelkar] Committee on Roadmap for Reduction in Import Dependency in Hydrocarbon Sector by 2030: Part I', New Delhi: Ministry of Petroleum and Natural Gas, Government of India, December 2013, http://petroleum.nic.in/sites/default/files/kelkar.pdf

14. Central Electricity Authority and Ministry of Power, 'Draft Report on Optimal Generation Capacity Mix for 2029-2030', New Delhi: CEA, and MOP, Government of India, February 2019, http://cea.nic.in/reports/others/planning/irp/Optimal_generation_mix_report.pdf

15. Power System Operation Corporation, 'POSOCO RRAS Merit Order Stack 16 June to 15 July, 2019', New Delhi: POSOCO, Ministry of Power, Government of India, https://posoco.in/download/rras-providers-rate-from-16th-jun19-to-15th-jul19/?wpdmdl=23521

16. Standing Committee on Energy (2018–19), 'Stressed/Non-Performing Assets in Gas-based Power Plants'.

17. The financial year in India is 1 April–31 March.

18. Standing Committee on Energy (2018–19), 'Stressed/Non-Performing Assets in Gas-based Power Plants'.

19. Central Electricity Authority and Ministry of Power, 'National Electricity Plan, Volume I: Generation', 2018.

20. NEP, Optimal generation mix reports of CEA, Tariff policy.

21. Author analysis.

22. Author analysis.

12

POWER: NICHE POTENTIAL?

RAHUL TONGIA

Centre for Social and Economic Progress Research Foundation

OVERVIEW

NATURAL GAS IS A SMALL fraction of India's electricity supply (3.6 per cent in financial year FY 2018–19). Less than 20 per cent of the total gas consumption goes to the power sector. This is not because of limited demand, but non-competitiveness with alternative energy supply options; coal when it comes to price; and renewable energy (RE) when it comes to both cleanliness and cost (for variable RE [VRE], without storage, which is competitive even with coal).

As of 2019, electricity supply is based off surplus coal capacity; virtually all the growth in capacity is for RE, albeit VRE. The key questions are: (1) what will it take to utilize existing gas-generation capacity (which is very underutilized, with an average capacity utilization factor, also called plant-load factor (PLF), of under 24 per cent in FY18–19); (2) under what scenarios could we see a growth of new gas-based generation capacity?

Input fuel price is one of two key variables for competitiveness, the other being expected PLF. Delivered LNG costs of $8/MMBtu

(Million Metric British thermal units) would translate to a generation cost of about ₹6/kWh for a PLF of about 50–60 per cent, corresponding to modest part-load operations. This cost is higher than the generation cost of power from new coal and even with a carbon tax of $40/tonne carbon dioxide which would add about ₹1.6/kWh to the cost, the generation cost of gas-based power would be higher than coal-based power assuming the gas is LNG. Such a high carbon taxation value is higher than expected in the foreseeable future and higher than some estimates of India's social cost of carbon.

The picture of base-load competitiveness is nuanced, varying heavily by location. In locations far from coal mines, gas may become competitive sooner than expected. Understanding these nuances is also critical to understanding structural differences across existing gas capacity, where access to cheaper gas determines output; and where all the sixteen or more gas-based power plants (totalling over a quarter of the capacity), that had zero output in FY18–19, were private sector plants.

While the cleanliness of gas power is important, most current pricing norms don't cover the differential with coal, even after adding about 30–50 paise/kWh to retrofit existing coal plants to meet local air-pollution norms. Another important characteristic of gas power, more so as the share of RE rises, is its flexibility and ability to ramp up and down quickly. Even here, while the ramping capability in percentage terms of gas is vastly superior to coal, the low operating capacity at any given time (often near 6–7 GW) means the absolute ramp-up capability of coal is much higher at a grid level (than at plant level). Over time, ramping and flexing roles may migrate to storage systems. Nonetheless, we find a disproportional value for gas for a peaking role. However, even with 100 per cent peaking utilization of existing capacity (as a bounding exercise), the volume of incremental gas required for such a role is very low, only about 3 per cent of the *current* total gas demand.

The real decisions will need to be taken a few years hence, when we know better what happens with rising electricity demand, changes in load curves (peaks versus off-peaks), compliance of coal plants with new emissions norms, RE deployments, storage costs and any 'surplus coal' (itself a function of retrofits, retirements and completion of under-construction plants). The problem is one of lead times, especially for infrastructure. Given the relative ease of locating a gas plant near supply and using the electricity transmission grid to ship power, it may be a lower risk option to leave the door open to coastal or otherwise on-pipeline power plants, rather than building pipeline infrastructure dedicated to or even focused on inland gas plants.

GAS IN THE CONTEXT OF THE POWER SECTOR IN INDIA

Natural gas plays a rather small role in India's electricity-generation mix. There are three distinct components of this equilibrium. First and foremost is techno-economic—how does it compare to alternatives? Second, is there enough gas available? Third, what are the special characteristics of gas-based power that can distinguish it from the dominant fuel (coal), viz., ramping and peaking capabilities and cleanliness? How are these signalled?

The share of natural gas generation in India's grid-based generation mix in FY2018–19 was only 3.6 per cent, despite a higher 6.8 per cent share of capacity (Figure 1).[1] If we add captive power to the mix, the share would be lower, since there are fewer captive power plants that are grid based, and the several gigawatts that exist, produce power at expensive rates. We see that the share has stabilized under 4 per cent from a high of 12 per cent in FY2010.

Figure 1: Gas in India's Electricity Generation Mix

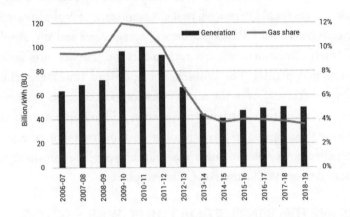

Source: Central Electricity Authority (CEA), Monthly summaries (March for multiple years), except 2006–07, where total generation to calculate gas share is based on Planning Commission data.

The earlier period tracked a rise in capacity, with a small bump in PLF, which peaked in FY2010 (Figure 2), which soon fell dramatically before stabilizing at a little over 20 per cent annually. While there were changes in gas supply, the ensuing period—FY11–16—saw enormous growth in coal-based generation capacity. This was partly due to capacity expansion by private companies in the power sector, displacing gas generation. Not only does India have sufficient (rather, surplus) coal-based capacity today, but also the marginal cost of coal beats almost all gas-based generation.

The average variable cost of generation of India's leading thermal generator, National Thermal Power Cooperation (NTPC), for instance, has been stable at just over ₹2/kWh for the last six years; this, despite a rising coal cess (presently at ₹400/tonne). Such averages mask a spread by location, with some pithead plants below ₹1.5/kWh and distant locations higher.

Figure 2: Gas capacity and utilization (annual PLF)

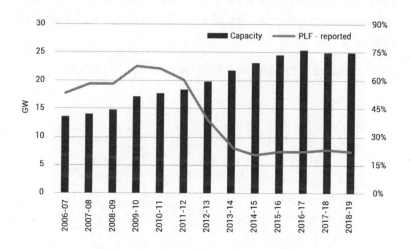

Source: CEA Monthly summaries.[2]

The average numbers for gas output and PLF mask a lot of important heterogeneity. Generation data from CEA show divergent PLFs for FY19 as shown in Table 1.

Table 1: Gas performance by sector, FY18–19

	Capacity Monitored (MW)	PLF
Central Plants	6,878	32.4 per cent
State Plants	6,713	27.0 per cent
Private/IPP Plants	10,292	15.6 per cent
Total	23,883	23.7 per cent

Source: CEA data CEA Annual Report on Fuel Supply, 2018–19.

None of the state- or Centre-run power plants have ever registered zero output (though two state units come close), *but about half the private-sector power plants had no output in FY18–19 (sixteen plants with 6.7 GW of capacity),* perhaps more if a few plants with missing data are estimated based on fuel allocations. If the private sector average rose from zero, it was predominantly because of a handful of plants with high PLF (Figure 3).

Figure 3: Plant-level utilization by sector (FY18–19)

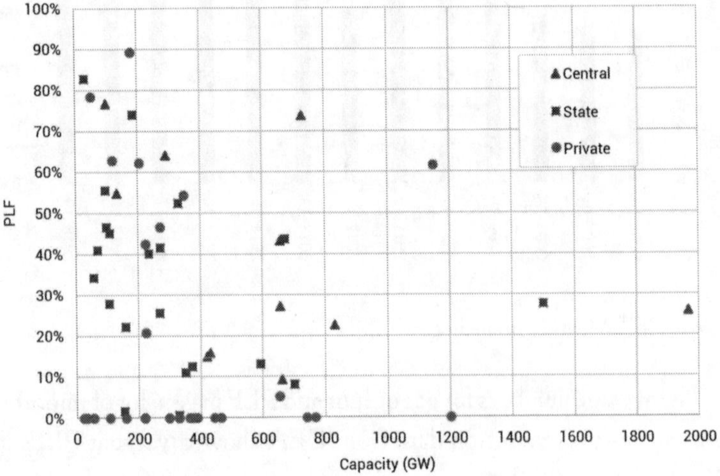

Source: CEA Annual Report on Fuel Supply, 2018–19.[3]

While low PLFs are a cause of many non-performing assets (NPAs), one has to be cautious in attributing the cause of low output. While the outage reports of Central Electricity Authority (CEA) and the Power System Operation Cooperation Ltd (POSOCO) show that a lot of gas plants have 'no fuel' as the reason for their nil output, it must be realized that no demand (itself a function of price) is an overlapping factor.

Official methodology only lists a single cause for 'zero output' for the day, even if there can be overlapping reasons. For plants with 'no fuel', even if fuel were available, their offtake might not rise due to high variable cost, due to which their output would not be called in the merit order despatch.[4]

Availability of fuel varies dramatically by source of gas. Comparing plant data for FY19, across administered pricing mechanism (APM)/ non-APM Krishna–Godavari–Dhirubhai (KGD) 6, and imported regasified LNG (RLNG), we see a wide gap between allotment versus usage (Table 2).

Table 2: Power Sector Natural gas allocation versus offtake
(FY18–19)

(MMscm/d)	Domestic Gas			RLNG (Imported)		TOTAL
	APM/ Non-APM/ PMT	KG-D6	Total	Long Term	SPOT	
Gas allotted	54.48	32.37	86.86	7.48	-	94.34
Gas Consumed/ Supplied	22.42	0	22.42	4.04	4.53	30.99
% Gas Consumed/ Supplied w.r.t Gas Allotted	41 per cent	0 per cent	26 per cent	54 per cent		33 per cent

Source: CEA Annual Report on Fuel Supply, 2018–19.[5]

Importantly, KG-D6, which was a third of allocated (expected) power sector gas, supplied zero. Those who were reliant on it suffered, and the same CEA fuel-supply report shows that in a few cases the impacted parties partially resorted to liquid fuels, which are likely to be more expensive.

Regarding imports, the consumption of RLNG was just over half the allocation under long-term contracts. However, the spot offtake more than made up for this gap, possibly taking advantage of low global LNG prices.

Examining the spread at a plant level, Figure 4 shows the severe structural difference between sectors. The private sector is by far worse off in terms of access to fuel.

Figure 4: Impact of no fuel on output by plant (FY18–19)

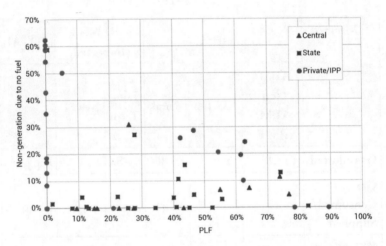

Note: This converts kWh outages reported due to no fuel and compares that to the output of the plant in the same period. This is as per reporting, and 'no fuel' may overlap with 'no demand'. Thus, even if the private plants with zero PLF got fuel, it is unlikely that they would find a corresponding offtake. We note that for the same range of mid-level PLFs, private plants faced greater 'no fuel' situations.

Source: Data from CEA's Annual Report on Fuel Supply, 2018–19.[6]

Current gas-based power purchase agreements (PPAs)—to the extent a power plant has such an offtake contract with a two-part tariff—separate fixed and variable costs. Fixed costs, which comprise return of equity (ROI), fixed operations and maintenance (O&M) costs, interest on debt and working capital, and depreciation are recoverable if the plant is 'available' as per a norm, even if it doesn't generate. Availability requires fuel, even if the output is expensive and the plant never gets called. Many contracts today pass fuel costs to buyers (utilities) once the PPAs are regulator approved, and thus those generators with a PPA are far better off than peers without a PPA.

One takeaway is that virtually all plants have reasonable supply capability margins (ability to increase output) *on average*. But public data doesn't disclose the time of day (peak vs off-peak) characteristics of when they supplied power. A hypothetical gas plant operating only three hours a day would have a 12.5 per cent PLF, but it may be running daily at full output during the peak. Alternatively, a plant may operate seasonally, or it may operate at part loads for much of its operations.

The next section attempts to examine issues of peaking and buffer capacity, using national-level data.

HOW MUCH GAS IS NEEDED FOR ELECTRICITY? DEPENDS ON HOW GAS OPERATES

There are two distinct aspects to gas-based electricity. The first is capacity and the second is generation (which leads to fuel requirements). The installed capacity of about 24 GW is already much more than today's generation at any given time and so represents 'surplus' capacity, which can easily produce more output at the margin. Of course, how any surplus declines as electricity demand grows is a large unknown, based on under-construction coal power plants, shifts in demand curves, and the rise of RE, especially dispatchable RE with storage.

How does gas perform? Data for 2019,[7] show that for an average all-India grid-level demand for a little under 150 GW (ranging from 97.6–184.5 GW over the calendar year), gas's output was for the most part between 4 and 6 GW (Figure 5), with some spikes pushing up the average compared to the median. For comparison, in FY19 (the last full year of generation data for gas that is available per CEA), gas capacity of 23.9 GW operated at 23.7 per cent PLF, which translates to an average output of 5.65 GW.

Figure 5: 2019 Gas-based generation all-India

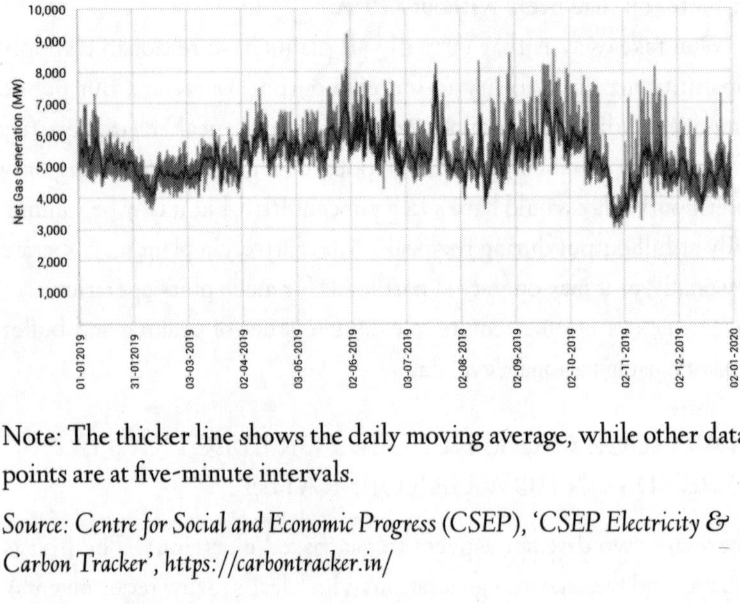

Note: The thicker line shows the daily moving average, while other data points are at five-minute intervals.

Source: Centre for Social and Economic Progress (CSEP), 'CSEP Electricity & Carbon Tracker', https://carbontracker.in/

While the daily outputs appear somewhat flat at this scale, especially compared to the installed capacity, which is about four times higher than typical output, there is a measurable daily variation of gas-based electricity output, as the close-up in Figure 6 shows. The daily swing correlates with evening demand peaks daily. The swings increased in the latter portion of the year (after the monsoon's effects were over). Even for the periods of maximum daily swing, the peak gas output is only about 50 per cent higher than the day's average and this peak only lasts a short period of time (two hours or less). Ramping also depends on total demand, for example, we see that weekends have lower total demand and lower gas ramping as well.

Figure 6: Daily all-India gas generation (detailed, period of maximum ramping)

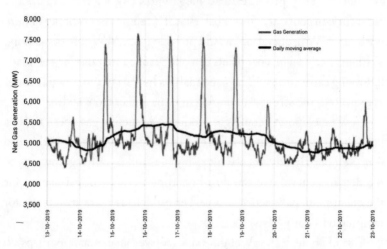

Note: While the peak is about 50 per cent higher for these days (high-peakiness), even here the average isn't more than ∼15 per cent higher than the low, confirming the duration of the peak is only about two hours. Weekend peakiness is measurably lower, even during lower ramping periods. Demand is lower overall for the weekends, but the impact is disproportionally on gas; even hydro, another strong peaker, shows less reduction in ramping during periods of lower demand (as per 2019 data).[8]

Source: Centre for Social and Economic Progress (CSEP), 'CSEP Electricity & Carbon Tracker', https://carbontracker.in/

Gas does provide value to the grid for ramping, and limited analysis shows that gas has a higher than average correlation between changes in net demand compared to coal (or nuclear).[9] This means that when demand swings, gas helps compensate.

While on a normalized (percentage) basis, gas ramps more than coal, the total grid value is modest, given the very low base of gas in operation. Thus, 6 GW of gas—even if it ramps 10 per cent per minute (which is an order of magnitude more than the actual ramp seen; just a theoretical estimate)—only provides 600 megawatts (MW)/min of support capability. In contrast, 'slow' coal, even if it ramps 1 per cent per minute with 120 GW in operation, would provide 1,200 MW/min of ramping. With proper design, coal plants can offer even more ramping and load-following capabilities.[10] The same analysis by Parray and Tongia shows, as expected, the strongest ramping in India comes from hydro.[11]

How much power could gas produce? Assuming gas doesn't play a base-load role where it would need to compete with coal, and hydro is maxed out already, then with rising demand (a shifting upwards of the demand curve), we can do a bounding exercise or estimation for the quantum of gas needed as a peaker (which also captures its use for ramping on a daily basis).

Out of about 24 GW of gas capacity, we can estimate perhaps 20 GW is available at any given time *if* both fuel and demand were present. From this, we can calculate the additional gas-based kilowatt hours generated if all the gas plants peaked at full capability (20 GW total) daily for one-and-a-half hours. Using generation data for 2019, such a peaking duty cycle translates to an additional 16 per cent generation.[12]

Assuming that the efficiency of gas generation for such duty cycles is the same as the average, as a first order, we can estimate the additional natural gas required. While we don't have granular time of day data for gas production over FY18-19, the total gas consumption (domestic plus imports) in FY18–19 stood at 60,798 million metric standard cubic metres per day (MMscm/d).[13] The power sector used 11,311 MMscm of gas for grid-connected utility power (i.e., excluding captive power),[14] or about 18.6 per cent of the total. Thus, growing power by 16 per cent for the peaking duty cycle (mentioned above) translates to about a 3 per cent increase in India's *present* gas consumption.

This is not to say that this modest growth as a peaker is of low value. As a peaker, utilizing existing capacity well is often the most cost-effective use of assets. While gas has a higher marginal cost than coal (for the most part), once existing but underused coal capacity is put into use and exhausted, or has ramping limits, gas can play a useful role for peaking. The value of such electricity could easily be double the average grid cost. One backstop for such value can be the cost of RE + storage— for meeting the evening peak, without building new coal power plants. Renewable energy without storage costs only approximately ₹2.75/ kWh for competitive grid-scale bids in favourable locations, and recent bids (late 2020) have come in under ₹2/kWh.

IS GAS COMPETITIVE FOR A LARGER ROLE IN ELECTRICITY?

The above calculation is for gas as a peaker, where the lower capital costs offset the higher variable costs when compared with coal. Building a coal power plant for just a few hours on average of daily use would be cost prohibitive. If we had inexpensive gas, then it could play a base-load role, especially in selected locations away from coal mines, but even for coal plants away from the mines, the variable costs of efficient coal power could be as low as approximately ₹3/kWh assuming access to notified price domestic coal. This includes all taxes and levies (such as the ₹400/tonne coal cess), as well as over-payments of at least 31 per cent to the railways for carrying coal (to offset or cross-subsidize their losses on passengers).[15]

How does gas compare?

Given below is a simple model for the economics of more efficient (but higher capital cost) combined-cycle gas power plants. The model emphasizes the importance of three key parameters: fuel cost, PLF and efficiency (which itself can depend on usage and duty cycle, closely

linked to PLF). Capital costs also matter naturally, but are not a variable
in that they are relatively fixed (and are a sunk cost in the case of existing
capacity). While the numbers used in the model are based on public
estimates of capital costs, the focus is on identifying trends or relative
importance, rather than specific generation cost numbers.

One of the trickiest challenges is estimating efficiency, which varies
not only by plant, vintage, etc., but also by operations. The same annual
PLF can be reached in infinite ways. It is not only part-loading but
also ramping that impacts heat rate (efficiency), namely, cycling up and
down, not to mention starts and stops. One indicator of how this plays
out in practice is to examine annual fuel consumption versus PLF of
existing plants.

For instance, CEA data for FY18–19 shows that gross efficiencies
(before auxiliary consumption) for gas plants, fell mostly between 40
and 50 per cent, but there was a small cluster of plants with efficiencies
around 20–30 per cent. Importantly, without 'time of day' data, we
cannot know the PLF versus heat rate (efficiency) penalty, since a 50 per
cent PLF could be either running at half load all the time, or full load
for half the year. However, this offers us a starting point for the analysis.

Figure 7: Gross efficiency versus utilization for gas plants (FY18–19)

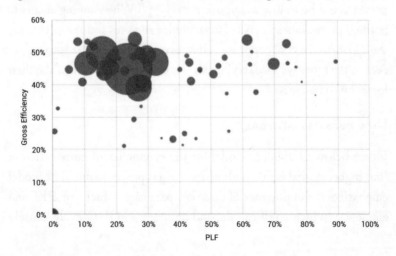

Note: The size of the bubble reflects the size of the plant. There are a number of plants with zero output, which are overlapping at the origin and hard to see. This reflects annual PLFs and doesn't directly show part-load operations. This assumes a net calorific value of 8,350 kilocalories per standard cubic metre (kcal/scm) for natural gas, which translates to 30.12 scm per MMBtu, and similar industry standard conversions for any reported use of naphtha or other liquid fuel (such as high-speed diesel).

Source: Underlying volume and generation data from the CEA Fuel Supply report 2018–19.[16]

For the model, we calculate fuel costs with a wide range of efficiencies parametrically, as well as penalties from nameplate (optimal) efficiencies as PLF falls. This heat rate penalty is a simplistic combination of steady-state, predictable efficiency falls with reduced output combined with the effects of ramping, start–stops. At an extreme, if the plants that are off are to turn on and only produce for a few hours in the evening before switching off, their efficiencies would be measurably lower than if they operated in a seasonal mode without a daily start–stop.

It is more straightforward to model costs at the plant level instead of fleet level, which would inherently have heterogeneity. We model a baseline 50 per cent gross efficiency plant, its efficiency falls to 42.5 per cent for 40 per cent PLF, with some cycling for the peak, as per the scenario above.

Using a range of fuel costs and PLFs, we find the variable costs of gas-based generation, post-auxiliary consumption of 3.5 per cent, to be as per Figure 8. For a representative delivered gas cost of $8/MMBtu, a 40 per cent PLF combined-cycle plant leads to variable costs of ₹4.7/kWh (using ₹71 per $ conversion). This is higher than the cost of coal power across India, even based on imported coal (except for importing coal plants that are far inland). For reference, the lowest cost pithead coal-based generation can be approximately ₹1.3/kWh fuel costs, inclusive of taxes and levies.

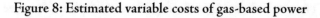

Figure 8: Estimated variable costs of gas-based power

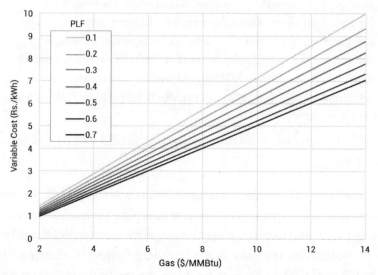

Note: These first-principle calculations by the author assume parameters as given in the text, including deterioration in efficiency with an aggregate fall in PLF as per the text.

Source: Author analysis.

While the variable cost penalty for lower PLFs is modest, the amortization of fixed costs becomes much worse at low PLFs.[17] Using reference cost structures for a combined-cycle power plant at ₹35 million/MW ($500,000/MW) overnight construction costs, and debt at 9 per cent returns, equity at 15 per cent and a 70:30 debt-equity ratio, we find a wide range of estimated per unit capital costs (Figure 9), which are strongly non-linear with PLF.

Figure 9: Estimated fixed costs of gas electricity generation

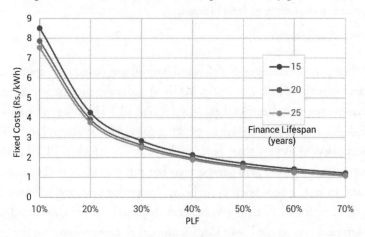

Note: These first-principle calculations by the author assume parameters as given in the text. The fixed costs are more or less constant, but spread over a lower base as PLF falls.

Source: Author analysis.

If we consider total costs (fixed plus variable), we find estimated costs as shown in Figure 10. Clearly, gas prices and PLF both matter enormously.

Figure 10: Estimated total gas-based power costs

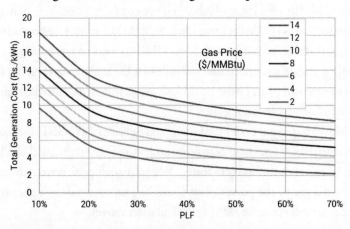

Note: These first-principle calculations by the author assume parameters as given in the text, e.g., long lifespan.

Source: Author analysis.

For plausible ranges of delivered natural gas based on imports (at least ₹559.36/MMBtu, or $7.87/MMBtu) under the current pricing and taxation regimes, base-load gas (50 per cent PLF) is going to be about ₹6/kWh ($0.08/kWh), while peaking gas could be above ₹10/kWh ($0.14/kWh). A very sharp peaking duty cycle, with a low PLF, has the highest value from a grid perspective, but this also leads to the highest costs. In fact, a new open-cycle plant is superior to a new combined-cycle plant for PLFs below 15 per cent (plausible for occasional and/or sharp peakers), as the lower CapEx more than compensates for the fall in efficiency.[18]

The major factors at play, viz., incoming gas costs and PLF, aren't independent. Assuming fuel availability, lower price fuel will also encourage a higher PLF, all else being equal. This has implications for policies for gas allocation—domestic (cheaper) versus imports. However, another important factor is location and most gas power plants are sited with fuel supply in mind.

For the base-load example, displacing coal also becomes a function of location. If we consider extremely low global (spot) gas prices, such as $1.5/MMBtu for Henry Hub and if we consider favourable delivery (liquefaction $2/MMBtu, transport $1.5/MMBtu only with mid-sea swap/arbitrage, regasification $0.5/MMBtu), that comes to just $5.5/MMBtu. Indian transportation and taxes are the remaining variables and so a theoretical plant onsite could find gas as low as $6/MMBtu, more so with favourable tax regimes.

Moves to put gas under the Goods and Services Tax (GST) are likely to materialize sooner than petroleum under GST, given the much smaller role of gas in state budgets today. Without such positive conditions, delivered gas to the power plant could be proportionately higher (and hence our reference $8/MMBtu calculation above).

Let us bound the problem by considering a near-to-supply 'best case', where \$6/MMBtu results in a variable cost of ₹3.34./kWh at 50 per cent PLF. While this appears competitive against non-pithead coal power plants (where variable costs can exceed ₹3.5/kWh), one has to also account for location-based PLFs. Far from the pithead, coal plants have low PLFs and similar pressures would apply on gas. For example, Karnataka's state-owned GenCo, Karnataka Power Corporation Ltd (KPCL), had a thermal PLF across its fleet of only 29.5 per cent in 2018–19.[19] At this PLF, the likely variable cost for combined-cycle gas plants (being built by KPCL just outside Bengaluru, in fact, since 2015) could be more than 10 per cent higher for the same incoming fuel. However, KPCL's incoming gas will not be as low as \$6/MMBtu.

As India moves towards pan-India electricity dispatch and markets (with testing having already begun), local competitiveness of gas versus local coal won't be sufficient—gas will have to compete with distant marginal costs of generation after factoring in electricity transmission costs, which are well under ₹1/kWh even for very long-distance transmission (excluding the north-east or mountainous areas).

Triangulating Duty Cycles with Supply Options

Optimal grid dispatch only looks at marginal costs once constructed, subject to transmission constraints,[20] which favours RE with near-zero marginal costs. On the other hand, this does not guide investment decisions. However, in the short run, India has surplus gas capacity.

If peaking and grid flexibility are the requirements, then combined-cycle plants are worse than open-cycle plants with regard to capabilities such as ramping, start–stop capabilities and cold starts. One alternative to traditional gas-based power plants is to use combustion engines that operate on gas—these can also operate on alternative liquid fuels if required. Such systems are multi-megawatt in size per unit, and scale to hundreds of MW in clusters.[21]

As per discussions with global providers of such solutions,[22] these have a capital cost lower than combined-cycle plants and can go from switched-off to full load in a few minutes, and can do multiple starts–stops per day. Their near full-load efficiency is reportedly close to 45 per cent, with low penalties for half-load operations. Planners should consider such technologies for grid balancing requirements.

What is missing for such technologies is a pricing signal that values such characteristics explicitly. Today, peak-time electricity is overwhelmingly priced at average prices (especially for power purchase agreements, or PPAs). The only time-based signals are for frequency-linked deviation settlement mechanism (DSM) payments for interstate central generation, or units purchased via the power exchange. Power markets covered only 3.5 per cent of grid-based electricity in FY17–18.[23] Signalling that reflects the state of the grid needs to grow to encourage peakers, which will also be required for storage solutions (including batteries).

It's worth observing that today's relatively low power exchange price, even during the grid peak, reflects a surplus in the grid and doesn't capture the true costs of peaking with new capacity expected to operate at low PLFs. Supply curves from other countries that have established power markets show an order of magnitude jump in supply costs for very high demand periods. However, the duration of such time periods is *much* lower than the daily peak estimates.

While hydro is an excellent peaker (and provides some inherent storage), land and socio-environmental constraints limit the growth of hydro. Alternatively, falling battery prices provide a backstop on gas for peaking. Batteries can offer the fastest response time, helping not just generation requirements but also frequency control support and other ancillary services. Tongia and Gross had estimated that even at $100/kWh delivered costs (inclusive of duties and taxes), the capital costs of a battery would be about ₹4/kWh.[24] With realistic duty cycles and adding O&M costs, the costs of a battery could be between ₹4.5–5/kWh at such a CapEx. Global costs of batteries (power electronics, inverter, etc.) were closer to \$250/kWh in 2019. However, even at today's higher high numbers, this translates to a maximum of ₹10–12.5/kWh, a bound that is falling, especially as cheaper finance is harnessed and economies of scale match duty cycle and location, in addition to the obvious learning-curve price reduction. Figure 10 above, shows that this leaves a small window for gas-based power. Yet another 'competitor' for gas peakers is demand-side management, including through demand response.

One other technology of possible importance is trigeneration (heating, cooling and electricity). It is more popular elsewhere, though India has piloted a few deployments. While attractive, thanks to its much higher system-level efficiency, the highest value proposition comes when all three components are in proportional demand. Otherwise, with limited heating (process or water heating) needs, that energy is 'wasted'. Even co-optimizing cooling and electricity is a challenge.

More than the competitiveness of trigeneration technology, one of the major challenges at a design level is scale. Most optimal solutions are medium sized, sizes larger than many Indian commercial establishments. Other countries talk of district-level trigeneration technology use, but issues of land, jurisdiction, and right-of-way (worse in India but a problem worldwide) complicate this optimal design.[25]

Environmental Aspects, including Carbon

Local air pollutants are a major concern in India, and the Ministry of Environment, Forest and Climate Change has issued strict emissions norms for coal power plants. Coal-based power is expected to become more expensive by several tens of paise/kWh, adding changes in both fixed and variable costs as the new norms come into force, necessitating upgrades or retrofits. However, this differential isn't sufficient to bridge the price gap between coal and gas in most cases (plants with cheap gas being an exception).

Can a carbon price make gas competitive? While there is no direct carbon price in India, the ₹400/tonne (\$5.63/tonne) coal cess is estimated at a little over \$3 per tonne of CO_2. This translates to electricity costs about 25 paise/kWh.[26] As Ali and Tongia have calculated in a forthcoming piece, even a coal cess at \$40/tonne of CO_2—a high figure unlikely to be in force for years in India—would impact coal by about ₹3/kWh (\$0.04/kWh), the differential to gas would only be about ₹1.7/kWh (\$0.02/kWh), given gas also emits CO_2.

Thus, it would take a high carbon cost to make gas competitive, that too only in some niches such as locations distant from coal plants and where reasonably priced gas is available. The ideal scenario for gas becomes strongly locational, ideally positioned where there is cheap fuel, but distant from coal and also in a low-RE region (wind is especially location-sensitive).

Conventional wisdom indicates that high delivered-coal costs in selected states, combined with low PLFs, means those plants will not find retrofitting to meet emissions norms viable and may simply shut down. Thus, any modest shift on average (at a national level) may be pronounced at a state level. Such niches appear to be a pathway for a rise in demand for gas-based power, beyond its role strictly for peaking. However, such futures could also signal a stronger transmission grid, or the faster rise of RE.

DISCUSSION: POWER WON'T BE AN ANCHOR TENANT FOR GAS DEMAND

As this chapter shows, not only is the share of electricity generated by gas-based power plants very low in India's power generation mix, even with a high peaking duty cycle, but this will also not change the picture much in terms of gas volume.

If we work backwards from the goal of tripling gas consumption by 2030, forget the much harder goal of tripling the *share of* gas in the growing energy basket and that electricity demand *won't* triple by 2030, its share in electricity generation has to grow. However, this is very difficult in the face of India's existing and underutilized coal capacity, and also because most of the growth in capacity at present comes not from gas, but from RE, which is effectively a 'must run' source.

We break down (sometimes overlapping) scenarios of the growth of gas for power generation, we find different levers or policy choices making these happen as (1) displacement of premium fuels; (2) peaking power; (3) base-load power; (4) cleaner power.

A first step for increased gas usage includes solving the supply problem. Gas plants that have to shut down due to 'no fuel' but have otherwise been competitive in the merit order should have fuel. An easy target is displacing liquid fuels used in gas-based power plants, with gas—those are expensive fuels so gas is viable for such generation. On the other hand, the use of liquid fuels by gas-based power plants is minuscule.

As we have seen, the upper bound for peaking power, based on existing plants, is about 3 per cent of today's total gas consumption. For this to materialize, other than finding cheaper input gas (today, domestic)—which is a driver for base-load gas as well—the electricity grid needs to signal grid conditions through 'time of day' pricing.

Instead of focusing on the volume of gas, policy should focus on maximizing the value proposition of gas, where, for example, in the power sector its peaking or ramping value is higher than the average cost of power. Basic policy gaps include the lack of or limited use of 'time of day' electricity pricing, more so for the grid (wholesale procurement), which is independent of consumer time-of-day pricing (a more complex undertaking that would require appropriate consumer metering hardware). Wholesale 'time of day' pricing is a niche today, as an estimated 88.3 per cent of FY2019 electricity was under PPAs that treat all electricity the same.[27]

Peaking power, high-ramping power, etc., are areas where gas has some modest role to play and these require new signalling and frameworks that go beyond 'rupees per kilowatt-hour' comparisons. While the volume may be modest, the value can be disproportional, perhaps two to three times higher. The grid needs to quickly shift to systems-level portfolio-level planning, instead of narrower competition based on levelized cost of energy (LCOE). Beyond just valuing special features of supply sources (like ramping), externalities also need to be signalled. A focus on cleaner sources can also help gas, but this would also help RE and batteries.

All these will take a few years to propagate, and the mid-2020s are also important for other reasons. First, the surplus disappears, even accounting for existing coal plants under construction.[28] Existing assets will be increasingly used, even if their PLF rise is modest. Second, RE will grow to a point where the existing grid, even with unconstrained transmission and perfect operations, cannot absorb all the RE—ToD issues will be paramount. Third, while some benefits can come from load shifting, net demand peaking in the evening means either battery technologies will have to be cost effective by then, or India will need 'something else'. Depending on what that 'something else' is, two to five years of advance planning may be required to get it ready for use by the mid-2020s.

Much of the discussion on gas for the power sector has been on the generation side, but there are additional linkages possible beyond basic generation. India has announced 100 smart cities, and we have city gas distribution (CGD) networks planned in 200 cities and towns. What, if any, is the coordination? Smart grids in the electricity sector are far ahead of smart infrastructure in gas and water, but these should synergize. Metering and billing is just one area where shared infrastructure can save costs (especially smart meters), but the linkages to a smart system may be more subtle and important. If we consider household CGD consumption, cooking is the real load, and not only is this bursty (concentrated disproportionately in the mornings and evenings), but it also leads to a low-utilization factor for the last-mile infrastructure. A more dynamic system may help with optimal pricing.

Ultimately, gas in the power sector is unlikely to grow much based solely on price: it may have a chance if we think value.

Notes

1. This is the generation from gas-based power plants, which can also run on naphtha or other liquid fuels, but the operations on liquid fuels—likely due to unavailability of natural gas—were only a tiny fraction of a per cent in FY19. Unless specified otherwise, this paper uses gas-based plants and gas generation interchangeably.

2. (The month of March over multiple years), except capacity for 2006–07, which is from the Ministry of Power's *Annual Report* 2006–07, showing capacity data for 31 January 2007. PLF is as reported, except for 2006–07, which is based on annual generation compared to a static (monthly capacity) for 2006–07.

3. Central Electricity Authority, Fuel Management Division, Annual report on fuel supply/consumption for gas-based power stations for the year 2018-19.

4. Muhammad Tabish Parray and Rahul Tongia, 'Understanding India's power capacity: Surplus or not, and for how long?', Research Paper No. 082019, New Delhi: Brookings India, 28 August 2019, https://www.brookings.edu/research/understanding-indias-power-capacity-surplus-or-not-and-for-how-long/

5. Central Electricity Authority, Fuel Management Division, Annual report on fuel supply/consumption for gas-based power stations for the year 2018-19.

6. Ibid.

7. Generation data, as seen on https://carbontracker.in/, which captures RLDC/NLDC data, accessed 12 February 2020.

8. https://carbontracker.in/ doesn't capture October 2018 or prior data, and October 2019 may not be representative of all time periods but it was the period of highest peaking output by gas and gives an illustrative example. Other years may have more peaking, but they may also have less peaking. These data are meant to be illustrative and help a bounding exercise.

9. Muhammad Tabish Parray, Rahul Tongia and Utkarsh Dalal, 'Insights from the Brookings India Electricity and Carbon Tracker', Discussion Note 092019, New Delhi: Brookings India, 17 September 2019, https://www.brookings.edu/research/insights-from-the-brookings-india-electricity-and-carbon-tracker/

10. Super-critical coal power plants, which are more efficient and represent virtually all new plants coming online, have the ability to ramp even more with appropriate design, but have to be designed to lower their output in absolute terms while maintaining super-critical operations, lest they become sub-critical operationally.

11. Parray, Dalal and Tongia, 'Insights from the Brookings India Electricity and Carbon Tracker', 2019.

12. This estimate allows for inherent variation, with some days of greater duration of maximum output, and some days less, e.g., on weekends.

13. Historical data via Petroleum Planning and Analysis Cell, New Delhi: Ministry of Petroleum, Government of India, accessed 29 January 2020, https://www.ppac.gov.in/WriteReadData/userfiles/file/NG-H-consumption.xls

14. Based on 30.99 MMscm/d as per Annual report on fuel supply/consumption for gas-based power stations for the year 2018-19, Fuel Management Division, Central Electricity Authority

15. Puneet Kamboj and Rahul Tongia, 'Indian Railways and Coal: An Unsustainable Interdependency', New Delhi: Brookings India, 17 July 2018, https://www.brookings.edu/research/indian-railways-and-coal/

16. Central Electricity Authority, fuel management division, Annual Report on fuel supply/consumption for gas-based power stations for the year 2018-19.

17. We treat most O&M costs as size-dependent fixed costs, such as salaries, annual maintenance contracts, etc.

18. This first order estimate assumes a base open-cycle gross efficiency of open-cycle systems as 33 per cent, falling slightly with PLF (analogous

to the fall modelled for combined-cycle plants), and capital costs of 2.5 crore/MW.

19. This includes the Yermarus Thermal Power Station (YTPS), a newer unit. Karnataka is also India's RE leader, but RE is also disproportionately higher in southern and western India, specifically in states far from coal mines. This calculation is based on Karnataka Power Company's 2018–19 Annual Report for generation and capacity. Power Company of Karnataka Ltd., '12th Annual Report 2018–19', Bengaluru: PCKL, Government of Karnataka, http://karnatakapower.com/wp-content/uploads/2019/12/kpcl_annual_report_2018_19.pdf

20. Grid constraints aren't just transmission bottlenecks, they are limits to how much the alternatives can reduce their output or back down (also termed flexible operations, or 'flexing'). Given that coal plants cannot turn-off and on easily, if they are required later (e.g., in the evening), then there is a limit to how low they can flex mid-day (at an RE peak). This limit is notified as 55 per cent output, but modern plants, with the right design, could go lower (albeit with an efficiency penalty).

21. These are medium-speed large-bore internal combustion engines in sizes of, say, 8–18 MW, distinct from the smaller, high-speed diesel generating sets often used by industry.

22. Wartsila has a large global fleet of such technologies, including marine applications.

23. Total power exchange volumes were much higher, in the order of 10 per cent, but most of that was not for day-ahead or term-ahead markets. See: Economics Division CERC, 'Report on Short-Term Power Market in India: 2017–2018', New Delhi: Central Electricity Regulatory Commission, Government of India, 2018, http://www.cercind.gov.in/2018/MMC/AR18.pdf

24. Rahul Tongia and Samantha Gross, 'Working to Turn Ambition into Reality: The politics and economics of India's turn to renewable power', Paper 4, Cross-Brookings Initiative on Energy and Climate Paper Series, New Delhi: Brookings India, September 2018, https://

www.brookings.edu/research/working-to-turn-ambition-into-reality/

25. Dubai's reported success with trigeneration technology has predominately 'for greenfield' deployments, or where land is accessible and plentiful.

26. Mohd. Sahil Ali and Rahul Tongia, 'Pricing Carbon Externality: Context, theory, evidence and lessons for India', in Tongia and Sehgal (eds), *Future of Coal India*, 2020.

27. This estimate is from IEX's presentation *Indian Energy Exchange October 2019*, online at https://www.iexindia.com/Uploads/Presentation/18_11_2019Presentation_Nov_2019.pdf. Of the remaining 12 per cent, only about 4 per cent was through markets, with the rest split between traders, unscheduled interchange, and direct bilaterals (in descending order).

28. About 30 GW of surplus, plus 20 GW of plants retired, plus 40 GW under-construction means about 50 GW of non-RE, non-hydro/nuclear capacity pipeline visibility. With an annual demand growth of about 10 GW, this will take five years.

13

CITY GAS DISTRIBUTION: EMERGING POTENTIAL?

ASHU SINGHAL

Chief GM (Corp. Strategy, Planning & Advocacy), GAIL;
Director, OPAL

RAJEEV MATHUR

Executive Director, GAIL (India) Ltd

INTRODUCTION

CITY GAS RETAIL STARTED IN India during the 1880s when the Calcutta Gas Company (formerly Oriental Gas) and the Bombay Gas Company began operations in Calcutta (now Kolkata) and Bombay (now Mumbai), respectively, with coal gas as the primary input. After a century of operations, the demand for coal gas, also known as synthesis gas, declined in Mumbai to the extent that the Bombay Gas Company was forced to close down its operations in 1980. In Kolkata, coal-gas supply continued and the original company, Oriental Gas was succeeded by the Greater Calcutta Gas Supply Corporation in 1987 and then by the Bengal Gas Ltd in 1962. Coal-gas supplies had spread to other states too. The Assam Gas Company was formed and in 1972,

317

the Vadodara Municipal Corporation started supplying coal gas to the city of Vadodara (then Baroda), in Gujarat.

The formation of the Gujarat Gas Company Limited (GGCL), Mahanagar Gas Limited (MGL, in Maharashtra), and Indraprastha Gas Limited (IGL, in New Delhi), which began operations in the late 1980s and the mid-1990s, gave a real thrust to the Indian city gas distribution (CGD) sector. As of 2020, CGD has a presence in 232 cities/geographical areas (GAs) and is expected to cover 53 per cent of India's geographical area and 70 per cent of India's population by 2030.

Access to energy is pivotal for any economic development and India's future development is heavily dependent on the sustainable growth of cities and access to clean and affordable energy. Growing urbanization and the consequential pollution poses serious threats, with catastrophic consequences in both rural and urban areas. Diesel-related pollutants are either already very high or rapidly increasing in Indian cities. As per the database released by the World Health Organization in May 2018, India had fourteen out of fifteen of the world's most polluted cities in terms of PM 2.5 concentration.[1] While carbon dioxide (CO_2) is responsible for global warming, it is the PM 2.5 particles and sulphur and nitrogen oxides (SOx and NOx) that are more dangerous for human health.[2] Studies have already established close links between exposure to fine particles and premature deaths from heart and lung disease.

The implementation of a nationwide CGD network is one way to tackle these problems without causing discomfort to its citizens. The ninth and tenth rounds of bidding for CGD, are significant initiatives to leapfrog to higher gas usage and to address urban pollution across the country. Due to lower emissions, switching to natural gas-based vehicles (NGVs), especially CNG, can help mitigate growing urban vehicular pollution. The first CNG station in India came up in 1992 in Surat, Gujarat followed by Delhi in 1993. Delhi and Mumbai started implementing CNG vehicle programmes on a large scale as a substitution for diesel during the late 1990s, when even Euro-I emissions standards were not in place and the sulphur content of diesel in India was as high as 5,000–10,000 ppm.[3] With fuel substitution, these cities were able to leapfrog to much cleaner emission levels, primarily targeting the most polluting segments on Indian roads that include diesel buses, three-wheelers, taxis and small commercial vehicles; CNG also offers the greater benefit of lowering CO_2 emissions, given the lower carbon content of the fuel.

Apart from vehicular pollution, many small and medium enterprises (MSMEs) emit harmful pollutants like CO_2 and other poisonous particles such as PM 10, arsenic, black carbon, formaldehyde, nickel and sulphur and nitrogen oxides. They consume cheaper but polluting fuels such as pet coke and furnace oil. A few Indian courts have recently banned the use of pet coke in states within their jurisdiction, but further actions are needed in this direction. The implementation of CGD projects can play a significant role in reducing localized pollution in urban spaces and can also contribute significantly towards lowering carbon emissions as a whole—CNG can act as a substitute for other polluting transport fuels and PNG can be used as domestic kitchen fuel as well as fuel for industries and commercial units.

According to a report published by Washington DC-based think-tank, Resources for the Future, the conversion of public transport to CNG made the 'most significant' impact on air quality in Delhi in fifteen years. A World Bank study published in 2004 also concluded that CNG had helped reduce the annual number of premature deaths—at least 3,629 in Delhi and at least 5,308 in Mumbai.[4]

In terms of cost, natural gas (as CNG) is 60 per cent cheaper than petrol and 45 per cent cheaper than diesel.[5] Similarly, as PNG, it is 40 per cent cheaper than LPG at market price. It almost matches the rate of LPG (based on prices in Delhi). An auto-rickshaw owner can save ₹7,000–8,000 ($100.1–$114.41) on his monthly fuel bill by converting to CNG from petrol.[6]

Rapid urbanization and increase in population demand sustainable and clean fuel. According to a report by the United Nations' World Urbanization Prospects in 2018, about 34 per cent of India's population now lives in urban areas, an increase from 30 per cent in 2011.[7] As more and more people move to urban areas, this results in the growth of urban clusters, where there is a constant demand for clean and affordable energy for mobility, heat, lighting and cooking by domestic, commercial and industrial users. In this regard, CGDs can provide a sustainable solution for urban energy needs.

This chapter aims to address the concerns that already exist or are likely to come up with the increased implementation of CGD networks.

ASSESSMENT OF EXISTING NETWORKS

GEOGRAPHIES SERVICED

By March 2020, 232 Geographic Areas (GAs) across India in 407 districts were covered under CGD networks, and about 6.07 million households and 3.375 million CNG vehicles were availing the benefit of clean fuel through existing CGD networks.

Prior to 2007, the CGD business in India was driven primarily by the active intervention of environmental groups and the judiciary, and dominated by a handful of entities including AGCL, IGL, MGL and GSPCL. In 2007, the Petroleum and Natural Gas Regulatory Board (PNGRB) envisaged the expansion of CGD networks to over 300 cities in India (from 30 cities in 2007), to ensure the availability of natural gas for urban consumers. Subsequently, the eighth bidding round was conducted till November 2016 and the number of CGD GAs increased to eighty-six in 2016.[8] Additional six cities were authorized to GAIL under Pradhan Mantri Urga Ganga (JHBDPL) project. By March 2018, the CGD network covered ninety-two GAs in twenty-three states/ union territories with a pipeline network of over 50,000 km. The PNG domestic customer base reached 4.26 million apart from over 26,000 commercial and 7,600 industrial connections. With all these rounds, CGD gas consumption as a proportion of total gas consumption rose from 1 per cent in 2000 to about 16 per cent in 2018.[9]

To further boost the CGD network, the PNGRB launched the ninth round of CGD bidding in April 2018 and the tenth round in November 2018. The ninth round was the largest of all the bidding rounds, with 86 GAs covering 174 districts across 22 states/union territories. It covered 26 per cent of India's population and 24 per cent of its area. After the ninth round of bidding, the potential coverage of CGD networks in India reached 50 per cent of the country's population, and over 35 per cent of its area.[10]

According to commitments made by various entities during the ninth round of bidding, around 200 million PNG (domestic) connections and 4,600 CNG stations are expected to be installed in the next eight years across the country. Further, under the tenth CGD round, work in another 50 GAs covering 124 districts (112 complete and 12 partial) in 14 states are in progress, accounting for 18 per cent of India's geographical area and 24 per cent of its population. It is expected that the CGD network will cover over 70 per cent of India's population and 53 per cent of the area after completion of work under both ninth and tenth round.[11] The eleventh round of CGD bidding is under consideration, with 44 additional GAs.

Figure 1: Gas Infrastructure Map, 2018

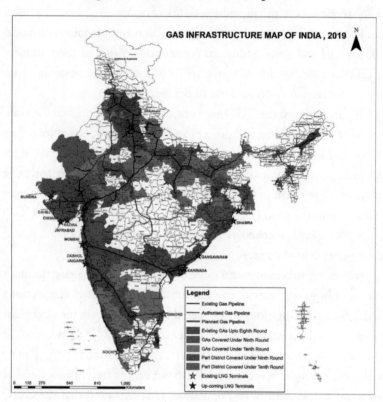

Source: PNGRB.[12]

Figure 2: Gas and percentage of population covered after the round of bidding

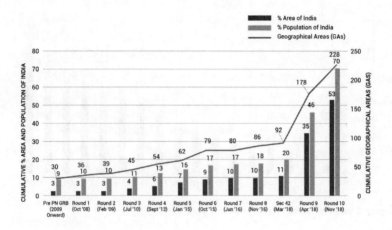

Source: PNGRB.[13]

GAS SUPPLY ALLOCATION

The Ministry of Petroleum and Natural Gas has accorded priority to domestic gas in the PNG (domestic) and CNG (transport) demand sector of the CGD network, as part of an allocation to push gas to substitute liquid fuel and LPG in urban areas. This priority on allocation of domestic gas makes CGD a key driver for India's natural gas consumption. As a result, the share of CGDs in the overall domestic gas consumption pie is on the rise and is likely to increase in the short-to-medium term. The new authorizations in the ninth and tenth rounds of bidding also ensure that CGD networks grow at a faster pace. Currently, CGD consumes over 16 per cent of India's natural gas consumption.

Figure 3: Increase in IGL gas sales over the years (MMscm/d)

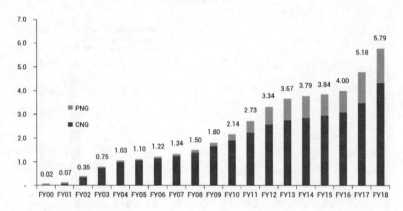

Source: Compiled from IGL Investors presentations (IGL, 2021).

Figure 4: IGL's historical Turnover, PAT and CapEx since inception (₹Cr)

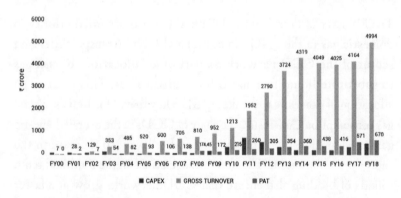

Source: Compiled from IGL Investor presentation (IGL, 2021).[14]

CHALLENGES IN EXPANSION OF CGD NETWORKS

While the sector is still developing in India, CGD businesses face some basic concerns which require intervention from various stakeholders. Although India has expanded its natural gas transfer pipeline infrastructure significantly in recent years, with a vision to complete the National Gas Grid (NGG), it needs further steps to create a robust CGD network. Apart from pipeline connectivity, CGD business needs huge investment with a long gestation period, as it takes time to complete the laying of networks and to develop the market in a new area. The end customers always have a choice of fuel and, therefore, CGD markets are intrinsically market-regulated. A long gestation period, coupled with initial low volume off-take, can adversely impact the CGD business. On average, investment in CGD networks is about ₹3–4 billion ($42–57 million) per city with an average demand for around 1.5 million metric standard cubic metres a day (MMscm/d). Cities with CGD networks have seen limited vehicular conversion to gas from liquids, owing to perceived gas price uncertainty and inconvenient access at retail stations.

Commercial Challenges

Demand in Tier II and Tier III towns

Despite the overwhelming response to the ninth and tenth rounds, there are still apprehensions about the adoptability and expansion of CGD in smaller cities. The feasibility of CGD is highly sensitive to capturing the latent demand in the GA and to policy and environmental regulations that support the adoption of natural gas. The CGD network is highly capital-intensive in nature. A typical CGD network requires an investment of ₹3–4 billion ($42–57 million) to service a volume of around 1.5 MMscm/d. Typically, the CGD network's consumer segment consists of four major segments—households, and the transportation, industrial and commercial sectors.

Transportation demand in a new GA has a naturally long gestation period due to initial low adaptation and conversion rate from liquid fuels to CNG. Domestic PNG connections are often used to measure success for CGD, but the ground realities are quite different. For every PNG connection, a CGD entity incurs a cost of around ₹18,000–20,000 and the customer pays around ₹5,000 as a refundable security deposit. It takes time to recover such PNG CapEx. Low and slow penetration (50–60 per cent even for long-established CGDs) and equally low consumption (less than 15 scm per month) makes it difficult for CGDs to recover CapEx and OpEx involved. Further, the sparse population density in Tier II/III cities increases the CapEx towards connecting a single household. Therefore, the long gestation period coupled with low volume off-take, can adversely impact the CGD business. The CGD operators counter this low-volume risk via bulk customers in industrial and commercial sectors. Therefore, the absence of such industrial/commercial clusters/establishments in Tier II and Tier III towns, along with poor awareness about cleaner energy options and laxity in implementation of stricter environment norms, can hamper CGD growth.

Infeasibility of aggressive bids

Given the challenge in meeting demand, the aggressive bidding in recent bidding rounds can affect the Internal Rate of Return (IRR) and the project investment rate of return for investors. Moreover, the slow build-up of revenue and volumes may lead to low debt serviceability of the new CGD companies and there is substantial risk that some CGD entities may become non-performing assets (NPAs) and be unable to complete infrastructure development plans as committed in the bids submitted to the PNGRB.

A similar situation occurred when projects in a common carrier natural-gas pipeline network authorized by the PNGRB, were later besieged with implementation problems, due to viability issues. In the future, we may see a lot of consolidation in the CGD sector to save cost and increase efficiency.

Skilled workforce availability

The increase in CGD capacity translates to significant skilled workforce requirements for operations, maintenance and commissioning jobs. The sector is projected to require around 55,000 people by 2023, due to exponential growth in pipeline infrastructure and the network, while the CNG/PNG marketing business needs close to 3,500 people.[15] Despite the overall technological advancement in the oil and gas sector, the availability of additional skilled workforce to undertake the expansion and the retention of this talent at this large scale is expected to be a challenge for the industry.

Low penetration of gas-based equipment and appliances

Gas-based equipment is not very popular in the Indian market and market penetration of gas-based water heaters, generators, and water pumps is quite low. This CNG market needs to be expanded further from focusing on three-wheelers, buses, and cars (given the potential of electric vehicles (EVs) as a competitor) to include heavy vehicles via LNG (as discussed in Chapter 16). Setting up LNG stations as a CGD bidding criteria can help to infuse LNG in the Indian transportation sector.

Logistical Challenges

The connectivity of GAs to trunk pipelines is another issue. The construction of many pipelines, authorized by the PNGRB, is running behind schedule as most developers are struggling with the viability of projects. The completion of these pipelines will be essential for the seamless supply of gas in new CGDs in the vicinity of those pipelines. In many cases, there is no pipeline connectivity to the allotted GAs and in other cases, one has to lay long-distance spur lines to provide connectivity or arrange alternate mechanisms (LNG by trucks, LCNG, etc.). As CGD entities have low gas consumption initially, there is little incentive for pipeline developers to lay a pipeline network. They are considered an anchor load in the current tariff regime. As the initial demand for new GAs is expected to be on the lower side, it is essential to provide a mechanism for GAs to ensure gas availability.

Regulatory Challenges

Multiple clearances

Permissions from different state, central and local authorities and varying high charges levied by these authorities, are the primary challenges to developing CGD infrastructure. Presently, many states seek annual lease rentals, plus property tax on the length of pipelines laid, which adversely affects the capacity of CGDs to develop infrastructure. Further, CGD authorization is controlled by central agencies like the PNGRB and states have limited say. The implementation of CGD requires close coordination and fast decision-making among all entities, to resolve ongoing issues facing development. It is important to make local governments enabling partners in the endeavour for speedy and successful implementation.

The speedy implementation of CGD projects in crowded urban areas faces many roadblocks. In most Indian cities, there is no provision for the availability of separate utility corridors for the laying of gas pipelines in the city. This results in the laying of pipelines along the roadsides or under pathways. This process results in taking clearances from city governments and other various government bodies and utilities such as corporations/municipalities/development authorities, other utility providers (water/telecom/electricity), other urban developers (road/bridge/rapid transit, etc.)

Bidding parameters

Bidding parameters in previous rounds focused on tariffs and quantum of performance guarantees and many bidders quoted close to zero tariffs with high-performance guarantees. As these tariffs were low and unviable, there may be no real development on the ground, leading to slow development of last-mile connectivity to domestic consumers.

As the previous CGD auctions were marred by bidders offering to charge a 'one paisa' tariff for the connections, the bidding parameters—for obtaining a licence to retail CNG and PNG in cities—were changed for the ninth round of bidding by the PNGRB. In the previous eight rounds on CGD bidding, companies were asked to quote tariffs for pipelines that carried gas within city limits. However, this bidding criterion did not include rates at which an entity would sell CNG to automobiles or PNG to households using the same pipeline networks. Since the rate of sale of CNG/PNG was not specified, it led to companies offering one paisa as the tariff to win licences.

The ninth round of CGD bidding gave more weightage to the physical work programme, i.e., domestic connection, CNG stations and the laying of pipelines. There was a greater focus on creating a higher number of CNG outlets and PNG connections. Higher marks were set for these two parameters, which were given 70 per cent of the bidding weightage. The tariff for CNG and PNG transportation within the city—previously the deciding criteria for winning a licence—was given just 10 per cent weightage.

The existing CGD model is a fixed bid tariff per unit of energy (MMBtu). However, the volume risk remains with the project investor. As the volume is low initially, investors are unable to recoup their cost during the initial years. Further, aggressive bidding has been seen in the ninth and tenth bidding rounds, where players promised to bid to cover 100 per cent of the population by PNG, which is very challenging.

Policy Challenges

Current tax regime

Natural gas is not under the good and services tax (GST) regime, which makes it expensive in comparison to alternatives. Under the current regime, the sale of natural gas attracts state value-added tax (VAT) and other charges which range from 0–20 per cent in various states.

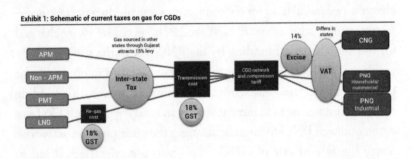

Exhibit 1: Schematic of current taxes on gas for CGDs

Source: GAIL and MOSL Analysis.[16]

For example, Delhi charges nil, while Maharashtra charges 13.5 per cent, Bihar 20 per cent and Gujarat charges 15 per cent. Apart from these, there are interstate taxes as well. For example, Gujarat levies 15 per cent on IGL and MGL for sourcing gas. When IGL sources its gas from Gujarat, it attracts 15 per cent interstate tax, 18 per cent GST on transmission and regasification—which results in an effective tax of 20 per cent on CNG, 11 per cent on PNG-domestic, and 15 per cent on PNG-industrial. On the other hand, MGL incurs an effective 31 per cent on CNG, 15 per cent on PNG-domestic and 25 per cent on PNG-industrial.[17] Further, CNG attracts an excise duty of 14 per cent, as it falls under manufactured goods. But as CNG is just a compressed form of natural gas, there shouldn't be any excise duty on it.

Exhibit 2: Summary of calculations for CNG and PNG-domestic

CNG price build-up (pre-GST)	IGL	MGL	GUJG
Domestic price (USD/mmBtu)*	3.8	3.8	3.8
INR/USD	69.0	69.0	69.0
Domestic price (INR/mmBtu)	260	260	260
Interstate tax (%)^	15.0	4.1	0.0
Interstate tax (INR/mmBtu)	38.9	10.7	0.0
Transmission cost (INR/mmBtu)@	85.0	30.0	30.0
GST on transmission (%)	18.0	18.0	18.0
GST on transmission (INR/mmBtu)	15.3	5.4	5.4
CNG sourcing cost (INR/mmBtu)	399	306	295
CNG sourcing cost (INR/scm)	15.8	12.1	11.7
CNG sales price excld excise (INR/kg)	36.8	35.7	38.7
Excise duty (%)	14.0	14.0	14.0
Excise on CNG (INR/kg)	5.2	5.0	5.4
CNG sales price incld excise (INR/kg)	42.0	40.7	44.1
VAT (%)	0.0	13.5	15.0
VAT on CNG (INR/kg)	0.0	5.5	6.6
CNG sales price incld VAT (INR/scm)	42.0	46.2	50.8
Total tax incurred (INR/kg)	7.2	11.1	12.0
Effective tax on sales price (%)	19.6	31.0	31.1

PNG Domestic price build-up	IGL	MGL	GUJG
Domestic price (USD/mmBtu)*	3.8	3.8	3.8
INR/USD	69.0	69.0	69.0
Domestic price (INR/mmBtu)	260	260	260
Interstate tax (%)^	15.0	4.1	0.0
Interstate tax (INR/mmBtu)	38.9	10.7	0.0
Transmission cost (INR/mmBtu)@	85.0	30.0	30.0
GST on transmission (%)	18.0	18.0	18.0
GST on transmission (INR/mmBtu)	15.3	5.4	5.4
PNG sourcing cost (INR/mmBtu)	399	306	295
PNG sourcing cost (INR/scm)	15.8	12.1	11.7
PNG sales price excld VAT (INR/scm)#	25.8	24.0	21.9
VAT (%)	5.0	13.5	15.0
VAT on PNG (INR/scm)	1.3	3.2	3.3
PNG sales price incld VAT (INR/scm)	27.1	27.3	25.2
Total tax incurred (INR/scm)	2.8	3.7	3.3
Effective tax on sales price (%)	11.0	15.3	15.0

*Assuming 22% PMT, rest at APM price; ^IGL gets all gas from Gujarat, MGL gets PMT from Gujarat; @indicative, not actual; #Excise is nil on piped natural gas

Source: MOSL Analysis.[18]

Exhibit 3: Summary of calculations for PNG-industrial/commercial

PNG Industrial/commercial price build-up (pre-GST)	IGL	MGL	GUJGA
CIF price (USD/mmBtu)@	10.3	10.3	10.3
INR/USD	69.0	69.0	69.0
Gas price (INR/mmBtu)	707.3	707.3	707.3
Interstate tax (%)	15.0	15.0	0.0
Interstate tax (INR/mmBtu)	106	106	0
Regas cost (INR/mmBtu)	48.0	48.0	48.0
GST on regas (%)	18.0	18.0	18.0
GST on regas (INR/mmBtu)	8.6	8.6	8.6
Transmission cost (INR/mmBtu)	85.0	30.0	30.0
GST on transmission (%)	18.0	18.0	18.0
GST on transmission (INR/mmBtu)	15.3	5.4	5.4
PNG sourcing cost (INR/mmBtu)	970	905	799
PNG sourcing cost (INR/scm)	38.5	35.9	31.7
PNG sales price excluding VAT (INR/scm)@	41.9	37.0	32.1
VAT (%)	5.0	13.5	6.0
VAT on PNG (INR/scm)	2.1	5.0	1.9
PNG sales price including VAT (INR/scm)@	44.0	42.0	34.0
Total tax incurred (INR/scm)	6.3	9.2	1.9
Effective tax on sales price (%)	15.0	24.9	6.0

Source: (MOSL, 2018).[19]

RECOMMENDATIONS AND THE WAY FORWARD

PNG CONNECTIONS

Piped Natural Gas (PNG) is an important focus area for India to provide affordable and clean energy to every household. It should be promoted at the time of the development of new residential neighbourhoods. Also, in order to increase the penetration of PNG connections, PNG connections should be made mandatory by municipal authorities while granting new building approvals in areas where CGD has been in existence for two to three years, particularly, for high-rise buildings. As PNG customers may not be ready to invest in connection charges, this amount may be provided as a grant to CGD entities through a financing agency, and the same may be recovered in instalments along with monthly charges over a two-year period for new PNG customers.

Marketing Exclusivity

It is observed in other gas distribution markets—developing countries, developed countries as well as cold countries where gas is important for heating purposes—that there is both supply/marketing and distribution exclusivity. As markets mature, a typically phased competition is introduced on supply/marketing. The exclusivity of infrastructure, over the term of the licence period, helps to avoid duplication of assets.

Promoting Gas-based Products

The government needs to look at promoting the adoption of gas-based equipment in urban areas. This can result in higher consumption in households and commercial establishments in CGDs. City Gas Distribution companies, along with equipment/appliance manufacturers need to increase their effort in this segment. Further, services offered by CGD companies may evolve in the future. They may offer a bundled energy solution to consumers, which could likely include emerging technologies such as gas engines for distributed power, micro-turbines, trigeneration, vapour-absorption chillers, water-heat recovery systems and fuel cells.

The GST on CNG vehicles may be reduced, registration charges for new CNG autos/taxis may be waived, and CNG may be mandated for public transportation. Further, state governments may encourage the procurement of CNG buses by bus transport departments/agencies wherever CNG is available. Gas-based generators may be mandated for commercial establishments/hospitals, etc., in CGD areas. Domestic gas may be allocated for new segments within the CGD sector, such as the MSME segment and gas-based generators, in RWAs/Mobile Towers.

Unified Planner (for CGD and Trunk Pipelines)

Despite the presence of the PNGRB, outcomes on CGD penetration so far have been mixed and in many cases have fallen short of expectations.

For the long-term development of the Indian gas sector, pipeline development and creating demand centres should go hand in hand. For this, it is necessary to separate the developmental and regulatory functions of the PNGRB, as recommended by NITI Aayog in its document 'Strategy for New India @ 75'.[20] While regulatory functions may be with the PNGRB, the development of gas network can be taken up by the Ministry of Planning and Natural Gas through the formation of a Gas Advisory Body (GAB). The policy for 'Development of Natural Gas Pipeline and City or Local Natural Gas Distribution Network' 2006 also recommended the creation of GAB, comprising all major stakeholders in the development of gas pipelines and CGD networks. This body can not only look at long-term planning for the natural-gas sector, but also be empowered to ease the number of permissions required by the CGD developers.

Single-window permissions and clearances for speedy implementation of CGD projects, putting online the process for obtaining permissions/licenses (such as obtaining a 'no objection certificate' from the district magistrate; a licence from the Petroleum and Explosives Safety Organization [PESO]) with a time limit, and no requirement of hard copies/paper copies, would help too.

UTILITY CORRIDOR

As land in urban spaces becomes more and more precious, there is an urgent need to set up utility corridors in cities, for the speedy implementation of infrastructure projects. In thriving metros (e.g., in cities like Bengaluru) implementing agencies get very little time to lay pipelines considering day-time traffic. With utility corridors, the cost of new urban infrastructure may be shared among various implementing agencies like water, sewage, electricity, gas and the cost of all utilities will be cheaper for consumers

The provision of a utility corridor will also save time and cost for all implementing agencies who have to take several permissions from various civic authorities. Apart from this, various civil agencies demand hefty charges against permissions for laying pipelines inside urban areas. This practice is significantly pushing up capital costs of building CGD infrastructure. Restoration charges should be rationalized for CGD in line with other utility services. Land should be allocated with cities at a reasonable rate for installing CNG stations/district regulating stations (DRS), metre regulating stations (MRS), etc. Further, 'Change in Land Use' (CLU) should be rationalized for setting-up CNG stations.

CGD Development Council

This council comprising key stakeholders—such as the PNGRB, the power and natural gas ministry, the Central and state governments, local authorities/municipalities, transmission companies and CGD entities—could be a game-changer. The council should be empowered to deliberate all critical issues creating bottlenecks. It should provide timely decisions binding upon all, including the laying down of a uniform policy on the grant of permissions and charges, applicable across all states on the theme of One India-One Policy; the allotment of land parcels for city gas stations and CNG stations at preferred rates; and should cut down the lag in achieving time-bound connectivity of GAs with transmission lines, which in many cases is as high as 70–80 km.

Green Push

From the standpoint of environmental sustainability, natural gas scores the highest among all competing hydrocarbon fuels. However, in terms of affordability to end-consumers, in the peak commodity-cycle phases, natural gas may not be able to compete with alternative fuels on price. Also, the consumer perception of uninterrupted availability of PNG or CNG is hard to build. Thus, a government mandate may be required to promote the usage of CNG and PNG.

The past experience of CNG usage in cities such as Delhi and Mumbai suggests that penetration of natural gas as CNG has taken-off only when it was mandated for public transport. Reciprocating the increasing availability of CNG infrastructure in many states/GAs, there is a need for state governments to boost efforts in making public transport infrastructure CNG compliant. A one-time investment to convert fleets to CNG would help in cutting down air pollution significantly and would also save public money. Restriction on polluting fuels (like petroleum coke and furnace oil) in CGD areas would encourage industrial/manufacturing consumers to switch to cleaner industrial PNG.

The benefits offered by CNG and PNG, such as a cleaner environment and reduced health costs are adequate drivers for the Government of India to mandate their use. Considering the social benefits of natural gas, taxes on fuel need to be reduced drastically to promote rapid adoption. The inclusion of natural gas under the GST net can solve the issue of the imperious movement of natural gas; CNG, PNG-domestic, and PNG-industrial may be treated differently under GST. This could enable better penetration of CNG and PNG-domestic through a possible increase in savings against alternate fuels. Another option could be keeping all segments under one GST rate.

Notes

1. World Health Organization, Global Ambient Air Quality Database, 2018, https://www.who.int/airpollution/data/cities/en/
2. PM or particulate matter consisting of arsenic, black carbon, formaldehyde and nickel.
3. International Council for Clean Transportation, 'India: Fuels: Diesel and Gasoline', Washington DCP: ICCT, 2018, https://www.transportpolicy.net/standard/india-fuels-diesel-and-gasoline/
4. Environment and Social Development Unit, 'For a Breath of Fresh Air: Ten Years of Progress and Challenges in Urban Air Quality

Management in India 1993–2002', New Delhi: South Asia Unit, World Bank, 2004.

5. CNG: ₹44.30/kg, Petrol: ₹72.81/Ltr, Diesel: ₹66.49, Commercial LPG: ₹62.36/kg in March 2019 in Delhi

6. Press Information Bureau, 2018. www.pib.nic.in/:www.pib.nic.in/ PressReleaseIframePage.aspx?PRID=1553241

7. UN Department of Social and Economic Affairs, '2018 Revision of World Urbanization Prospects', New York: United Nations, 16 May 2018, https://www.un.org/development/desa/ publications/2018-revision-of-world-urbanization-prospects. html#:~:text=Today%2C%2055%25%20of%20the%20 world's,increase%20to%2068%25%20by%202050.&text=The%20 level%20of%20urbanization%20in,population%20living%20in%20 urban%20areas.

8. Authorized geographical area (GA) means the area as defined under the Petroleum and Natural Gas Regulatory Board (Authorizing Entities to Lay, Build, Operate or Expand City or Local Natural Gas Distribution Networks) Regulations, 2008

9. McKinsey & Company, 'Unlocking gas potential: new business models', Paper presented at Petrotech-2019: Shaping the New Energy World through Innovation & Collaboration, 13th International Oil & Gas Exhibition, 10–12 February 2019, Greater Noida, https:// www.igxindia.com/wp-content/uploads/Theme-Session-McKinsey-Unlocking-gas-potential.pdf

10. Press Information Bureau, 'Hon'ble Prime Minister to lay Foundation Stones of City Gas Distribution (CGD) Projects in 65 Geographical Areas (GAs) in 129 Districts under the 9th CGD Bidding Round', New Delhi: PIB, 20 November 2018, 'Shri Dharmendra Pradhan distributes Letters of Intent', https://pib.gov.in/Pressreleaseshare. aspx?PRID=1553241

11. Ibid.

12. Gas Infrastructure Map of India, https://www.pngrb.gov.in/pdf/FinalGAsFullDistric-Map_14-02-2020.jpg

13. PNGRB brochure for 10th bidding round, https://www.pngrb.gov.in/pdf/cgd/bid10/brochure.pdf

14. https://iglonline.net/english/Default.aspx?option=article&type=single&id=35&mnuid=163&prvtyp=site

15. Infraline, 'Challenges in Natural Gas Distribution Sector of India', Infraline (blog) 12 October 2018, http://www.infraline.com/infraline-energy/blogs/185/3/home.aspx

16 https://www.motilaloswal.com/site/rreports/636670969386633069.pdf

17. Swarnendu Bhushan and Abhinil Dahiwale, 'Oil & Gas: Sector Update', 2018, *Motilal Oswal*, https://www.motilaloswal.com/site/rreports/636670969386633069.pdf.

18. https://www.motilaloswal.com/site/rreports/636670969386633069.pdf

19. https://www.motilaloswal.com/site/rreports/636670969386633069.pdf

20. NITI Aayog, 'Strategy for New India @ 75', New Delhi: NITI Aayog, Government of India, November 2018, https://niti.gov.in/sites/default/files/2019-01/Strategy_for_New_India_2.pdf

14

FERTILIZERS: A REGULATORY DILEMMA?

ASHOK GULATI

Infosys Chair Professor for Agriculture

PRITHA BANERJEE

ICRIER

BACKGROUND

INDIA'S SUCCESS IN TRANSITIONING FROM a 'ship-to-mouth' situation on the foodgrain front in the mid-1960s, to a self-sufficient country in basic staples (rice and wheat), and even a net exporter of cereals later, is well known. Today, India stands as the largest exporter of rice, exporting roughly 12 metric million tonnes (MMt) every year, valued at more than $7 billion per year, and India's granaries are overflowing. Stocks of cereals with the Central government stood at more than 81 MMt as of 1 July 2019, against a buffer stock norm of 41 MMt. All this would not have been possible without the Green Revolution (GR) in 1966–67.

The GR technology was a package of high yielding variety (HYV) seeds of wheat and rice. The new HYVs responded very well to higher doses of fertilizers, giving a response ratio of grains-to-fertilizer use as high as thirteen in the initial years of GR. In a way, therefore, one can say, at the least, that fertilizers played a catalytic role, along with HYV seeds and irrigation, in converting India from a hugely deficit country in staples to a country comfortably in surplus.

Keeping in mind the catalytic role of fertilizers, one of the key objectives of policymakers has been to ramp up the production of fertilizers at home. But as things stand on the raw material front, India is wholly dependent on imports for potassic (K) and phosphatic fertilizers (P) (either imports of rock or finished products). Therefore, the major focus of policymakers in ramping up domestic production capacity was for nitrogenous fertilizers (N), especially urea. Today, India produces roughly 24 MMt of urea in thirty urea plants in the country. The prime feedstock of the urea industry is natural gas, accounting for about 94 per cent of urea production, with the remaining 6 per cent coming from naphtha-based plants.

To encourage farmers to use chemical fertilizers, Indian policy for long has been to subsidize them for the benefit of farmers, i.e., selling fertilizers below the normative cost of production and distribution. The subsidy is given to fertilizer plants. In the Union budget of 2019–20, the fertilizer subsidy is provisioned at roughly ₹800 billion ($11.44 billion). The fertilizer industry claims this is severely under-provisioned as they already have dues of more than ₹390 billion ($5.5 billion), which have not been paid by the government.[1]

Among the fertilizers that are used in India, urea is the most heavily subsidized product. Almost 75 per cent of its costs are covered by government subsidies, while di-ammonium phosphate and muriate of potash carry a subsidy of about 25 per cent over their cost. This translates to about two-thirds of the total subsidy in the Union budget of 2019–20 being directed to urea while the remaining subsidies go to other nutrients. As a result of this massive subsidization of urea, its consumption increased from 14.1 MMt in 1990–91 to 23.9 MMt in

2018–19.[2] Despite increasing consumption, domestic production of urea has stagnated after 2009–10,[3] due to increased uncertainty over incentives for the industry, thereby increasing import dependency.

Increasing consumption has resulted in the amount of subsidy for urea also rising. In the last twenty years (from 2000–01 to 2018–19), urea subsidy (annual) has escalated from ₹94.81 billion ($1.35 billion) to ₹449.95 billion ($6.43 billion) at current prices. The subsidy on urea has been rising for both indigenous and imported urea consumption. While the subsidy on imported urea is related to the fluctuations in its world price, the increasing subsidy on indigenous urea is linked to rising costs of production, primarily driven by the escalating price of natural gas supplied to the sector.

Against this background, this paper attempts to dig deeper into the role of natural gas in the urea sector and how its pricing and the allocation of domestic gas across various consuming sectors, impacts urea subsidies. Accordingly, the second section examines the landscape of natural gas in India: its production, import and consumption, its allocation across various consuming sectors (especially that of domestic gas), its pricing and implications for urea subsidy, etc. In the third section, we take up the issue of the 'Make-Buy' option and evaluate the global competitiveness of India's urea industry.

This raises interesting questions about the five new plants being taken up, cost estimates of which are likely to be between $400 and $500/Mt while existing plants produce urea at around $332/Mt. On the basis of the analysis carried out in the previous sections, the last section suggests a way forward, by giving fertilizer subsidies directly to farmers on a per-hectare basis and by freeing up the fertilizer and gas sectors from all controls. It makes a case that the time to reform is now when India is hugely surplus in basic cereals.

THE LANDSCAPE OF NATURAL GAS IN INDIA

Production, Consumption and Imports

If one looks at the domestic production of natural gas in India since 2001–02, one observes three strands: (a) production was largely stagnant during 2001–02 to 2007–08; (b) it increased sharply during 2008–09 to 2010–11; and (c) since 2011–12 to 2017–18,[4] it experienced a declining trend (Figure 1). The consumption of natural gas, however, increased over the entire period from 28 billion cubic metres (Bcm) in 2001–02 to 52.84 Bcm in 2017–18. The consumption and domestic production of natural gas largely matched each other during 2001–02 to 2010–11, but thereafter, domestic production did not keep pace with demand resulting in increasing imports of liquefied natural gas (LNG). (Figure 1)

Figure 1: Domestic production and consumption of natural gas in India (increasing import dependency)

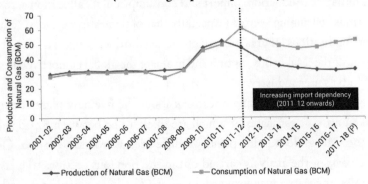

Source: Constructed using the data in Energy Statistics 2019, Ministry of Statistics and Programme Implementation, Government of India, 2019.[5]

Sector-wise Offtake of Natural Gas in India

In 2017–18, the fertilizer sector was the largest consumer of natural gas in India (28 per cent of total offtake) followed by power (23 per cent), transmission and distribution (16 per cent), refinery (12 per cent) and petrochemicals (8 per cent). These five sectors together constitute almost 87 per cent of the total offtake of natural gas in the country (Figure 2).

Over the last ten years, there has been a change in the share of different sectors (Figure 2)in the offtake of natural gas. Up to 2012–13, the power sector used to be the highest consumer of natural gas in India (almost 30 per cent in 2012–13), while the fertilizer segment was the second highest (almost 27 per cent in 2012–13). In 2017–18, the situation reversed, and the fertilizer industry has now become the highest consumer of natural gas.

Figure 2: Sector-wise offtake of natural gas: Changes over the last ten years

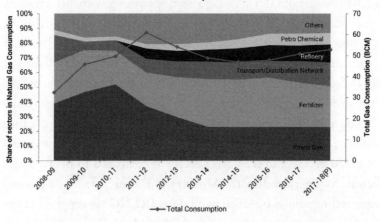

Source: Constructed using the data in Energy Statistics 2019, Ministry of Statistics and Programme Implementation, Government of India, 2019.[6]

Relative Shares of Major Consuming Sectors in Domestically Produced Natural Gas

The fertilizer industry is the most prioritized sector for the distribution of natural gas in India. According to government guidelines in 2010, for pricing and commercial utilization of natural gas,[7] the first three sectors in order of priority are gas-based fertilizer plants, LPG plants and power plants supplying to the grid. It was also decided by an empowered group of ministers (EGoM) in 2013 that the fertilizer sector would get 31.5 million metric standard cubic metres per day (MMscm/d) of domestic gas, which would be distributed to power and other sectors only after the supply to the fertilizer sector was ensured. However, as per the Ministry of Power's report, as well as data obtained from the Fertilizer Association of India (Figure 3), it is clear that the share of the fertilizer sector in total domestic gas production has been declining continuously.[8] The report also states that the share of power and city gas distribution (CGD) in total domestic gas, along with their absolute values, have increased considerably from 2015–16 to 2017–18.[9] This is a puzzling development, especially since after CGD, fertilizer has been identified as the sector with the highest priority for the distribution of gas. Domestic gas supplied to the fertilizer sector (absolute value and the share in domestic production) has been declining for the last few years.

Not only is the power sector getting a larger share of cheaper domestic gas, but it is also being supplied at a lower rate (estimated weighted average) to the power sector as compared to the fertilizer sector. As mentioned by the Ministry of Power,[10] domestic gas and imported regasified liquefied natural gas (RLNG) is supplied to the power sector at a price of $4–5.5 per Million Metric British thermal unit (MMBtu),[11] and $10–12/MMBtu,[12] respectively. Given that in 2017–18, only around 22 per cent of the gas consumed in the power sector was imported, the weighted average price of gas in the sector would come to around $7/MMBtu, while the pooled gas price in the fertilizer sector was $9.7/MMBtu.

Figure 3: The changing share of sector-wise distribution of domestic natural gas

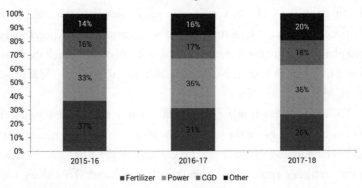

Source: Gulati and Banerjee (2019),[13] constructed using the data in Standing Committee on Energy (2018–19): Sixteenth Lok Sabha, Government of India (2019).[14]

INCREASING PRICE OF NATURAL GAS SUPPLIED IN THE FERTILIZER SECTOR AND ITS REASONS

Before 2015, the fertilizer sector used to get domestic gas at an administered price of $4.2/MMBtu on the basis of net calorific value (NCV). As per the new domestic gas pricing formula adopted in 2015, domestic gas prices have since declined over time. During the period from April to September 2015, it was declared as $4.66/MMBtu on a gross calorific value (GCV) basis.[15] The declared domestic price for gas was $3.36/MMBtu on a GCV basis,[16] from October 2018 to March 2019.[17]

Despite declining prices, the fertilizer sector has been receiving gas at higher prices since 2015 for two reasons. The first reason is the pooling of gas prices, of both domestically produced and imported gas. Experts have argued for this particular policy measure (pooling of gas prices) for long because different urea plants were getting gas at different prices due to varying combinations of domestic gas and imported RLNG. The costs of production for different plants were thus dependent not only on the conversion efficiency of plants but also on gas prices. Hence, there was a need to bring uniformity to gas prices for all fertilizer plants. In March 2015, the Cabinet Committee on Economic Affairs approved the pooling of gas prices supplied to fertilizer plants. All gas-based urea plants now got their feedstock at a uniform price, which increased from \$9.8/MMBtu on an NCV basis in 2015–16 to \$12.3/MMBtu on an NCV basis in 2018–19.

The second reason relates to the fact that in the last few years, the share of domestic gas in the total gas consumption of the fertilizer sector has been declining. In 2012–13, 76 per cent of the total gas consumed in the fertilizer sector was domestically produced. This share went down to almost 62 per cent in 2014–15, i.e., just before the pooling of gas prices was implemented. Since then, the share has fallen even more. In 2018–19, only around 38 per cent of the total gas consumed in the sector was domestically produced. In the first quarter of 2019–20, the share of domestic natural gas stood at around 30 per cent of the total gas consumption in the sector (Figure 4).

Figure 4: Share of domestic and imported natural gas in fertilizer sector

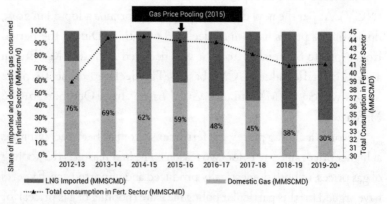

*Up to July 2019

Source: Gulati and Banerjee (2019)[18]; data from Fertilizer Association of India (FAI).

The Implications of Increasing Gas Price on Urea Subsidy

Following the answer to a question in the Lok Sabha regarding fertilizer subsidy,[19] the translation of increasing gas prices to subsidies can be explained as follows:

The weighted average energy norm for all gas-based plants in India taken together is 5.86 giga calories per million tonnes (Gcal/Mt) (FAI). We know that 1 Gcal is equal to 3.96 MMBtu, or approximately 4 MMBtu. This means that India would need 23.44 MMBtu of gas (5.86 * 4 = 25.99) on average to produce 1 MT of urea (FAI).

If gas prices increase by \$1/MMBtu, assuming a rupee-dollar exchange rate of around ₹70/\$, the additional subsidy liability for that increase becomes around ₹1,640.8/MT (23.44 * 1 * 70 = 1,640.8) since the sale price to the farmers is the same. So, for the level of urea production in the country (23.5 MMt) between 2018 and 2019, the subsidy liability will increase by (\$550 million) ₹38.5588 billion (1,640.8 * 23.5 * 10^6 = 38.5588 * 10^9) if the gas price increases by \$1/MMBtu.

The fertilizer sector is either importing urea (around 23 per cent of recent urea consumption is imported) or is importing its main feedstock, gas, in the form of RLNG ($\sim$65–70 per cent). This invariably drives up the cost of production, thereby increasing subsidy liabilities for the government. This has significant implications for the 'Make-Buy' policy option.

'MAKE-BUY' OPTION IN THE UREA SECTOR

To achieve an efficient allocation of resources, one of the economic arguments is that self-sufficiency in all sectors is neither feasible nor desirable. One must weigh, well in advance, whether it is cheaper to produce that commodity at home or to import it, therefore, making a 'Make-Buy' decision. Yet, two problems arise with this argument when applied to the urea sector, as often argued by the Indian fertilizer industry: (a) while domestic costs of urea can be easily assessed and kept within reasonable bounds, the international prices of urea are volatile. Deciding which international price to use as a point of comparison with the domestic cost of production remains an issue for countries that aim for relative stability in their urea sector and consequently their food sector; (b) it is possible that when large countries like India enter the global market and introduce a higher demand for urea, the international urea prices are unduly pushed up. To avoid price increases, it might be better to target self-sufficiency in urea production.

Both these arguments are somewhat overplayed. Experience has shown that businesses often perform better and achieve higher levels of efficiency when they are exposed to global competition, with due diligence to avoid any dumping. While international prices of all commodities fluctuate, most decision-making in various sectors is based on an 'open economy environment' that includes 'Make-Buy' options in decision-making. So, there is a continuous effort to project future prices, develop future markets, have long-term contracts and so on. Shutting down the 'Make-Buy' option leads to cumulative inefficiency in the system and to high-cost structures that need to be avoided.

There is some truth to the argument that global prices would increase if India were to enter the global urea market with a large demand, especially given that global supplies are limited at any given point in time. If India were suddenly to announce that it needs to import, for example, 7 MMt of urea, prices will naturally shoot up as supplies cannot be stretched much in the short run. However, this can be tackled to a large extent. First, why should India suddenly announce that it needs to import 7 MMt or 5 MMt of urea, after a meeting of the steering committee of secretaries? Why not keep imports of urea de-canalized (stopping the practice of importing urea on government account through only two state trading enterprises) and allow importers to keep importing at varying times and in small quantities whenever they feel prices are low?

Second, if India is to be a large importer of urea in the long run and if the world is to be made aware of this, there will be enough global investment to satisfy India's urea demand. There is ample gas available across the world, after the discovery of coal-bed methane in Australia and shale gas in the US[20] and there is great capital floating around looking for investment opportunities such as this. But investors will need stability in policies to continue investing in new urea plants. Indian producers must also be ready to establish new plants in Gulf countries, where gas is available at lower prices and urea can then be supplied from there to India.

Third, it may be noted that it is not the 'either-or' game, but the 'Make-Buy' option which operates at the margin. India will not completely stop the domestic production of urea, and nor will India become completely dependent on imported urea. There are plants that are technically as efficient as any others, in terms of global standards (for example, the Babrala plant of Yara meets global standards on energy efficiency). The trade is at the margin and to know how much can be efficiently traded (imported) rather than produced at home, we need a supply curve of domestic urea production, constructed on the basis of production by each urea plant and its concession price (the price at which it gets its production/delivery costs covered).

We have done so in Figure 5, based on data from 2018–19. The weighted average cost (excluding tax) for the gas-based plants was ₹22,408/MT ($320.5/MT) while the weighted average cost for the three naphtha-based plants was ₹36,185/MT ($517.5/MT). However, only around 6 per cent of the total domestic urea production comes from naphtha-based plants. So, for all the plants taken together, the weighted average cost (excluding tax) for urea production in India stood at ₹23,226/MT ($332.2/MT) in 2018–19. Compared to the import prices of urea, which were at \$284.6/MT, the cost of production of urea seems considerably higher. But to get a real import parity price, one needs to add handling charges and bagging costs of urea at the port in the cost insurance and freight (CIF) price. This would be about \$15/MT, making the import parity price roughly \$300/Mt. In 2018–19, there were only seven plants producing 18.9 per cent of the total domestic production with a before-tax cost of production of \$300/MT. In Gulati et al.,[21] we had shown that in 2014–15, seventeen urea plants were producing at a cost less than \$300/Mt when the import price (CIF) was \$287.5/Mt. So, in the past four years, the costs of production of urea plants have increased considerably.

One main reason behind this is, as mentioned earlier, the increase in the price of natural gas supplied to the fertilizer sector. The consequence of this argument is that the global competitiveness of India's urea sector depends to a large extent on the price at which it can procure natural gas, which in turn depends upon how much natural gas it can get from domestically produced sources and how much it has to import as RLNG. The higher the share of imported gas, assuming that the import parity of gas is higher than the price of domestically produced gas, the higher the price of pooled gas will be, leading to an overall higher cost of production of domestic urea, and thus, lower global competitiveness. In such a situation, from an efficiency perspective, it may be better to import urea directly. Else, India can allocate more domestic gas to the urea sector to keep its cost of production low, which will also make it a globally competitive sector. In that case, many Indian urea plants could even export urea.

Figure 5: Supply curve of urea in India 2018–19

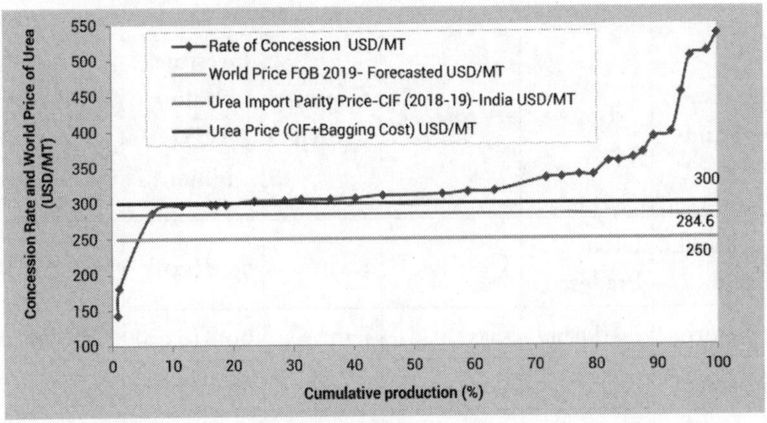

Source: Gulati and Banerjee (2019),[22] authors' analysis based on Production and Cost: FAI; Exchange Rate: (Government of India, 2019)[23]; Forecasted World Price: World Bank Pink Sheet (World Bank, 2019)[24]; and Import Parity Price calculated by the Directorate General of Commercial Information and Statistics (DGCIS, Government of India, various years).[25]

Interestingly, notwithstanding this type of Make-Buy option analysis, the Government of India recently planned to revive five urea plants, to decrease the import dependency of the sector. Each of these urea plants will have a capacity of producing 1.27 MMt of urea. At 100 per cent of their capacity, other things being equal, the total domestic production of urea will increase by 6.35 MMt—almost substituting the import of urea completely. An estimated total investment of ₹396.51 billion ($5.6 billion) will be required to revive those plants (Table 10). But if there is no domestic gas available and if they have to rely on imported gas, their production costs will be very high, compared to global urea prices. Initial estimates suggest that production costs will range between $400 to $500/MT, vis-à-vis an import parity price of about $300/MT. This does not seem to be a very rational decision purely from the perspective of economic efficiency (Make-Buy).

Table 1: Gas plants for revival: A Snapshot

New Plants	State	Feedstock	Capacity (MMt)	Investment ₹billion (USD billion)	Expected date of commissioning
Gorakhpur	Uttar Pradesh	Gas	1.27	70.9 (1.01)	Feb-'21
Sindri	Jharkhand	Gas	1.27	69.8 (0.99)	May-'21
Barauni	Bihar	Gas	1.27	70.5 (1)	May-'21
Ramagundam	Telangana	Gas	1.27	52.54 (0.75)	Dec-'19
Talcher	Odisha	Coal-Gasification	1.27	132.77(1.8)	Sep-'23
Total			6.35	396.51 (5.6)	

Source: FAI, also presented in Gulati and Banerjee (2019).[26]

THE RATIONAL WAY TO MOVE FORWARD

Based on the discussion above, what could be a rational way to move forward? Economic efficiency cannot be ignored in the name of self-sufficiency, especially when India is short of resources for investment. This rationale becomes even more compelling since India is a net exporter of cereals, with Prime Minister Narendra Modi himself talking about his vision of halving urea consumption by 2022,[27] and giving priority to zero budget natural farming (ZBNF) as indicated in the Union budget of 2019–20.

It is all the more important that we produce and use urea in the most cost effective and environmentally sustainable way. It has been shown that the higher subsidy levels on urea vis-à-vis di-ammonium phosphate and muriate of potash, have led to the overuse of nitrogen (N) vis-à-vis phosphorous (P) and potassium (K) in several states, lowering the response ratio to as low as three in recent years.[28] Moreover, given that urea granules are subsidized but not are soluble, it is estimated that almost 75 per cent of N applied in granular form evaporates either into the atmosphere in the form of ammonia (NH_3), nitrogen (N_2), or nitrogen oxide (NO_x) gases or percolates into groundwater as nitrates (NO_3).[29]

The release of excess nitrogen into the atmosphere and nitrates into groundwater are equally detrimental to the environment. Nitrous oxide (N_2O) is one of the main causes of stratospheric ozone depletion and it is also 300 times more potent ('radiatively reactive')[30] than carbon dioxide (CO_2) as a greenhouse gas. As for groundwater pollution by N, excess nitrate (NO_3) contamination in groundwater causes 'blue baby syndrome'. Studies have found that many states in India (Punjab, Haryana, Karnataka, and Tamil Nadu, for example) have NO_3 levels that are much higher than the safe limits prescribed by the World Health Organization.[31] Apart from these, excess nitrogen in the soil causes acidity and it could affect the biodiversity adversely in water bodies. Thus, by encouraging disproportionate use of urea via subsidies, India is actually subsidizing pollution by nitrogen which must stop.

Further, the current subsidy regime does not induce innovations in fertilizer products, e.g., soluble fertilizers to be used in fertigation. The best way forward, therefore, will be to give fertilizer subsidies directly to farmers on a per hectare basis[32] and to allow the fertilizer sector to be fully exposed to market forces, i.e., let retail prices of all fertilizers be market-determined. But this cannot happen so easily unless gas pricing is freed from government controls. Since roughly 45 per cent of natural gas is being imported (2017–18) and its import parity price is generally about two-and-a-half to three-and-a-half times higher than domestically produced gas, this will raise the overall price of domestic gas. It will also allow more profits to domestic gas producers and, hopefully, more investments in domestic exploration will follow soon. Big gas players would also like to tie up with players in large consuming sectors like fertilizer and power for their own stability and assured markets. Thus, a new regime will emerge with de-canalized imports of gas as well as fertilizers, the freedom to produce urea at home (based on domestic gas or imported gas or a mix of two), and the possibility of exporting fertilizers. This will promote efficiency in a market-driven system. Farmers' interests will be taken care of by giving them subsidies directly on a per hectare basis.

If this transition from highly controlled and regulated fertilizer and gas sectors seems too bold a step to be carried out in one go, one may choose the second option of allocating more gas from domestically produced sources to the fertilizer sector on a priority basis, in line with the recommendations of the empowered group of ministers (EGoM) in 2013. In a dual pricing regime, with much lower prices of domestically produced gas, the overall cost of urea can be kept under check. This would improve the global competitiveness of Indian urea and would lead to the automatic import substitution of urea. In such a scenario, it would not be surprising to see many urea plants eager to export urea.

But in that case, other sectors like power and oil refinery will have to compete for more imported gas. The bottom line is that the production of domestic gas must increase to cope with its consumption. This will happen only when more investments flow into the exploration of domestic gas, which would require improvement in the gas pricing regime, moving gradually towards import parity pricing.

The big question is: can India manage this transition? India has played with controls and regulations for too long and that has not led to higher efficiency or faster growth. In fact, much of the urea industry feels saddled, especially when arrears from the government take years to materialize. Unleashing market forces can stimulate growth and promote efficiency, making the Indian urea industry a vibrant one. This is the time to do it, especially when India is comfortably placed on the foodgrain front. The fertilizer industry will find its own equilibrium and a new vibrancy. Farmers will be fully compensated with direct income support on a per hectare basis. This will be less distortionary and will promote efficiency and growth in the fertilizer sector, which India must aspire towards.

Notes

1. Fertiliser Association of India, *Annual Review* 2018–19, New Delhi: Fertiliser Association of India, 2019.

2. Fertiliser Association of India, *Fertiliser Statistics* 2017–18, New Delhi: Fertiliser Association of India, 2018; also see Fertiliser Association of India, *Annual Review* 2018–19.

3. It increased for one year in 2015–16, then again declined and stagnated thereafter.

4. The increase was mainly due to the discovery of a large reserve in the Krishna–Godavari basin (KGD6), but the enhanced production did not sustain for long.

5. Government of India. *Energy Statistics* 2019. New Delhi: Ministry of Statistics and Programme Implementation (MOSPI).

6. Ibid.

7. Ministry of Petroleum and Natural Gas, 'Guidelines for pricing and commercial utilization of non-APM Gas produced by National Oil Companies (NOCs) from their nominated blocks', No. L-12018/23/2011-GP-II, New Delhi: Ministry of Petroleum and Natural Gas, Government of India, 3 December 2011, http://petroleum. nic.in/sites/default/files/Pricing%20and%20commercial%20 utilization%20of%20non-APM%20gas%20produced%20bby%20 NOC%27s%20from%20their%20nominated%20blocks%20dt%20 23.12.2011%20%26%2028.06.2010_0.pdf

8. Ministry of Power, 'Standing Committee on Energy (2018–19): Sixteenth Lok Sabha', New Delhi: Ministry of Power, Government of India, 2019.

9. In part because of the e-bid RLNG scheme that allowed power producers to pool lower spot LNG with domestic gas.

10. Ministry of Power, 'Standing Committee on Energy (2018–19): Sixteenth Lok Sabha', 2019.

11. Including basic price, transportation cost and various taxes and duties.

12. Including imported gas price at port, regasification cost, transportation cost marketing margin and various taxes and duties.

13. Ashok Gulati and Pritha Banerjee, 'Rejuvenating Indian Fertilizer Sector', Paper presented at the FAI Annual Seminar - New Approach to Fertilizer Sector, December 2-4, 2019, New Delhi.

14. Ministry of Power, 'Standing Committee on Energy (2018–19): Sixteenth Lok Sabha', New Delhi: Ministry of Power, Government of India, 2019.

15. Alternatively $5.18/MMBtu on net calorific value (NCV) basis— since NCV is 90 per cent of GCV (according to the conversion chart provided by the Petroleum and Planning and Analysis Cells).

16. Alternatively, $3.73/MMBtu on NCV basis.

17. $3.23/MMBtu on GCV Basis for the period October 2019 to March 2020; and $3.69/MMBtu on GCV basis for April to September 2019.

18. Ashok Gulati and Pritha Banerjee, 'Rejuvenating Indian Fertilizer Sector', Paper presented at the FAI Annual Seminar - New Approach to Fertilizer Sector, December 2-4, 2019, New Delhi.

19. Ministry of Petroleum, 'Guidelines for pricing and commercial utilization of non-APM gas,' produced by national oil companies (NOCs) from their nominated blocks, No. L-12018/23/2011-GP-II, Ministry of Petroleum & Natural Gas, Government of India: New Delhi, 2011, http://petroleum.nic.in/sites/default/files/Pricing%20and%20commercial%20utilization%20of%20non-APM%20gas%20produced%20bby%20NOC%27s%20from%20

their%20nominated%20blocks%20dt%2023.12.2011%20%26%20 28.06.2010_0.pdf

20. Tim Boersma, Akos Losz and Astha Ummat, 'The Future of Natural Gas in India: A Country at a Crossroads', Working Paper, Columbia Global Energy Dialogues, New York: Centre on Global Energy Policy, Columbia | SIPA: New York, April 2017, https://energypolicy. columbia.edu/sites/default/files/The%20Future%20of%20 Natural%20Gas%20in%20India%20-%20A%20Country%20at%20 a%20Crossroads%200417.pdf

21. Ashok Gulati and Pritha Banerjee, 'Fertilizer Pricing and Subsidy in India', in Ashok Gulati, Marco Ferroni and Yuan Zhou (eds), *Supporting Indian Farms the Smart Way*, New Delhi: Academic Foundation, 2018, pp. 91–148.

22. Ashok Gulati and Pritha Banerjee, 'Rejuvenating Indian Fertilizer Sector', Paper presented at the FAI Annual Seminar - New Approach to Fertilizer Sector, December 2-4, 2019, New Delhi.

23. Department of Economic Affairs, *Economic Survey, 2018-19*, New Delhi: Ministry of Finance, Government of India, 2019.

24. World Bank, 2019, *World Bank Pink Sheet*, worldbank.org/en/research/ commodity-markets.

25. Government of India, *EXIM Data Bank*, commerce-app.gov.in/eidb/

26. Ashok Gulati and Pritha Banerjee, 'Rejuvenating Indian Fertilizer Sector', Paper presented at the FAI Annual Seminar - New Approach to Fertilizer Sector, December 2-4, 2019, New Delhi.

27. *Mann ki Baat*, Prime Minister Narendra Modi, 26 November 2017, https://pib.gov.in/newsite/PrintRelease.aspx?relid=173860

28. P.P. Biswas and P.D Sharma, 'A New Approach for Estimating Fertilizer Response Ratio: the Indian Scenario', *Indian Journal of Fertilisers*, Vol. 4, No.7 (2008): pp. 59–62.

29. R. Prasad, 'Efficient fertiliser use: The key to food security and better environment', *Journal of Tropical Agriculture*, Vol. 47, Nos. 1–2 (2009).

30. M.A. Sutton et al., *Our Nutrient World: The challenge to produce more food and energy with less pollution*. Global Overview of Nutrient Management, Edinburgh: Centre for Ecology and Hydrology, 2013; on behalf of the Global Partnership on Nutrient Management and the International Nitrogen Initiative.

31. S.K. Gupta, R.C. Gupta et al., 'Methaemoglobinemia in Areas with High Nitrate Concentration in Drinking Water', *National Medical Journal of India*, Vol. 13, No. 2 (2000): pp. 58–61. Also see P.S. Datta, D.L. Deb, and S.K. Tyagi, 'Assessment of groundwater contamination from fertilisers in Delhi area based on O-18, NO_3 and $K+$ composition', *Journal of Contaminant Hydrology*, Vol. 27, No. 3 (1997): pp. 249–262.

32. That is, to shift to income policy of supporting farmers instead of price policy, since the latter is regressive in nature. Department of Economic Affairs, *Economic Survey 2014–15, Volume 1*, New Delhi: Ministry of Finance, Government of India, February 2015, pp. 53–56, https://www.indiabudget.gov.in/budget2015-2016/es2014-15/echapter-vol1.pdf

15

THE PETROCHEMICAL AND MICRO, SMALL AND MEDIUM ENTERPRISES SECTORS

AMIT MEHTA

Head-Gases, Reliance Industries Limited

BACKGROUND

NATURAL GAS IN INDIA IS used to a limited extent in the petrochemical industry and the micro, small and medium enterprises (MSME) sector. The consumption of gas in the petrochemical industry increased from 3 per cent in 2008–09 to 8 per cent in 2018–19. The International Energy Agency (IEA) in its 2018 report on the future of petrochemicals states that the global demand for plastics—the most familiar group of petrochemical products—has outpaced that of all other bulk materials (steel, aluminium, cement) and has nearly doubled since 2000.[1] The IEA report projects that by 2030, petrochemicals will consume an additional 56 billion cubic metres (Bcm) of natural gas, equivalent to about half of Canada's total gas consumption today.

While the highest per capita demand today comes from Korea (100 kg/capita), developing economies like India and China are catching up and are expected to sharply increase their share of plastic consumption, in comparison to advanced economies. The petrochemical sector plays a vital role in all key areas of the economy in India, including infrastructure, agriculture, healthcare, textiles and consumer durables. Petrochemical products, such as polymers, cater to the entire spectrum of items of daily use and provide critical inputs which enable other sectors to grow. While the demand for petrochemicals is increasing, the growth in shale production in the United States of America (the US) continues to drive down prices of some key inputs used in manufacturing units, particularly natural gas liquids (LPG and ethane). In India, the expectation of economic growth and consumer sentiments, both augur well for the petrochemical industry since its growth is directly related to that of the economy.

Meanwhile, the Indian micro, small and medium enterprises (MSME) sector is the backbone of the nation's economic structure and comprises around 63.4 million units.[2] As reported by the Central Statistics Office of the Ministry of Statistics and Programme Implementation, the share of the MSME sector in the all-India GDP during 2017–18 was 29.7 per cent. As reported by the Directorate General of Commercial Intelligence and Statistics, the share of MSME related products in total exports during 2018–19 was 48.10 per cent.[3]

Table 1 shows the current classification of MSMEs in accordance with the provision of the Micro, Small & Medium Enterprises Development (MSMED) Act, 2006. Covid-19 has created an unprecedented situation across the globe and India. The resultant lockdowns announced by the Government of India have caused a severely disrupted the Indian economy, and MSMEs have been the worst affected.

Table 1: Classification of the MSME Sector

Enterprise Type	Current Criteria: Investment Limit (₹)	Post Covid-19 Proposed Criteria: Investment and Annual Turnover
Micro	Less than ₹2.5 million ($35,000)	Investment less than ₹10 million ($143,000) and turnover less than ₹50 million ($710,000)
Small	From ₹2.5 million ($35,000) up to ₹50 million ($710,000)	Investment from ₹10 million ($143,000) up to ₹100 million and turnover from ₹50 million ($710,000) up to ₹500 million
Medium	From ₹50 million ($710,000) up to ₹100 million ($1.43 million)	Investment from ₹100 million ($1.43 million) up to ₹200 million ($2.86 million) and turnover from ₹500 million ($7.15 million) up to ₹1 billion ($14 million)

Source: Cabinet Committee on Economic Affairs (CCEA)[4]

Out of 63.4 million MSME units, the micro sector with 63.05 million estimated enterprises accounts for more than 99 per cent of the total estimated number of MSMEs. The small enterprises sector with 0.33 million accounts for 0.52 per cent of the total estimated MSMEs and the medium enterprises sector (with 0.005 million estimated enterprises) for 0.01 per cent of total estimated MSMEs. Around 32.488 million MSMEs (51.25 per cent) are in rural areas and 30.9 million MSMEs (48.75 per cent) are in urban areas.[5]

India's GDP increased by 6.8 per cent in 2018–19.[6] The country's industrial production accelerated at an average growth rate between 3.3–4.4 per cent from 2015–16 to 2017–18 (Figure 1). The MSME sector has, however, consistently maintained a growth rate between 8.5–10 per cent during the aforesaid period.[7]

Figure 1: Industrial production growth

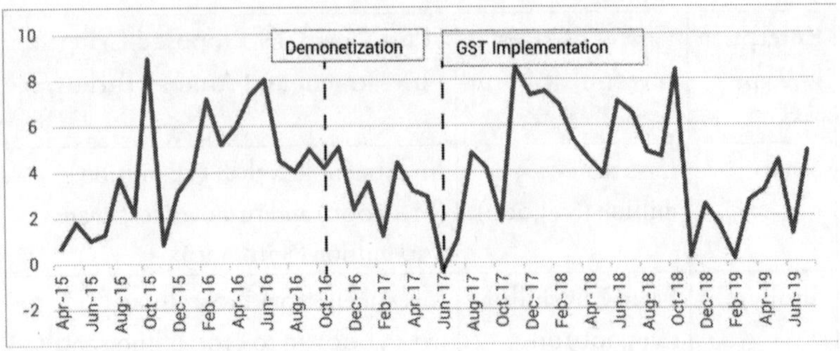

Source: National Statistical Office, Ministry of Statistics and Programme Implementation, Government of India.

While there is limited public data to prove energy consumption in the MSME segment, a study carried out by the Bureau of Energy Efficiency (BEE) during the Eleventh Five Year Plan period (FY 2007–12), shows the estimated total energy consumption to be at ∼19.9 millions of tonnes of oil equivalent (Mtoe; ∼64 million metric standard cubic metres per day (MMscm/d) of natural gas (NG) equivalent) for all major MSME clusters in India. Figure 2 below shows the energy mix in 2012 which accounted for manufacturing products in MSME and is predominantly powered by coal.[8]

Given this background, this chapter seeks to analyse the current and expected demand from the petrochemicals and MSME sectors; the likely reasons for the low penetration of natural gas in these sectors; the conditions that enable the increase in gas consumption and the kind of demand that will be met via natural gas as fuel and feedstock.

Figure 2: Energy Mix (2012) in major MSME clusters

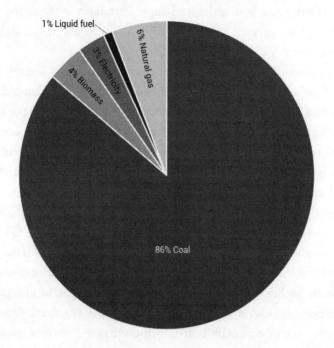

Source: Bureau of Energy Efficiency.

ASSESSING DEMAND OUTLOOK

PETROCHEMICALS

Sector Outlook (Near- And Long-Term)

Indian ethylene demand as of 2018 was ∼6.7 million metric tonnes (MMt), with an expected growth of 4 per cent till 2024. On the supply side, another 1,200 kilo tonnes per annum (kt/a)of capacity is likely to be added in 2021–22 by Hindustan Mittal Energy Ltd. In 2020, Covid-19 led to a delay in projects which could push completion timelines beyond 2022. Thus, the ethylene demand-supply scenario in the near-term (2018–24) is expected to remain more or less balanced and tighter towards 2023–24 (Figure 3).

Propylene production capacity was ~7242 kt in 2018 and ~1200 kt/a of capacity addition is likely to be added by 2022. Demand for propylene in 2018 was ~5.1 MMt, expected to grow at ~7 per cent till 2024. Therefore, the growth in demand is expected to outpace the planned capacity addition in India. In the long term, the growth of the petrochemical industry is primarily dependent on the economic activity in India and is directly correlated to the growth in GDP.

The demand for polymers (like polyethylene and polyvinyl chloride [PVC]) and for intermediates (like monoethylene glycol [MEG]) are key consumer segments for ethylene, which is most relevant for natural gas demand. Almost all other building blocks and intermediates would be met by naphtha crackers and refineries. In the near-term, except for a brief period of Covid-19 recovery for the first three quarters (Q1–Q3 FY 2020–21), we expect the near-term growth in 6–8 per cent range for the period up to 2022. Based on long-term projections,[9] the demand for polymers is estimated to grow from the current ~13.5 Mt/a to ~29.6 Mt/a by 2030 and ~49.7 Mt/a by 2040 as highlighted.

Similarly, the demand for MEG, the other key consumer for ethylene is expected to more than triple from the current ~3179 kt/a to ~10744 kt/a by 2040 (Table 2).

Figure 3: Domestic ethylene and propylene demand (kt/a)

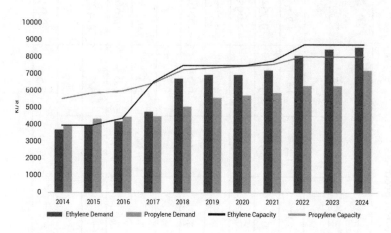

Source: Author's estimates.

PETROCHEMICAL FEEDSTOCKS AND NATURAL GAS DEMAND

The petrochemical industry uses different sources of feedstock such as naphtha, natural gas (NGL, ethane, propane, butane) and LPG. The choice of feedstock is dependent on the availability, economics, product portfolio and power consumption related to each feedstock. The continuous supply of feedstock and uninterrupted high-quality power are critical for the petrochemical industry. For feedstock, naphtha is used when a wide range of co-products (including propylene and butadiene derivatives) are manufactured while natural gas and NGL are preferred when the ethylene output of a cracker needs to be maximized since they yield a higher proportion of ethylene (Table 3).

Table 2: Expected demand for petrochemical products

	Unit	2018	Growth in per cent	2022	Growth in per cent	2030	Growth in per cent	2040
GDP growth			6.1		6.3		6.3	
Population	Bn	1.3	1.15	1.4	1.13	1.5	1.10	1.7
HDPE	KTA	2,885	6.1	3,662	6.3	5,987	5.0	9,752
LDPE	KTA	797	6.1	1,012	6.3	1,654	5.0	2,695
LLDPE	KTA	1,692	6.1	2,147	6.3	3,510	5.0	5,717
Overall PE	KTA	5,374	8.0	6,821	7.6	11,151	6.0	18,164
PVC (Pipes)	KTA	2,359	7.5	3,146	7.0	5,393	5.5	9,211
PVC (other rig)	KTA	281	8.8	393	7.6	707	6.0	1,266
PVC (Flexibles)	KTA	618	8.1	843	7.0	1,444	5.5	2,467
PP	KTA	4,900	6.8	6,364	7.0	10,911	5.5	18,637

	Unit	2018	Growth in per cent	2022	Growth in per cent	2030	Growth in per cent	2040
Other PP Der	KTA	86	5.9	108	5.1	160	4.0	237
Total Polyolefins	KTA	13,532	6.7	17,567	6.7	29,606	5.3	49,746
Total Polymers (excl. PET)	KTA	13,532	6.7	17,567	6.7	29,606	5.3	49,746
MEG	KTA	3,179	6.1	4,034.9	6.3	6,596	5.0	10,744
Total	KTA	16,711		21,602		36,202		60,490

Source: Author analysis.

Table 3: Typical yield of major petrochemical feedstocks

Feedstock	Ethylene in per cent	Propylene in per cent	Crude/C4's in per cent	Pygas in per cent	Hydrogen in per cent	Fuel Gas in per cent	Fuel Oil in per cent
Ethane	80.4	1.7	2.8	2.5	6.2	6.2	0.3
Propane	42.0	17.0	4.0	7.0	2.0	27.0	1.0
N-Butane	40.0	17.0	10.0	7.0	2.0	22.0	2.0
LT Naphtha	31.0	16.0	9.0	19.0	2.0	19.0	4.0
Gasoil	21.0	15.0	9.0	19.0	1.0	10.0	25.0

Source: Author analysis.

In India, most crackers use naphtha and propane as major raw materials for the production of ethylene, propylene and other petrochemicals. Ethane is currently imported by Reliance Industries Limited (RIL) as feedstock and other gas crackers extract ethane from the rich gas from ONGC's western offshore fields and from liquefied natural gas (LNG). Naphtha is sourced locally from refineries and imported. An additional naphtha-based capacity is required to absorb the national surplus.

Table 4: Existing petrochemical crackers

Company	Location	Feed	Ethane Source	Capacity (KTA)
GAIL	Auraiya, Pata, Uttar Pradesh	Ethane	LNG-based	950
Haldia	Haldia, West Bengal	Naphtha	-	670
Indian Oil	Panipat, Haryana	Naphtha	-	857

Company	Location	Feed	Ethane Source	Capacity (KTA)
Reliance Industries	Dahej, Gujarat	Ethane/ Propane	US Ethane	500
Reliance Industries	Nagothane, Maharashtra	Ethane/ Propane	US Ethane	500
Reliance Industries	Vadodara, Gujarat	Naphtha	-	180
Reliance Industries	Hazira, Gujarat	Naphtha/ Ethane	US Ethane	955
Reliance Industries	Jamnagar, Gujarat	Refinery Off Gases	-	1,560
OPAL	Dahej, Gujarat	Ethane/ LPG/ Naphtha	LNG-based	1,100
BCPL	Assam	Ethane/ LPG/ Naphtha	Domestic Gas	220
Total				7,492

Source: Author analysis.

Among all petrochemical products, extracting ethane from natural gas is the most economically competitive option to meet the demand for ethylene. Propylene and other blocks are predominantly supplied by refineries, naphtha or LPG-based crackers. To meet the estimated demand for consumer products using ethylene in 2040, an additional ethylene capacity of ~19,879 kt/a would be needed. This translates to a demand for ~100 MMscm/d of natural gas, towards shrinkage, within which the quantity of rich gas is ~1,248 MMscm/d (~330 Mtpa of LNG).

Meanwhile, the potential demand for natural gas as fuel would be dependent on the building blocks of the cracker, type and the level of downstream integration. The typical fuel gas demand for a stand-alone gas-based cracker is estimated to be ~1.2 MMscm/d per million ton of cracker capacity. Fuel gas demand for integrated crackers with downstream complex is estimated to be ~2.2 MMscm/d per million-ton of cracker capacity. Thus, the estimated demand for gas as fuel for a capacity of 19,879 kt/a is estimated be in the range of ~24 MMscm/d to 44 MMscm/d. Moreover, meeting this demand would require an addition of thirteen new world-class crackers by 2040.

Table 5: Projected additional ethylene capacity by 2040 (kt/a)

Product	Additional Demand (2018–40)	Additional Ethylene capacity
PE	12,790	12,918
PVC	9,686	2,422
MEG	7,565	4,539
Total	30,042	19,879
Ethane required	24,848 kt/a	

Source: Author analysis.

Using natural gas as feedstock in crackers is dependent on a number of factors, including the availability of a large volume of rich gas; the competition from other fuel-based crackers and refineries; the economics of gas vis-à-vis other feedstocks; product portfolio and its demand profile. This will be discussed in greater detail in the next few sections.

MICRO, SMALL AND MEDIUM ENTERPRISES

Sector Outlook (Near- and Long-term)

The contribution of MSMEs to the country's total manufacturing output has remained consistent at ~30 per cent,[10] in the last five years. The National Manufacturing Policy under the Department of Industrial Policy & Promotion, Government of India, envisages raising the share of the manufacturing sector in GDP from 16 per cent to 25 per cent by the end of 2022.

To fulfil this vision, the contribution of MSMEs needs to increase to ~52 per cent, i.e., more than half by 2022. One could look at the transformation in the policy environment witnessed in China for small and medium enterprises (SMEs) in the recent past, where SMEs constitute an overwhelming majority of the enterprises. They are key to China's economic development, as they represent more than 90 per cent of all market entities, over 80 per cent of nationwide employment, more than 70 per cent of patents, over 60 per cent of GDP and more than 50 per cent of tax revenues.[11]

The MSMEs have been severely impacted by economic activities coming to a halt due to the prolonged lockdown in India in the wake of Covid-19. In the global supply chain, the lockdown has led MSMEs to face shrinkage of exports, cessation in production, non-availability of manpower, uncertainty of consumption and a liquidity squeeze in the market. In response to this, the Government of India and the Reserve Bank of India (RBI) have announced a slew of measures to support the sector:

- Liquidity measures such as collateral-free automatic loan (₹3,000 billion [$42.9 billion]) with a four-year tenure and a twelve-month moratorium on principal repayment so that they can meet the operational liabilities that have built up, buy raw materials and restart the business.

- ₹200 billion ($2.8 billion) as a subordinate debt to stressed MSMEs.
- Equity infusion of ₹500 billion ($7.15 billion) to help MSMEs expand in size as well as capacity.
- Global tenders to be banned for government procurement up to ₹2 billion ($20 million)
- The RBI has also announced a moratorium on term loans, has eased working capital financing and has put off interest payment on working capital facilities without an asset classification downgrade.[12]

To make MSMEs competitive and help the sector grow, a number of initiatives have been taken in the past including:

- Several announcements to promote ease of doing business.
- In-principle approval for loans up to ₹1 crore within fifty-nine minutes through online portals.
- All Central public sector undertakings (CPSUs) to compulsorily procure at least 25 per cent from MSMEs.
- Single consent under air and water pollution laws.
- Allocation of ₹75.72 billion ($1.08 billion) for the MSME ministry for FY2021.
- ₹10 billion ($140 million) to MSMEs in pharmaceuticals, auto components and others for technology upgradations, research and development (R&D), business strategy to make them export competitive.
- Micro-Units Development and Refinance Agency Banks (MUDRA) and Startup India.

Natural Gas Demand

The BEE study commissioned under the Eleventh Five-Year Plan by government-identified energy sources and the consumption of 19.9 Mtoe (∼65 MMscm/d) across major MSME clusters in the country (Table 6).

Table 6: Major energy source across different clusters in India as per the BEE study in 2012

Sector	Clusters	Product/Process	Major Energy Source
Glass	Firozabad	Glass products	Natural gas
Brass	Bhubaneswar	Utensils	Coke/coal, firewood
	Jagadhri	Brass, aluminium	
	Jamnagar	Extrusion, foundry, machining	
Brick	Varanasi Fired clay bricks		Coal
Ceramics and refractories	Morbi	Wall tiles, vitrified tiles, sanitaryware, floor tiles	LNG, coal gasifiers, LPG
	East & West Godavari	Refractory bricks, ceramic jars	Coke/coal, firewood
	Khurja	Ceramic and pottery	
Chemical	Ahmedabad	Chemicals and dyes	Firewood, Coke/Coal
	Vapi	Chemicals and dyes	Firewood, coke/coal

Sector	Clusters	Product/Process	Major Energy Source
Dairy	Gujarat	Chilling and pasteurization	Electricity, furnace oil
Foundry	Batala, Jalandhar and Ludhiana	Foundry	Firewood, coke, electricity
	Belgaum	Cupola, induction	
	Coimbatore	Cupola, induction	
Galvanizing and wire-drawing	Howrah	Galvanizing, wire drawing	Coal, HSD/LDO
Ice making	Bhimavaram	Ice blocks	Electricity
Paper	Muzaffarnagar	Kraft paper	Biomass (various forms)
Rice mill	Ganjam	Rice	Rice husk, electricity
	Vellore	Rice	
	Warangal	Raw rice	
Sponge Iron	Orissa	Sponge iron	Coke/coal, electricity
Tea	Jorhat	Coal and natural gas based	Coal, natural gas
Textiles	Solapur	Towels and blankets	Coke/coal, lignite, natural gas, electricity
	Surat	Sarees and dress materials	
	Tirupur	Compacting, dyeing, knitting	

Source: Bureau of Energy Efficiency.

The MSME sector recorded a growth of over 10 per cent in 2008–09. However, post the global financial crisis of 2008, this growth fell sharply and hovered around 4–7 per cent.[13] In the last few years though, the sector has consistently maintained a growth rate between 8–10 per cent.[14] Further, as per the seventieth round of the National Sample Survey (NSS) conducted during 2015–16, units in the MSME sector have grown at a compound annual growth rate (CAGR) of ∼6.4 per cent from 2006–07 to 2015–16. Considering the volatility in the growth pattern, a conservative growth rate has been considered—in tandem with a projected IEA growth rate of 6.5 per cent for India—for projecting the energy demand in MSMEs.

Using the BEE study as a benchmark, and extrapolating the same at an average growth rate of 6.5 per cent per annum, it is projected that the energy consumption of key MSME clusters for 2019–20 works out to ∼31 Mtoe (∼101 MMScm/d of NG equivalent). If the current energy mix pattern continues (Figure 2), 90 per cent of this demand will be met via coal, other solid fuels, and biomass and restricts the current addressable demand for natural gas to ∼8 MMscm/d.

The long-term demand for natural gas depends on the conversion of coal and other solid fuels to natural gas, which has been very slow due to the significantly lower cost of coal, vis-à-vis natural gas. Given increasing environment concerns, the government and judiciary have mandated a ban on the use of 'dirtier' fuels. In March 2019, the National Green Tribunal (NGT) mandated all ceramic units in the Morbi ceramic region that operated on coal gasifiers to switch to gas or shutdown. This meant an increase in gas consumption in the region to 6.5 MMscm/d,[15] from ∼2.5 MMscm/d in 2019. This increase represented 80 per cent of the total potential gas demand ∼8.0 MMscm/d, in Morbi.

The following scenarios were considered for coal-to-gas switching, to determine the long-term potential for natural gas in the MSME sector.

- Base Case: 30 per cent coal-to-gas switching by 2040, driven by the increasing concern for the environment.

- Low Case: 10 per cent coal-to-gas switching by 2040, no significant policy initiatives and a business-as-usual (BAU) scenario.

- High Case: 60 per cent coal-to-gas switching by 2040, an aggressive policy stance by government and judiciary, and similar to the NGT order in Morbi, Petcoke/fuel oil (FO) ban in the National Capital Region (NCR).

A Working Paper titled 'India's Energy and Emissions Outlook, 2017–18',[16] brought out by NITI Aayog in July 2019, assumed three growth-rate numbers for GDP till 2047—low growth rate of 5.8 per cent, a medium growth rate of 6.7 per cent and a high growth rate of 7.4 per cent. According to the Organization for Economic Cooperation and Development (OECD), India's GDP growth rate will be less than 5 per cent in the 2030s and less than 4 per cent in the 2040s.[17]

However, amidst the present Covid-19 pandemic, impacting economic activities in India, the International Monetary Fund (IMF) has reduced India's growth for 2020–21 to 1.9 per cent.[18] Similarly, the credit ratings major, Fitch, downgraded India's growth forecast to 0.8 per cent in 2020–21. The agency, however, did expect growth to rebound to 6.7 per cent in 2021–22.[19] Growth in the MSME sector thus was expected to be significantly lower in 2020–21 due to the impact of Covid-19, but beyond that, was expected to be in tandem with India's long-term GDP growth projections. Accordingly, the potential gas-demand growth in MSMEs was considered at around 2 per cent for 2020–21 and around 6 per cent beyond that up to 2030, and 5 per cent from 2030 to 2040. Based on this, the potential demand for natural gas over the next two decades in the MSME sector is as per Figure 4.

Figure 4: Natural gas demand under different scenarios

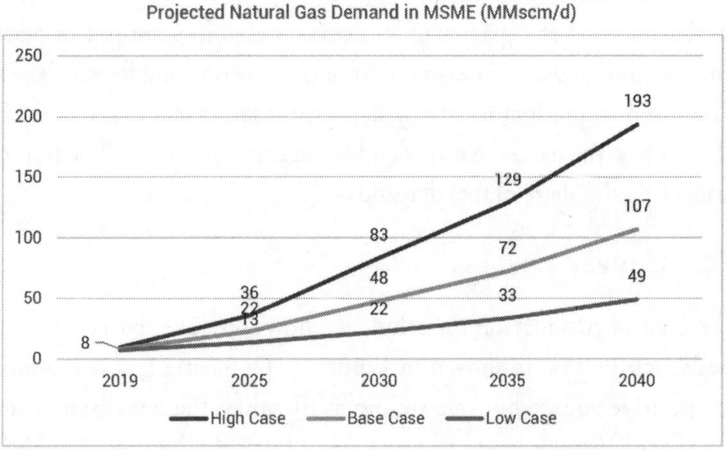

Projected Natural Gas Demand in MSME (MMscm/d)

Source: Author analysis.

KEY ISSUES HAMPERING NATURAL GAS CONSUMPTION

LIMITED RICH GAS AVAILABILITY

Gas demand for feedstock in petrochemicals is dependent on the availability of rich gas. India has a limited availability of rich gas from domestic sources and most supplies from western offshore fields have dwindled to insignificant levels for existing gas-based cracker units in western India. The current natural gas consumption by the petrochemicals sector is ∼9 MMscm/d, the majority of which is supplied by regasified LNG or RLNG (∼7 MMscm/d), and the balance by domestic gas (∼2 MMscm/d) from ONGC's western offshore gas fields. These crackers have moved to LNG and Reliance India Limited (RIL) has started ethane imports from the US.

Also, India has not been able to source rich LNG, except for the first 5 Mtpa LNG contracts with RasGas, Qatar. Going forward, while India is expected to see a significant increase in gas availability from domestic sources, most of this will be lean gas. Also, LNG suppliers do not offer rich LNG for exports. Hence, the availability of rich gas will be low. Therefore, it is unlikely that India will enhance its additional gas-based cracker capacity unless certain enablers are put in place. This means that one can expect most of the new demand for ethylene to be catered to predominantly by naphtha-based crackers and some by LPG. Thus, the natural gas demand for petrochemicals will be limited to meeting the share of fuel demand only.

Cost Competitiveness

The cost of production for ethylene and propylene, based on 2019 feedstock prices, is shown in Figure 5. Domestic gas is the most competitive source but due to low availability, the next best option is naphtha, which leads to local air pollution. Currently, naphtha demand is lower than production from refineries and as a result, India is currently a net exporter of naphtha. Moreover, the cost of production of ethylene from LNG (extraction of ethane) is high, vis-à-vis other feedstock. Given these factors, despite the increased availability of cheap alternative feedstock for cracking, naphtha is expected to remain the dominant feedstock for petrochemical production in Asia, with only a partial amount of its market share eroded by Ethane and LPG.

Figure 5: Comparison of feedstock prices

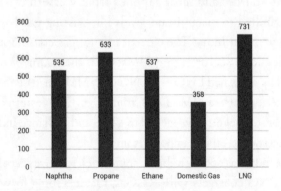

* Based on 2019 feedstock prices

Source: Author analysis.

A structural shift in the MSME sector, from coal and other solid fuels to natural gas, can primarily be driven by environmental concerns and policy-induced changes. Typically, MSMEs have very low margins and the cost of fuel plays an important role in determining these margins. Historically, coal has been the cheapest alternative, vis-à-vis natural gas and other fuels, as seen in Figure 6.

Figure 6: Pre-Covid-19 long-term[20] landed cost of alternate fuels versus gas in \$/MMBtu (at 2019 average Brent @\$65).[21]

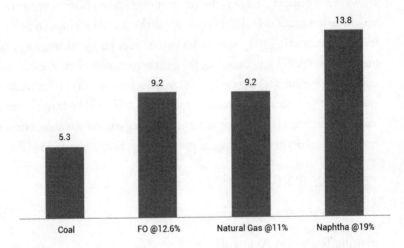

Source: Author's analysis.

Gas Infrastructure

Inadequate gas infrastructure (pipelines, spur lines and city gas distribution (CGD) networks) have hampered uptick, particularly in the MSME sector. Since ~60 per cent of the MSME units are rural based and with limited availability of gas infrastructure, the share of gas in the sector has remained muted. An additional 13,500 km gas pipeline is underway, along with an expansion in the CGD network, covering around 303 districts in about twenty-two states as a part of the ninth and tenth CGD bidding rounds. The execution of the same is critical to ensure increased access to natural gas for MSMEs.

POLICY CONCERNS

Policies to encourage gas use by the MSME sector have been limited to specific regions (Gujarat and Delhi), where gas is available due to the existing gas pipelines and CGD networks. The recent NGT order to ban the use of coal gasifiers has forced many units to shift to natural gas. However, a greater focus on the environment and industrial pollution would help enable this shift. Other areas that need a change in policy include: facilitating gas usage in industrial sectors by addressing tax inefficiencies (GST); unbundling the gas transmission, distribution and marketing businesses to create a level playing field for all marketers and ensure non-discriminatory access to pipelines and CGD infrastructure; and introduction of gas hubs/exchanges to bring gas-on-gas competition to enable competitive sourcing of gas by key industries and MSMEs.

THE WAY FORWARD

PETROCHEMICALS SECTOR

Making Rich Gas Available

India has a limited availability of rich gas and no incremental rich gas supply is expected from existing known and upcoming domestic sources. The Government of India must ensure the use of all available volumes of rich gas (estimated $\sim$10 MMscm/d) to gas-based cracker units before it is burnt as fuel. Rich gas, via the Hazira–Vijaipur–Jagdishpur integrated pipeline (HVJ), is currently being used as fuel before the extraction of ethane and propane. Such practices should be discontinued.

Importing Rich LNG

Imported LNG contains 6–10 per cent of ethane and propane along with methane. Depending on the quantity of ethane/propane contained in the LNG, it is called lean gas (lower C_2-C_3 content $\sim$6 per cent), or rich gas (higher C_2-C_3 content $\sim$8–10 per cent). An Ethane Propane Recovery Unit (EPRU) can separate ethane and propane from LNG. The Oil & Natural Gas Corporation (ONGC) has a facility at Dahej, where it separates C_2-C_3 from the rich LNG received at the Petronet LNG terminal. Reliance has an EPRU at Dahej which is currently mothballed but can be put to use if rich LNG is made available.

Ethane and propane are feedstock for steam thermal crackers, which convert this feed to ethylene and propylene: building blocks for the polymer industry. After the extraction of ethane and propane from the rich gas, the lean gas can then be used for other gas consumers. Thus, importing rich LNG can benefit the petrochemicals industry. But currently, most LNG suppliers do not offer rich LNG and prefer to extract ethane and propane before liquefaction. Therefore, these imports are only possible via bilateral dialogue and negotiations.

Import Incentives for Ethane/Propane (C_2-C_3)

Crude oil also contains associated gas or NGLs (natural gas liquids) viz., ethane, propane and butane. After extracting LPG (propane and butane), there is a stream of ethane and some propane (C_2-C_3) left, which can be used as a petrochemical feedstock. For example, RIL receives a C_2-C_3 feed from ONGC's Uran plant for its Nagothane cracker plant. Such a C_2-C_3 stream can be imported from the Middle East. If incentives are given for ethane-propane imports, it can help develop polymer and its downstream industries in the country.

MICRO, SMALL AND MEDIUM ENTERPRISES

Gas Supplies and Availability

Adequate gas availability for MSMEs on competitive terms and access to gas sources through transmission and distribution infrastructure are important drivers for switching to gas from alternate fuels and increased gas consumption. Unbundling transportation and marketing activities enables such access. Moreover, implementing third-party access to pipelines and non-discriminatory access to CGD infrastructure where market exclusivities no longer exist will also aid gas supplies to MSMEs.

Domestic gas is the most competitive source for MSMEs and growth in gas consumption in the sector will depend on increased production from domestic sources. As per the commitments made under the ninth and tenth CGD bidding rounds conducted in July 2018 and February 2019, the winning CGDs have committed to set up gas distribution pipeline networks to connect major industrial estates, including MSMEs. While signs of progress will be visible only over the next three to four years, this network across different geographical areas (GAs) will be useful in providing access to gas supplies.

Cost Competitiveness

Natural gas emits ~50 per cent less carbon vis-à-vis coal/lignite and ~30 per cent less than liquid fuel such as naphtha. Therefore, a suitable policy framework to introduce carbon tax and/or an emission trading system (ETS) is required to promote gas and reduce the carbon footprint in the MSME sector. The point is that bottom lines must account for the social cost of carbon and its abatement. Ideally, the tax rate on coal should take into account the full cost of using coal, including air and water pollution, emissions and an estimate of the costs that would maximize the overall welfare for society.

Coal has been included in the GST since its implementation in 2017, but natural gas has not yet been included in the GST regime. The exclusion of gas from GST has not only increased the complexity of the taxes on gas but also put it at a disadvantage, compared to 'dirtier' fuels such as FO, coal, and pet-coke. To provide a level playing field to natural gas, it should be included under GST at the earliest and be subject to lower tax vis-à-vis coal to provide incentives for switching.

In the immediate term, it should be set at least at the same GST rate as coal (5 per cent currently).

Contractual Flexibility to MSMEs

- Stringent gas supply contracts (take-or-pay) lead to financial liabilities in the case of small gas consumers in the MSME sector, because of severe fluctuations in their downstream demand patterns. To facilitate an increase in gas usage in MSMEs, suppliers should introduce innovative structures to offer flexibilities in the initial period of setting-up/commissioning to get them accustomed to their usage of gas as fuel, the pattern of and fluctuation in, their gas usage, their actual plant demand during summer or winter, etc.

- Making contracts flexible for MSMEs may include flexibility on 'take or pay' (TOP), i.e., the supply basis should be on minimal TOP levels or without any TOP commitments. Key aggregators and distributors can offer flexibilities in gas pricing to protect against any volatility in gas offtake by MSMEs—based on fluctuations in their downstream demand owing to factors like seasonality, impact in the downstream value chain due to various local/global factors, etc.,—and levy no penalties for such daily fluctuations.

Policy and Institutional Interventions

The MSME sector has largely remained unorganized, with $\sim$99 per cent units in the micro-segment and more than 60 per cent rural-based units. Due to this, MSMEs are subject to severe information asymmetry. The lack of information on various schemes deprives MSMEs of the benefits offered by the government, banks and other agencies. While there are numerous institutions in the country to provide support to the MSME sector and to facilitate its growth, the formulation of targeted policies and their effective implementation has been a challenge for such institutions.

Accelerating growth and enabling outreach

With a view to promoting ease of business, the government has introduced an online filing system under the Udyog Aadhaar Memorandum (UAM) to register new MSMEs based on self-declared information. The utilization and reach of various schemes as well as credit support is constrained due to the lack of formalization and low levels of registration of MSMEs under UAM. Awareness about UAM, especially in rural areas, needs to be created and its implementation formalized at the national level.

Facilitating access to credit and risk capital

Due to their informal nature, MSMEs lack access to formal credit as banks face challenges in credit-risk assessment owing to the lack of financial information. Further, very few MSMEs can attract equity support and venture capital financing. The government should encourage lending to MSMEs through suitable institutional frameworks.

Removing infrastructural bottlenecks and development of clusters

Bottlenecks to access infrastructure affect the competitiveness of MSMEs (just as in the case of the gas industry and access to gas infrastructure), and reduces their ability to venture into domestic as well as global markets. The development of MSME clusters has been largely confined to government organizations with low levels of private investment. There is a need to assess cluster development and increase funding from the private sector. China has witnessed the rapid growth of industrial clusters in accordance with the principles of socialization, specialization and market-orientation. Local government bodies provide an enabling environment, including financial incentives through appropriate policies and vital infrastructure required for business. One such example is Shenzhen, a technology hub in China, where the local municipal government has made it a priority to encourage more innovation-led start-ups by introducing several financial incentives.[22]

Regulatory mandates due to environment concerns

In the long term, economic growth in the MSME sector will also be linked to energy usage, considering increasing concerns over climate change, largely attributed to fossil-fuel use. Driven by environmental concerns and momentum on energy transition, it is expected that MSMEs too will prefer the use of cleaner fuels like natural gas and renewables. Globally, governments have started promoting the use of cleaner forms of energy through regulatory mandates, for example, China's programme for switching from coal to natural gas for its power, industrial and residential sector. In India too, the judiciary has shown increased concern towards the environment and has mandated a ban on the use of 'dirtier' fuels. The NGT has been actively taking steps to tackle pollution levels in recent months and has ordered strict enforcement to reduce industrial pollution in critically and severely Polluted Industrial Areas (PIA). Timelines on some of the key NGT actions undertaken are:

December 2018: The NGT ordered all the State Pollution Control Boards (SPCBs) to finalize action plans within three months to bring pollution levels down in identified PIAs to acceptable limits.

July 2019: The NGT argued for immediate and necessary measures to stop polluting activities. Key provisions of the order were:

1. Central Pollution Control Board (CPCB) and SPCBs to prohibit polluting activities in identified clusters within three months

2. No industrial expansion allowed in critically polluted areas
3. SPCBs to consider recovering compensation from polluting units for the past five years

November 2019: The NGT asked for strict compliance by CPCB and SPCBs and reiterated a three-month deadline (by February 2020) to implement their action plans and report compliance, failing which they could face punitive action. This has been delayed given the Covid-19 crisis.

1. Further, some key interventions by the government/Supreme Court/NGT, resulting in an increase in gas consumption in MSMEs/industrial customers are as follows.
2. On 6 March 2019, the NGT ordered the closure of industrial units (~500 units) in Morbi that operated using coal gasifiers.
3. In all, 292 MSMEs were ordered to change over to natural gas as an industrial fuel in Firozabad (TTZ) using the Uniform Gas Pooled Price.
4. The environment bench of the Supreme Court ordered a ban on the industrial use of pet-coke and furnace oil in Uttar Pradesh, Haryana and Rajasthan on 24 October 2017 along with the existing ban on their usage in the NCR area.

Hence, for long-term benefits, the government should continue to promote the use of natural gas through a mandated policy programme and offer fiscal incentives for conversions to natural gas by the MSME sector.

Notes

1. International Energy Agency, 'The Future of Petrochemicals: Towards a more sustainable chemical industry', Technology report—October 2018, Paris: OECD/IEA, 2018, https://www.iea.org/reports/the-future-of-petrochemicals

2. Ministry of Micro, Small and Medium Enterprises, 'Annual Report 2018–19, New Delhi: MSME ministry, Government of India', https:// msme.gov.in/sites/default/files/Annualrprt.pdf

3. Lok Sabha Unstarred Question No. 2863 answered by the Ministry of Micro, Small and Medium Enterprises.

4. https://pib.gov.in/PressReleasePage.aspx?PRID=1628344

5. Ministry of Micro, Small and Medium Enterprises, 'Annual Report 2018–19'.

6. National Statistical Office, Ministry of Statistics and Programme Implementation.

7. Lok Sabha, Unstarred Question No. 2412 answered by the Ministry of Micro, Small and Medium Enterprises.

8. Bureau of Energy Efficiency, 'BEE-SME Programme: Situation Analysis in 35 SME Clusters', Project Report, New Delhi: Ministry of Power, Government of India, 2012, https://beeindia.gov.in/sites/ default/files/Situation%20analysis.pdf

9. The key drivers and assumptions for growth include GDP growth. As per the IEA, India is expected to grow at an average rate of ~6.5 per cent till 2040. GDP growth rates are considered on a conservative basis (between 6.1 per cent to 5 per cent); polyethylene (PE) demand growth: growth in urbanization, and packaging material requirements were expected to grow in tandem with GDP; PVC demand growth: agricultural growth, construction activities, and pipelines are expected to grow higher than GDP; PP demand growth: growth in urbanization, automobiles, packaging, industrial polymers, etc.; MEG growth is expected to grow in tandem with GDP; Near term growth rates are based on industry estimates.

10. Ministry of Micro, Small and Medium Enterprises, 'Annual Report 2018–19'.

11. CBN Editor, 'SMEs Account for over 60% of China's GDP, Beijing Mulls Inclusion of Loans as MLF Collateral', *China Banking News*, 22

June 2018, http://www.chinabankingnews.com/2018/06/22/smes-account-60-chinas-gdp-beijing-mulls-inclusion-loans-mlf-collateral/

12. Reserve Bank of India, 'Covid-19 Regulatory Package', Notification, DOR.No.BP.BC.47/21.04.048/2019-20, New Delhi: RBI, 27 March 2020, https://www.rbi.org.in/Scripts/NotificationUser.aspx?Id=11835&Mode=0

13. U.K. Sinha, 'Report of the Expert Committee on Micro, Small and Medium Enterprises', New Delhi: Reserve Bank of India, June 2019, https://rbidocs.rbi.org.in/rdocs/PublicationReport/Pdfs/MSMES24062019465CF8CB30594AC29A7A010E8A2A034C.PDF

14. Ministry of Micro, Small and Medium Enterprises, 'Annual Report 2017–18', New Delhi: MSME Ministry, Government of India, https://msme.gov.in/sites/default/files/MSME-AR-2017-18-Eng.pdf

15. Sunil Raghu, 'Sources Say Gujarat may cut Gas Prices for Morbi Cluster by 10 Per Cent', *Cogencis*, 28 June 2019, http://www.cogencis.com/newssection/sources-say-gujarat-gas-may-cut-gas-prices-for-morbi-cluster-by-10/

16. Simi Thambi, Anindya Bhatacharya and Oliver Fricko, 'India's Energy and Emissions Outlook: Results from India's Energy Model', Working Paper, New Delhi: Energy, Climate Change and Overseas Engagement Division, NITI Aayog, 2019, https://niti.gov.in/sites/default/files/2019-07/India%E2%80%99s-Energy-and-Emissions-Outlook.pdf

17. Thambi, Bhatacharya and Fricko, 'India's Energy and Emissions Outlook: Results from India's Energy Model', 2019.

18. International Monetary Fund, 'Transcript of April 2020 Asia and Pacific Press Department Briefing', Washington DC: IMF, 15 April 2020, https://www.imf.org/en/News/Articles/2020/04/16/tr041520-transcript-of-april-2020-asia-and-pacific-department-press-briefing

19. Fitch Wire, 'Coronavirus Damages India's Growth and Fiscal Outlook', *FitchRatings*, 27 April 2020, https://www.fitchratings.com/research/sovereigns/coronavirus-damages-indias-growth-fiscal-outlook-27-04-2020

20. Longer than three years.

21. Percentage indicates the average linkage to Brent at which n and natural gas trade.

22. Sinha, 'Report of the Expert Committee on Micro, Small and Medium Enterprises', 2019.

16

TRANSPORT: A SUBSTITUTE FUEL?

GAUTHAM BABU DASARI

India Gas Advocacy and Regulations Lead, Shell Energy

SARAH KHOO

Asia Head – Market Advocacy & Regulations, Shell Energy

INDIA FACES A STIFF CHALLENGE. Its growing energy requirement, coupled with rapid economic expansion, has contributed to deteriorating air quality leading to alarmingly high health and social costs. Indian cities have been consistently ranked among the most polluting in the world by various domestic and international agencies. The transport sector is a significant contributor to this pollution. Studies by independent think-tanks and by the Central Pollution Control Board (CPCB), show that medium and heavy commercial vehicles (MCVs and HCVs) constitute 2.5 per cent of the vehicular population, but contribute to 60 per cent of the pollution levels. The older fleet (more than ten-years-old), which accounts for about 15 per cent of the total fleet, not only suffers from poor energy efficiency but also pollutes ten to twelve times more than newer vehicles.[1] Considering the adverse impact of air pollution on health, there is an urgent need to adopt suitable policies by increasing the share of cleaner fuels, promoting fuel efficiency and modernizing fleets to meet the mobility requirements of the growing population.

Globally, liquefied natural gas (LNG) is becoming a preferred fuel for long-haul transport, especially MCVs and HCVs. While China is at the forefront of adopting LNG as a transport fuel, many European countries, as well as the US, have increasingly started promoting a switchover to natural gas and LNG, by undertaking suitable policy initiatives and providing incentives.

This chapter explores the potential of LNG-fuelled vehicles in the MCV and HCV segments in India. It discusses the challenges in the adoption of LNG as a transport fuel, the policies needed to support adoption, and proposes a few recommendations to mitigate these challenges.

LNG ENGINE TECHNOLOGIES

There are currently two different engine technologies for heavy-duty LNG vehicles that fulfil the European exhaust emission standards, Euro VI (stoichiometric petrol/gas engines [spark-ignition or SI engine] and high-pressure direct injection [HPDI] engines). Stoichiometric SI engines can be easily designed for gas or LNG. Three-way catalysts can be used for cost-effective exhaust gas after treatment in SI engines.

The HPDI engine works in the same way as a diesel engine and auto-ignition is initiated with a smaller amount of diesel (5 to 10 per cent) consumption. Even though HPDI diesel engines offer the highest efficiency and the lowest emissions, SI engines are likely to propel the seeding of the market, as the incremental cost vis-à-vis the diesel engine is the lowest. Dual-fuel engines will lead the retrofitting market. Diesel engines can be retrofitted to dual-fuel engines with additional costs for cryogenic tanks, engines and peripherals. A CNG engine can be easily modified to an LNG engine with the addition of a storage tank and safety valves.

Emissions: LNG versus Diesel

The Natural & BioGas Vehicle Association (NGVA), Europe, commissioned a study in 2017 to perform an industry-wide greenhouse gas (GHG) intensity analysis (well-to-wheel) of supplying and using natural gas at Euro VI, mainly focusing on the road transportation sector. As per this study, the well-to-wheel GHG emissions for heavy-duty vehicles are 6 per cent and 15 per cent lower than the diesel baseline, for LNG SI and HPDI engines, respectively.

Figure 1: GHG intensity of Natural Gas

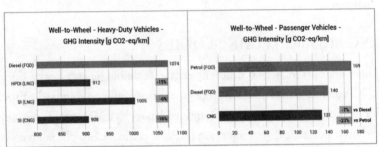

Source: NGVA Study on Greenhouse Gas Intensity of Natural Gas in Transport(2017).[2]

In India, the adoption of BS VI, which is comparable to Euro VI, will put diesel vehicles on par with LNG vehicles, with respect to nitrogen oxide (NOx) emissions. However, LNG also continues to emit three times lower levels of sulphur oxides (SOx) and CO_2 emissions, as evidenced by the NGVA study.

Table 1: Vehicle population (domestic sales year-on-year) in India

(Millions)	2012	2013	2014	2015	2016	2017	2018*	2019*
Passenger Vehicles	2.63	2.69	2.50	2.60	2.79	3.05	3.29	3.38
MCV, HCV-Passenger*	0.05	0.05	0.04	0.04	0.04	0.04	0.05	0.06
MCV, HCV-Goods*	0.30	0.22	0.16	0.19	0.21	0.22	0.26	0.30
LCV*	0.46	0.52	0.43	0.39	0.44	0.46	0.55	0.64
Three-wheelers	0.51	0.54	0.48	0.53	0.54	0.51	0.64	0.70
Two-wheelers	13.41	13.80	14.81	15.98	16.46	17.59	20.20	21.18
Total	17.4	17.8	18.4	19.7	20.5	21.9	25.0	26.3

* - CV breakup between MHCV and LCV based on historical average from 2016–17 onwards

Source: MoRTH Annual Reports & Society of India Automobile Manufacturers (SIAM) Statistics.[3]

India: Market Potential for LNG in Road Transportation

Diesel consumption in India has been increasing at a compound annual growth rate (CAGR) of ~4 per cent since 2012. Total consumption touched approximately 84 million metric tonnes (MMt) in 2018–19. While this represents the opportunity universe, the realizable LNG demand in the MCV and HCV segment is estimated under three scenarios (low, base and high), assuming different levels of penetration, driven by scenarios of infrastructure rollout, regulatory support, enabling policies and incentives impacting LNG's economic case vis-à-vis diesel.

Key Assumptions

- Annual vehicular additions: 2.5 per cent, 4.5 per cent and 7 per cent (low, base, high)
- Target penetration rates—MCV and HCV—goods carriers and passenger vehicles/bus:
- By 2030: 5 per cent, 7.5 per cent and 12.5 per cent (low, base, high) in year-on-year new vehicle additions
- Average mileage (km/l): 2.92
- Average distance travelled per day (km): 262.5
- Diesel(/ltr) and LNG(/kg) energy equivalence: 1:1

Figure 2: LNG demand-projection-scenarios for India

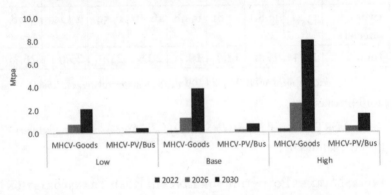

MHCV: Medium and heavy commercial vehicles; PV: Passenger vehicles

Source: Industry inputs and analysis.

While typically only new builds are favoured in the EU and China, retrofitting has great potential to accelerate the adoption of LNG-fuelled vehicles, as in the case of CNG. In India, retrofitting is yet to be developed on a commercially viable scale.

ECONOMICS OF LNG IN ROAD TRANSPORT

The incremental cost of LNG vehicles is expected to be ~₹4–7.5 lakh more than the BS IV diesel trucks, depending on the vehicle weight rating. The incremental cost of LNG vehicles vis-à-vis BS VI diesel trucks is expected to be lower by about 40–50 per cent. The LNG retrofit for truck/buses is expected to cost ~ ₹10 lakh. While these cost estimates are based on industry inputs from pilot projects and enquiries for low volume orders (<5), mass production is expected to reduce the unit costs by at least 15–20 per cent.

INCREMENTAL TCO PAYBACK: LNG VERSUS DIESEL VEHICLES

A payback period is presented as the time required for recovering incremental upfront costs and differential operating expenditure (OpEx) for LNG vehicles versus diesel vehicles (differential total cost of ownership). As fuel savings are a key driver for the switchover, the payback period for vehicle owners is presented at different LNG and diesel prices under prevailing tax and duty regimes. The payback period is sensitive to various factors, including the average distance travelled by the vehicle, exchange rates, the location of Retail Outlet (RO), Goods and Services Tax (GST), financing options (D/E split).

Figure 3: Payback Period for Incremental TCO (Diesel Vs LNG)

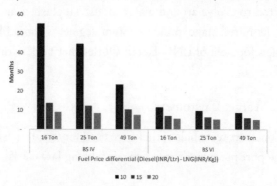

Source: Industry inputs and analysis.

The payback (incremental TCO) for trucks of 16 tonnes; 25 tonnes and 49 tonnes vis-à-vis BS IV trucks is between one to five years. Such high payback periods would not make LNG trucks attractive for truck operators. A payback between six months to a year-and-a-half is generally considered attractive enough for truckers to switch over.

The payback period for LNG vehicles is expected to decrease substantially vis-à-vis BS VI diesel vehicles, since these vehicles are 10–15 per cent more expensive than BS IV diesel vehicles.

As LNG prices are completely market-driven, fleet owners would make switchover decisions by assuming conservative LNG prices and, hence, financial incentives are required to cover extreme price fluctuations. While LNG-fuelled vehicles offer lower TCO in comparison with diesel-propelled vehicles over their life cycles, the upfront incremental capital expenditure (CapEx) is a significant barrier during the initial stages of market development. A financial incentive— in the form of lower GST (at 5 per cent instead of 28 per cent), or cash subsidies to meet 50 per cent of the incremental cost—can bring down the payback period to under six months.

Target Market

The selection and prioritization of routes and clusters will determine the growth trajectory of LNG in road transportation in India. The market is expected to evolve around major industrial clusters and corridors. During the initial stage, point-to-point segments should be targeted for the development of LNG Retail Outlets network in order to seed the market.

Potential Target Customers

- Container terminals: Trucks are used for cargo transport within the port premises; the major ports being Jawaharlal Nehru Port

(JNPT) at Mumbai and the ports of Chennai, Vizag, Cochin and Tuticorin.

- Mining trucks: Tippers are used to transport raw coal or metal ore from the mine to the warehouse. Target areas: Odisha, Jharkhand, Madhya Pradesh, Chhattisgarh and Andhra Pradesh.

- Automobile carriers: Car carriers are used to transport cars from the plant to various locations. Major manufacturing centres: Halol, Sanand and Pune.

- Petroleum products transport trucks: Trucks are used to transport LPG to bottling plants. Last-mile transportation of Motor Spirit (MS) and High-Speed Diesel (HSD) from the depot to the RO by trucks.

- Inter-city buses: Inter-city buses operated by state transport corporations (STCs).

- Milk carriers: Suitable target to switchover to LNG considering fixed running pattern and daily frequency of running. Target clusters in Gujarat.

The major corridors/clusters with sizeable diesel consumption (say, current annual consumption $>$ 0.5 MMt) include Mumbai–Delhi, Mumbai–Belgaum, National Highway (NH) 44-South, NH44-North, states or state clusters with high heavy-duty vehicle (HDV) diesel consumption such as Maharashtra, Gujarat, Rajasthan, Haryana–Punjab, UP–Bihar, and cities such as Kakinada, Chennai and Kolkata.

CHALLENGES FOR MASS PENETRATION

Despite enabling regulations, except for a few pilot projects on a very limited scale, the market for auto LNG is yet to take off. The challenges faced by various stakeholders for fuel switching are discussed below.

Technology/Safety/Environmental

There is no one technology on models, as original equipment manufacturers (OEMs) in global markets have launched a variety of models using matured LNG engine technologies (SI, dual and HPDI) which are compliant with Euro VI standards. Multiple Indian auto manufacturers have also developed prototypes and applied for type approvals. Retrofitting (diesel to LNG) is not widely encouraged globally. The EU/national regulations for retrofitted dual-fuel vehicles are yet to be approved, and the EU countries prefer certifying retrofitted vehicles on a vehicle-to-vehicle basis due to concerns around methane slip and compliance with Euro VI standards.

Additionally, the United Nations Economic Commission for Europe (UNECE) Regulations (Amendment to R115) for LNG retrofit vehicles is yet to be approved. In India, while emission regulations for type approval are in place, the potential of retrofits complying with BS VI standards is yet to be tested. Based on the European experience, it can safely be concluded that retrofits would deliver a significantly superior emissions performance, vis-à-vis Euro IV/BS IV, and their potential to contribute to air quality by displacing the old BS I-IV trucks/bus fleet shouldn't be ignored. The requisite safety standards for transportation, storage and dispensing of LNG are in place.

Infrastructure

Apart from the existence of a robust economic case for all stakeholders, fuel availability is a critical factor for adoption. Vehicle owners will want LNG fuel-retail infrastructure to be in place before they switch from conventional oil-based fuels, while infrastructure developers and auto manufacturers will want evidence of robust demand for the new fuel, before they invest in developing ROs and manufacturing facilities.

This stalemate can be addressed if one or more stakeholders in the value chain play a role in multiple parts of the chain, or if the government steps in to mitigate the uncertainty through enabling policies including financial/non-financial incentives.

Economics

Vehicle owners

The upfront (incremental) CapEx is a key barrier for the switchover decision. The preference of the vehicle owner to assume this exposure is dependent on the ecosystem assuring a relatively short payback period, say, less than one year.

India's MCV and HCV market is highly fragmented, with about 70–80 per cent of the market dominated by fleet owners with less than five trucks. Such vehicle owners would typically join the bandwagon only after the market stabilized in all respects—the availability of fuel, sustained price advantage over alternative fuel, development of service centres and availability of spares.

Such small players are unlikely to participate in market seeding, unless the burden of the incremental CapEx is eliminated or decreased, by way of financial incentives by the government. Even large fleet owners are hesitant to diversify their fleet by inducting a few LNG trucks, as they are unsure about exposure to LNG price volatility and retail infrastructure availability.

While STCs have a relatively bulk demand, they would be unwilling to incur additional upfront costs for LNG buses as most of these corporations are not in sound financial condition. In the absence of financial support through schemes like Faster Adoption and Manufacturing of (Hybrid) Electric Vehicles (FAME) for electric vehicles (EVs), STCs have adopted the wait and watch mode with interest in LNG buses limited to only pilot projects.

Retail infrastructure developers

It is difficult to attract private investors to develop either stand-alone LNG ROs or LNG + LCNG [liquefied compressed natural gas] stations, as the return on their investment is a function of uncertainty in multiple factors including demand growth, LNG and alternative fuel prices and fiscal and environmental policies. While the new fuel marketing policy provides for co-locating conventional and green fuel-ROs, and potentially enhancing prospects for economic returns on cost-sharing/marginal-cost basis, retail infrastructure developers would be encouraged more if they could have stakes in other parts of the chain (LNG supply, captive demand or transportation).

Auto manufacturers

While many OEMs have developed prototypes for LNG trucks/buses, they are not committing investments and dedicated assembly lines for manufacturing LNG trucks in the absence of a sizeable demand. In the absence of a clear roadmap from the government to promote various cleaner fuels, they have been focusing on introducing BS VI compliant models. The aggressive promotion of EVs has made it more difficult for LNG trucks, despite various studies indicating the inflexion point for EVs to compete with LNG in the HDV segment is likely to come only after 2025 in the US and the same could be beyond 2030 for India.

LNG suppliers

Petronet LNG Limited (PLL), Indian Oil Corporation Limited (IOCL) and Shell Energy India Private Limited (SEIPL) have been operating truck-loading bays for small-scale LNG. All other LNG terminal operators are either currently developing LNG bays or have committed investments at their terminals to meet the demand of industrial customers for the supply of LNG by trucks. While the supply infrastructure required to seed the market is in place, a slow ramp-up may force terminal operators to revisit further investment plans.

LNG *transporters*

Even though the supply of LNG by cryogenic tankers started nearly a decade ago, the market hasn't expanded and is being serviced by only a few players. While LNG for trucks has the potential to augment the existing demand for cryogenic tankers, players are unlikely to commit investments until they are certain of the demand, technology and committed orders from demand owners and/or LNG suppliers.

Policies and Regulations

In the absence of a central energy ministry or a coordination body, different ministries are responsible for managing different fuels. Competitive inter-fuel dynamics may lead to the promotion of any specific fuel or mobility option at the expense of other options, and without due consideration for commercial and technical maturity. This also translates into disparities in financial incentives and taxation policies, which would, in turn, signal sub-optimal investment decisions for other fuels.

Even though LNG is a mature, commercially and technologically cleaner fuel option available for long-haul MCV and HCVs (based on global experiences), the government is yet to develop a plan to promote this fuel, in the public sector undertakings (PSUs) and state transport undertakings segments, along the lines of FAME for EVs. Dedicated budgetary allocations to provide financial incentives (subsidies on the purchase of vehicles, IT exemptions on loans, customs duty waivers on raw material and equipment imports) have helped to lessen the burden of high upfront costs and TCOs for vehicle owners and have played a great role in kick-starting the market for EVs. While EVs are not mature enough to offer commercially/technically viable solutions for MCVs and HCVs and for long-haul transport, similar financial incentives (even at a much lower scale) would have helped in seeding the market for LNG vehicles.

POLICY AND REGULATORY DEVELOPMENTS

The Ministry of Road Transport and Highways and the Department of Heavy Industry (under the Ministry of Heavy Industries and Public Enterprises), are the nodal ministries for the transportation and auto sectors. While the road and highways ministry focuses on the formulation of policies and regulation relating to motor vehicles and the State Road Transport Corporations (SRTC), the Department of Heavy Industry focuses on policies relating to various engineering industries including the automotive sector. Key policies and regulations impacting the growth of auto LNG are as under.

NATIONAL AUTO POLICY

The draft National Auto Policy (2019) provides a vision for the growth of the automotive industry to achieve various social, economic and environmental targets (such as the objectives of green mobility). This includes achieving GHG reduction targets set under the nationally determined contributions (NDCs), by adopting policies to increase the share of zero- or low-emission vehicles. Natural gas-based mobility is one of the identified green mobility options along with biofuel, EV and hydrogen alternative fuels. The draft policy proposed various recommendations which could propel the growth of natural gas-based mobility, including auto LNG in the country.

Green Mobility Roadmap

- Finalize a technology-agnostic green mobility roadmap, through the evolution of emission regulations.
- Define the long-term roadmap for incentives and infrastructure investments for green mobility.

Drive Green Mobility Demand in the Public Domain

- Mandate a minimum share of green vehicles among new vehicles purchased by Central and state government agencies and municipal corporations, including:
  - ○ 25 per cent of all vehicles from 2023, and 75 per cent of all vehicles from 2030 procured by the central and state government
  - ○ 50 per cent of all vehicles from 2023, and 100 per cent of all vehicles from 2030 procured by municipal corporations in metros
- Use the government e-Marketplace portal to aggregate all green vehicle orders with standard specifications over three months and enable bulk procurement.

Advanced and Extensive Green Mobility Infrastructure Network

- Conduct a detailed study on the requirement of public infrastructure for green vehicles.
- Based on the study, define a national plan for the establishment of public infrastructure for green vehicles.

FUEL RETAIL MARKETING POLICY

The Fuel Retail Marketing Policy (2019) aims at enhancing fuel availability by augmenting the retail fuel network in remote areas, customer service levels and the participation of the private sector. In line with the Government of India's objective of encouraging green fuels, the policy mandates the installation of facilities for marketing at least one new generation of alternate fuels (such as CNG, LNG, biofuels), and EV charging points at the proposed retail outlets, within three years of operationalization—subject to the entity complying with various other statutory guidelines (of the Petroleum and Natural Gas Regulatory Board (PNGRB), Central Electricity Authority (CEA), Petroleum and Explosives Safety Organization (PESO), etc., as applicable). The PNGRB recently issued a clarification that any entity can set up an LNG station in any area, including CGD licensed geographical areas. This is likely to encourage the proliferation of required facilities.

TECHNICAL AND SAFETY REGULATIONS

The Ministry of Petroleum and Natural Gas declared LNG as a transport fuel in 2017, as part of remedial measures to tackle the menace of air pollution. Since then, various necessary technical and safety regulations have been amended to facilitate the use of LNG as a transport fuel (Annexure 1).

The PNGRB has recently issued a comprehensive regulation covering technical and safety aspects of LNG/LCNG retail outlets, providing an authoritative guide to assuring safety for operators and the community in the use of natural gas-fuelled vehicles.

GLOBAL EXPERIENCE

CHINA

Chinese cities used to regularly figure in the list of the world's most polluted cities during the early years of the last decade. The Chinese government has tackled the menace of air pollution by promoting cleaner fuels, including natural gas, through proactive and targeted policy measures. The aggressive adoption of natural gas has played an important role in reducing emissions and improving air quality in their cities.

Out of 19 million tonnes (Mt) of LNG supply by trucks in 2018, approximately 6.7 Mt was sold as transport fuel to nearly 3.5 lakh trucks and buses through a network of more than 2,500 retail outlets supplied from coastal LNG terminals, as well as domestic mini-liquefaction plants. The remainder was supplied to commercial and industrial consumers not connected to the pipeline grid.

The Chinese government has also issued a series of policies since their Twelfth Five-Year-Plan, to build a lower carbon and lower emission transportation system. The policies and incentives have included offering cash subsidies, demonstration projects and allowing a moderate over-construction of LNG refuelling facilities. China witnessed a record high of 75,000 units in LNG truck sales in 2017. This was the result of the impact of several regulations—enforcement of control over truck size and overloading, diesel vehicle emissions upgrade to National VI in 2019 and the prospect of diesel truck bans in certain areas such as the main ports in the Beijing–Tianjin–Hebei region from October 2017. As a result, many truck owners chose LNG trucks, which already met the more stringent emissions requirement, instead of diesel trucks.

The strong growth of the auto LNG market in China can be largely attributed to a clear policy vision on transportation fuels, stricter enforcement of emission norms, and fiscal incentives as enablers by the government. Additionally, the collaboration among LNG suppliers, OEMs and investors has also played a crucial role in the development of retail infrastructure, thus overcoming the typical chicken and egg conundrum between which one should come first, the infrastructure or the market.

The European Union

The EU is the newest market for auto LNG, and respective governments are promoting auto LNG through a slew of incentives and enabling policies in the absence of substantial price differential between imported LNG and other liquid fuels.

The auto LNG market and infrastructure development kicked-off only after the approval of the Alternative Fuels Infrastructure Directive (AFID) by the European parliament in 2015. The directive mandated

EU member states to develop national policy frameworks for developing CNG and LNG refuelling points on the main corridors of the Trans-European Network for Transport by 2025 (LNG Blue Corridors) and set binding targets for each state. Several EU member countries are also providing incentives for the purchase of LNG vehicles. For example, Germany earmarked €10 million for funding LNG vehicles in 2018 (subsidy per lorry and tractor is €8,000 for CNG and €12,000 for LNG); Spain offered subsidies towards the purchase of new NGVs (€1,200 for a car and €12,000 for a bus or truck) and development of new refuelling facilities in 2017/18; the Netherlands is developing an LNG-based transportation corridor along the Rhine through Germany to Switzerland.

While there are several differences in the resource mix and paths for achieving economic growth and environmental targets, India could still adopt several policies and regulatory initiatives undertaken globally to create a sustainable ecosystem for the development of the auto LNG market in India.

A CNG Case Study

Critical factors that played a key role in the adoption of CNG in Mumbai and Delhi provide a blueprint for the development of the LNG market for MCVs and HCVs.

- Judicial and regulatory interventions, driven by environmental and health imperatives, laid the foundation for seeding CNG markets.
- Allocation of cheap domestic gas and favourable taxation sustained the price advantage over vis-à-vis diesel/petrol.
- Assurance of availability of fuel was provided by developing refuelling networks and financial incentives for conversion kits.

Case Study: Mumbai

Enabling Conditions

- Proximity to domestic gas landfall point in Mumbai (Uran) and existing gas pipeline networks and allocation of domestic gas.

- Establishing a robust CGD market to develop during the initial phase.

- Judicial intervention to phase out older transport vehicles within stipulated time-limits, pursuant to a writ filed by environmental activists.

- An eight-year extension of the vehicle licence when it was converted to CNG, created a demand for the conversion of approximately 15,000 diesel Premier Padmini taxis in 2002.

- 50,000 petrol-run taxis also converted over time to CNG, driven by inter-fuel price advantages. Similar orders in subsequent years helped to extend the useful lives of light commercial vehicles (LCVs) and three-wheelers.

- Government support by providing financial assistance for the conversion of three-wheelers and taxis under the Seed Capital Scheme and reduction of sales tax on CNG kits by 50 per cent.

- Favourable price differential driven by differential taxation and continued domestic gas allocation ensured that the payback period remained less than one year for three-wheelers, taxis and LCVs.

Effective Results

- Robust market potential attracted auto manufacturers to launch CNG models, ensuring the development of an ecosystem for the whole supply chain and after-market services.

- Development of a CNG retail network ensured the availability of CNG and contributed to the growth of the market. Mahanagar

Gas Limited (MGL) has been supplying gas to ~7.5 lakh CNG natural gas vehicles (NGVs), through its network of over 256 CNG stations in Mumbai and Thane.

Case Study: Delhi

Enabling Conditions

- Availability of cheap domestic gas due to the GAIL trunk pipeline helped to seed the CNG market during the initial phase in the mid-1990s.
- Judicial intervention by the Supreme Court in a public interest litigation filed by M.C. Mehta, aided conversion of public transport (taxi, three-wheeler and bus fleets to CNG) within a stipulated timeline based on the recommendations of the Environment Pollution (Prevention and Control) Authority in 1998.
- Sustained inter-fuel price differentials also helped the CNG market to flourish.

Effective Results

- Indraprastha Gas Limited (IGL) has been supplying CNG to ~ 11.5 lakh CNG vehicles, through its robust network of over 550 CNG stations in Delhi and NCR.

Case Study: Gujarat

Enabling Conditions

- Promotion by the state government and enabling policies encouraged private investors to build CGD networks in the early 1990s.

- Favourable inter-fuel differential prices coupled with proximity to RLNG terminals and landfall points of Mumbai's offshore domestic gas.

Effective Results

- Developed intrastate pipeline networks enabled the adoption of CNG in cities like Surat, Ahmedabad and Vadodara in the late 1990s.

RECOMMENDATIONS FOR LNG IN ROAD TRANSPORT

It is clear that LNG can play a significant role as a suitable fuel—economically and environmentally—in the MCV and HCV segments for long-haul transportation, as it offers better performance vis-à-vis diesel vehicles. While EVs are widely anticipated to become the mainstay in the two/three/passenger car segments for intra-city transport over the next five to eight years, the development of suitable technology for a mass-scale adoption in the MCV and HCV segments for long-haul transportation is unlikely to be available until the end of next decade. Against this backdrop, the adoption of LNG for long-haul transportation has the potential to not only address emissions from the transportation sector but also provide attractive economics for all stakeholders including the national and state governments.

Stakeholder-wise Recommendations

Government of India

- Reduce GST/Tax on LNG to 5 per cent, equal to GST on coal (polluting fuels).
- The GST rate on LNG-fuelled HDV/MDVs should be reduced from 28 per cent to 5 per cent—on par with EVs. The reduction of

GST rates on new LNG vehicles, as compared to diesel vehicles, will help in reducing the incremental cost of the vehicle and motivate fleet operators to purchase the same.

- Provide infrastructure status to LNG stations, long-term and short-term tax-incentives and faster depreciation, as incentives to LNG retail station operators.
- Government grants/subsidies should be provided for the incremental vehicle cost to state transportation corporations, to enable them to switch over to LNG.
- Promote indigenous manufacturing of tanks and LNG RO dispensing equipment through incentives.
- Encourage government departments/public enterprises to use LNG vehicles for long-distance transportation.

Ministry of Petroleum and Natural Gas and the PNGRB

- The ministry should collaborate with other key stakeholders to create an integrated roadmap for faster adoption of LNG as a transport fuel.
- The ministry may issue necessary guidelines for collaboration between entities setting up LNG and LCNG stations and provide a level playing field for both entities. With the declining domestic gas production, which is available at administrative price mechanism (APM) prices, the government will have to review existing gas allocation rules and may have to explore domestic gas and RLNG pooling for CGD priority segments as well.
- Create a cryogenic vehicles research centre and provide R&D grants for associated research.

Ministry of Road Transport and Highways

- The vehicle scrapping policy may be amended to provide incentives to vehicle owners to switch to LNG vehicles. Replacement of old diesel vehicles by LNG vehicles can be encouraged by levying a lower GST rate on new LNG vehicles against a scrapped diesel vehicle under the 'voluntary vehicle fleet modernization plan,' which is expected to be launched shortly.

- Provide incentives to manufacturing set-up either by international manufacturers or as joint ventures with Indian companies. This will increase the availability of more models in the Indian market.

- Waiver of road tax for LNG vehicles on par with EVs by the state governments.

Petroleum and Explosives Safety Organization

- The retrofitting of existing diesel vehicles to LNG, could provide the initial impetus for the growth of auto LNG as in the case of the CNG market development in Mumbai and Delhi. This will extend the life of old diesel vehicles at a fraction of the cost of replacement by BS VI compliant vehicles. Petroleum and Explosives Safety Organization (PESO) should notify the standard checklist and tests to be conducted for the type approval and put in place a mechanism for time-bound approvals. Additionally, the regulator should notify guidelines for the authorization of service providers to provide retrofitting services. This will help LNG penetration flourish through after-market services.

- PESO should approve the use of ISO tankers for LNG transportation. Transportation through railway tank wagons can ensure supply to industry corridors at cheaper rates of transportation, thus reducing the fuel cost as well.

- Permit mobile LNG stations (LNG RO on wheels) to operate in India. Mobile ROs can help in faster penetration of LNG and create seed markets for setting up conventional ROs. Additionally, they will help new CGD operators to develop CNG markets and support the development of pipeline infrastructure.

Other Stakeholders

- LNG in the transport sector can only realize its potential with the collaboration of all players in the value chain by sharing risks suiting their appetite and return expectations.
- LNG suppliers and clean energy investors should explore models for funding the incremental cost of vehicles and retail stations, subject to minimum consumption assurance and/or sharing the price differential between LNG and diesel under suitable commercial models.

Integrated Roadmap

Ministry of Road Transport and Highways, the Department of Heavy Industries and the Ministry of Petroleum and Natural Gas should create an integrated roadmap to promote LNG as a transport fuel in collaboration with other government, regulatory and industry players/bodies.

Figure 4: Stakeholders towards an integrated road map

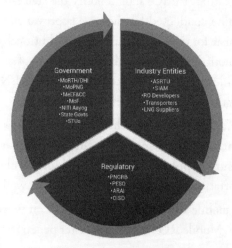

Government: Ministry of Road Transport and Highways, Department of Heavy Industries, Ministry of Petroleum and Natural Gas, Ministry of Environment, Forest and Climate Change, Ministry of Finance, NITI Aayog, State Governments and State Transport Corporations

Industry Entities: Association of State Road Transport Undertakings, Society of Indian Automobile Manufacturers, Retail Outlet Developers, Original Equipment Manufacturers

Regulatory: Petroleum and Natural Gas Regulatory Board, Petroleum and Natural Gas Regulatory Board, Automotive Research Association of India, Oil Industry Safety Directorate

ANNEXURE 1

TECHNICAL AND SAFETY REGULATIONS FOR LNG AS TRANSPORT FUEL

LNG Engine and Storage

- Central Motor Vehicles (Tenth Amendment) Rules, 2017: Design and emission standards.
- Gas Cylinder (Amendment) Rules, 2018: Specification for cylinder.

LNG Dispensing Station and Road Transportation

- Static and Mobile Pressure Vessels (Amendment) Rules, 2018: Setting up and operating standards and safety standards of LNG dispensing stations; requirements and safety standards for road transportation.

LNG Terminal

- Static and Mobile Pressure Vessels (Amendment) Rules, 2018: Specifications of LNG storage vessels, piping, fitting and valves and safety standards.

LNG Vehicles

- Automotive Industry Standard - 024 and 028 (Amendments) 2018: LNG vehicle components including fitment of cylinder on vehicle, regulator, vaporizer, LNG receptacle, joints, connections, compartment or sub-compartment, automatic shutoff valve, ventilation, gas-air mixture and gas injector.
- Central Motor Vehicles Rules, 1989 (Amendments) 2018/19: Type approval requirements for OE or converted LNG and dual-fuel vehicles.

Notes

1. MoRTH Concept note on Voluntary Vehicle Fleet Modernization Programme & NCAP, National Clean Air Programme 2019, https://morth.nic.in/sites/default/files/Concept_Note_on_Voluntary_Vehicle_Fleet_Modernization_Programme.pdf
2. http://ngvemissionsstudy.eu/
3. SIAM, https://www.siam.in/publications.aspx?mpgid=42&pgidtrail=45
   https://morth.nic.in/road-transport-year-books; https://morth.nic.in/annual-report; https://morth.nic.in/sites/default/files/Concept_Note_on_Voluntary_Vehicle_Fleet_Modernization_Programme.pdf; http://ngvemissionsstudy.eu/; https://www.siam.in/publications.aspx?mpgid=42&pgidtrail=45; https://morth.nic.in/road-transport-year-books; https://morth.nic.in/annual-report

SUPPLY AND INFRASTRUCTURE

17

DOMESTIC PRODUCTION

RAJEEV KUMAR

Vice President, Business Development and Integration, bp India

INTRODUCTION

INDIA HAS BEEN PRODUCING GAS for over a century. Historically, however, gas has generally been considered a by-product of oil production and has consequently not enjoyed the same strategic significance as oil. Discoveries consisting solely of gas had often been dismissed as relative failures. The consumption of gas was mainly confined to local areas, with its utilization remaining stagnant at around 4–5 million metric standard cubic metres per day (MMscm/d). The late 1980s and early 1990s marked the beginning of the development of gas sectors in India, with the commissioning of the Hazira–Vijaipur–Jagdishpur (HVJ) pipeline in 1987-88, leading to a significant jump in production. This was followed by the major gas-only field, Bassein, coming into production in 1988. The late 1990s saw a significant rise in production, though suboptimal pricing prevented discoveries from being developed.

Over the last three decades, the sector has seen a series of policy reforms in the upstream industry—pre-NELP exploration regime, pre-NELP small, medium-sized and discovered fields; a coal-bed methane (CBM) policy and subsequently, the launch of the New Exploration Licensing Policy (NELP) in 1999. These were aimed at reducing the dependence on the import of both oil and gas, as well as meeting the energy needs of a growing population. Several changes in market development and pricing transformed the gas sector in the 1990s, resulting in a significant growth in demand, a dramatic reduction in flaring and substantial increase in production.

Between 1991 and 1996, government intervention provided the required impetus to open avenues for exploration and production in the oil and gas sector in India. In 1991, the oil and gas sector was opened up to private sector participation under the pre-NELP exploration regime and pre-NELP small, medium-sized and discovered fields.

The liberalized policy adopted by the Government of India necessitated an appropriate agency to regulate and oversee the upstream activities in the petroleum and natural gas sector and also advise the government in these areas. The Directorate General of Hydrocarbons was set up in 1993 to oversee and review oil and gas field development programmes to encourage exploration and production.

Before NELP was launched in 1999, twenty-eight exploration blocks were awarded to private companies, with the Oil and Natural Gas Corporation (ONGC) and Oil India Limited (OIL) retaining the rights to participate in the blocks after hydrocarbon discoveries. The Government of India offered twenty-eight small and medium-sized discovered fields (proven reserves discovered by ONGC and OIL) to the private sector during the same period. Production sharing contracts (PSCs) awarded in 1992–93 had the distinctive feature of private companies being operators with ONGC/OIL retaining participating interests. This resulted in production and revenue-sharing issues in the awarded blocks. Therefore, in order to further encourage investment in the exploration and production (E&P) sector both by private and public companies, NELP was introduced by the Government of India in 1999. Some key features of this policy included:

- The clause for mandatory state participation through ONGC and OIL or any carried interest of the state was removed.
- ONGC and OIL would compete with private sector companies to obtain petroleum exploration licences (PELs), unlike the earlier grant of PELs (for public sector units) on a nomination basis.
- Companies were given the freedom to market crude oil and natural gas in the domestic market.
- Cess (levied earlier on crude oil production) was abolished.
- Licences were awarded through a process of international competitive bidding.
- No signature discovery or production bonus needed to be paid.
- Full cost recovery was allowed, with an unlimited carry-forward period on a contract area basis.

Between 1999 and 2016, nine rounds of NELP saw the Government of India signing 254 contracts with national oil companies as well as private and joint venture companies. These contracts resulted in 172 discoveries—sixty-six oil and 106 gas. Upstream reforms resulted in several gas discoveries, mostly in deep water but most of them were either not commercial or the estimated resources were less than expected.

While NELP did succeed in opening up the upstream sector to private and international players, it failed to deliver a sustained increase in gas production or attract any substantial investment due to multiple challenges, viz., a prolonged award process, hurdles in getting requisite approvals, an inflexible contractual framework, policy clarity, a perceived risk of state intervention in pricing and marketing terms and below-ground factors. As a result of these, more than 80 per cent of NELP contracts have been relinquished, and only forty-five contracts out of 254 are operational. This led to a new policy framework in 2016 under the Hydrocarbon Exploration and Licensing Policy (HELP).

Despite numerous changes in the upstream sector, India's production profile for natural gas has not seen substantial increase. In fact, since 2010, domestic production has either declined or remained stagnant. If natural gas consumption is to increase, a corresponding increase in domestic production becomes a natural prerequisite. For this to happen, a number of changes still have to be initiated in India's upstream policy. This chapter seeks to identify pressure points along the upstream value-chain and provide recommendations that could facilitate domestic production.

INDIA'S NATURAL GAS PRODUCTION PROFILE

India's natural gas production saw a continuous increase till 2010, with the recognition of gas as an important energy source. Since then, the figures have been alternating.

Figure 1: Timeline of policies in India

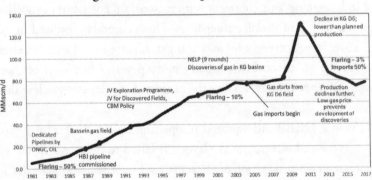

Source: Analysis based on data from the Ministry of Petroleum and Natural Gas, Government of India.

Domestic production in the country consists of output from nominated blocks under ONGC and OIL, from pre-NELP exploration, pre-NELP producing fields and NELP blocks under the PSC regime. Over the last decade, the nomination blocks of ONGC and OIL have been the dominant suppliers of domestic gas. Balance supplies have come in from private and JV fields like the Panna–Mukta–Tapti basin, blocks operated by Vedanta (Cairn), and from the fields awarded under NELP like Reliance Industries Limited (RIL) and British Petroleum's (BP) KG-D6. The commercial production of coal-bed methane (CBM) in India commenced in Raniganj, West Bengal, from 2007, with five producing blocks currently. The gas is being supplied from fields located in western and south-eastern areas, viz., the Hazira basin, Mumbai offshore and the KG basin as well as the north-east region (Assam and Tripura).

The year 2010 saw an upward trend in the supply of gas from the KG basin and then a subsequent decrease till 2017, due to a decline in production from the KG basin and not much additional production from other NELP blocks. Gas production has shown an increase over the last two years, led mainly by a growth in output from ONGC's marginal fields in eastern offshore regions, and new development projects in western offshore areas. In 2019, offshore fields accounted for approximately ~67 per cent of gas production. The remaining natural gas production, including CBM, was from ten states—Andhra Pradesh (3 per cent), north-eastern states (15 per cent), Gujarat (4 per cent), Rajasthan (5 per cent), Tamil Nadu (4 per cent) and CBM from Jharkhand, Madhya Pradesh and West Bengal (2 per cent).

Figure 2: Production profile of gas in India

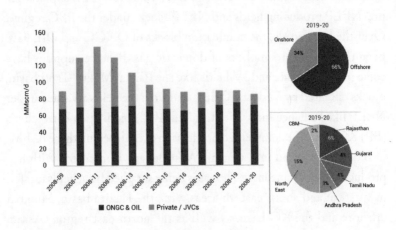

Source: Ministry of Petroleum and Natural Gas.

ESTIMATION OF GAS RESOURCES

Despite declining domestic production, India is estimated to have significant resources. IHS bp E&P Resource Study estimated the total gas resource potential in India until 2050 at over 100 trillion cubic feet (Tcf) or greater than 20 billion barrels of oil equivalent (Bboe). This comprises conventional (41 per cent), unconventional (17 per cent), technology impact (14 per cent), yet-to-find (14 per cent) and frontier yet-to-find (14 per cent). The DGH report provides an almost similar total. As per its E&P activity book for 2018–19, there is about 7 Bboe (or 47 Tcf) of already discovered gas resources. Undiscovered prognosticated resources are estimated at 600 Tcf (50 per cent gas of the total resource potential). With a 25 per cent chance of success and 60 per cent recovery, yet-to-find recoverable resources for gas are ~100 Tcf.

The scope for technology to increase recovery is estimated at 3.7 Bboe (around 20 Tcf), which is largely driven by subsurface and imaging (43 per cent), with contributions from wells (construction and intervention) and recovery. Digital technologies contribute ~25 per cent of the volume uplift.

Figure 3: Gas resources in India

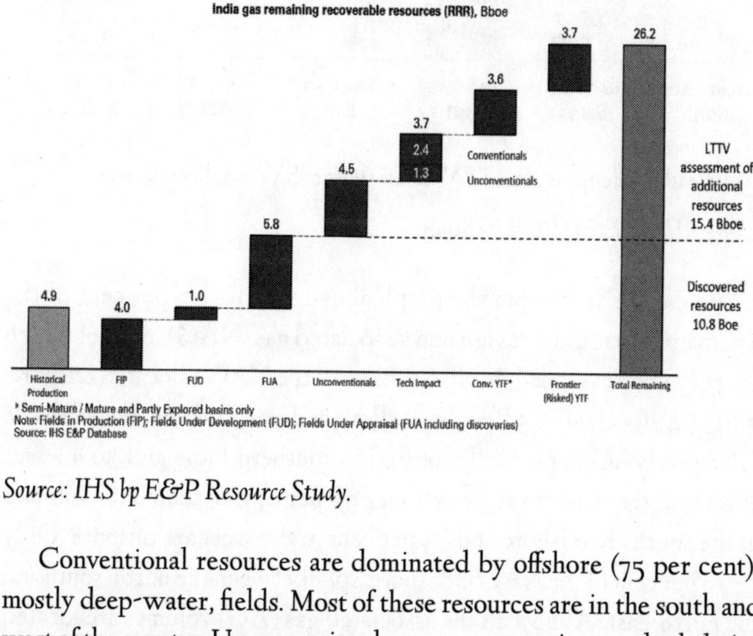

India gas remaining recoverable resources (RRR), Bboe

> Semi-Mature / Mature and Partly Explored basins only
> Note: Fields in Production (FIP); Fields Under Development (FUD); Fields Under Appraisal (FUA including discoveries)
> Source: IHS E&P Database

Source: IHS bp E&P Resource Study.

Conventional resources are dominated by offshore (75 per cent), mostly deep-water, fields. Most of these resources are in the south and west of the country. Unconventional resources comprise mostly shale (75 per cent) and CBM. In terms of exploration potential, 3.6 Bboe (~20 Tcf) arises in proven basins with a further 3.7 Bboe of risked opportunity in unproven frontier areas. Yet-to-find resources from proven basins are mainly from the KG basin, with the Cauvery constituting more than 60 per cent. Yet-to-find resources from the frontier basins have a success rate of 5–10 per cent, mainly coming from the Indus fan, the Mahanadi River, the Punjab shelf and the Andamans.

Figure 4: Discovered conventional gas resources (MMboe)

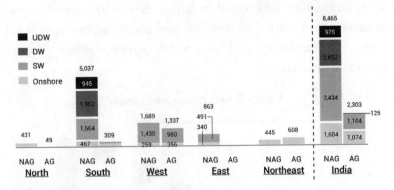

UDW: ultra-deep-water; DW: deep water; SW: shallow water

Source: IHS bp E&P Resource Study.

As can be seen from the graph above, almost 80 per cent of the discovered gas resources are non-associated gas (NAG), most of which are yet to be developed. In all, 6.9 Bboe of the NAG is located offshore, with 3.4 Bboe and 2.5 Bboe in shallow and deep waters, respectively. Offshore NAG is primarily located in southern India and, to a lesser extent, in the western regions. Over 90 per cent of the NAG volumes in the south are offshore and 85 per cent in the west are offshore. Only ~20 per cent of the NAG is onshore, split between the north, south and the north-east. Almost all the associated gas (AG) volumes are located onshore and in shallow waters in oil dominant regions—the west and north-east—with almost all of them being in production.

There is substantial unconventional in-place gas resource potential, although risked recoverable resources are far more modest. While un-risked in-place resources are estimated to be about 174 Bboe, risked recoverable resources are estimated to be 4.5 Bboe. Unconventional sources are concentrated in Cambay, Cauvery, Krishna–Godavari and the Assam shelf. The most important tight/shale oil and shale gas plays are in the west and south. The eastern region holds important CBM plays. The potential for gas hydrates is large in the Bay of Bengal but very uncertain, as evidenced by a survey 'The Indian National Gas Hydrate Programme Expedition 02', undertaken in 2015.[1] The challenges faced by unconventional development are mostly factors above ground level as well as modest geological potential, due to the kerogen quality and maturity risks.

While there is significant potential in both the level of exploration activities and the development of the discovered resources, that potential has not been realized due to suboptimal gas pricing policies, coupled with issues related to contract management. Companies have focused more on oil discoveries and their development, especially since oil producers are being offered import parity prices.

KEY ISSUES THAT HAMPER INCREASED PRODUCTION

THE UNIQUE NATURE OF E&P PROJECTS

Figure 5 depicts a typical cycle for an oil and gas field development in a deep-water field. Given that the Indian hydrocarbon basin is medium to high risk, as can be seen below, only about 10 per cent of exploration activity is successful and goes into development. Barring a few exceptions, it usually takes at least seven to ten years to complete the exploration and appraisal process before the field is ready for development. Development projects for offshore fields take an additional four to five years for a greenfield gas development.

While exploration costs are about 10 per cent of the E&P life cycle cost, the biggest cost component is taken up by development that accounts for over 80 per cent of the total life cycle cost. Therefore, while contractors can incur initial exploration expenses at their own risk, depending on the probability of success, it becomes critical to have clarity around future revenues and pricing, before large amounts of capital expenditure for development are committed.

Figure 5: Typical cycle for oil and gas field development in deep-water field

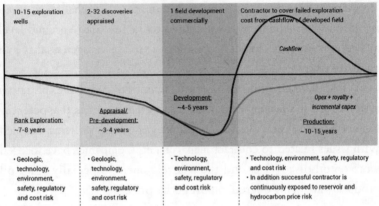

Source: Analysis by author.

Hence the prices of oil and gas must account for the costs of finding oil and gas resources, the business risks involved and costs for developing and operating the fields along with any statutory duties. In addition, prices should also provide a reasonable return to the investor on the overall E&P portfolio.

COST OF SUPPLY

The cost of supply can range widely from $4/Boe to $77/Boe, i.e., $1/MMBtu (one million British Thermal Units) to $13/MMBtu. Most resources require an average cost of supply in the range of $5/MMBtu to $8/MMBtu (Figure 6 below).[2]

To be able to fully develop and produce India's potential gas resources, gas price is extremely critical. First, over 90 per cent of this potential is non-associated gas. The development of such resources would be the same as that of crude oil. Second, most of these resources are in difficult areas—deep water, ultra-deep water, offshore, etc. This will further increase the cost of development. Hence, it is important that these gas resources are explored and developed as long as they can be produced at prices lower than landed liquefied natural gas (LNG). Fiscal stability and predictable regulatory frameworks are also critical, given the long gestation period of an E&P project.

Figure 6: Range of the cost of gas supply ($/Boe)

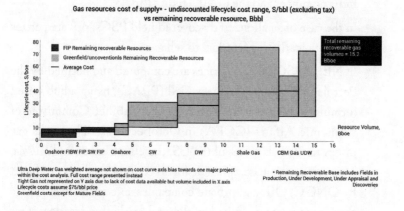

Gas resources cost of supply* - undiscounted lifecycle cost range, S/bbl (excluding tax) vs remaining recoverable resource, Bbbl

Ultra Deep Water Gas weighted average not shown on cost curve axis bias towards one major project within the cost analysis. Full cost range presented instead
Tight Gas not represented on Y axis due to lack of cost data available but volume included in X axis
Lifecycle costs assume $75/bbl price
Greenfield costs except for Mature Fields

* Remaining Recoverable Base includes Fields in Production, Under Development, Under Appraisal and Discoveries

Source: IHS bp E&P Resource Study.

PRICING ISSUES

Despite commercially untenable gas prices, domestic gas in India has been regulated and priced below the cost of supply. Over the years, multiple pricing regimes have been introduced by the Government of India.

- Historically, in some pre-NELP PSCs for exploration blocks, the government allowed pricing freedom (but without marketing freedom). Gas was sold at market-determined prices discovered/ negotiated by contractors.

- In the case of mid-sized discovered field PSCs, the government agreed to a market-related price, which was derived based on a pre-agreed fuel-oil basket linked formula in PSCs with a provision for periodic price revision. In the Panna–Mukta–Tapti basin, the price formula for gas is linked to an internationally traded fuel-oil basket, with a specified floor and ceiling price with provision to revise the ceiling price after seven years from the date of first supply. In these PSCs, gas is being sold to Government of India nominees and the GAIL (India) Ltd.

- In the case of small-sized discovered field PSCs, private parties are given marketing freedom to sell gas.

- In NELP PSCs, the gas prices are computed and notified by the Petroleum Planning Analysis Cell (PPAC), using a hub-based formula, which was approved by the Cabinet Committee of Economic Affairs (CCEA) in October 2014. This links gas prices to the hub prices of the US, the UK, Canada and Russia. This price regime is applicable for all conventional gas produced by ONGC, OIL and private companies, except in cases where the Government of India has allowed marketing freedom. Gas is sold at a 40 per cent discount in the north-eastern region, which is reimbursed from the Union budget. This formula leads to significantly lower gas prices as it is based on prices from gas surplus countries, even though India is a net importer of gas. According to economic principles, domestic prices must align with international prices, which is the true opportunity cost of gas to the economy.

- Most domestic gas (85 per cent) is priced using the formula mandated by the Central government in 2014. For other kinds of gas (~10 per cent of domestic sales or 10 MMscm/d) companies have been given marketing freedom or in the case of some PSCs, the gas price formula, linked to liquid fuels, has been agreed upon in the respective PSC itself. In addition, about 50 per cent of natural gas consumed in the country is imported in the form of

LNG under long-term/short-term contracts as well as on-the-spot contracts. However, even with this type of regime, there are several concerns regarding gas pricing:

○ Cost of production versus end-use gas price: The existing gas production is restricted to a few areas (western offshore, parts of Cambay, KG offshore and the north-east), and the bulk of these volumes are from mature fields. The lack of market-driven gas prices for old fields disincentivizes investments, which could extend field life and increase production. While India imports ∼50 per cent of its gas requirements, gas prices continue to be linked to gas prices of gas surplus countries with prolific geology and a high proportion of onshore and associated gas, all of which create downward pressure on prices. The impact on profitability has a compounding effect on the ability to fund existing and new projects in India. It is important to note that, while historically most of the gas production was by way of associated gas, present discoveries are largely non-associated gas and hence need a market-based price to ensure that they are developed. The cost of the development of these non-associated gas discoveries is the same as that of crude oil. Further, development and operating costs vary across shallow and deep-water projects and a view of full life-cycle costs, including decommissioning expenses, need to be taken.

○ Treatment of oil vis-à-vis gas: The price of gas has always been at a significant discount to oil. For FY20, the average price of domestic allocated gas of $3.46/MMBtu translates into an oil equivalent price of $20/Bbl; at a time when the average Brent price was $61/Bbl. It is also pertinent to note that oil produced under the same regime is linked to Brent/Bonny Light and priced almost at import parity. This makes it unattractive for developers to invest in gas production.

- Natural gas has been excluded from GST, which has a twin impact on gas markets, by increasing the capital cost for investors and increasing the cost for buyers.

Inadequate Supply Infrastructure

The existing gas pipeline infrastructure, particularly in south and east India is limited. The presence of a bundled entity (involved in both transportation and marketing) distorts the competitive functioning of the gas market by creating a monopoly with entry barriers. This in turn creates price distortion and prevents true transparent price discovery.

There are also some regulatory/governance challenges that have impacted the production of gas.

- Lack of incentive to develop difficult resources: Most discovered resources were in difficult to produce areas (and depths), which made development under the government-controlled prices unviable. While the development cost of gas discoveries was linked to the crude oil price (services and procurement cost are driven by oil), the controlled gas price was much lower than the equivalent crude oil price (on calorific value equivalent basis), leading to multiple discoveries not being developed.
- Lack of clarity on PSC interpretation: As some PSCs progressed into the production phase, the focus began to shift from activities to revenues, which resulted in considerable scrutiny from statutory agencies, severely impacting decision-making. Some basic decisions went through multiple decision windows, delaying both exploration and development. The lack of clarity around gas pricing (the significant difference between domestic price and import price, gas utilization policy, etc.) also delayed the development of the gas sector, impacting both the supply and the market.

- Cross-subsidies: The prevailing regime of domestic gas pricing allows for cross-subsidies to other sectors like fertilizers, power and CGD, which has suppressed the domestic pricing of gas. It is well accepted and documented that subsidizing end-use industries via the price of feedstock (in this case natural gas), is one of the most price-distorting approaches.

RECENT POLICY REFORMS

In recent years, policy decisions and major reforms have been taken to address many policy-related issues, to arrest production decline and attract new investments. In March 2016, the government implemented the Hydrocarbon Exploration & Licensing Policy (HELP) under which blocks are awarded via the Open Acreage Licensing Policy (OALP). Bids submitted under HELP are assessed based on the work programme committed to and potential government revenue share post-royalty; OALP gives companies the flexibility to carve out blocks of their choice and submit an expression of interest (EOI) at any time of the year (accumulated twice a year and invited for bids).

The key features of HELP are:

- Single licence that covers the exploration and production of all types of hydrocarbon, viz., conventional oil and gas, CBM, shale oil, gas hydrates, etc.
- Revenue-sharing contracts with two monitoring parameters for the government revenue and production of the contractor, no cost recovery and hence, micro-management by the government.
- Reduced and graded royalty rates.
- Full marketing and pricing freedom of gas (on 'an arm's length' basis).

- Extended period for exploration and production, i.e., eight years for on-land/shallow water and ten years for deep-water/frontier areas.
- Exploration throughout the contract period.

In order to incentivize the production of gas from difficult areas, the Government of India has approved marketing freedoms, including gas pricing for high-pressure/high-temperature (HP/HT), deep and ultra-deep-water discoveries/fields. A price ceiling is set for commercial production that has commenced on or after 1 January 2016. The ceiling is linked to the alternate fuel. Marketing and gas pricing freedom has been provided for future bidding rounds, including for gas pricing under HELP and Discovered Small Field (DSF).

Marketing and pricing freedom has also been provided for CBM gas and new gas discoveries for which the field development plan has yet to be approved as of March 2019. So far ninety-four blocks have been awarded up to OALP IV, and OLAP V and VI have been launched. In addition to the HELP policy, the government also took up some further reforms:

- Fast tracking the monetization of existing discovered resources: A DSF policy was introduced to fast-track the monetization of undeveloped small fields/discoveries of National Oil Companies (NOCs), awarded under the nomination regime and relinquished discoveries under the PSC regime. A DSF Bid Round-I was launched in 2016, under which thirty-one blocks were awarded in February 2017. These contracts consisted of forty-four fields with estimated in-place volumes of 424 MMBoe. The DSF Round-II was launched in 2018, with twenty-five contract areas on offer, covering fifty-nine discovered oil and gas fields, spread over 3,000 sq. km, with an in-place volume of 1.39 Bboe. Of these, twenty-three contracts were awarded in March 2019.

- Improved access to information on sedimentary basins: Additional steps have been initiated to strengthen the collection and dissemination of seismic data on sedimentary basins to provide geologists with easy access to more extensive data. A reassessment of the hydrocarbon potential of India's sedimentary basins was undertaken by a multi-organization team (ONGC, OIL and DGH) in twenty-six sedimentary basins, based on the geo-scientific data generated over several decades. The total conventional hydrocarbon reassessed volumes estimated for twenty-six sedimentary basins and offshore areas is about more than 300 Bboe as compared to the hydrocarbon resource of ∼205 Bboe assessed earlier, signifying an increase of 49.1 per cent in resource estimates. Out of this about 73 per cent is in the yet-to-discover category.

- Policy initiatives to resolve legacy issues: A number of policy initiatives aimed at unlocking production from existing acreage have been undertaken in the recent past. For example, a PSC extension policy for pre-NELP exploration blocks; an extension policy for small and medium-sized discovered fields to private JVs; a policy framework for relaxations, extensions and clarifications at the development and production stage under the PSC regime and an enhanced oil recovery (EOR) policy. Based on these policy reforms, several legacy issues have been resolved and additional production can be accessed.

Several additional policy measures were rolled out in February 2019 to accelerate exploration and maximize production from existing resources. Key features of these reforms are:

- In category 2 and 3 basins (where presently there is no commercial production), exploration blocks will be bid out exclusively based on exploration work programmes, without any revenue or production share to the Government of India, for revenue up to $2.5 billion in a financial year.

- Marketing and pricing freedom for all the new gas discoveries where the field development plan is yet to be approved.
- Enhance production from existing nomination fields of ONGC and OIL, allowing them to induct private sector partners.
- Lower royalty rates for early production.

With these key policy reforms, the E&P sector has seen considerable new investment commitment both for the development of discovered gas resources as well as a commitment of around ₹175 billion ($2.3 billion) under OALP up to Round-IV. Pricing and tax distortion continue to be a major constraint impacting investment in the exploration and production of gas.

INTERNATIONAL CASE STUDIES

Brazil

Brazil has, for a long time, priced domestic gas on a fuel-oil-parity basis. However, as more and more E&P companies are developing new gas supplies, the conditions are now conducive for gas-on-gas competition. Accordingly, Brazil has begun to permit E&P producers to negotiate with buyers independently, thereby transitioning to gas-on-gas competition and market-driven pricing.

Also note that over the past thirteen years, the Brazilian gas market has grown threefold without having to rely on any subsidies. What made this possible was pricing gas at fuel-oil parity at the burner tip. This was also the import parity price of pipeline imports from Bolivia and the price of substitute fuel. The fuel-oil-parity-pricing policy ensured that gas prices increased in line with oil prices and cost escalation, thereby maintaining the economic incentive to explore for and produce natural gas and to increase domestic production in line with demand.

Oil-linked wellhead prices have kept pace with rising upstream capital costs. Gas prices linked to oil substitutes have encouraged both consumption and supply responses. New offshore associated 'pre-salt' gas has the potential to replace LNG imports.

INDONESIA

In Indonesia, we are observing a shift from gas being exported to being consumed at home. Given the need to meet domestic demand, Indonesia recognizes that it needs to attract investments into its upstream E&P sector in order to maintain and increase indigenous gas production. It has not been successful so far due to uncompetitive PSC terms in the current regime where pricing is administered using a cost-plus approach. It has not kept pace with rising upstream costs.

To meet domestic gas demand, an increasing share of new supplies are being allocated to serve the domestic gas market through a mandated policy called the domestic market obligation (DMO). The DMO poses serious challenges to the commercialization of key resource plays and risk-deterring future investments, as its policy on pricing is uncertain. Uncertainty exists because domestic gas prices are agreed upon through negotiations on a field-by-field basis with the regulator. The government is working to improve allocation mechanisms, boost efficiency in the gas industry and reduce its overall fuel subsidy burden. However, Indonesia regularly goes back and forth on regulations regarding the oil and gas industry, thereby deterring investment.

KEY RECOMMENDATIONS AND WAY FORWARD

Meeting a significant portion of future gas demand from domestic resources is possible, perhaps up to 50 per cent through 2050, if there are successes in higher risk frontier and unconventional basins. The potential exists to grow production to almost 7–8 billion cubic feet per day (Bcf/d) from the present level of ∼2.5 Bcf/d. The recoverable resource potential is estimated at ∼100 Tcf, and comprises conventional, unconventional, exploration, frontier exploration and technology upside. Exploration potential includes opportunities within existing basins (e.g., Krishna–Godavari) and higher risk frontier basins (e.g., the Andaman Sea).

Figure 7: Potential gas production MMscm/d (2018–40) in Optimistic scenario

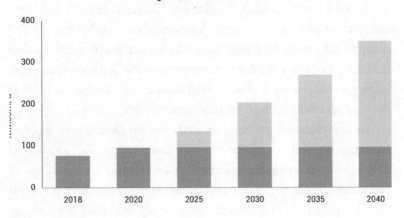

Source: IHS bp E&P Resource Study and author's assessment

Recent policy initiatives by the government—deep-water and CBM gas price deregulation, HELP/OALP policies, DSF rounds and allowing price and market freedom for the development of new gas discoveries—will provide an impetus to natural gas production in the country. Currently, various gas projects are under development from existing discovered resources that could add additional production starting 2020 onwards.

Technology can be used to have a positive impact on developing these resources. Subsurface and imaging technologies, in particular, have the potential to provide a resource boost of over 24 per cent. The impact of technology is typically greater for offshore and unconventionals. Digital technologies will contribute to cost reduction across all gas resources and have a pronounced effect in deep and ultra-deep water. Sub-basalt imaging could unlock resources, particularly, frontier plays. Small-scale hydraulic fracturing on mature onshore fields is a practice that has been used in the Permian basin in the US in recent years and could yield a further 10 per cent factor on mature onshore fields.

Figure 8: Technology potential impact on gas recoverable resources excluding YTF

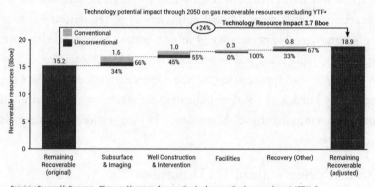

Technology potential impact through 2050 on gas recoverable resources excluding YTF*

Remaining Recoverable Resources - 2F recoverable resource for conventional and unconventional resource classes in LTTV India
*Excluding political factors, assuming current source market and prices

Source: IHS bp E&P Resource Study

However, to access India's total untapped yet-to-find potential, it is crucial to provide predictability in the appropriate contractual, fiscal and regulatory framework. It also requires a process that grants players non-discriminatory access to both marketing and infrastructure. Within the right policy framework, the Indian market will have access to domestic gas supply on a long-term sustainable basis. As the energy mix changes, countries will have to compete for capital and India will need to attract investment, technology and streamline the ease of doing business.

What Is Required?

The results of the 'Global Petroleum Survey' of 2018 by the Fraser Institute Global Petroleum,[3] indicate that the extent of positive sentiment regarding key factors driving investment in the oil and gas sector has increased in many regions around the world, thus leading to increased exploration and production activities. The US remains the most attractive region for investment globally, followed by the EU. Despite the fact that India was ranked sixty-first among eighty countries in 2018 (an improvement from previous years), it still appears in the lower half of the list mainly due to taxation, administrative uncertainty, interpretation and enforcement of regulations, cost of regulatory compliance, quality of infrastructure, geological database, regulatory duplication and inconsistencies and legal system processes. While there is an appreciation of the government's effort to reduce the regulatory burden, the survey indicates that much more is required in the areas mentioned above. Accordingly, key suggestions in this regard are listed below.

Market Pricing Without Tax Distortions

A predictable long-term market-based pricing policy with no tax distortions will enable gas to reach the right value in parity with other alternate commodities. The inclusion of natural gas under GST is key to achieving this. The GST rate should either be uniform with competing fuels for the sector, or lower to account for fewer GHG emissions per energy unit.

While market and pricing freedom has been provided for all new domestic production, this should be implemented in the true sense without any restriction or constraints and, more importantly than ever, the government must continue to stay its course. Unless the government adopts remunerative pricing, investors will not invest to monetize gas.

Predictable, Stable and Attractive Contractual and Fiscal Terms

Many projects are deferred in volatile commodity markets because of the way they are assessed on the risk and return curve. A stable and attractive fiscal regime could make a big difference to project efficiencies. This is particularly important in this sector, given that oil and gas businesses are multi-decade projects.

For basins that are not proven, differentiated HELP terms can be offered. In this regard, the recent policy announcement by the central government to bid out exploration exclusively based on exploration work programmes, without any revenue or production share to the government in category 2 and 3 basins (where presently there is no commercial production), is a positive step.

Market Infrastructure to Access the Market

India is a demand-led investment story. Market structure reforms to ensure that producers can access the pipeline infrastructure and serve customers on a non-discriminatory basis are required to unlock the potential in the E&P sector. This will not only provide producers with a fair market price but also require the Government of India to enforce the existing PNGRB regulations to separate content (gas) from the carriage (pipeline) and provide the PNGRB adequate power to ensure fair market practices. Doing this will help to overcome the current market structure and lead to the creation of a vibrant gas market.

Ease of Doing Business

India has made notable progress in the ease of doing business index. However, in the oil and gas sector, given the nature of contractual agreements, there is still the need to further simplify the existing regulatory framework. India needs to streamline processes. To this end, the government has announced the following initiatives:

- Strengthen the DGH including the delegation of power for effective contract management and expediting approvals.
- Create an alternate dispute resolution mechanism through a committee of eminent persons/experts to avoid arbitration.
- Initiate the process of fast track approval through 'Ease of Doing Business' guideline.

Notes

1. Kuldeep M. Sukla et al., 'National Gas Hydrate Programme expedition 02: Identification of gas hydrate prospects in the Krishna-Godavari Basin, offshore India', *Marine and Petroleum Geology*, Vol. 108 (2019): pp. 167–84, https://doi.org/10.1016/j.marpetgeo.2018.11.013

2. The discounted cost of supply analysis is point forward basis using a discount rate of 7 per cent. New asset costs are discounted back to their first year of spend. Producing asset costs were discounted to 2017. No capex or E&A (Exploration & Appraisal) costs were applied.

3. Ashley Stedman and Kenneth P. Green, 'Global Petroleum Survey 2018', Vancouver: Fraser Institute, 29 November 2018, https://www.fraserinstitute.org/sites/default/files/global-petroleum-survey-2018.pdf

List of citations

- IHS bp E&P Resource Study
- India's Hydrocarbon Outlook - A Report on Exploration & Production Activities – published by DGH
- Indian Petroleum and Natural Gas Statistics – published by MOPNG (numerous years)

18

PIPELINE NETWORK

ASHU SINGHAL

Chief GM (Corp. Strategy, Planning & Advocacy); Director, OPAL

RAJEEV MATHUR

Executive Director, GAIL (India) Ltd

INTRODUCTION

India has come a long way from the commissioning of the Hazira–Vijaipur–Jagdishpur (HVJ) pipeline in 1987. Natural gas pipeline networks and facilities have been augmented and the country has a ~17,900 km-long gas pipeline network at present. Most of the infrastructure is concentrated in the west, north and south-east parts of India, connecting subsequent gas markets. The transmission network facilitates delivering gas to various customers from different onshore and offshore sources. This chapter is aimed at addressing the challenges faced by the Indian gas sector. It also focuses on gas infrastructure and efforts to fulfil the vision of a gas-based economy.

The Government of India formed Gas Authority of India Limited in 1984, known as GAIL (India) Ltd, since 2002 with the following objectives:

- To augment and set up infrastructure for utilization of natural gas.
- To transport, treat, fractionate, purify and market natural gas fractions.
- To formulate plans for proper utilization of natural gas fractions in close coordination with the Government of India and concerned agencies, including industrial users.
- To plan, design and construct pipelines, systems and related facilities for collection, treatment, fractionation and marketing of natural gas fractions.
- To promote research and development in transmission, treatment and processing.

The HVJ pipeline (1986–87 Phase-I) was planned, developed and commissioned to supply large volumes of natural gas from the Bombay High fields to fertilizer and power plants along west and northwest India. The proximity to markets and grid and the promise of inclusive growth, development and geographical equity played an important role in deciding the location of fertilizer and power plants. The HVJ natural gas transport pipeline has become the lifeline of these fertilizer and power plants and also spread positive socio-economic externalities of environment-friendly industrial development in the western and northern parts of the country.

The 1990s saw a period of consolidation and augmentation of gas pipeline networks. In May 1992, the Oil and Natural Gas Corporation (ONGC) transferred all gas pipelines and marketing functions relating to natural gas to GAIL. In March 1994, the HVJ upgradation project was approved at a total cost of ₹23,760 million ($339.8 million), which increased the pipeline flow capacity from the then existing 18.2 metric million standard cubic metre per day (MMscm/d) to 33 MMscm/d. This was undertaken by increasing capacities of existing compressor stations at Hazira and Jhabua and setting up two new compressor stations at Vaghodia and Khera, together with laying an additional 505 km pipeline between Vijaipur and Dadri. In the late 1990s, the Ministry of Petroleum and Natural Gas allocated 0.6 MMscm/d of natural gas for supply to industries in Agra and Firozabad in order to improve the environment and to protect the Taj Mahal, one of the seven wonders of the world, from pollution.

In July 1997, the Government of India approved a joint venture company (JVC) for securing competitive liquefied natural gas (LNG) supply and developing facilities for its import and utilization. Accordingly, Petronet LNG Ltd was formed in 1998 as a JV by India's four major oil and gas public sector undertakings (PSUs), led by GAIL. In 2004, Petronet LNG Ltd set up South-east Asia's first LNG receiving and regasification terminal at Dahej in Gujarat, with an original nameplate capacity of 5 million metric tonnes per annum (MMtpa). It signed an LNG sale and purchase agreement with Ras Laffan Liquefied Natural Gas Company Ltd (RasGas), Qatar for the supply of 7.5 Mtpa LNG, and the first lot reached India in 2004. Later, the Dahej–Vijaipur pipeline (DVPL) and the Vijaipur–Dadri pipeline (under the Gas Rehabilitation and Expansion Project or GREP) were upgraded, integrating them with HVJ to support additional volume from Dahej.

The Petroleum and Natural Gas Regulatory Board (PNGRB) was established in 2007, under the PNGRB Act 2006, to grant authorization to entities to lay, build, operate or expand gas pipeline as common carriers or contract carriers in the country. The PNGRB defined the eligibility criteria for entities, including GAIL, to lay pipelines as a common or contract carrier under the PNGRB (Authorizing Entities to Lay, Build, Operate or Expand Natural Gas Pipelines) Regulations, 2008.

ASSESSMENT OF THE EXISTING NETWORK

At present, ~17,900 km of trunk pipelines pass through various states/ union territories (UTs) (Annexure I). Three major pipeline entities are engaged in natural gas transportation across India as of now—GAIL, Reliance Gas Transportation Infrastructure Ltd (RGTIL)/Pipeline Infrastructure Ltd (PIL) and Gujarat State Petronet Ltd (GSPL). GAIL operates over 12,800 km of trunk pipelines comprising ~72 per cent of the pan-India pipeline network. This includes the HVJ, DVPL, Dahej– Uran–Panvel–Dhabol Natural Gas Pipeline Network (DUPL/DPPL), Dadri–Bawana–Nangal and Dabhol–Bengaluru trunk pipelines, which will evacuate domestic gas, as well as imported regasified liquefied natural gas (RLNG).

In addition, GAIL also operates regional gas pipeline networks in Maharashtra, the Krishna–Godavari basin, Cauvery basin and Gujarat. The PIL and Reliance Gas Pipeline Ltd (RGPL) operate ~2,100 km of pipelines (about 11 per cent of the pan-India network), namely, the East–West pipeline (EWPL) to evacuate gas from the KG-D6 field in Andhra Pradesh and the Shadol–Phulpur pipeline. The GSPL is mainly focused in the state of Gujarat and operates ~2600 km of gas pipelines (14.5 per cent of total).

Table 1: Pipeline operators and network capacity

S. no.	Transporter	Length (km)	Percentage share
1	GAIL	12828	71.9 per cent
2	PIL	1784	10.0 per cent
3	GSPL	2593	14.5 per cent
4	AGCL/DNPL	105	0.6 per cent
5	IOCL	140	0.8 per cent
6	ONGC	24	0.1 per cent

S. no.	Transporter	Length (km)	Percentage share
7	RGPL	302	1.7 per cent
8	Gujarat Gas	73	0.4 per cent
	Total	17849	100.0 per cent

Source: PNGRB, PPAC, GAIL.

To provide an impetus for gas-grid development, the Government of India is also considering support to fund pipeline projects. The 'Vision 2030' document by the PNGRB, formulated a plan to develop a national gas-grid ecosystem across the country,[1] with another over 16,500 km of additional gas pipeline to be laid out to complete the grid and are already been authorized. Some sections of these projects are at various stages of implementation.

An action plan prepared by the Ministry of Petroleum and Natural Gas, subsequent to the declaration of a national gas grid.

The existing major cross-country natural gas pipelines transport gas to the west, north and east (under execution) of the country. At present, there is no provision for connecting pipelines from central, north-east and the east coast of India, to sources in other parts of the country. There are also a few isolated networks in the southern region. Hence, measures need to be taken to ensure the equitable distribution of natural gas nationwide. Regional imbalances in access to natural gas have to be rectified if clean and green fuel is to be provided throughout the country.

Despite the eventual building of a national gas grid, the underutilization of existing gas pipelines (pan-India gas pipeline utilization ~50 per cent) is a bottleneck to both efficient operations and further expansion. Slow expansion, in turn, jeopardizes the efficient construction and operation of LNG terminals. The next few sections identify bottlenecks in increasing infrastructure capacity under the existing framework.

CHALLENGES UNDER EXISTING FRAMEWORK

Natural gas pipeline infrastructure is highly capital intensive. Without an anchor, i.e., load customers like power and fertilizer companies, capital investment in pipeline networks cannot get the required returns. An uncertain demand-supply scenario further amplifies risk on proposed pipeline projects, making them economically unviable.

So far, GAIL has been the only entity to make substantial progress in the execution of national gas-grid pipelines and the majority of the pipelines awarded by PNGRB are yet to witness any notable progress. The reasons for slow or no progress may be summarized as follows.

COMMERCIAL/INDUSTRY CHALLENGES

Slow progress is in part attributable to the uncertainty of demand risk. For natural gas pipelines, the ambiguity on demand risk currently lies with the developer.

The design capacity of existing gas pipelines in India stood at 369 MMscm/d on 1 April 2018. Suboptimal flow rates led to an average of 45 per cent effective capacity utilization, with large variations across regions (the high-demand region of Mumbai utilized up to 91 per cent of pipeline capacity, while the 1,000 km Dabhol–Bengaluru pipeline utilized a low 8 per cent).

Some other challenges include:

- Reduction in domestic gas supply and lack of visibility in the increase of domestic gas production
- Low demand tie-up, due to non-affordability of imported regasified liquefied natural gas (RLNG)
- Stranded gas-based power plants due to paucity of domestic natural gas

- Lack of new anchor customers (fertilizers and power plants) to increase offtake
- Lack of reforms in end-user sectors leading to lower price affordability with respect to competing fuels
- Low and uncertain financial return on investments.
- Low prices of polluting competitive fuels (coal/liquid fuels versus gas)
- Natural gas is kept out of the Goods and Services Tax (GST) regime. End consumers don't get tax credit on value-added tax (VAT) paid, resulting in increased cost of production for gas-based industrial consumers.

REGULATORY CHALLENGES

Major enablers of growth and capacity utilization in the transmission pipeline segment include government policy and regulation and regular access to multiple sources of gas and demand centres across the network.

Regulations are expected to provide a fair and level playing field for operators, while ensuring that customers get regular supply at reasonable prices. At the same time, regulations must facilitate investment and network expansion by serious players keeping economic viability in view. When such growth enablers are stifled, this has a direct impact on the creation as well as utilization of pipeline capacity.

The low capacity utilization of existing networks, alongside implementation delays of upcoming pipelines, is a testament to this issue. Though the government laid out ambitious plans to double the pipeline network and Indian pipeline companies have obtained authorization for a number of pipelines through the PNGRB, the progress of construction of these pipelines has been very tardy, as reflected by the data.

Table 2: Status of under-construction pipelines for the national gas grid (more than 3 years from authorization)

Network/Region	Entity	Length (km)	Design Capacity (MMScm/d)	Year of Authorization by PNGRB	Status
Mallavaram–Bhilwada	GSPC India Transco Ltd	2042	78	July 2011	Partially laid upto Ramagundam in Telangana
Mehsana–Bhatinda	GSPL India Gasnet Ltd	2052	77	July 2011	Partially laid
Bhatinda–Srinagar	GSPL India Gasnet Ltd	725	42	July 2011	Partially laid
Kakinada–Vizag–Srikakulam	A P Gas Distribution	391	90	July 2014	NIL
Ennore–Nellore	Gas Transmission India Pvt. Ltd	250	36	December 2014	NIL
Ennore–Thiruvallur–Bengaluru Puducherry–Nagapattinam Madurai–Tuticorin	Indian Oil Corporation Ltd	1385	85	December 2015	Partially laid to be completed by 2021
Jaigarh–Mangalore	H-Energy Pvt. Ltd	635	17	June, 2016	NIL

Source: PPAC, PNGRB.

The existing model for natural gas pipelines in India is a bidded tariff per unit of energy (MMBtu) for twenty-five years for PNGRB-bidded pipelines. For pipelines authorized by state/central governments, the PNGRB determines tariff as per regulations, where tariff is computed with 60 to 100 per cent capacity utilization in the first five years of the pipeline to derive a twelve per cent return on capital deployed.

In either situation, the volume risk remains with the project investor. To begin with, the volume is low and the investor is not able to recoup his cost during the initial years. Further, the additive/pancaking tariff methodology employed by the PNGRB results in high pipeline tariffs, which when passed on to consumers makes the fuel unaffordable in new/remote areas. Eventually, it impacts capacity utilization of existing pipeline infrastructure, resulting in substantially low returns on investment as against the intended return (12 per cent post tax) in PNGRB regulations. Other challenges include issues related to right of use/right of way acquisition in various states.

Financial Viability/Sustainability of Pipeline Projects

Pipelines involve large capital investment, which is coupled with significant risk in terms of financial viability and returns on investment. The development of the natural gas market is still in a nascent stage in the central, eastern and north-eastern parts of India. Further, the practical difficulties of pipeline project execution, right-of-use acquisition, highly cost intensive, etc., makes it imperative that adequate security of investment be envisaged during the techno-commercial planning of pipelines.

In order to reduce project costs, to make the investment financially viable and also to make the tariff affordable to customers—particularly to fertilizer plants, power plants, city gas distribution (CGD) entities and small industrial consumers—Central and state governments could consider viability gap funding or capital support to develop natural gas pipeline infrastructure as a public good. For example, in the ongoing

Jagdishpur–Haldia and Bokaro–Dhamra Pipeline (JHBDPL) project, execution began only after the Cabinet Committee on Economic Affairs (CCEA) approved numerous enabling factors to make investment commercially viable:

- Capital grant of 40 per cent
- Unified tariff on GAIL's interconnected cross-country pipelines
- Signing of gas supply and transportation agreement (GSTA) with three fertilizer plants
- Approval for the development of seven cities en route to the JHBDPL project

ENABLERS TO DEVELOP GAS INFRASTRUCTURE IN INDIA

Funding Models

Viability Gap Funding

The 2014 Union budget announced the construction of an additional 15,000 km of gas pipelines on a public-private partnership (PPP) basis, along with viability gap funding (VGF). The success of a gas pipeline under this mode would depend on aligning availability, demand, pricing of gas, and gas transportation (tariff), to create a win-win situation of for all stakeholders. Viability gap funding would hedge the associated risk. Infrastructure projects have long gestation periods and, in most cases, are not financially viable on their own. Primarily, VGF is meant to reduce the capital cost of projects by credit enhancement and to make them viable and attractive for private investment through supplementary grant funding.

As discussed earlier, in 2016, the Government of India provided 40 per cent VGF as a capital grant for the ₹129.4 billion ($1.85 billion) natural gas pipeline from Jagdishpur to Haldia and Bokaro to Dhamra

(JHBDPL), along with the promise of creating anchor-load customers along the pipeline. However, much more is needed to create the nation's gas highways to ultimately achieve the ambition of 15 per cent share of natural gas in the country's fuel mix.

Public-Private Partnership Models

Based on the learning from other sectors, stakeholder expectations from converting the partnership and risk-allocation framework into appropriate PPP structures and contractual arrangements ought to be clearly spelt out. The roles and responsibilities of various stakeholders—including the regulator, the Central and state governments, sponsoring authority and private investors—need to be laid down and clearly defined.

Equitable risk-sharing, based on forecast risks regarding a pipeline's design, build, finance, operation and maintenance can make projects succeed. An acceptable equitable risk allocation scheme can transfer a considerable amount of project risk away from pipeline developers to private/public partners. Considering the innovative structures being deployed by the National Highways Authority of India (NHAI), it is evident that there are viable models that can be extended to the natural gas sector as well, on how to de-risk the demand issue and accelerate infrastructure development.

The various models employed by NHAI look at different combinations of risk/reward profiles to suit different projects ranging from engineering, procurement and construction (EPC) where projects are fully funded by NHAI, to the build, operate and transfer (BOT) model where the rights to build, operate and collect tolls on a project get assigned to the concessionaire for a defined period. The hybrid annuity model (HAM) combines both models, wherein NHAI supports 40 per cent of the project costs and the investor bears the remaining 60 per cent, reducing upfront funding requirements for the concessionaire. More importantly, the demand-uncertainty risk is taken up by NHAI which retains the rights to levy and collect tolls from the project, while making fixed annuity payments to the investor throughout the life of the project.

Rationalization of Pipeline Tariff as Enablers

Currently distinct tariffs, for each separately authorized/accepted pipeline, lead to tariffs being added up for the use of multiple pipelines. This means higher cost gas and higher tariffs for consumers in the hinterland, while also placing new regions in a competitively disadvantageous position. On the other hand, unified or rationalized tariffs mean far-flung customers do not have to pay high cascaded tariffs and this leads to inclusive geographical equity in terms of industrial development and socio-economic growth across the country.

The following benefits accrue from a unified tariff.

- No disparity in tariff among customers in terms of distance or in terms of new versus old customers
- Level playing field for all connected LNG terminals
- Improvement in the competitiveness of gas vis-à-vis alternate fuels
- Substantial reduction in tariff for customers on pipelines like JHBDPL
- Entities become more viable to carry out the development of infrastructure

INDEPENDENT REGULATORY OVERSIGHT

India's aim of competitive markets cannot be achieved without effective independent oversight. Statutory regulators must be put in place for coal, oil and gas (upstream), on the same lines as with electricity.

Policy Push

New policies are required to manifest in the way they are desired—i.e., the gas sector will incentivize gas producers, gas pipeline companies,

marketers and consumers equally. To meet the growing energy demand
over the next few years, India will have to enhance its energy security
by procuring energy supplies at affordable prices. While the country
has surplus idling natural gas pipeline capacity, and sufficient planned
capacity utilization is in progress, major investments are required in the
domestic upstream industry and to acquire hydrocarbon reserves abroad.

A more conducive policy environment coupled with an effective
regulatory regime is the basis for accelerated growth in domestic
resources. The concept behind this must be to allow the common-carrier
capacity of natural gas pipelines to be utilized by any entity on a non-
discriminatory basis.

INFRASTRUCTURE CREATION

The concept of natural monopoly in the transportation of natural gas
is universally accepted in view of its capital-intensive nature, safety
benefits and protection of consumer interests. The national interest is
protected by avoiding infructuous investment; by optimum utilization
of infrastructure of natural gas pipelines and by allowing the 'common-
carrier' capacity of a natural-gas pipeline to be utilized by any entity on
a non-discriminatory basis.

Globally, countries with well-developed gas markets are
characterized by the creation of infrastructure such as LNG terminals
and gas transmission pipelines. Infrastructure creation reduces or
removes risks for gas importers, gas marketers and LNG terminal
investors. Over time, the network provides a push to setting up gas-
based industries and promotes the development of industrial zones,
corridors and clusters. However, in India, it is observed that private
investors are sceptical about developing infrastructure, as there is a
risk of this infrastructure remaining unutilized or underutilized in the
absence of firm tie-ups with regard to sourcing gas and gas offtake.
Unless new mechanisms/models support investors to secure their return,
the expectation of private investment in the gas pipeline infrastructure
will not materialize.

Public-private partnership (PPP) schemes are required to be explored as a means of attracting private-sector participation and investment for the development of capital-intensive gas transmission projects which have a long gestation period. Through this, the prospective private investor could receive financial support by way of a government grant to improve the commercial viability of projects.

Experiences of developed gas markets, both global and in the EU, show that gas transmission and marketing activities were unbundled after attaining a level of maturity. In these countries, the prerequisite was a well-developed, competitive, liberalized gas market with mature regulatory regimes. Globally, only a few of the top gas-consuming economies have undertaken the unbundling exercise under market reform till date. Insights from such global cases can be applied to the Indian context to ensure a better transformation.

Globally, the right prerequisites were available—a well-developed pipeline network, developed demand, adequate availability of domestic and pipeline gas, high share of gas in the energy mix, mature regulatory environment with a strong framework for open access, etc.—for successful outcomes. Unbundling in these cases led to the emergence of multiple gas marketers and a marginal increase in gas share in the primary energy mix.

However, there is no clear evidence of an increase in the pace of infrastructure development, post unbundling. Successful global examples also indicated that unbundling is a long journey and a phased approach followed over many years is critical to achieving the ultimate objectives of unbundling. We have real-life examples of failure while implementing deregulation and unbundling in immature markets. Elsewhere (as in Japan, South Korea, China, Russia, Iran, UAE, etc.) unbundling hasn't been taken up, yet the gas market flourishes due to supportive policies.

Gas markets in India are far from mature. The number of participants, including gas consumers, gas producers and shippers is not large enough for competitive forces to set in. Policies and regulatory reforms are still at a nascent stage and yet to take shape. Gas prices are not market-driven, thus creating distortions and asymmetries in information and leading to incorrect market signals. Unless the markets attain maturity with regard to these basic building blocks, the primary objective for which unbundling is required will not be met.

RECOMMENDATIONS AND THE WAY FORWARD

EXPEDITING THE PROCESS

Permissions have to be sought from state, municipal, and local authorities—multiple clearances and permissions are required from many agencies. Providing single-window clearances even at the district level, for the gas-pipeline network is a key factor for the expeditious implementation of the gas infrastructure.

RATIONALIZATION OF PIPELINE TARIFF

Pipeline tariff rationalization would entail the pooling of capital expenditure and operating expenditure across various pipelines. Allocating this sum over total gas volumes could make gas-transmission costs feasible for new pipelines and could help develop gas markets in new geographies, like the north-east region of India. Currently, tariff is calculated over individual pipelines and if capital expenditure is high, the pipeline's tariff is high, despite low volumes of gas being transported. Hence, the move is expected to bring parity to the price of gas across networks.

INNOVATIVE MODEL TO ATTRACT PRIVATE INVESTMENT IN INFRASTRUCTURE

The Indian gas industry needs to consider various models particularly being used in other infrastructure sectors. It must look at new and innovative models that encourage the fast development of infrastructure. This could be through:

- Capital grants by the Government of India
- Public-private partnership along with VGF through bidding
- A fixed annuity-based model, the amount of which may be discovered by public bidding. This takes away the volume risk from the investor enabling him to raise low-cost funds. However, the government would need to commit funding the gap between annuity payable to the investor and tariff recovered from the customer during initial years. Further, some pipelines may earn tariffs higher than the annuity liability which can be transferred to the government.

Policies for Enhancing Downstream Demand

- Reform is needed in the gas-based power sector to revitalize the sector and to anchor gas demand, as Discoms are not scheduling power generated from gas-based power plants from RLNG.
- Natural gas is identified as one of the primary fuels for the integration of renewable energy (RE). Gas-based power is more suited to provide intermittency and variability support than coal-based power. It is estimated that the Indian power system would require 20 Bcm ($\sim$55 MMscm/d) of gas to integrate 175 GW of RE by 2022 and 30 Bcm ($\sim$82 MMscm/d) of gas to integrate 350 GW of RE by 2030.
- Formulation and enforcement of peaking power policy. Currently, utilities do not have an obligation to serve and thereby tend to shed load during peak hours or in the face of a sudden increase in demand or decrease in generation. However, this can be avoided by introducing a 'peaking power policy' under which utilities

are incentivized to purchase power required to serve consumers round-the-clock. Power purchased under peaking policy should be allowed to be passed through in tariff. Through 'peaking power policy', gas-based power can be promoted in the economy.

- The power system development fund (PSDF) scheme should be re-introduced to incentivize the pooling of domestic gas with LNG.

- Mandatory gas-based power purchase obligation should be introduced in states in line with renewable power obligation.

- Sale of power from gas-based power plants to neighbouring power deficit countries must be encouraged.

GOVERNMENT MANDATE FOR ENVIRONMENTALLY BENIGN FUEL

Natural gas plays a relatively minor role in the Indian energy mix. Gas use is projected to grow in many sectors, such as power generation and transport, while retaining an important role as a feedstock for the fertilizer industry. However, despite its versatility and low environmental footprint compared with coal and oil, its relatively high price compared to competing fuel in different sectors is thwarting growth in gas demand.

From an environmental sustainability standpoint, natural gas scores the highest among all competing hydrocarbon fuels. However, as the externalities of these fuels are not internalized—in terms of affordability to end-consumers—in the peak commodity cycle phases, natural gas may not be able to compete with alternative fuels on price. Distortion and misalignment in the existing tax structure also does not help gas to grow, thus putting it at a disadvantageous position vis-à-vis competing polluting fuels.

It is pertinent to mention that externalities of competing fuels are not being fully internalized and thus natural gas is not finding its rightful place in the energy basket of India, despite a slew of positive externalities. This implies that unless regulatory reforms and policies are taken to support internalization of externalities of the competing fuels, natural gas will play a limited role in India's energy future.

Thus, government efforts to recognize externalities and reflect the same in tax and regulatory policies would be crucial for natural gas and growth in natural gas infrastructure. Government mandates may also be required to promote natural gas usage, thereby leading to a growth in the natural gas market. Past experience of CNG usage in cities such as Delhi and Mumbai suggests that penetration of natural gas as CNG took off only when it was mandated for public transport.

RATIONALIZATION OF FUEL PRICES

Relative prices play the most important role in the choice of fuel and choice of energy form that promotes efficient fuel choices and facilitates appropriate substitution so that resulting inter-fuel choices would be economically efficient.

ANNEXURE I

Gas Pipeline Network as of January 2020 (Source: PPAC, PNGRB, GAIL)

Details of existing Natural Gas Pipelines in the country					
S. No	Name of the Natural Gas Pipeline	Authorized Entity	CPSE/ State PSU/ Pvt	Length (Km)	States through which it passes
1	Hazira-Vijaipur-Jagdishpur -GREP (Gas Rehabilitation and Expansion Project)-Dahej-Vijaipur, HVJ/ VDPL	GAIL	CPSE	4587	Uttar Pradesh, Madhya Pradesh, Rajasthan, Gujarat
2	Dahej-Vijaipur (DVPL)-Vijaipur-Dadri (GREP) Upgradation, DVPLII & VDPL	GAIL	CPSE	1326	Uttar Pradesh, Madhya Pradesh, Rajasthan, Gujarat
3	Dahej-Uran-Panvel-Dhabhol	GAIL	CPSE	929	Gujarat, Maharashtra
4	Agartala regional network	GAIL	CPSE	61	Tripura
5	Mumbai regional network	GAIL	CPSE	131	Maharashtra
6	Assam regional network	GAIL	CPSE	1	Assam

Details of existing Natural Gas Pipelines in the country					
S. No	Name of the Natural Gas Pipeline	Authorized Entity	CPSE/ State PSU/ Pvt	Length (Km)	States through which it passes
7	K.G. Basin network(+RLNG + RIL)	GAIL	CPSE	892	Andhra Pradesh, Puducherry
8	Gujarat regional network(+RLNG + RIL)	GAIL	CPSE	636	Gujarat
9	Cauvery Basin network	GAIL	CPSE	276	Puducherry, Tamil Nadu
10	Rajasthan regional network	GAIL	CPSE	153	Rajasthan
11	Dadri-Bawana-Nangal (DBNPL)	GAIL	CPSE	867	Punjab, Haryana, Uttar Pradesh, Uttarakhand, Delhi
12	Chhainsa-Jhajjar-Hissar (CJHPL)	GAIL	CPSE	304	Haryana, Rajasthan, Punjab
13	Dabhol-Bangalore (DBPL)	GAIL	CPSE	1130	Maharashtra, Karnataka, Goa
14	Kochi-Koottanad-Bangalore-Mangalore (Phase I)	GAIL	CPSE	450	Kerala

	Details of existing Natural Gas Pipelines in the country				
S. No	Name of the Natural Gas Pipeline	Authorized Entity	CPSE/ State PSU/ Pvt	Length (Km)	States through which it passes
15	Jagdishpur-Haldia Pipeline Phase-1 (JHBDPL)	GAIL	CPSE	770	Uttar Pradesh and Bihar
16	Auraiya-Phulpur Pipeline (APPL)	GAIL	CPSE	315	Uttar Pradesh
Sub- Total (GAIL)				12828	
17	Uran-Trombay	ONGC	CPSE	24	Maharashtra
18	Dadri-Panipat	IOCL	CPSE	140	Haryana, Punjab, Uttar Pradesh
19	EWPL (Kakinada-Hyderabad-Uran-Ahmedabad)	PIL	Pvt	1784	Andhra Pradesh, Gujarat, Maharashtra, Telangana
20	Shadol-Phulpur	RGPL	Pvt	302	Madhya Pradesh, Uttar Pradesh
21	Hazira-Ankleshwar	Gujarat Gas	State PSU	73.2	Gujarat
22	GSPL's Gas Grid including spur lines	GSPL	State PSU	2593	Gujarat

Details of existing Natural Gas Pipelines in the country				
S. No	Name of the Natural Gas Pipeline	Autho-rized Entity	CPSE/ State PSU/ Pvt	Length (Km)	States through which it passes
23	AGCL's Assam regional network	AGCL	State PSU	105	Assam
Sub-Total (Others)				5021	
Total				17849 (~17900 Km)	

*Competitive Bidding

(*Source:* PNGRB,PPAC, GAIL)

LIST OF APPROVED NATURAL GAS PIPELINE PROJECTS UNDER DEVELOPMENT

A. Pipelines under execution by GAIL

S. No.	Pipeline	Length (Km)	State through which it passes
1	Jagdishpur-Haldia & Bokaro-Dhamra	1905	Bihar, Jharkhand, West Bengal, Odisha and Assam
2	Baruni-Guwahati	729	
3	Dhamra-Haldia	240	Odisha and West Bengal
4	Kochi-Koottanad-Bangalore-Mangalore (Ph-II)	437	Kerala, Tamil Nadu and Karnataka

S. No.	Pipeline	Length (Km)	State through which it passes
5	Vijaipur-Auraiya	352	Madhya Pradesh and Uttar Pradesh
6	Sultanpur-Jhajjar-Hissar section of CJHPL	135	Haryana
7	Haridwar-Rishikesh-Dehradun section of DBNPL	54	Uttarakhand
8	Srikakulam- Angul	690	Andhra Pradesh and Odisha
9	Mumbai-Nagpur-Jharsuguda	1755	Maharashtra, Madhya Pradesh, Chhattisgarh and Odisha
10	North East Gas Grid	1656	Assam, Meghalaya, Tripura, Mizoram, Arunachal Pradesh, Nagaland, Manipur and Sikkim
Total		7953	

Pipelines under execution by Other Entities

S. No.	Pipeline	Name of Entity	CPSE/ State PSU/ Pvt.	Length (Kms.)	State through which it passes
1	Ennore-Thiruvallur-Bengluru-Puducherry-Nagapatinam-Madurai-Tuticorin	Indian Oil Corporation Ltd	CPSE	1,385	Tamil Nadu and Karnataka
2	Bhatinda - Jammu - Srinagar	GSPL India Gasnet Limited	State SPV	729	Punjab, Jammu & Kashmir
3	Mehsana – Bhatinda	GSPL India Gasnet Limited	State SPV	2,052	Gujarat, Rajasthan, Haryana and Punjab
4	Mallavaram - Bhopal - Bhilwara via Vijaipur	GSPL India Transco Limited	State SPV	2,042	Andhra Pradesh, Telanagana, Chattisgarh, Madhya Pradesh, Maharashtra and Rajasthan
5	Kakinada - Vizag - Srikakulam	AP Gas Distribution Corporation	State SPV	391	Andhra Pradesh

S. No.	Pipeline	Name of Entity	CPSE/ State PSU/ Pvt.	Length (Kms.)	State through which it passes
6	Nellore-Vizag-Kakinada	IMC Ltd	Pvt	525	Andhra Pradesh
7	Ennore - Nellore	Gas Transmission India Pvt. Ltd	Pvt	430	Andhra Pradesh and Tamil Nadu
8	Jaigarh-Mangalore	H-Energy Pvt. Ltd	Pvt	749	Maharashtra, Goa and Karnataka
9	Kanai Chhata to Shrirampur	H-Energy	Pvt	315	West Bengal
Total				8,618	

Notes

1. Industry Group, 'Vision 2030: Natural Gas Infrastructure in India', Report by Industry Group for Petroleum and Natural Gas Regulatory Board, 2013, https://www.pngrb.gov.in/pdf/vision/vision-NGPV-2030-06092013.pdf

19

LNG REGASIFICATION TERMINALS

PRABHAT SINGH

CEO, Petroneting

OVERVIEW

AS DISCUSSED IN EARLIER CHAPTERS, India is dependent on liquefied natural gas (LNG) imports to meet its natural gas demand, given that it imported more than 50 per cent of its total consumption in FY 2019–20. With this dependence on imports, regasification terminals have been a crucial aspect of the supply chain, while meeting the gas demand across the country. As Table 1 shows, the country's existing regasification capacity (which stood at 42 MMtpa in the first quarter of 2020), is expected to increase by 19 MMtpa in the near future.

Further, with another 10.5 MMtpa of capacity in various stages of implementation, suffice it to say that if all these projects are implemented, India's regasification capacity will increase to 72 MMtpa by 2030.

Table 1: Regasification Terminal Capacity

No.	TERMINAL	DEVELOPERS	CAPACITY (MMtpa)
		Existing Terminal	
1	Dahej	Petronet LNG Limited	17.5
2	Hazira	Royal Dutch Shell, Total Gaz Electricite	5.0
3	Dabhol	GAIL, NTPC	5.0
4	Kochi	Petronet LNG Limited	5.0
5	Ennore	Indian Oil Corp	5.0
6	Mundra	GSPC, Adani	5.0
	TOTAL EXISTING		**42.5**
		Under Construction	
7	Jaigarh (FSRU)	H Energy	4.0
8	Dhamra	Adani	5.0
9	Jafrabad (FSRU)	Swan	5.0
10	Chhara	HPCL & Shapoorji Pallonji	5.0
	TOTAL UNDER-CONSTRUCTION		**19.0**
		Proposed	
11	East coast	Petronet LNG Limited	5.0
12	Kolkata/Digha Port	H Energy	2.5
13	Karaikal	AG&P	3.0
	TOTAL PROPOSED		**10.5**
	GRAND TOTAL		**72.0**

FSRU: Floating storage regasification unit; HPCL: Hindustan Petroleum Corporation Ltd.

Source: Author compilation

India imports close to 21 Mtpa via long-term LNG contracts balance via short-to-medium-term (ST) contracts. A study by Petronet LNG Ltd and Deloitte (2018–19) expected gas consumption to increase to 251–326 MMscm/d by 2030 (Figure 1).[1] Of this, the supply from existing and projected domestic gas is expected to be between 106–126 MMscm/d (an increment of 35–55 MMscm/d over current production). Therefore, the total LNG requirement in 2030 would be in the range of ~40–56 Mtpa (145–200 MMscm/d). Considering our existing imports of ~31 Mtpa, the incremental LNG requirement is expected to be ~10–26 Mtpa.

Figure 1: India's Gas demand in 2030

India's gas demand is expected to grow from 145 MMSCMD to ~251-326 MMSCMD

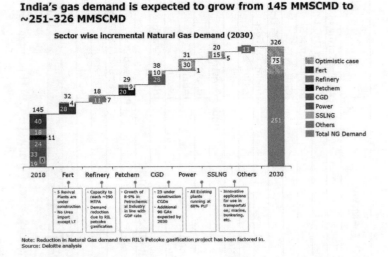

Note: Reduction in Natural Gas demand from RIL's Petcoke gasification project has been factored in.
Source: Deloitte analysis

Source: Petronet LNG Ltd and Deloitte (2018–19).[2]

This increasing demand will necessitate the creation of LNG regasification terminals, along with associated infrastructure (trunk pipelines as well as intra-city pipelines and LNG dispensing stations along major highways). However, building regasification terminals has seen its fair share of challenges. This chapter seeks to understand the challenges that existing and under-construction regasification terminals face. It highlights the forthcoming technology in the regasification space that will enable smoother delivery to end-consumers and provides recommendations that will enable increasing the share of gas and, more importantly, LNG in the energy sector.

CHALLENGES IN INCREASING REGASIFICATION CAPACITY

PLANNING ISSUES

India's regasification capacity (current, under-construction and proposed) stands at 72 Mtpa. If gas consumption in the country were to increase to 15 per cent (as per the target set by the Ministry of Petroleum and Natural Gas) by 2030, from the existing 6.5 per cent, it would lead to a total gas requirement of $\sim$700 MMscm/d. This is an incremental consumption of 350 MMscm/d over the projected gas requirement up to 2030 (Figure 1). This would translate to an additional regasification capacity of at least 100–125 Mtpa (to support, at least, 400–450 MMscm/d of gas requirements) when India has planned only for 72 Mtpa. India has not done enough planning in terms of terminal capacity to meet this target in the next nine years.

FINANCIAL ISSUES

Financing regasification terminals can be a challenge in the future. Setting up terminal capacity and the associated infrastructure nearby (roads leading to and within the plant, pipeline networks, etc.) is a capital-intensive exercise. Today, given that India's regasification capacity is limited, margins are not a problem for terminal operators. However, if all 72 Mtpa of capacity were to come up, we will see an increase in competition which will impact margins negatively. This will eventually make financing additional capacity a challenge for terminal operators.

The price of the molecule plays a crucial part in a price-sensitive economy like India. If the LNG price forward market is in contango and if substitutes or alternatives to backward price movements are available, then this will impact the economics of the entire project, along with the internal rate of return (IRR) and payback periods for the companies investing in this part of the value chain.

Furthermore, the global market is moving towards a merchant model, meaning that financing regasification infrastructure will be similar to financing the construction of refineries, not necessarily backed up by long-term tie-ups of volumes or capacity. Such financing would be based on the fundamentals of demand supply and connectivity to markets. This will lead to a new era in the financing of terminals. Creating gas hubs in India will assist in financing, as this will imply the commoditization of gas in the country, similar to the Americas and Europe.

Return on Investment

If regasification terminals are not connected to the end consumer by any means, the entire asset is classified as stranded. Further, low utilization also impacts terminal operations. The operator is expected to keep the terminal functioning despite low operating incomes, high operation cost, inability to service loans and risks of the plant being impaired after the commencement of production.

Pipeline Access and Last-mile Connectivity

Connecting terminals to the national gas grid has been especially challenging in the southern region of India. The LNG terminals in Kochi and Ennore are unutilized and operating at less than 25 per cent of their installed capacity, respectively, since these terminals are either not connected to the grid or are unable to use the pipeline network as third-party access is a problem. Pipeline access and last-mile connectivity for regasification terminals suffers from the chicken and egg problem in India. Going forward, it is critical to answer the question of who will pay for the infrastructure—pipeline operators or terminal operators.

Further, land acquisition and the terrain play a role in the development of connectivity till the last mile of the individual household. The best solution offered during current times is to make the landowner the companion to the growth trajectory and the development of the infrastructure. If we share the pie with him, he might start thinking along the lines of a prospective resource developer and entrepreneur. The idea is to bring everybody on to the same platform to think, work and solve problems together. It will be a win-win situation for all.

Regulatory Challenges

Issues related to double taxation on the small portion of shipping component in LNG imports, value-added tax (VAT) versus inclusion in the Goods and Services Tax (GST) are some of the issues that will need to be resolved. Further, the rationalization of pipeline tariffs will be critical to improving the competitiveness of LNG versus other alternatives.

TECHNOLOGY AND INNOVATIONS

Building LNG Carriers

Given India's dependence on imports, building its own fleet will allow for the presence of the LNG regasification trade across the entire value chain and secure and provide the most affordable molecule to users of gas, including non-volatile transportation costs.

The indicative calculation of the vessels required for free-on-board (FOB) deals is illustrated below:

Table 2: Breaking down voyage metrics for Indian LNG ships

Days in a year	Round trips days per voyage	Expected Trips in a year	MTPA loaded in a year
330	9	36.7	3.3
330	22	15.0	1.4
330	52	6.3	0.6
Average	28	19.3	1.8

Source: Author analysis.

As Table 2 indicates, the minimum number of days for a round trip is assumed as nine and the maximum number of days for a round trip is assumed to be fifty-two, with an average of 330 operating days in a year for the ships to carry the volume.

There are three options for the Indian subcontinent depending upon the vessel size. A vessel of 170,000 cubic metres (m^3) to 210,000 m^3, on average can pick the load from 0.60 Mtpa to 3 Mtpa in a year. Based on these numbers, India will require approximately around 50–60 LNG vessels depending upon the size (from 170,000 m^3 to 210,000 m^3 capacity) to cater to the increasing LNG requirement and to meet 15 per cent of the gas-based energy structure of the country.

Apart from this, since the activity and orders are huge, and each vessel will cost around $200 million, India's LNG import industry (LNG importers, regasification plant owners, gas marketing companies) can also aid the country's manufacturing capacity by building 50 per cent of the total orders of LNG shipping vessels under the 'Make in India' umbrella. This will serve as a bi-directional development for the economies of both the ship-builder and buyer. As we shift towards the buyer's market regime, any proposition which is on a fifty-fifty basis on the vessel building side seems doable and will be acceptable in years to come.

Breaking Standard-Sized LNG Cargoes into LNG ISO Tank Containers

LNG containers are built to transport cryogenic bulk liquids from LNG regasification terminals. After cooled LNG is loaded, it can be transported through rail, road or vessels in containers. Under present conditions, it becomes difficult to look into ISO containers (LNG on wheels) since the economics (loading, rail and road freight, trucking to consumer and the cost to transport the empty container back) are not feasible in a price-sensitive economy like India.

However, there is a case for investing in this process, given that it can help bring LNG to under-served regions in the country while the pipeline infrastructure is still being built. The ISO container itself can play a pivotal role in developing the zones by developing LNG markets in and around the country—if the fuel is available till the last mile for every user group, consumption will increase resulting in the overall development of the zone.

As both an innovation and a concept, ISO containers have the potential to break many barriers, along with the more conventional LNG trucks.

Case study: China

China is the world's second-largest importer of LNG but lacks natural gas pipelines and storage infrastructure, similar to India. China National Offshore Oil Corp (CNOOC) is working with a railway company to deliver LNG by rail, on a trial basis. The two-year trial will involve sending LNG to central China from four terminals—Guangxi, Zhuhai, Zhejiang and Tianjin. Ideally, trucks carrying ISO tanks can serve distances of 500 km and trains can service longer distances of over 1,000 km.

As per trial reports each ISO tank can carry 17–18 tonnes of LNG, with trains being able to carry fifty such tanks. As one of China's largest

LNG importers, CNOOC aims to transport 1 Mtpa of LNG in ISO tank containers by 2021. It will increase this to 2 Mtpa by 2022–23. It also plans to use ISO tanks for LNG storage. As per internal surveys, ISO tanks are about 30 per cent cheaper than current storage facilities, besides being extremely efficient at saving space.[3]

Apart from this, LNG is globally imported through containers under a ground-breaking agreement. In China's case, Fortis BC Energy Inc. will export Canadian LNG produced by the company's small-scale LNG terminal in British Columbia, in standard-sized shipping containers starting in 2021.

Uberization of LNG

Previously, the LNG industry was more than 90 per cent of long-term trade, driving with point-to-point movement. The industry is witnessing a major change, with its share of spot and short-term LNG contracts increasing to around 30 per cent. With the advent of new technologies like artificial intelligence (AI) and the Internet of Things (IOT), it will not be long before trading in LNG will be carried out digitally or via an app, similar to the Uber model, i.e., available on call with very few days' notice, especially since there will be vessels floating across various geographical locations. These vessels not only act as floating storage but also provide optimization opportunities, reducing the cost of transportation by swaps.

Democratizing the Handshake between Producers and the Consumers

Today, major suppliers and terminal owners play the role of aggregators. With the support of technology including the use of blockchain, it will be possible to carry out end-to-end mapping. This would mean that a small gas producer in a country with a surplus of gas would be able to access liquefication abilities and ship a portion of its molecules in

LNG vessels. Similarly, a small consumer would be able to source such molecules directly from a producer and book capacity in terminal and pipelines to get molecules at his doorstep.

RECOMMENDATIONS AND THE WAY FORWARD

ADDRESSING FINANCIAL ISSUES: CAPITAL VGF FOR REGASIFICATION TERMINALS AND PIPELINES

A severe challenge to the development of pipelines and regasification terminals is the return on investment or the internal rate of return. Viability gap funding by the government will help address this challenge and help in laying the building blocks of the LNG trade. Further, it will also lead to development along the supply chain, the region where terminals are located, employment creation and overall industrial development.

OPERATIONAL GAP FUNDING (YEARLY OPERATIONAL BREAK-EVENS)

Another funding option is for the government to provide operational and guaranteed commitments to the regasification and pipeline developers. This guaranteed cover for annual expenditure will ensure zero cash loss for the pipeline developer. The idea for the operational breakeven is not for the entire life cycle of the regasification terminal. It should only work for the first four or five years and within this time the regasification terminal operator should make the best efforts to get the terminal to stand on its feet economically.

INVESTMENT IN THE UPSTREAM LNG VALUE CHAIN

The landed cost of LNG sourced under existing long-term contracts (gas- or oil-linked) is in the range of $8–10/MMBtu. In order to reduce the landed cost of LNG, investment in the upstream value chain can be a potential option. Currently, the US is a developed and free-market economy and is at the forefront of technological innovation, especially in the field of hydraulic fracking. This alternate sourcing model involves investment in upstream gas fields, booking capacity in a midstream pipeline and investment in downstream liquefaction terminals. On the basis of initial high-level research, the landed price is expected to be around $5–6/MMBtu, thereby increasing the affordability of gas, compared to alternative competitive fuels.

TAXATION REFORMS

Inclusion of Natural Gas in GST

The exclusion of natural gas from the GST's purview has complicated the issue, especially since this, as well as staying within VAT, has made gas an expensive fuel to use and consume. Apart from this, a barrier has been erected between gas and other competitive fuels.

If the aim is to make India a gas-based economy, there must be reforms especially on the taxation front, in order to make the structure less complex for the users of LNG. According to the usage of the sectoral value chain, most end users are under the GST regime, while LNG remains included only in the pre-GST regime. Bringing natural gas under GST so that industry and micro, small and medium enterprises (MSMEs) can avail of the benefits of the taxes paid, without bearing the burden of the cascading impact of multiple taxes.

Custom Duty Waiver

Custom duty rates on LNG, as well as on equipment for building regasification terminals/pipelines/associated infrastructure imported into India, should be reviewed. A duty waiver will add to the development of the sector. As the lowest polluting fuel among other fossils, LNG should be taken out of the customs net and some duty credits/drawbacks should be provided to the users of LNG for promoting the usage of non-polluting fuel.

LNG- Fuelled Vehicles

The seeding of LNG vehicles in India must be facilitated by the exemption of customs duties on the import of LNG-fuelled vehicles and capital equipment to manufacture vehicles and for pilot development for initial five years, as Indian manufacturers do not have a business case for introducing new truck modelled on LNG.

Extended Tax Incentives and Reduction in Port Charges

Kerala is an ideal location to promote the LNG terminal-port as an LNG bunkering hub for marine traffic, with tax incentives for the bunkering hub. This will increase in view of the International Maritime Organization (IMO) 2020 regulations. As seen in other ports around the world, such as Colombo and Singapore, the government must work towards reducing port charges in India, for vessels that call for bunkering or gas cool-down services.

Pipeline development for enhanced utilization of the regasification terminals

The deeper the city gas distribution (CGD) connectivity, the more enhanced the utilization of gas in the energy mix of the nation. The key lies in its availability at the doorstep of every household.

Skills Development

Skill development in the hydrocarbon sector is the need of the hour and should be an integral part of the development of the gas industry. Petronet LNG Limited has set up a unique learning centre, the LNG Academy, at Kochi's LNG Terminal. The LNG Academy imparts training on the entire LNG and gas value chain. It also organizes workshops to share the experience of LNG professionals, covering various aspects of the LNG vertical right from upstream, liquefaction, shipping, regasification, and pipeline transmission/distribution, to burner tip consumption.

The academy endeavours to enhance and update knowledge and impart practical hands-on experience to aspirants. We have already conducted successfully a few well-attended programmes with contributions from known industry experts.

Notes

1. Petronet LNG Ltd and Deloitte, 'India's Current Demand (Optimistic) Domestic Supply Scenario', New Delhi: PLL& Deloitte, 2018–19, https://petronetlng.com/NaturalGasOverView.php
2. Ibid.
3. Muyu Xu and Shivani Singh, 'China's CNOOC to trial LNG delivery by rail: Executive', Reuters, 15 October 2019, https://www.reuters.com/article/us-china-energy-gas-cnooc/chinas-cnooc-to-trial-lng-delivery-by-rail-executive-idUSKBN1WU11F

COMMERCIAL

20

PRICING: A COMPLEX EVOLUTION

ANUPAMA SEN

Oxford Institute for Energy Studies

INTRODUCTION

THE PRICING OF DOMESTIC GAS in India has been a contentious issue for several years, with domestic pricing reform undergoing several reconfigurations. At first glance, gas pricing in India appears notoriously complicated. There are a variety of different prices at the well head.

To put it in simple terms, for many years the price of domestic gas to producers was set according to the terms of the fiscal regime that governed a specific producing field. India has had multiple fiscal regimes in place at different points in time—including the 'nomination regime', the pre-New Exploration Licensing Policy (pre-NELP) regime, the NELP and the Hydrocarbon Exploration Licensing Policy (HELP; the ruling regime which now includes an 'open acreage' licensing system)[1]—therefore a multitude of prices have existed simultaneously. Transportation costs, marketing margins and Central and state taxes were then added to this well-head price to obtain the delivered price for gas. As states have considerable fiscal autonomy over indirect taxation, these tax rates have tended to vary across states.

There have been numerous attempts at reforming domestic gas prices.[2] The latest configuration of domestic gas pricing reform, implemented in October 2014, has broken with the previous system (which was based on oil price linkages), with a linkage to a twelve-month trailing (with a lag of one quarter), physical volume-weighted average of four international 'benchmark' gas prices—the US Henry Hub price, the UK National Balancing Point (NBP) price, the Russian domestic gas price and the (Canadian) Alberta reference price for gas. Transportation tariffs and indirect taxes are then applied as before. The formula is adjusted bi-annually and although this simply adds to the multitude of pricing regimes for domestic gas, previous regimes are expected to eventually converge to this new pricing regime.

It can be argued that these numerous attempts at reforming domestic gas pricing have been mainly predicated around managing the price level, rather than establishing a logical basis for price formation, which reflects the dynamics of the Indian economy—in other words, they have focused on price levels as opposed to pricing mechanisms.

This chapter summarizes the policy discussion on the need to move to a pricing mechanism for Indian gas, and in doing so addresses the following research questions:

- How should domestic gas be priced for the Indian market?
- What are some of the key trade-offs that policymakers face in gas pricing and what are the underlying distortions?
- Is there a general framework of guiding principles for natural gas pricing that can be applied to the Indian market?

At the time of writing, India is grappling with the global coronavirus pandemic, facing a severe economic contraction due to lockdowns imposed to control the spread of the virus. Policymakers around the world are facing a choice on where to direct fiscal stimulus packages to catalyse economic recovery—at 'traditional' carbon-intensive industries, or at industries that could facilitate a transition to environmentally sustainable economic growth. Gas features prominently as an option in these debates, particularly in European economies, given its potential for decarbonization via several technological pathways,[3] without the requirement for new investments in network and storage infrastructure.

The next section sets out some general guidelines around the design of a gas pricing mechanism. The following section reviews the trade-offs faced in designing a pricing mechanism, after which the discussion moves to highlighting some key distortions that have resulted from the existing system. The penultimate section sets out policy options to consider going forward and is followed by the concluding section. Other chapters in this publication deal with issues relating to the end-user sectors in detail. However, this chapter is meant to frame the problem and suggest broad policy options to resolve it.

GENERAL GUIDING PRINCIPLES ON GAS PRICING

The literature on pricing suggests that there are a set of distinct economic principles which can serve as a general guide to determining price mechanisms. Summarizing from the works of Peng and Poudineh,[4] and Reneses, Rodriguez and Perez-Arriaga,[5] these are described as follows:

- Sustainability: The price should enable a regulated company to finance its businesses and new investment required for future operations.

- Efficiency: The price should act as a signal that incentivizes consumers to use the amount of resources that are efficient for the system.

- Equity: An equitable price does not unduly discriminate against one group of consumers in service provision and cost allocation.

- Transparency: The price should be communicated (e.g., published) in clear and understandable terms.

- Simplicity: The price should be easy to understand and accept.

- Stability: The price should be based on a calculation methodology that is consistent over time.

- Consistency: The price should be coherent with the industry structure and regulatory framework in place in the country at any given time.

Having set out these principles, it is important to note that there are trade-offs between them and it is extremely difficult to meet them all simultaneously. Peng and Poudineh, for instance, contend that equity (also referred to as the fairness principle) has the most ambiguous definition and has been interpreted differently in different countries.[6] In some instances, policymakers use it to subsidize energy access for low-income consumers. However, this is because equity is often confused with affordability (or the ability of low-income consumers to pay) of gas. Instead, equity implies that all consumers should face the same calculation methodology for price regardless of whether they pay the same charges. Further, the principle of economic efficiency may conflict with the principles of equity, sufficiency or simplicity. For instance, company operations need to be planned around efficiency (ensuring the company's medium- and long-term viability) and sustainability/ sufficiency (ensuring that resources have been allocated optimally in the company's operations) but the price for consumers needs to balance equity, efficiency (in terms of signals to end-consumers) and sufficiency (ensuring that prices allow sufficient revenues) say Peng and Poudineh.[7] Thus, policymakers may need to find a balanced compromise between the various principles.

There are two broad approaches towards setting prices: a top-down approach begins with the cost of production, adding margins on top, etc. A bottom-up approach begins with pitching consumer prices and then working backwards. Either way, the incidence of taxation should be such that it preserves the signal of the economic price to buyers and sellers along the value chain.

In addition to the above guiding principles, another important factor is the basis upon which a price mechanism is determined. Here again, the literature provides some useful examples. Julius and Mashayekhi, for instance, propose three options to determine the basis for an economic price of natural gas based on the availability of gas reserves in any specific country.[8]

- A gas-surplus country is one in which the demand-supply balance is such that the point of 'economic depletion' of gas is very far into the future.[9]

- A country short of gas, or one with a gas deficit, is one in which the potential availability of gas is projected never (or only briefly) to exceed the potential demand for it.

- A country with a window of surplus, is one in which the planning period includes times of both gas surplus and gas shortage. The point of economic depletion is projected to fall within this period or clearly in a foreseeable timeframe beyond it.

For gas-surplus countries in which depletion is far from imminent, the basis for the price mechanism is usually the long-run marginal cost of production (LRMC)—or the cost of meeting a future increment in demand over a long period.[10] There are two broad methods of estimating LRMC. Some authors advocate the Average Incremental Cost (AIC) method for gas (estimated by dividing the discounted incremental costs of meeting future projected demand by the discounted volume of projected future incremental output over the same period).[11] In surplus-window countries, the pricing mechanism must take into consideration an estimate of the depletion premium for gas—which is the present value of foregone consumption—in addition to the extraction cost. In gas-deficit countries, the recommended basis for deriving a price mechanism is its replacement value in the marketplace.

GAS PRICING MECHANISMS: KEY TRADE-OFFS AND DISTORTIONS

How do these general principles apply in practice? At the heart of the gas pricing issue is one key trade-off that is faced by all policymakers attempting to develop a market for gas in their countries. Markets for gas need to be developed with prices low enough (relative to alternatives) to stimulate demand, but high enough to justify the considerable infrastructure expenditure needed to create a market for gas.[12]

This perceived dilemma can be summed up in two seemingly opposing views, illustrated in Figure 1 below:

Figure 1: Key trade-off in development of a domestic gas market

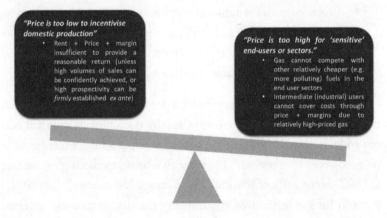

"Price is too low to incentivise domestic production"
- Rent + Price + margin insufficient to provide a reasonable return (unless high volumes of sales can be confidently achieved, or high prospectivity can be *firmly* established *ex ante*)

"Price is too high for 'sensitive' end-users or sectors."
- Gas cannot compete with other relatively cheaper (e.g. more polluting) fuels in the end user sectors
- Intermediate (industrial) users cannot cover costs through price + margins due to relatively high-priced gas

Source: Author analysis.

On one side of the trade-off, the price, margins and proportion of rent earned from gas extraction (for upstream companies, if this is part of their fiscal contract with the government or owner/custodian of the resource) are collectively deemed too low to provide a regulated company an expected return (potentially violating the principle of sustainability/sufficiency). On the other side, gas cannot compete with other (sometimes potentially more polluting fuels, e.g., coal) substitutes in the end-user sectors, or, industrial intermediate gas users cannot cover their costs due to relatively higher-priced gas (potentially violating the principle of equity).

This trade-off is underpinned by some key characteristics of a developing gas market; namely, high infrastructure costs, asset specificity and elements of monopoly power along the supply chain. As a result, governments tend to intervene in the supply chain to capture rent,[13] and correct some of these distortions, but these interventions then become conflated with other government objectives, including energy security and income distribution, creating numerous points of further intervention and distortion along the supply chain (potentially violating the principle of efficiency).

A look at the domestic gas supply chain in India (Figure 2) can help illustrate this.

Figure 2: Domestic gas supply chain in India

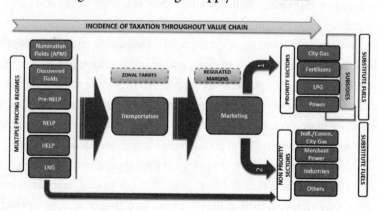

Source: Author analysis.

Reading Figure 2 from the left, as stated in the introduction, India's gas prices have been determined by the upstream regulatory regime governing any producing field. There have been frequent revisions to the regime, which began with a cost-plus regime dominated by the National Oil Companies (NOCs) until the early 1990s (Nomination Regime). This was followed by a regime that permitted private companies to participate with a 30 per cent carried interest for NOCs (Discovered Fields or pre-NELP regime). This was then replaced with a liberalized profit-sharing upstream fiscal regime in 1998 (NELP), followed by a revenue-sharing regime in 2016 (HELP; with an open acreage licensing system). This has resulted in a multiplicity of upstream gas prices, as different producing fields operate under different regimes, creating inefficiency.[14]

Transportation tariffs are additionally added to pipelines that are further down the supply chain. For existing pipelines, these have been set based on a regulated rate of return of 12 per cent for transportation companies, with users charged in a zonal pricing system with percentage increments on every additional 300 km of pipeline from the starting point—increments are applied on a telescoping basis, with every successive increment being smaller than the previous one. Longer distances increase the likelihood that more than one zone will be crossed, which would increase the total transmission cost. Thus, tariffs for consumers further away from the point at which gas enters the pipeline, are more expensive.[15] A supplier transporting gas to a load in a different zone from the point of entry would have to pay the charges for the zone of origin and the zone of delivery and also for any intervening zones. This accumulation of zone access charges is called 'pancaking'.[16]

Marketing margins (the next stage of the supply chain) are regulated and added to the price. Sales of domestic gas to end users are then effectively rationed, with different prices in different sectors—which receive subsidies directly through, as well as outside of the gas pricing mechanism. Domestic gas is first sold to priority sectors with the remainder sold to non-priority sectors. The imports of liquefied natural gas (LNG) are sourced directly at market prices by non-priority sector users to make up the deficit. These sectors have their own dynamics (discussed later). Indirect taxes are repeatedly applied throughout the value chain, at the federal and state level, often with tax rates differing across states, creating a cascading effect.[17]

DISTORTIONS CREATED THROUGH THE PRICING SYSTEM

There are three main distortions that have been created, as the pricing system for domestic gas has been used to meet multiple objectives.

Lack of Consistent Pricing that is Sustainable through the Supply Chain

Table 1 shows a summary assessment of multiple domestic pricing systems, broadly viewed against the guiding principles described earlier in this chapter. Under the nomination regime (covering the period from Independence to the early 1990s, when exploration and production were carried out exclusively by the NOCs) prices were fixed by the government under its administered price mechanism (APM) on a cost-plus basis—or costs plus a regulated rate of return. There were some exceptions to this: gas sold to India's north-eastern states, historically considered to be underdeveloped, was at a 40 per cent discount on the APM rate, with the difference paid as a subsidy to the NOCs. Similarly, the government permitted gas from certain designated fields operated by the NOCs to be sold at non-APM prices or notional market prices ranging from $4.20-$5.25/One Million British Thermal Units (MMBtu). The price of gas produced under the Nomination Regime was deliberately kept low, in order to subsidise certain industries, and by extension, their consumers.

Table 1: Assessment of domestic pricing mechanisms

	Nomination regime (administered pricing mechanism)	Discovered fields/ pre-NELP	NELP	HELP/OALP
	Cost-plus regulated rate of return	Linkage to twelve-month average of fuel-oil prices with floor and ceiling	Linkage to Brent Crude price with floor and ceiling: 'S' curve: Selling price = $2.5 + (ceiling price for Brent − 25)^{0.15} + C.	Physical volume weighted average of Henry Hub, UK NBP), Russian domestic gas price, and Alberta reference price for gas
Sustainability	Sustainable if revenue requirements consistently reviewed; however, APM production eventually stagnated	Relatively sustainable as production continued	Unsustainable; resulted in a static formula and falling production	Indeterminate at present

	Nomination regime (administered pricing mechanism)	Discovered fields/ pre-NELP	NELP	HELP/OALP
Efficiency	Not efficient from a supply-chain perspective; plus, high transaction costs	Not efficient from a supply-chain perspective, all gas sold to GAIL for onward marketing (at APM rates)	Inefficient, as floor/ceiling were not varied in line with international price movements	Not efficient from a supply-chain perspective, as end users do not face the same price
Equity	Not equitable as applicable differently to different consumers	Not equitable; all gas sold to GAIL for onward marketing (some at APM rates)	Not equitable from a supply-chain perspective, as originally based on bids from a small group of end users	Relatively equitable compared with previous regimes, but end users still face different prices
Transparency	Not transparent; prices determined by regulator	Not transparent; prices determined within contractual terms	Not transparent; rationale underpinning the formula not clearly explained	Transparent; price and sources of data regularly published

	Nomination regime (administered pricing mechanism)	Discovered fields/ pre-NELP	NELP	HELP/OALP
Simplicity	Complex; involves multiple and regular assessments of companies' costs and required return	Relatively simple, as linkage to clear benchmark	Simple to calculate, linkage to a (static) benchmark	Simple to calculate
Stability	Dependent upon regulator	Indeterminate, as prices were subject to contractual terms	Formula was in place for five years, as per NELP terms; however, a pricing dispute undermined stability	Stable; revised every six months
Consistency	Inconsistent with move to a market-oriented system	Consistent with move to a market-oriented system, but oil linkage less relevant	Consistent with move to a market-oriented system, but oil linkage less relevant	Consistent with move to a market-oriented system, gas linkage more relevant

Source: Author analysis.

Prices under the pre-NELP regime were determined by production sharing contracts (PSCs) between exploration companies and the government and linked to an average of fuel-oil prices over the previous twelve months, subject to a ceiling, which was frequently revised. Under the NELP regime, the domestic gas price was set according to the formula in Table 1, where SP represented the selling price (in $/MMBtu), $2.5 was a constant representing the base price of gas, and CP was the lagged price of Brent Crude, subject to a floor and a ceiling. 'C' was a constant representing the outcome of bids (presumably as a proxy for demand) invited from consuming sectors in the original discovery exercise, which was later set to zero by the government.[18] The exponent (0.15) gave rise to an 'S' curve with relative inelasticity at the upper and lower ends, meant to work in favour of buyers or sellers, respectively—although it has been argued that the curve worked asymmetrically.[19] When approving the formula, the government set the ceiling and floor prices for Brent at $60 and $25. Brent breached the $60 ceiling soon after the adoption of the formula and subsequently reached twice that level, which rendered the formula outdated.[20] The resulting price of $4.20/MMBtu was adopted in 2009 for a five-year period and was meant to be reviewed in April 2014. Jain provides a description of the ensuing dispute over the NELP price.[21]

The formula under the HELP regime introduced a dynamic element to the mechanism for domestic gas pricing, with its biannual price adjustments and its applicability to gas produced from all upstream regimes (barring those subject to existing contractual price clauses). Its linkage to gas prices rather than oil prices reflects the changing structure of the market for internationally traded gas,[22] but the benchmarks used in the formula have little relevance to Indian gas market dynamics.[23] This multiplicity of prices obscures the emergence of a dominant signal for determining the demand for gas and the consequent investment needs of the sector.

Pricing in a Two-tier Market

A second key distortion created through the pricing system is the existence of a two-tier market for gas. The structure of demand can be analysed starting with the different consuming sectors categorized in the government's 'gas utilization policy' which supports the rationing of domestically produced gas to certain priority sectors before it is released for sale to the wider Indian market. The first tier comprises, in order of priority:

- City gas for households (piped natural gas or PNG) and transport (compressed natural gas or CNG)
- Fertilizer manufacturing plants using gas as an input
- LPG plants using gas as an input
- Gas-based power plants that supply gas to grid-connected power distribution utilities

The priority order for tier-1 consumers has remained largely unchanged over the last decade, apart from one major adjustment in July 2015, when city gas was moved to the top of the tier from the bottom, displacing fertilizers. All domestic gas left over is then released into a more general second tier of consumers, which includes:

- Steel, refineries and petrochemical plants
- City gas for industrial and commercial consumers
- Captive and merchant power plants
- Other consumers, feedstock and fuel

It can, therefore, be argued that the tier-1 sector sets the dynamics of demand for gas. Figure 3 illustrates this two-tier structure. Just over 80 per cent of domestic gas is consumed by tier-1 sectors, and close to 50 per cent of LNG imports.[24]

Figure 3: Two-tiered market structure

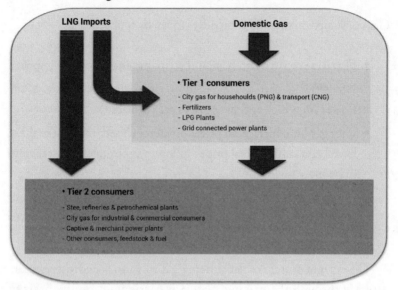

Source: Author analysis.

As the whole Indian gas market comprises two segments—one using gas allocated at government-controlled prices and the other paying market prices for imported LNG—no confident assessment of the latest gas demand in India has been possible so far. Some degree of overlap between the two segments makes the picture even messier. Consequently, government projections of future demand have tended to be over-optimistic and international assessments by multilateral agencies cautious, yet confused, with the differences between low and high forecasts widening to as much as 100 billion cubic metres (Bcm).[25] This structure violates the principle of efficiency, impedes the emergence of a clear pricing signal and makes it difficult to assess future capacity requirements. Although the gas utilization policy was meant to end when 'supply matched demand',[26] economic logic dictates that supply is unlikely to match demand in a rationed market.

PRICE SENSITIVITY IN END-USER SECTORS

Gas consumption in India is broadly driven by four sectors:

- Fertilizers (in which manufacturing and retail prices are regulated)
- Power (in which end-user prices are regulated)
- City gas (in which retail prices are deregulated, but where there have been rollbacks to prices following consumer resistance to price increases)
- Other industries, (comprises refineries, petrochemicals, iron and steel and merchant/commercial consumers of gas; in which prices are deregulated).

The current system of subsidizing gas to various end-user sectors directly through the pricing system is carried out on the basis of arguments around 'price sensitivity' for these sectors, which has led policymakers to prevent price rises or shield these sectors from any price fluctuations—all of which runs against most if not all of the general principles on pricing and the creation of a market for gas.

In the fertilizer sector, for instance, the price of fertilizers is set on the assumption that the cost of gas will range from $6.5/MMBtu to $14/MMBtu (a range fixed by government policy). Fertilizer companies receive government subsidies to offset higher gas prices and additionally the retail price of fertilizers is subsidized by the government. The evidence shows, however, that fertilizer companies, rather than being passive recipients of pricing subsidies, also make input choices based on minimizing input costs (which, in turn, minimize the government subsidy bill) among competing substitutes. This includes not just domestic gas but also imported LNG, imported urea and imported naphtha.[27] Price pooling was introduced in 2015, whereby urea manufacturing plants communicate their gas requirements to a pool operator, which sources any imported LNG needed to meet incremental demand for gas in the sector.[28] The imported LNG is pooled with domestic gas and sold to manufacturing plants at an average uniform price. Sen shows that this scheme raised urea production, reduced the urea subsidy bill and raised LNG imports.[29]

In the power sector, where gas plants comprise roughly 8 per cent (25 GW) of installed capacity (with roughly 14 GW of this made idle due to the poor competitiveness of gas with coal in the power sector),[30] gas cannot compete with coal in the merit order dispatch above a threshold price.[31] The price pooling scheme was implemented for the power sector from 2015–17. Under this, reverse e-auctions were conducted for generators to source LNG imports, which were offered waivers or discounts on taxes, transportation tariffs and the marketing margin. Imports were pooled with domestic gas and sold to distribution utilities at an average price. A quantum of the federal budget funding was allocated to finance this initiative, with the assumed gas price under the scheme capped at $6.5/MMBtu (or a delivered price of nearly $8/MMBtu) and the resulting power tariff capped at ₹4.70/kWh ($0.067/kWh) (hence financial incentives and/or support was provided up to a tariff of ₹4.70/kWh [$0.067/kWh]). Sen shows that this briefly raised the utilization of gas-based plants.[32]

The current system of subsidizing different users through the pricing mechanism and the fact that prices are not allowed to vary, does not reveal the true price elasticity of demand for different sectors—this elasticity is arguably also indicative of the competitiveness of various end-user sectors, which could be taken into account when establishing a pricing mechanism (for instance on the basis of prices of competing, and sometimes more unsustainable, inputs).

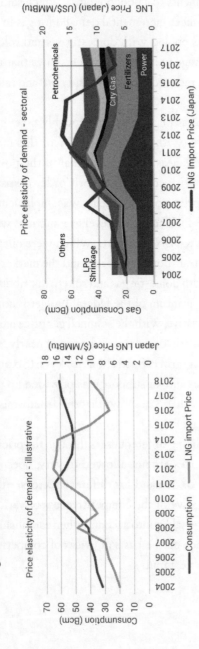

Figure 4: Illustrative price elasticity of demand for gas – total (LHS) and sector wise (RHS)

Source: Author analysis

Figure 4 above utilizes Asian LNG prices—which are arguably closer to some sort of opportunity-cost-based market price—to illustrate the price elasticity of demand in various consuming sectors. In practice, however, the complex systems of controlled prices and cross-subsidies contribute to the opacity of latent demand, preventing accurate price signals from emerging.

MOVING TOWARDS A RATIONAL PRICING MECHANISM: POLICY OPTIONS

The medium-term policy objective of the Indian government is to increase the share of natural gas from 6.5 per cent of the energy mix at present to 15 per cent by 2030. It can be presumed that the underlying rationale is to increase the share of natural gas, potentially displacing more polluting fuels and achieving energy security (of physical supplies, as well as fiscal balance). In the longer term, pricing reforms should prepare the gas industry to be long-term competitive in moving to a low carbon energy sector and economy, through catalysing the development of new technologies and potential for sector coupling.[33]

Finally, it can be assumed that another key government objective is to ensure that gas is affordable to as wide a range of end-consumers as possible. This section addresses two questions: how can the distortions be addressed in keeping with public policy objectives? And, what are the incremental versus the long-term changes that would be required?

PRICING FOR A SUSTAINABLE SUPPLY CHAIN

It is clear from the discussion in the previous section that market conditions for gas in India conform to a gas-short or gas-deficit situation,[34] in which case the preferred basis for determining a domestic gas pricing mechanism should be its replacement value in the market place.[35] This implies that in the short term:

- The base price of gas should in some way reflect the price of substitutes that it is meant to be replacing in the economy.
- The price should also reflect the opportunity cost of producing gas domestically.

In the first case, domestic price should be linked to the primary inputs in end-user sectors, which are the main competing substitutes to gas. In the second instance, the price should be linked to the price of the major proportion of LNG imports. Figure 5 below illustrates the Indian gas price relative to the cost of importing LNG (the arrow is one representative measure of the opportunity cost).

Figure 5: Indian gas prices versus international gas prices

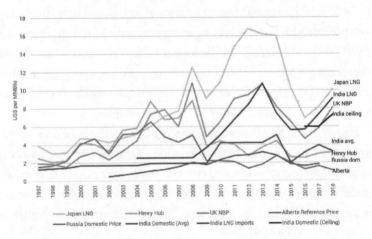

Source: Author analysis.

In April 2016, the government introduced a ceiling price for gas produced from difficult, high-temperature, high-pressure deep-water fields. This price was the lowest of: (a) the landed price of imported fuel oil; (b) the weighted average landed import price of coal, fuel oil and naphtha (with weights set at 30 per cent, 40 per cent and 30 per cent, respectively); and (c) the landed price of imported LNG. The linkages were based on twelve-month averages and included a 5 per cent mark-up to reflect freight, insurance, etc. This mechanism provides a structural starting point for a gas-pricing mechanism which could be simplified or adjusted for factors such as fuel-efficiencies, differential capital costs or externalities. Finally, the incidence of taxation should be re-evaluated.

In the long term, measures should be taken towards reforming transportation tariffs to facilitate competition in the gas market. This would include moving from a zonal to an entry-exit system under which, specific entry and exit points are identified in the transmission network system by a regulator. The capital and operating costs for transmission companies that are serving specific zones are worked out and allocated across these designated entry and exit zones.

In the UK, entry tariffs are set based on auctions of entry points to gas suppliers (i.e., shippers or traders), whereas exit tariffs are set by the regulator—the idea being that transmission companies can recoup their required return from these total revenues. Entry-exit tariffs are also meant to facilitate easier trading of gas within a designated entry-exit zone (suppliers pay just one charge to enter a zone and another to exit; once in a zone they can trade with multiple buyers), and in a sense act as a virtual hub. However, the volumes of gas traded in the economy need to increase in order to introduce such a system (and for it to be truly competitive).

CORRECTING FOR A TWO-TIER MARKET

In the medium term, the two-tier structure needs to be consolidated for a single dominant price signal to emerge. The experience of China provides some lessons in this regard, where a gradual process of restructuring and price adjustments contributed to the development of a market.[36] China had multiple well-head prices and several segmented end-user sectors to which gas was supplied on a heavily regulated basis. In 2005, reforms were initiated to streamline the wellhead prices into just two types: tier-1 and tier-2 fields, and also to consolidate end users into a smaller number of groups (the broad distinction between end-users was between residential and non-residential consumers).

These reforms were primarily aimed at establishing a link between the well-head price and the price of competing fuels and finally, at raising gas prices and reducing the differential between the different well-head prices. While tier-1 prices were set on a government-regulated cost-plus basis, the prices for tier-2 fields were linked to the prices of competing fuels through a basket of crude oil, LPG and coal prices, with an 8 per cent annual limit on any price increase. The declared aim was that tier-1 prices would steadily reach tier-2 prices through an annual adjustment process over three years (which took much longer).

By 2008, China's average wellhead price was around one quarter of the average international gas price while prices to consumers were some 10–15 per cent lower than the wellhead price, even excluding transport costs, while residential prices (usually lower than other prices), varied widely depending on the province.[37] In 2010, producers and large consumers were allowed to negotiate prices around a benchmark price based on the wellhead price, which itself could vary by as much as 10 per cent in either direction. At the end of 2011, another major round of reform was implemented, aimed at moving the price point from the wellhead to the city gate, based on a netback formula—and at the establishment of a single city-gate price ceiling for each province—applying to all onshore pipeline gas.

Shanghai was selected as the base point for pricing, with prices in other provinces calculated based on the Shanghai hub price, with adjustments for differential pipeline transmission tariffs compared to the costs of gas delivered to Shanghai. The formula set out by the National Development and Reform Commission (NDRC) was:

$$PGAS = K * ((\alpha * PFO * HNG/HFO) + (\beta * PLPG * HNG/HLPG)) * (1+R)$$

Where, PGAS was the tax-inclusive city-gate price in Shanghai in RMB/cubic metres; K was a constant discount factor to encourage the use of gas; α and β were the weights of fuel oil (60 per cent) and LPG (40 per cent) in China's energy supply; PFO and PLPG were the average imported fuel oil and LPG prices in RMB/kg; HNG, HFO and HLPG were the heating values of gas, fuel oil and LPG (8,000 Mcal/kg, 10,000 Mcal/kg and 12,000 Mcal/kg); and, R was the value-added tax (VAT) rate for natural gas. Over time, city-gate prices based on the formula were established in each province as the ceiling price for gas—which was later changed to the benchmark price.

From 2013 onwards, the Chinese government introduced the two-tiered pricing system for the end users, specifically for non-resident consumers, applying the netback pricing formula (above) to incremental volumes (i.e., volumes deemed in excess of a base volume established by the 2012 consumption level). This translated into a price increase to non-resident consumers in China. While the price of the base volumes was still regulated, the steadily growing incremental volume share of non-residential gas consumption was priced by a netback linkage to international energy prices. The stated aim was that by 2015, the two prices would converge towards the fully market-based price used for the incremental volumes and China would then effectively be pricing its gas at market prices.[38] There continued to be increases in the base price and the city gate price over the next few years. By using data, O'Sullivan shows that the average city gate price in China moved in conjunction with the Shanghai price.[39]

In 2015, following the global fall in oil and later gas prices, the government merged the two pricing tiers for non-resident users into one to create a single price for sales to all non-resident users. In May 2018, the government announced that it would unify the price of residential gas (which had hitherto been well below non-residential prices) with that of non-residential gas. City-gate tariffs for residential users, which had not changed since 2010, were freed from government control and increased to the level of non-residential prices in June 2018. Since then, the national oil companies (NOCs) have been able to negotiate prices around that benchmark with the gas distributors.

After June 2019, household prices were, in theory, to be allowed to rise to a level 2 per cent above the non-residential prices, although price cuts could be of any amount. In practice, consumers—whether residential, industrial or in other sectors—do not pay the city-gate prices, which are regulated by the NDRC. Local gas distributors (such as ENN Energy, China Gas Holdings and Kunlun Energy) buy the gas at the city-gate from major oil companies, transmit it through their citywide pipeline networks and are allowed to charge a price by sector that delivers them a government-approved rate of return. Some larger industrial customers negotiate directly with the gas suppliers (principally China's three major oil companies).

The local pricing bureau set the end-user prices across China.[40] Tiered pricing was extended for residential consumers based on the amount of usage (smaller volumes to larger volumes), in terms of coverage, a base tier-1 covered those households which together made up 80 per cent of residential demand. Tier-2 covered households using the next 15 per cent of gas volumes while tier-3 covered the last 5 per cent of demand.[41] China's gas pricing at the end-user level remains fragmented and complex and the recent trade war with the US has influenced government priorities in terms of reducing dependence on LNG imports and focusing on domestic gas and bilaterally negotiated pipeline imports.

The governance structure in China is, of course, not directly applicable to India, but the Chinese experience illustrates that reform of the pricing mechanism (e.g., the implementation of a formula reflecting the replacement value of gas in the marketplace) can be carried out alongside the consolidation of the two tiers towards some clear medium-term goals. As price pooling has been an acceptable solution to increase the availability of gas (and thus its utilization in end-user sectors) in the past, it could be used once again with a view to this end (merging the two tiers, or raising prices in one tier to meet the other). The process could be market-oriented (through auctions, for instance) and could begin with specific parts of the end-user value chain, eventually extending to include the entire chain. Any such process would require mitigating measures, but these should be aimed at protecting end-consumers rather than sectors.

IMPROVING PRICE SIGNALS IN END-USER SECTORS

It is important to recognize that well-functioning market mechanisms can deliver efficiency, but not affordability. Objectives on income distribution (an important part of government policy and socio-economic development) should, therefore, be met outside the pricing system and market, rather than directly through it. This already occurs to an extent wherever subsidies are being delivered directly to the end consumer, rather than through a subsidy on the wholesale or retail price and would entail its implementation across different end-user sectors/end consumers.

Another important element to creating a clear price signal to incentivize the use of gas is to price in environmental externalities, particularly where gas is disadvantaged against more polluting fuels. For instance, in the power sector, the tax (cess) on coal production (at around \$6/tonne) is nowhere near enough to incentivize coal to gas switching.[42] Sen carried out an analysis of coal to gas switching using the following assumptions:

- An average selling price for power estimated at around ₹3.20/kWh (\$0.045/kWh)
- A fixed cost of ₹1.35/kWh (\$0.019/kWh) based on the capital costs for a medium-sized power plant

- An increase of $1.3/MMBtu in the delivered price of gas to power, and an increase of roughly ₹0.45/kWh in the variable cost for every $1/MMBtu increase in gas prices.[43]

At a gas price of $5.50/MMBtu, the tax per tonne of coal production would have to be roughly four-and-a-half times higher (namely around $27/tonne) to incentivize coal-to-gas switching. As this would require a nearly 30 per cent increase in electricity tariffs (or an equivalent increase in subsidies), it may not be a politically acceptable way of pricing in externalities. Instead, incorporating externalities into the pricing formula per se may be one way of incentivizing relative competition between fuels.

Taking the Chinese city-gate pricing formula as one example, the heating values could be adjusted in some way to take account of relative emissions from different fuels. In the UK for instance, a combination of the EU Emissions Trading System (€20/tonne) and the UK carbon price floor (£18/tonne) have resulted in a carbon price that has seen coal plants disappear from the generation mix for days or even weeks at a time over 2019, with the system balanced through a combination of gas and renewables.

However, some analysts have estimated that a much higher carbon price, exceeding $40/tonne, would be needed for gas to be able to compete with coal. Based on an existing coal tax of ₹0.25/kWh for coal-fired power, a $40/tonne CO_2 (carbon dioxide) price would take the coal-fired tariff to ₹3.3/kWh for coal, or ₹1.3/kWh for gas (thus ₹1.7/kWh spread to coal). Additionally, LNG-based gas cannot compete on a marginal cost basis with existing coal close to pithead locations. The potential tariff increases that would be required through the incorporation of a higher coal cess or carbon dioxide price once again raise concerns around their distributional impacts on poorer consumers who have largely been shielded from tariff increases.

Depending on the mechanism that is used to price in externalities, revenues could be used to support mitigating measures for the most vulnerable consumers from higher electricity prices.[44] For instance in the UK, while gas is sold at market-determined rates to all consumers,[45] the UK government provides an ex-market payment to make gas affordable to vulnerable consumers in the form of a winter heating allowance. This is a one-off tax-free payment of between £100 and £300 to elderly citizens of pensionable age, to help with their winter heating bills as prices tend to be higher in the winter on the back of higher demand for heating (and, therefore, for gas). The allowance amount is graded according to factors such as age of the recipient (persons eighty years or older receive a higher payment) and his/her other sources of income (persons living on their own receive a higher payment relative to those living with someone who has an income). This allowance is paid directly into the bank account of eligible consumers. Payments are made automatically as eligible consumers are registered on the UK's well-developed social security system, but consumers can also make claims for payments if they feel they are eligible. The payment is funded through revenues from general taxation in the national budget. This allowance was introduced in 2009.

Figure 6: Framework for sustainable domestic gas pricing in India

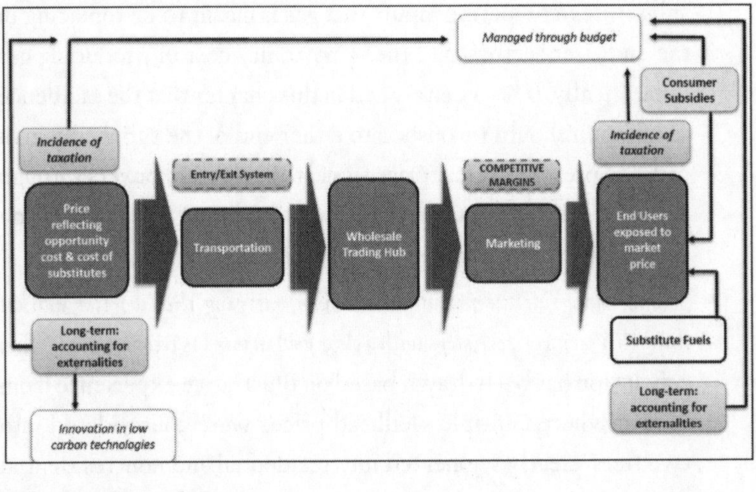

Source: Author analysis.

CONCLUSION

This chapter has identified the key trade-offs before policymakers in the development of a gas market, namely—markets for gas need to be developed with prices low enough (relative to alternatives) to stimulate demand, but high enough to justify the considerable infrastructure expenditure needed to create a market for gas. It has assessed historical and current pricing systems, based on a set of general economic principles and identified three key distortions that have resulted from the same. These are—a lack of sustainable pricing through the supply chain, a two-tier market structure that obfuscates assessments of latent demand and consequently of pricing and investment signals, and price sensitivity in end-user sectors that is imposed rather than inherent, which should ideally be capitalized upon to construct a competitive pricing mechanism for gas.

In order to address these distortions:

- *First, it is concluded that the pricing mechanism for gas should have, as its basis, a linkage to the replacement value of gas in the market place.* This can be simulated through a linkage to the prices of the main substitutes/competing inputs that gas is meant to be replacing in the end-user sectors, and the opportunity cost of producing gas domestically. It has been argued in this chapter that the incidence of taxation should be pushed to either end of the supply chain in order to preserve a clear price signal to sellers and buyers through the supply chain. In the longer term, a reform of transportation tariffs to the more competitive entry-exit system is advocated.

- *Second, alongside the pricing mechanism, merging the two-tier market through a series of clear steps with a clear goal in mind is recommended.* This conclusion has been drawn based on illustrative experience from China, where multiple wellhead prices were consolidated into two tiers, clearly segmented into residential and non-residential consumers, with tier-1 prices gradually adjusted upwards to meet tier-2 prices for all non-residential consumers. And finally a single city-gate price (varying by province) for non-residential and residential consumers.

- *Finally, it is recommended that measures to improve price signals in end-user sectors be put in place.* These should meet all distributional objectives from outside the market; mitigating measures should protect consumers rather than sectors; and pricing in environmental externalities should be employed to improve the relative competitiveness of gas vis-à-vis other more polluting fuels.

Figure 6 provides an illustrative example of a framework for domestic gas pricing in India that reflects these changes and lends itself to crafting policies in each part of the gas-supply chain. The 2020 pandemic, ongoing at the time of writing, induced a unique situation, creating a rare opportunity for 'root and branch' reforms—an abundance of fossil-fuel supplies combined with a sharp contraction in energy demand. This situation, one could argue, created an opportunity to introduce mechanisms to price in environmental externalities in the economy *without* a significant impact on prices for final consumers, and therefore on demand. It remains to be seen, at the time of writing, whether governments will choose to direct policy reforms and fiscal stimulus towards shifting their economies on to a more sustainable path of economic growth.

Notes

1. More on these in the section on reviewing the trade-offs faced in designing a pricing mechanism.
2. These are discussed in the section that highlights key distortions that have resulted from the existing system, and are summarized in Table 1.
3. These pathways include hydrogen production by methane reforming with carbon capture utilization and storage, hydrogen production

via electrolysis from excess renewable electricity, and biomethane production.

4. Donna Peng and Rahmatallah Poudineh, 'Sustainable Electricity Pricing for Tanzania', Working Paper, E-40305-TZA-1, London: International Growth Centre, LSE/University of Oxford, August 2016, https://www.theigc.org/wp-content/uploads/2016/08/Peng-Poudineh-2016-Working-Paper.pdf

5. Javier Reneses, Maria-Pia Rodriguez and Ignacio-Perez Arriaga, 'Electricity Tariffs', in Ignacio-Perez Arriaga (ed.) *Regulation of the Power Sector*, London: Springer-Verlag, 2013, pp. 397-441.

6. Peng and Poudineh, 'Sustainable Electricity Pricing for Tanzania', 2016.

7. Ibid.

8. DeAnne Julius and Afsaneh Mashayekhi, *The Economics of Natural Gas: Pricing, Planning and Policy*, Oxford: Oxford Institute for Energy Studies, Oxford University Press, 1994.

9. Gas is a depletable commodity as a country has a fixed stock. A consumption of 1 Btu today implies forgone consumption 1 Btu at some future date.

10. In economic terms, the cost of supplying an additional unit of production, assuming all factors of production can be varied. This is in contrast with short-run marginal cost (SRMC), in which at least one factor of production cannot be varied. SRMC is considered more efficient, whereas LRMC is considered to be more realistic.

11. Julius and Mashayekhi, *The Economics of Natural Gas: Pricing, Planning and Policy*, 1994.

12. Jonathan Stern and Christopher Allsopp, 'The Future of Gas: What are the analytical issues related to pricing', in Jonathan Stern (ed.), *The Pricing of Internationally Traded Gas*, Oxford: Oxford Institute for Energy Studies, Oxford University Press, 2012.

13. Governments utilize these rents to supplement fiscal income from other sources.

14. See Anupama Sen, 'India's Gas Market Post-COP21', OIES Paper: NG120, Oxford: Oxford Institute for Energy Studies, June 2017, for a full exposition.

15. See Petroleum and Natural Gas Regulatory Board (Determination of Natural Gas Pipeline Tariff) Regulations, New Delhi: Government of India, 2008.

16. Steven Stoft, Carrie A. Webber and Ryan H. Wiser, *Transmission Pricing and Renewables: Issues, Options and Recommendations*, Berkeley: Environmental Energy Technologies Division, Ernest Orlando Lawrence Berkeley National Laboratory, University of California, 1997.

17. This reinforces the incentive for vertical integration and disincentivizes competition.

18. Bids were received only from two sectors: power and fertilizers. See Anil Kumar Jain, *Natural Gas in India: Liberalization and Policy*, Oxford: Oxford Institute for Energy Studies, Oxford University Press, 2011, p. 116.

19. Anil Kumar Jain, *Natural Gas in India*, 2011.

20. Ibid.

21. Ibid.

22. Fulwood and Boersma, writing in this book (see Chapter 4), state that 'gas-on-gas' pricing now accounts for nearly 50 per cent of traded gas. The relevance of Henry Hub may increase if it becomes India's 'swing supplier' on the margin, but it currently accounts for negligible volumes.

23. See Anupama Sen, 'Gas pricing reforms in India: Implications for the Indian gas landscape', OIES Paper: NG96, Oxford: Oxford Institute for Energy Studies, 2015, pp. 15–16 for an analysis. In April 2016, the government introduced a 'ceiling price' for gas produced from 'difficult' high temperature, high-pressure deep-water fields. See Section 5 for details.

24. This number may, of course, vary, based on international gas prices.

25. This number may vary, based on international gas prices.

26. Sen, 'Gas Pricing Reform in India – Implications for the Indian gas landscape', 2015.

27. This is a small proportion since over 90 per cent of urea manufacturing plants are now gas-based. See Sen 'India's Gas Market Post-COP21', 2017, pp. 8–9, for a detailed explanation of the fertilizer-sector strategy.

28. Press Information Bureau, 'Pooling of Gas in Fertilizer (Urea) Sector', New Delhi: PIB, Government of India, 2015.

29. Sen, 'India's Gas Market Post-COP21', 2017.

30. Standing Committee on Energy (2018–19), 'Stressed/Non-performing Assets in Gas-based Power Plants', Forty-Second Report, New Delhi: Ministry of Power, Government of India, January 2019, http://www. indiaenvironmentportal.org.in/files/file/16_Energy_42.pdf

31. In 'India's Gas Market Post-COP21', 2017, Sen estimates this price to be $4.55/MMBtu (at an electricity price of around ₹3.0/kWh on a variable cost basis for an existing medium-sized plant); this is in line with government pronouncements $5/MMBtu as a 'viable proposition' for gas in the power sector (see Singh, S. 'India exploring long-term gas contracts at $5/MMBtu', *The Economic Times*, 22 April 2016.

32. Sen, 'India's Gas Market Post-COP21', 2017.

33. For instance, in the UK, a target to move to net zero emissions is catalysing the decarbonization of not only electricity but also heating and transport, in which decarbonized gas technologies (including biogas, bio-methane, power-to-gas (hydrogen) and methane with carbon capture and storage) are being tested by the industry in terms of their development to commercial scale.

34. India is not a 'gas-rich' country, with 0.7 per cent of global gas reserves.

35. One would argue that given the global carbon constraint, this should be the preferred option for even 'gas surplus' countries, as reserves in the ground no longer hold a 'depletion premium' in the conventional way in the long term.

36. See Stephen O'Sullivan, 'China's Long March to Gas Price Freedom: Price Reform in the People's Republic', OIES Paper, NG138, Oxford:

Oxford Institute for Energy Studies, University of Oxford, November 2018.

37. Ibid.

38. Ibid.

39. Ibid.

40. Ibid.

41. Ibid.

42. And in fact, one could argue that it is not a 'carbon tax' as it does not explicitly tax emissions.

43. See Sen, 'India's Gas Market Post-COP21', 2017.

44. Chapter 24 in this publication looks at the issue of externalities in greater detail.

45. See Patrick Heather, 'The Evolution and Functioning of the Traded Gas Market in Britain', OIES Working Paper, NG44, Oxford: Oxford Institute for Energy Studies, University of Oxford, 2010, for a detailed exposition of the liberalization of the UK gas market.

21

TAXATION

NEETU VINAYEK

Partner, Ernst & Young LLP

SANTOSH SONAR

Executive Director, B S R & Associates LLP, Mumbai

HITEN SUTAR

Director, Ernst & Young LLP

THE OIL AND GAS SECTOR is among the eight core industries in India[1] and plays a major role in influencing decision-making for all other important sections of the economy. To encourage investments in the sector, the Government of India has provided various direct and indirect tax incentives to entities operating in the sector. However, the sector has experienced several challenges on account of various factors, such as the non-inclusion of oil and gas in the Goods and Services Tax (GST) regime, removal of tax holidays and litigation on existing incentives. To attract better traction and investments, it is important to tackle these issues to provide certainty and clarity. This chapter is divided into two sections: direct taxes and indirect taxes, the challenges faced under each and the best international practices which can be adopted to encourage investments in the sector.

INDIRECT TAXES

As discussed in earlier chapters, one of the major reasons for high gas prices in India is its taxation policies—in particular, indirect taxation. Since natural gas is not under the purview of the GST regime, there are a number of levies that consumers have to pay while utilizing gas. The indirect tax framework of the oil and gas sector has the following features:

- Multiple indirect taxes (excise duty, sales tax/value-added tax [VAT], Central sales tax [CST], National Calamity Contingent Duty and Oil Industry Development Board Cess, among others) levied on the production or sale of petroleum products
- Higher and varying tax rates across states
- Restriction on input tax credit to producers/suppliers
- Restriction on input tax credit to buyers/end users
- Exemption on first sale to notified oil marketing companies
- Cascading of tax

CHALLENGES FOR GAS CONSUMPTION UNDER THE CURRENT INDIRECT TAX REGIME

Overview

The Government of India introduced a unified dual GST regime in India from 1 July 2017, with the objective of achieving 'One Nation, One Tax, One Market'. However, given the dependence of the states on the oil and gas sector for revenue, natural gas (along with petrol, diesel and aviation turbine fuel) was excluded from the GST regime and continues to be governed by respective Central/state laws.

Central government taxes

Table 1: Indirect taxes currently levied by Government of India on natural gas

Product	Customs (on imports in India)		Excise Duty (on production)
	Basic Customs Duty (BCD)*	Countervailing Duty (CVD)	
Liquefied Natural Gas (LNG)	2.5 per cent**	Exempt	Exempt
Natural gas in gaseous state (other than CNG)	5 per cent	Exempt	Exempt
Compressed Natural Gas (CNG)	5 per cent	14 per cent	14 per cent

* Apart from the applicable BCD, an additional surcharge—the 'Social Welfare Surcharge'—is also levied @ 10 per cent on BCD. As per the Notification No. 51/2017- Customs, dated 30 June 2017, special additional duty of customs [of 4 per cent] is exempted on petroleum crude, petrol, diesel, petroleum gases and fuels, and compressed natural gas for use in the transport sector. Further, National Calamity Contingent Duty (NCCD) and Oil Industry Development cess (OIDB cess) is not chargeable on natural gas.
** Nil rate when imported for generation of electricity by electricity-generating company (not for a captive power plant).

The interstate supply of natural gas is chargeable to CST at a concessional rate of 2 per cent against the issuance of Form C. Form C can be issued by specified persons for prescribed usage, i.e., by a registered dealer for resale, for use in manufacturing goods for sale, or generation of electricity. With regard to interstate sale, a concessional rate of 2 per cent is available, however, the CST paid on procurement is not available as an input tax credit to the buyer.

State government taxes

Besides the levy of taxes by the Central government, state governments also levy VAT on the intrastate sale of natural gas. This ranges from about 3 per cent (as in Maharashtra, for use in manufacture), to 20 to 25 per cent (Bihar, Chhattisgarh, Uttar Pradesh, Uttarakhand). Thus, VAT rates and related compliance provisions vary from state to state. Many states restrict input tax credit to buyers when natural gas is used as fuel. An illustrative list of VAT applicable in some states is as under.

Table 2: VAT applicable in some states

State	VAT Rate
Chhattisgarh	25 per cent
Uttarakhand	20 per cent (Concessional rate of 5 per cent is prescribed for local sale of natural has (other than CNG) to a registered dealer for use in the process of manufacture of taxable goods under the Uttarakhand GST Act)
Gujarat	15 per cent
Maharashtra	13.5 per cent (Concessional rate of 3 per cent on the local sale of natural gas to a registered dealer for use as fuel or as raw material in the manufacture of goods, subject to certain conditions)
Andhra Pradesh	14.5 per cent (Rate for piped natural gas for domestic use is 5 per cent)
Assam	14.5 per cent

While natural gas was also subject to entry tax in some states, for instance in Gujarat, pursuant to the introduction of GST the entry tax has been abolished with effect from 1 July 2017. Thus, high tax rates—coupled with restrictions on input tax credit—have led to the cascading effect of tax and this consequently affects the ultimate price of natural gas to the consumer. Based on this brief overview of the indirect tax framework of natural gas, let us evaluate the impact of such a taxation framework on various stakeholders and their challenges.

IMPACT ON STAKEHOLDERS

Impact on Producers and Distributors

To boost the natural gas sector, the Government of India has provided a concessional tax regime. Under this regime, basic customs duty is nil and the integrated GST or IGST is 5 per cent for the import of specified goods required in connection with specified petroleum operations (subject to certain conditions, including submission of an Essentiality Certificate from the Director-General of Hydrocarbons).

Further, if the goods are imported on a lease basis, then the IGST on import of goods will be exempted, provided that the IGST on lease rentals is also paid by the importer. Similarly, various other goods and services procured by exploration and production (E&P) companies are liable to GST at applicable rates (ranging from nil to 28 per cent). Further, a lower rate of 12 per cent is prescribed for contract services in relation to E&P operations in offshore locations beyond 12 nautical miles.

Therefore, the output (natural gas) is liable to excise duty and VAT/CST, and the procurement of goods and services is generally liable to GST. The E&P player cannot claim input tax credit of GST paid on the procurement of various goods/services against the output liability of excise duty/VAT/CST. This leads to a cascading effect of taxes on the cost of production of natural gas and ultimately affects prices of natural gas in the market. Concurrent management and compliance with various tax legislations/pre-GST and GST regimes add to the compliance burden of such companies.

Table 3: An illustration of impact of inclusion of natural gas under GST on producers (E&P)[2]

Particulars	As per current tax structure (in ₹)	If included under GST regime (in ₹)
Procurement		
Procurement of goods/ services (**A**)	80	80
Ineligible Input Tax Credit (**B**) GST @ 5 per cent on ₹30 on goods GST @ 18 per cent on ₹50 on services (Refer note 1 & 2 of Endnotes 2)	10.5	0
Eligible Input Tax Credit (**C**) GST @ 5 per cent on ₹30 on goods GST @ 18 per cent on ₹50 on services	0	10.5
Total Cost of procurement (**D = A+B**)	90.5	80

Sale of Natural Gas		
Sale Price (exclusive of taxes) (E) (Refer note 3 of Endnote 2)	100	100
VAT @13.5 per cent (F) (Refer note 4 of Endnote 2)	13.5	-
GST@18 per cent (F) (Refer note 5 of Endnote 2)	-	18
Total Sale Consideration (G = E+F)	113.5	118
Net impact on profit (H = E-D)	9.5	20

Net Tax Outflow on sale to the Company (B-F)		
VAT	13.5	
GST		7.5

Note: As can be seen from the illustration, the exclusion of natural gas from GST affects the cost of production and considering assumptions, the ineligible input tax credit affects cost to the extent of approximately 13 per cent. As depicted above, since goods/services procured by E&P companies are chargeable to GST (which cannot be offset against output tax liability in the nature of VAT/CST that can be levied on natural gas), GST becomes an additional cost for these stakeholders. As in the case of companies involved in E&P operations, various inputs and input services procured by distributors for the conversion of LNG are liable to GST. This includes GST paid on infrastructure that is set up—regasification terminals, construction of storage tanks, laying of pipelines, etc. Such GST is also not creditable to distributors (traders of natural gas) leading to an increase in the overall cost of operations for such distributors. This impacts companies using natural gas for electricity generation.

In the GST regime, consumers of natural gas also face issues in obtaining Form C for the procurement of natural gas at the concessional rate of 2 per cent, as was permitted under the CST Act. In a few states, the state authorities have taken the view that Form C can be issued only if natural gas is used either for resale or for the manufacture of specified petroleum products. However, upon appeal, high courts have granted relief to buyers—holding that they continue to be eligible for the concessional rate of 2 per cent and state authorities have to issue Form C.

For instance, in the case of Caparo Power Ltd versus the state of Haryana and others, the Punjab and Haryana High Court directed tax authorities to issue Form C in respect of natural gas purchased by the petitioner from oil companies in Gujarat and used for the generation or distribution of electricity at power plants in Haryana. It is reported that the above decision was also upheld by the Supreme Court.

Although the matter has been settled in most states, this approach has been disruptive to trade and adds cost and burden to the operation of companies.

Table 4: An illustration of impact of inclusion of natural gas under GST, on companies using natural gas as fuel for the production of goods[3]

Particulars	As per current tax structure (in ₹)	If included under GST regime (in ₹)
Input Side		
Procurement of goods/services (A)	80	80
Ineligible Input Tax Credit (B) VAT paid on Natural Gas @ 3 per cent of ₹10 (Refer note 1 of Endnote 3)	0.3	-

Eligible Input Tax Credit (C) GST on other procurement of input/input services at 18 per cent (Refer note 2&3 of Endnote 3)	12.6 (on balance ₹70)	14.4
Total Cost of procurement (D = A+B)	80.3	80

Sale of Goods		
Sale Price (E) (Refer note 4 & 5 of Endnote 3)	100	100
GST@ 18 per cent (F)	18	18
Total Sale Consideration (G = E+F)	**118**	**118**
Net impact on profit (H = E-D)	19.7	20

Net Tax Outflow on sale to the Company (F-C)		
GST	5.4	3.6

Source: Authors' analysis.

Note: Although the impact may not appear to be significant in the above illustration, the same shall vary depending on state-wise VAT rates as applicable on natural gas, and the actual quantum of natural gas procured by the company. Further, the incremental costs of VAT paid on natural gas may be more in absolute terms than in relative terms.

Impact on Companies Using Natural Gas as Feedstock

As discussed in the chapter 'Fertilizers: A Regulatory Dilemma', the fertilizer sector is one of the largest consumers of natural gas. Restrictions to availing of input tax credit of VAT paid on natural gas, against GST payable on final products in the form of fertilizers, results in the increase in overall costs of production. This, in turn, negatively impacts fertilizer companies and increases the subsidy bill.

Table 5: An illustration of impact on inclusion of natural gas under GST, on a fertilizer company[4]

Particulars	As per current tax structure (in ₹)	If included under GST regime (in ₹)
Input Side		
Procurement of goods/services (A)	80	80
Ineligible Input Tax Credit (B) VAT paid on Natural Gas @ 3 per cent of ₹70 (Refer note 1 of Endnote 4)	2.1	-
Eligible Input Tax Credit (C) GST on other procurement of input/input services at 18 per cent (Refer note 2 and 3 of Endnote 4)	1.8 (on balance ₹10)	14.4
Total Cost of procurement (D = A+B)	82.1	80
Sale of Fertilizer		
Sale Price (E) (Refer note 4 and 5 of Endnote 4)	100	100
GST(@ 5 per cent for use as fertilizer) (F)	5	5
Total sale consideration (G = E+F)	**105**	**105**
Net impact on profit (H = E-D)	17.9	20

Net Tax Outflow on sale to the Company (F-C)		
GST	3.2	Accumulation of Input Tax Credit due to inverted duty structure, i.e., the rate on the final product is lower than the rate on inputs

Source: Authors' analysis.

As depicted above, there is an incremental cost of around 3 per cent on account of ineligible input tax credit for fertilizer companies. These incremental costs will be higher in states where VAT rates on natural gas extends to 14.5 per cent and above. Further, in order to regulate the prices of fertilizers, the government pays a subsidy to fertilizer companies. From 2018–19, the government paid a fertilizer subsidy of around ₹730 billion ($10.44 billion).[5] The inclusion of natural gas under the GST regime will lead to an overall reduction in the cost of fertilizers and accordingly, a reduction in subsidy payouts to the sector by the Central government.

Impact on the Transportation Sector

Compressed natural gas is used to fuel passenger cars and city buses and has the potential to fuel heavy-duty trucks as LNG. Currently, petrol and diesel are not under the GST regime. However, natural gas is a cleaner fuel, as compared to both petrol and diesel and including it under GST will help reduce the overall cost. However, since services provided in form of transportation of goods or passengers are liable to GST, the excise duty/VAT paid on natural gas becomes a cost for the sector.

Table 6: An illustration of impact of inclusion of CNG under GST, used for passenger transportation[6]

Particulars	As per current tax structure (in ₹)	If included under GST regime (in ₹)
Input Side		
Procurement of goods/ services (A)	80	80
Ineligible Input Tax Credit (B) VAT paid on CNG @ 13.5 per cent of ₹60 (Refer note 1 of Endnote 6)	8.1	-

Eligible Input Tax Credit (C) GST on other procurement of input/ input services at 18 per cent (Refer note 2 and 3 of Endnote 6)	3.6 (on balance ₹20)	14.4	
Total Cost of procurement (D = A+B)	88.1	80	
Sale of services			
Sale Price (E) (Refer note 4 and 5 of Endnote 6)	100		100
GST@ 18 per cent (F)	18		18
Total Sale Consideration (G = E+F)	**118**		**118**
Net impact on profit (H = E-D)	11.9		20
Net Tax Outflow on sale to the Company (F-C)			
GST	14.4	3.6	

Source: Authors' analysis.

From the above illustration, it is evident that the ineligible input tax credit affects the cost of transportation to the extent of around 10 per cent. Hence, in order to promote cleaner fuels in the transportation sector and reduce the overall cost for the sector, natural gas should be covered under the ambit of the GST regime.

Impact on Households

Piped natural gas is liable to excise duty at the rate of 14 per cent. Since distributors and companies involved in E&P operations are ineligible to avail of the input tax credit of GST paid on various inputs and input services, the overall cost of natural gas supplied to households is higher. Despite LPG coming under the GST regime (5 per cent bracket), the cost of PNG is at par with a subsidized LPG cylinder and lower than the price of non-subsidized LPG cylinders. Thus, even though both fuels are used for domestic uses by the end-consumer, the difference in the tax treatment changes their price structure.

Impact on Government Revenues

Taxes on the production and sale of natural gas, are the main source of revenue for states as well as the Central government. The total sales tax collected by state governments from Central Public Sector Enterprises (CPSEs) on crude oil, natural gas and petroleum products (which contribute around 90 per cent of the total state revenue from these products) during 2017–18 amounted to ₹1,718.37 billion ($24.57 billion). Out of the state tax collection, the amount collected towards natural gas (both CNG and PNG) amounted to ₹50.39 billion ($720 million) in 2017–18, which is around 3 per cent of the tax collected.[7]

Further, 80 per cent of the taxes from natural gas are attributable only to three states—Gujarat, Uttar Pradesh and Maharashtra. The following table shows the portion of revenue earned by state governments from natural gas products.

Table 7: Revenue earned by state governments from natural gas products as portion of total state revenue from oil and gas taxes

State	Amount (₹billion)	State Revenue (per cent)
Gujarat	20.84	41.4
Uttar Pradesh	12.7	25.2
Maharashtra	6.81	13.5
Andhra Pradesh	1.87	3.7
Assam	1.80	3.6
Kerala	1.48	2.9

State	Amount (₹billion)	State Revenue (per cent)
Rajasthan	1.47	2.9
Madhya Pradesh	1.21	2.4
Haryana	1.13	2.2
Tripura	0.44	0.9
Tamil Nadu	0.43	0.9
Delhi	0.11	0.2

Sources: Economics & Statistics Division, 'Indian Petroleum & Natural Gas Statistics 2017–18', New Delhi: Ministry of Petroleum and Natural Gas, Government of India, September 2018, http://petroleum.nic.in/ sites/default/files/ ipngstat_0.pdf

It is expected that the inclusion of petroleum products under the purview of GST may negatively affect government revenue. While the income from tax collected from natural gas is not significantly high (as compared to other petroleum products), bringing it under the purview of GST may change this. It will result in higher tax collections from natural gas and may be able to balance the collection from the fuels it displaces (though in absolute terms for a while at least, there could be a dip in overall tax revenues, given that gas is priced cheaper than other petroleum products).

A Case for Including Natural Gas in GST

With the intent of bringing in a harmonized system of indirect tax structure in India, GST was introduced in 2017, subsuming all tax levies applicable on goods and services, with a few specified exclusions.

The very objective behind the introduction of GST was to:

- Bring in a simpler tax system in the country
- Mitigate cascading effects by subsuming multiple taxes under a single tax regime

- Reduce prices of goods and services by eliminating the cascading effect
- Reduce compliance costs.

Extensive discussions have been undertaken for the inclusion of natural gas in the GST regime. But concerns over the loss of significant tax revenues and loss of flexibility to increase tax rates are the main deterrents. But at the same time, the increased costs of petroleum products (due to non-inclusion in the GST) lead to increased costs of final products in various industries. Hence, industries have repeatedly asked that natural gas should be included in the GST regime. As the illustrations in the previous section indicate, the effective cost of operations is higher in the current tax structure—vis-à-vis on the inclusion of natural gas in GST—in both upstream and downstream industries.

To summarize, the overall benefits of including natural gas in the GST regime will be as follows:

- Free flow of input tax credit, which is the basic premise of the introduction of GST leading to efficiency across the supply chain
- Reduced cost of extraction, production and distribution of natural gas
- Reduction in the overall cost of goods produced by company using natural gas as fuel for generation of electricity
- Promotion of the use of a clean fuel for electricity generation, as compared to other fuels such as coal
- Reduction in the overall cost of production of companies using natural gas as feedstock, such as fertilizer companies
- Reduction in compliance costs because of a single taxation system
- Reduction in the transportation cost of passengers/goods

- Increased revenue to state governments from natural gas, once consumption increases

DIRECT TAXES

At present, the Income-tax Act, 1961, (ITA) is the Central Act that governs provisions regarding income-tax in India. There are huge expectations from the industry for a simplified tax law, reduction in tax rates, extension of tax incentives currently available and the granting of greater fiscal incentives for oil and gas operations.

CURRENT TAX REGIME AND TAX INCENTIVES

India has a simplified tax regime for direct taxes, where profits of Indian companies are taxable at 34.94 per cent,[8] and profits of foreign companies are taxable at 43.68 per cent.[9] Profits for this purpose are to be computed after considering adjustments under Indian direct tax laws. There is also an alternate mechanism for computing taxation, where taxes are computed on adjusted profits as per financial statements, i.e., minimum alternate tax (MAT) at 17.47 per cent,[10] in the case of Indian companies and at 16.38 per cent[11] for foreign companies. In case the amount payable as per MAT exceeds taxes computed under the Act, a taxpayer is required to pay tax under MAT. The excess tax paid under MAT is available as a credit to a taxpayer, which can be carried forward for a period of fifteen years and can be offset against the tax payable under normal tax provisions. Due to the MAT regime, a company may be required to pay taxes, even during the tax holiday period.

The Government of India reduced corporate tax rates with the intention of making India both globally competitive and an attractive investment destination. Domestic companies are now given an option to opt for a lower tax rate of 25.17 per cent,[12] subject to certain conditions. Further, a domestic company incorporated after 1 October 2019 and engaged in the manufacturing or production of any article and research in relation thereto, which commences manufacturing operations before 31 March 2023 can opt for a lower tax rate of 17.16 per cent.[13] The aforementioned option once exercised, cannot be withdrawn subsequently.

The provisions of MAT are not applicable to a domestic company opting for the aforementioned regime. Consequentially, the provisions of MAT credit are also not applicable to such companies.

CHALLENGES FACED BY OIL AND GAS COMPANIES ON DIRECT TAXES

Because of the peculiar nature of industry, certain tax incentives are granted to the companies engaged in the sector (Refer Appendix 1). However, while claiming such incentives, certain challenges are faced by these companies.

This section highlights the challenges that oil and gas companies face during production, import and transportation.

Deduction of Exploration and Drilling Expenditure Denied on Technical Grounds

Section 42 of the ITA provides an additional deduction for companies involved in E&P. However, this deduction requires that the production sharing contract and revenue sharing contract entered into with the Government of India, be tabled before each House of parliament. It has been observed that such contracts are not tabled before parliament immediately upon signing and at times, it takes years before they are tabled. Accordingly, companies face serious challenges in tax proceedings when claiming allowances under Section 42 of the ITA.

Another common issue faced by companies is the lack of clarity to offset losses from one non-producing field against income from another producing field. It is common for E&P companies to undertake exploration or extraction activities in multiple fields. While the ITA does not restrict off-setting losses from a non-producing field against the business income from a producing field, in some cases this position is questioned by income-tax authorities, especially if the contracts do not have specific enabling clauses.

In view of the above, E&P companies are burdened with the payment of taxes on income arising from producing fields. They are also not allowed to offset losses suffered on account of the expenditure incurred on non-producing fields. Such losses are allowed to be carried forward and offset only for a period of eight years. This results in a loss to companies.

Denying Presumptive Tax Regime to Certain Service Providers

The presumptive taxation regime as provided in Section 44BB of the ITA is applicable only to non-residents. The applicability of presumptive tax regimes to certain foreign companies are challenged and, in many cases, the benefits of presumptive taxation are denied on grounds such as:

- Services rendered by foreign companies do not have proximate nexus to field operations (for e.g., design and engineering done outside India)
- Foreign companies engaged by sub-contractors are not eligible for presumptive taxation
- If a foreign company is rendering a bouquet of services, only the income earned from certain services is eligible for a presumptive basis of taxation.

Lack of Clarity on Cross-Country Pipeline

A 100 per cent deduction for capital expenditure is available for companies engaged in laying and operating cross-country natural gas or crude or petroleum oil pipeline networks. However, there is a lack of guidance on the application of the aforesaid provision. The scope of the term 'cross-country' is unclear. It must be clarified whether this provision can be applied to pipelines used within the city gas distribution (CGD) network, or whether it can be applied for pipelines spanning one state to another.

Interestingly, the Petroleum and Natural Gas Regulatory Board (PNGRB) rules,[14] define natural gas pipelines to include spur lines but exclude pipelines in a city or local natural gas distribution network. Accordingly, there is uncertainty about whether the aforesaid deduction can be claimed by companies engaged in the business of operating a cross-country pipeline under India's domestic tax laws.

Denial of Tax Holiday

A 100 per cent tax holiday is available for seven consecutive years for profits from the commercial production of natural gas. However, it has been generally seen that such tax holidays have been questioned/denied by tax authorities for various reasons. These include the kind of income that is derived from business operations, whether there is a nexus between the income and the eligible business and whether the business has been set up by splitting the operations of a business already in existence. A majority of the issues mentioned above are caused by differences in interpretation/lack of clarity about the provisions of ITA. It would be in the interest of the sector if the aforesaid issues are appropriately addressed.

GLOBAL OVERVIEW OF TAX INCENTIVES

To refine and improve existing incentives, it would be advisable if some international best practices are considered and fiscal incentives are devised considering the same. Incentives provided by different gas-producing countries are discussed below.[15]

Australia

Income tax is charged at 30 per cent on the taxable income of a company engaged in exploration and production activity (reduced tax rates can apply for some low turnover entities). The determination of taxable income allows an immediate deduction for revenue costs (e.g., operating costs, general and admin costs) as well as certain specified capital expenditure (e.g., exploration, environmental protection costs). Other capital costs will generally be depreciable for income tax over time. Income tax losses incurred by the tax payer can be carried forward indefinitely, subject to the satisfaction of continuity of ownership test or the same business test.

Petroleum Resources Rent Tax (PRRT) is a 40 per cent tax imposed on oil and gas production revenues. In determining the amount upon which PRRT is imposed, a deduction is allowed for both capital and revenue expenditure. For the purpose of deduction of capital expenditure, the expenditure is categorized as exploration expenditures (exploration drilling costs, seismic survey), general project expenditures (development expenditures, costs of production), closing-down expenditures (environmental restoration, removal of production platforms), resource tax expenditure (state royalties and excise), acquired exploration expenditure and starting base expenditure. Any carried forward unused deductions can be carried forward and augmented at rates that differ depending on this categorization.

Canada

A minimum of 10 per cent deduction is allowed for the costs incurred by oil and gas companies to acquire rights in foreign oil and gas fields in a year. The maximum permissible deduction in any year is income earned from the foreign resource or 30 per cent of the expenditure incurred for such foreign sources. The cost incurred on the acquisition of oil and gas property in Canada is accumulated in an account and a maximum deduction of 10 per cent of the accumulated balance in the account is allowable in a year.

Norway

A company can claim a refund of the tax value of exploration expenses for each year, including direct and indirect expenses related to exploration activities. The refund is to be issued within three weeks after the issuance of the final tax assessment. For example, If a company spends NOK 100 million on exploration expenses in 2018, it can claim a cash refund of NOK 78 million no later than three weeks after 1 December 2019. This is regardless of whether the drilling is successful or not.

Saudi Arabia

Additional tax deductions are provided for investment in six regions,[16] for a period of ten years from the start of the project. These deductions are inter-alia in the form of tax deductions of training and salary costs incurred for the nationals of Saudi Arabia.

The incentives provided in these countries have played a significant role in aiding domestic production. While they cannot be exactly replicated as far as India is concerned (given the differences in the taxation regime), it still provides policymakers with a direction.

We also looked at countries with gas consumption similar to that of India, in terms of parameters such as the ratio of import of natural gas by per capita GDP. Tabulated below is the comparison of import by different countries and their per capita GDP.

Table 8: Comparison of import by different countries and their per capita GDP

Country	Natural gas imports[17] (cubic meters)	Per Capita GDP in USD[18]	Natural gas import/per capita GDP
Germany	119,500,000,000	50,800	2,352,362
Japan	116,600,000,000	48,256	2,416,279
China	97,630,000,000	7,162	13,631,667
United States	86,150,000,000	53,643	1,605,987
Italy	69,660,000,000	35,108	1,984,163
Turkey	55,130,000,000	14,922	3,694,545
The Netherlands	51,000,000,000	54,412	937,293
Mexico	50,120,000,000	10,287	4,872,169
South Korea	48,650,000,000	27,631	1,760,704
France	48,590,000,000	44,465	1,092,770
United Kingdom	47,000,000,000	42,554	1,104,479
Spain	34,630,000,000	32,331	1,071,108
Canada	26,360,000,000	50,960	517,268
India	23,960,000,000	1,915	12,511,749
Taiwan	22,140,000,000	50,500	438,416
The United Arab Emirates	20,220,000,000	68,600	294,752

Country	Natural gas imports[17] (cubic meters)	Per Capita GDP in USD[18]	Natural gas import/per capita GDP
Belgium	18,090,000,000	46,313	390,603
Belarus	17,530,000,000	6,413	2,733,510
Russia	15,770,000,000	12,388	1,273,006
Poland	15,720,000,000	17,011	924,108

Source: Central Intelligence Agency, 'Country Comparison: Natural Gas – Imports,' The World Factbook

As can be observed, Germany, Japan and Italy have similar natural gas imports per capita GDP (almost half of Mexico's imports per capita GDP). While it appears that Japan and Germany offer no special incentives to companies operating in the oil and gas sector, Mexico offers a beneficial rate of depreciation. For example, 100 per cent depreciation is allowable on the original investment amount for exploration, secondary and enhanced oil recovery and non-capitalized maintenance; 25 per cent on investments for the development and exploitation of petroleum; and 10 per cent on investments in infrastructure, storage, and transportation that is essential for the contract, oil and gas pipelines, and terminals among others. Net operating losses incurred in the execution of deep-water contracts are eligible to be carried forward for a period of fifteen years as against ten years applicable to other companies. Italy allows a deduction for all costs related to oil and gas exploration.

Given India's population density and aggregate and potential demand, it is essential to have stability in terms of availability. Accordingly, it is necessary to give an impetus to domestic E&P and additional incentives must be considered for these companies.

POLICY RECOMMENDATIONS (INDIRECT AND DIRECT TAXES)

- The section on indirect taxes makes it self-evident that gas has to be brought under GST. This will aid not only producers but also consumers, and will lead to an overall increase in gas consumption.

- Allowance for offsetting inter-field losses in upstream gas operations would eliminate the disparity between E&P taxpayers and other normal taxpayers in India.

- Allow the option of claiming deduction of capital expenditure by E&P companies on a straight-line basis under Section 42 of the ITA. In other words, exploration expenses may be allowed as a deduction over the life of PSC or for a pre-defined duration. This would ensure that certain losses, which lapsed after eight years of incurrence, would still be available for set-off against future profits.

- Carry forward offset of losses indefinitely (currently such carry-forward is limited to eight years).

- Consider extending eligibility of lower tax rates to foreign companies operating through a branch/project office in India in the sector. Such companies bring techno/commercial capabilities required in complex E&P operations. Usually, such companies do not set up a permanent/long-term presence in India by establishing a company. Accordingly, given the need to encourage such foreign companies, the Government of India may consider extending the benefit of lower tax rates to foreign companies operating in the sector.

APPENDIX 1: SPECIAL DIRECT TAX INCENTIVES PROVIDED TO OIL AND LAND GAS COMPANIES

1. Deduction of Exploration and Drilling Expenditure under Section 42 of the Income Tax Act
2. Deduction for 'farm-in' expenditure: Depreciation can be claimed on the farm-in value at prescribed rates while computing the profits for the oil and gas company.[19, 20]
3. 100 per cent tax holiday for production of natural gas for seven years: This is for New Exploration Licensing Policy VIII blocks and coal-bed methane (CBM) blocks licensed under the fourth round.[21]
4. Presumptive taxation of companies engaged in providing services to E&P operations
5. Site Restoration Fund

Notes

1. Oil and Gas Statistics, *Make In India*, http://www.makeinindia.com/sector/oil-and-gas
2. This is an illustration to indicate additional tax cost. The actual impact will vary depending upon various factors, including the quantum of procurement and related supply chain of the given company. Assumptions for the illustration are as follows:

   1: Out of the total procurement of ₹80, the goods portion is assumed as ₹30 and the balance amount is considered towards procurement of services. As specified above—since most of the goods procured for E&P operation are chargeable to the concessional GST rate of 5 per cent—GST has been calculated at 5 per cent on goods. GST has been calculated at the rate of 18 per cent on services required for exploration activities.

   2: Impact of BCD/SWS is not considered in the impact assessment above, as the same is a constant cost in both scenarios.

3: For analysing the impact, the sale price under the GST regime has been assumed to be the same as under the current tax structure.

4: The VAT rate on the sale of natural gas has been considered as 13.5 per cent, as applicable in the state of Maharashtra (other than industrial consumers).

5: The proposed GST rate on the sale of natural gas has been assumed at 18 per cent.

3. Assumptions for the illustration:

1: In the current tax structure, the VAT rate on the purchase of natural gas is 3 per cent in Maharashtra, if used as a raw material/ fuel for manufacture of goods. For illustration purposes, out of the total procurement of inputs of eighty, the portion of natural gas is assumed as ten and the balance amount is considered towards other procurements liable to GST.

2: The GST rate on natural gas has been assumed at 18 per cent.

3: Impact of BCD/social welfare surcharge (SWS) is not considered a constant cost in both scenarios in the impact assessment above.

4: For analysing impact, the sales price under the GST regime has been assumed to be the same as under the current tax structure.

5: The GST rate on goods is considered at 18 per cent for illustration purposes.

4. Assumptions for the illustration:

1: In the current tax structure, the VAT rate on the purchase of natural gas is 3 per cent in Maharashtra if used as a raw material/fuel for the manufacture of goods. For illustration purposes, out of the total procurement of inputs of eighty, the portion of natural gas is assumed as ten and the balance amount is considered towards other procurements liable to GST.

2: The GST rate on natural gas has been assumed at 18 per cent.

3: Impact of BCD/social welfare surcharge (SWS) is not considered a constant cost in both scenarios in the impact assessment above.

4: For analysing impact, the sales price under the GST regime has been assumed to be the same as under the current tax structure.

5: The GST rate on goods is considered at 18 per cent for illustration purposes.

6: The fertilizer sector is eligible for subsidy granted by the Government of India. The same is not considered in the sale price.

5. Press Information Bureau, Statement issued by Ministry of Chemicals and Fertilizers, New Delhi: PIB, Government of India, 19 July 2019.

6. Assumptions for the illustration:

1: In the current tax structure, the VAT rate on the purchase of natural gas is 3 per cent in Maharashtra, if used as a raw material/fuel for the manufacture of goods. For illustration purposes, out of the total procurement of inputs of eighty, the portion of natural gas is assumed as ten and the balance amount is considered towards other procurements liable to GST.

2: The GST rate on natural gas has been assumed at 18 per cent.

3: Impact of BCD/social welfare surcharge (SWS) is not considered a constant cost in both scenarios in the impact assessment above.

4: For analysing impact, the sales price under the GST regime has been assumed to be the same as under the current tax structure.

5: The GST rate on goods is considered at 18 per cent and the GST rate on passenger transportation services is considered at 18 per cent for illustration purposes.

7. Economics & Statistics Division, 'Indian Petroleum & Natural Gas Statistics 2017–18', New Delhi: Ministry of Petroleum and Natural Gas, Government of India, September 2018, http://petroleum.nic.in/sites/default/files/ipngstat_0.pdf

8. Highest rate of 30 per cent (including surcharge at 12 per cent, and cess of 4 per cent on tax and surcharge) for income above ₹100 million.

9. Highest rate of 40 per cent (including surcharge at 5 per cent, and cess of 4 per cent on tax and surcharge) for income above ₹100 million.

10. 15 per cent after the introduction of the Ordinance dated 20 September 2019 (plus surcharge at 12 per cent for Indian companies for income above ₹100 million and cess of 4 per cent on tax and surcharge).

11. 15 per cent after the introduction of the Ordinance dated 20 September 2019 (plus surcharge at 5 per cent for foreign companies for income above ₹100 million and cess of 4 per cent on tax and surcharge).

12. Including surcharge of 10 per cent and cess of 4 per cent on tax and surcharge.

13. Including surcharge of 10 per cent and cess of 4 per cent on tax and surcharge.

14. Petroleum and Natural Gas Regulatory Board (Authorizing Entities to Lay, Build, Operate or Expand Natural Gas Pipelines) Regulations, 2008.

15. Taxation regimes of other countries have been summarized, based on desktop research undertaken.

16. These six are: Ha'il, Jazan, Najran, Al-Baha, Al-Jouf and Northern Territory.

17. Central Intelligence Agency, 'Country Comparison: Natural Gas – Imports,' The World Factbook, 7 January 2021, https://www.cia.gov/the-world-factbook/field/natural-gas-imports/

18. Central Intelligence Agency, 'Country Comparison: GDP – Per Capita (PPP)', The World Factbook, 7 January 2021, https://www.cia.gov/the-world-factbook/field/gdp-per-capita-ppp

19. Depreciation @ 25 per cent of written down value.

20. Circular No 20/2019 dated 19 August 2019 issued by the Central Board of Direct Taxes.

21. Section 80-IB(9) of the Income-tax Act, 1961, subject to satisfaction of prescribed conditions.

SECTION E

REGULATION AND SUSTAINABILITY

22

REGULATORY FRAMEWORK

SUDHA MAHALINGAM

Raja Ramanna, Chair Professor, Energy and Environment Programme,
National Institute of Advanced Studies, Bangalore and former Member,
Petroleum and Natural Gas Regulatory Board, India

INTRODUCTION

THE PARTIAL MARKET OPENING AROUND the mid-1990s led to
select oil and gas fields being given to private consortia for exploration
and production. Investors were also given marketing freedom to sell
gas that they might discover, although that meant utilizing pipelines
already operated by GAIL (India) Ltd for transporting new discoveries
or building new pipelines. In 1997, the government fully opened up
upstream activities to private investors and put in place transparent
policies and mechanisms, including international competitive bidding
processes to award exploration licenses. Increased supply would
necessitate the construction and commissioning of the national gas grid
(NGG) as well as markets where gas could be consumed. In tune with
trends elsewhere in the economy (in the 2000s)—where network
industries such as electric supply and telecommunications, hitherto
reserved for the public sector, were being thrown open to private

capital)—the Government of India decided to open up to private investors, pipeline construction and operation as well as construction, operation, marketing and sale of gas through city gas distribution (CGD).

With the Hazira–Vijaipur–Jagdishpur pipeline (HVJ), the main trunk pipeline under government ownership, non-discriminatory open access to market participants would be required. This entailed the separation of carriage from content at the first instance, followed by the unbundling of the (then) Gas Authority of India Limited (GAIL). A national pipeline policy was also put in place to ensure that all future pipelines would have 33 per cent open access capacity for use by third-party shippers.[1]

With many private players entering the gas business, an impartial regulator would be required to oversee the transition from state to markets. The primary task of the proposed independent regulator would be to incentivise private investors to construct new domestic gas pipelines and expand existing pipelines. The regulator would also develop new markets for gas by incentivizing investors to build city or local gas distribution networks. With the government owning the dominant transportation-cum-marketing entity, an impartial regulator working at arm's-length from all stakeholders would be required.

Thus, began the task of drafting a law that would establish and empower a new regulator for India's downstream hydrocarbon industry. In 2006, the Indian parliament passed the Petroleum and Natural Gas Regulatory Board Act. The Petroleum and Natural Gas Regulatory Board (PNGRB) was formally set up in July 2007.

THE PNGRB AS A REGULATOR

The PNGRB Act, 2006 confers extensive powers on the regulator to perform the following key functions:

- License entities to build, expand and operate natural gas pipelines and CGD networks
- Monitor implementation of the licences issued by it, and ensure compliance with conditions of the licence
- Unbundle GAIL into transportation and marketing segments
- Determine common carrier/contract carrier capacity in existing and new pipelines, mandate open-access and enforce compliance
- Determine tariffs for common carrier pipelines and CGD networks
- Settle disputes between stakeholders in the sector, including disputes of a class action character[2]

The downstream hydrocarbon regulator would, through appropriately designed regulations, incentivize private capital to build the missing pipelines in order to form a comprehensive NGG. The second major task envisaged for the regulator was to identify and declare existing pipelines to be common carriers and determine tariffs for the third party use of a common-carrier capacity. Multiple shippers could then use common-carrier capacity to supply gas to end-consumers. To enable the regulator to perform this function, Sections 20 to 22 of the PNGRB Act confer extensive powers on the regulator.[3] The PNGRB would also have to lay down rules of access and enforce them. It would set technical and safety standards and monitor compliance by entities with these standards. This function is crucial to market-making.

Finally, the PNGRB would decide disputes between petroleum and natural gas companies as well as disputes between the government and companies, brought to it for resolution. Consumer-related disputes of class action character would also be decided by the PNGRB, although individual consumer disputes were outside its purview. Appeals from regulatory decisions lie with the Appellate Tribunal for Electricity (APTEL), the appellate body for electricity and gas for certain matters and with the civil courts for others.[4] The regulator, according to the PNGRB Act, has been given extensive powers by the civil courts to enable it to discharge its duties and enforce its orders. It is noteworthy that the design and remit of the PNGRB conforms to the good governance parameters, devised by Stern and Holder for the World Bank.[5]

Regulatory Performance: 2007–18

Assessing regulatory performance in terms of the objectives for which the PNGRB was set up, is the first step to understanding how the gas industry has fared under the new regulatory regime.

During the first twelve years of its existence, the PNGRB put in place twenty-nine regulations, adopted after following due process of consultation with concerned stakeholders.[6] Of these, four pertain to licensing functions. Once regulations were in place, the PNGRB began the process of awarding licences to lay/build/operate trunk pipelines and CGD networks through a structured process of competitive bidding. Till November 2018, the PNGRB held ten rounds of bidding for CGD, and awarded a total of 228 licences to build local area distribution networks covering 70.47 per cent of the population and 52.73 per cent of the land area.[7] During the same period, the PNGRB licensed thirteen trunk pipelines. Even prior to the establishment of the PNGRB, the government licensed ten other pipelines.[8] Together, these pipelines would constitute a gas grid reaching substantial parts of the country, after they were built.

However, till date, not a single pipeline licensed by the PNGRB has been commissioned, except in limited stretches (as opposed to the entire length of the pipeline licensed). Some are under construction.[9] The only pipelines that were fully commissioned after the PNGRB came into existence were those that had been licensed by the government, prior to the establishment of the regulator.[10] Similarly, of the 228 CGD networks/Geographical Areas (GAs) licensed by the PNGRB till date, only 43 have been commissioned according to the Petroleum Planning & Analysis Cell (PPAC), a government body affiliated to India's petroleum ministry,[11] (more on this in the next section).

In 2016, in a highly controversial move, the Ministry of Petroleum and Natural Gas bypassed the PNGRB and through a directive issued under Section 42 of the PNGRB Act, 2006, awarded licences to GAIL to build a 2,539 km pipeline network in eastern India (the Jagdishpur-Haldia and Bokaro-Dhamra Pipeline or JHPDPL). It also awarded six CGD licences (Khordha, Cuttack, Patna, Ranchi, East Singbhum and Varanasi) along this pipeline network to GAIL, without going through the competitive bidding route. It further sanctioned GAIL, a viability gap fund of ₹51.76 billion ($740 million). This measure was an acknowledgement of a lacuna in the regulatory design that prompted the government to not only issue a directive to the PNGRB, awarding GAIL the licence to build the JHPDPL pipeline and the six CGD networks along this pipeline, but also provide viability gap funding (VGF) to support the initiative. This move further diminished the salience of the regulator and eroded its authority and legitimacy.

A decade would be considered a long enough time for the regulator to initiate market-opening measures to introduce competition in the natural gas supply business. It might be instructive to point out that unbundling of integrated electric utilities, equally complex, was accomplished in record time, whereas the unbundling of India's integrated gas utility has remained a non-starter. During the twelve years of its existence, the PNGRB never initiated any steps in this direction. It has still not drafted any unbundling regulations, although it has framed regulations laying down the rules of access to GAIL's pipelines already declared as common carriers. Even here, the PNGRB has seen only limited success in enforcing rules of access because GAIL, the single buyer of gas from most sources—domestic as well as imported liquefied natural gas (LNG)—has frequently denied access to competitors, citing technical obstacles. This is evident from the number of disputes filed with the

PNGRB by frustrated shippers.[12] Market-making, a key regulatory objective, has been a casualty in the process.

The CGD Regulations under PNGRB

The PNGRB has unambiguous licensing powers enshrined in Sections 16 to 19 of the PNGRB Act, 2006. However, Section 16 was notified only three years after the PNGRB was set up, delaying the start of pipeline and CGD. [13] As explained in Chapter 13, the thrust of the bid design until the eighth bidding round was to incentivize the successful bidder to connect as many households as feasible and to charge as low a price for cooking gas, without jeopardizing the economic viability of the project. In other words, weightage given to household connections assumed priority in the licensing for CGD.[14] The franchisee would be free to cross-subsidize between consumers.

Issues with the Initial Bidding Process

Thirteen cities and towns were offered CGD licences in the first three rounds. Not many bidders participated in the initial rounds because the knowledge, expertise and financial muscle to build gas infrastructure were limited to incumbent public sector companies. In the first two bids, investors quoted a very high number of household connections (it had the highest weightage) and very low tariffs (the second-highest weightage) in order to win the licence. It would have been unrealistic for them to invest in constructing the necessary infrastructure for supplying so many households, while simultaneously charging very low tariffs. Yet, because the final price of gas was not regulated it allowed the investor to transfer the cost of the infrastructure to the final gas price, especially for non-household uses.

However, the third bidding round for nine CGD areas threw up several irrational bids that quoted near-zero tariffs.[15] This round had to be cancelled and no licences were issued because of the irrationality of the entire process. The fourth round of bids was kept in abeyance till these teething problems were taken care of. This unforeseen stalling of licensing can be laid at the door of the regulator for setting ambitious bidding criteria by giving maximum weightage to household connections and announcing it transparently ex-ante.

What prompted irrational bids, however, was a loophole in the design of reforms. The PNGRB has no control over gas prices, but only the tariff. The winner of the CGD licence, a monopoly franchisee in its CGD area with exclusive marketing rights for five years, could transfer the cost of building the network on to the gas price. This anomaly was not foreseen in the regulatory design because 'competition for the market' was expected to take care of any abuse of market power by the monopoly franchisee.

Despite the award of licences, the infrastructure roll-out was slow for a variety of important reasons, including lack of cheaper domestic supplies, the approvals and clearances for laying gas pipelines in their respective franchise areas, leading to delays and hold-ups.

Course Corrections and Their Implications

- **Gas allocation policy:** In August 2014, the Ministry of Petroleum and Natural Gas changed the gas allocation policy such that PNG and CNG consumers were given preference over all for low-priced domestic gas. Further, CGD entities were asked to pass on the benefit of price control to the final consumers.[16] The consumer bill would henceforth indicate the break-up, showing gas prices separately from transportation/distribution tariff and taxes. This move was to ensure that gas allotted for PNG was not diverted to industrial uses. Although it is a salutary move from the viewpoint of domestic consumers, it diverted gas already committed from other regulated sectors (power and fertilizer), which now had source LNG to meet their needs. As the CGD networks expand, they are likely to absorb most, if not all domestic production for supply to PNG connections and CNG, leaving the bulk consumers to rely on imported LNG.

- **Public utility status**: In 2018, the Ministry of Labour and Employment accorded the gas industry public utility status. It also directed the Ministry of Housing and Urban Affairs and public sector enterprises (PSEs) to ensure the provision of piped cooking gas in their residential complexes countrywide.[17] Public utilities, despite earning profits, are part of the public service landscape and are, therefore, heavily regulated. Public utility status pre-empts labour strikes and as such, shields CGD franchisees.

- **Easing clearance hurdles:** In 2018, the Ministry of Housing and Urban Affairs ordered that all state governments should earmark land plots for the development of CNG stations at the planning stage of town/city and the same should be specified in the revised Master Plan. They were also to modify building by-laws for providing gas pipeline infrastructure in residential and commercial buildings at the architectural design stage. These measures are expected to speed up clearances for laying pipelines within cities reducing delays in rolling out CGD networks.

- **Changed bid parameters:** The PNGRB amended bid parameters to preclude zero-tariff bids, although the emphasis continues to be on domestic PNG connections and CNG for vehicles. The new parameters reflect the aggressive thrust on the expansion of cooking-gas connections. As it stands, CGD is envisaged as a utility industry servicing a large number of consumers, each consuming modest quantities of gas, rather than as a bulk supplier of fuel to industries.

- **Marketing and expansion of Geographical Areas:** PNGRB extended the period of marketing exclusivity for CGD licensees to eight years for entities licensed from 2018 onwards, to provide a modicum of comfort to investors by allowing enough time to recoup investments made in constructing and operating CGD networks.[18] The franchise area for CGD from cities and urban settlements was also expanded to include rural areas. This could facilitate the setting up of small and medium industries in rural areas and provide the CGD franchisee with a mix of consumers, necessary for the business to be profitable and attractive to private investors.

FINDINGS, CONCLUSIONS AND THE WAY FORWARD

To ensure that gas consumption in India increases, it becomes necessary to increase the PNGRB's powers and add important functions to its arsenal.

(a) **Infrastructure Planning:** Building a nationwide gas grid requires a degree of planning and nudging potential investors to take their businesses to areas hitherto not served. However, planning infrastructure is a tool that is missing in the regulatory toolkit. The regulator can only signal, but not force, the market to build pipelines to areas that are not served. In developed countries, infrastructure was built at the behest of governments, such as in Europe where the entities are government-owned or the regulator (as in the US) accorded some degree of central planning as to where the pipelines should be built. In India, as things stand now, planning for infrastructure is politically driven, rather than market-driven. There is a case for entrusting planning to the regulator.

Licences could be awarded on the basis of competitive bidding where the bid parameter itself could be VGF. Competitive bidding provides superior outcomes. Even the budgetary outflow in the form of VGF could be minimized through this process. Therefore, planning and awarding licences based on VGF should be made part of regulatory remit by amending the PNGRB Act 2006. If the government decides to offer VGF for the construction of pipelines, the task of identifying investors should be left to the regulator which, of course, must follow transparent bidding processes.

(b) **Pricing Function:** Given increasing gas consumption, it becomes necessary, in the interest of transparency, that end-consumers are aware of the price they are paying. Cooking-gas prices are currently pegged to APM and imported LNG is sold to bulk consumers at variable prices depending upon CIF [cost, insurance and freight] price, market demand, price of substitutes, etc.

In June 2020, gas trading through an exchange was launched enabling price discovery, especially for LNG. It is a salutary move. Eventually, India will have to move to gas-to-gas competition when the existing gas sales and purchase contracts expire. Under this scenario, to ensure fair market practices, the regulator must ensure that the consumer is provided with a detailed break-up, listing the gas purchase price, transmission and distribution tariffs, marketing margins and taxes where applicable. Any disputes relating to the components of a bill could perhaps be referred to the Competition Commission of India. This will enable the shipper to pass on the cost of imported LNG/non-APM gas whilst also providing transparency to the consumer, since it hampers the ability of the shipper to inflate the consumer bill beyond what is warranted.

(c) **Marketing exclusivity clause:** A period of eight years offered to CGD licensees is still inadequate to recoup investments in infrastructure in rural or semi-urban franchise areas. Instead of a uniform marketing exclusivity period, a differential time-frame could be considered, wherein franchisees with large rural populations are given longer marketing exclusivity.

(d) **Cancelling licences:** Licences issued to franchisees who won the bid quoting zero or negligible tariffs should be cancelled and these GAs rebid, since these networks are unlikely to get built. There are sufficient enabling clauses in the licences which empower the regulator to cancel the licenses of a licensee not complying with licence conditions.

(e) **Unbundling:** GAIL has to be unbundled in a phased manner so as to prevent a conflict of interest. When the same entity acts as both transporter and marketer, the temptation to accord priority to one's own customers over third-party competitors using the pipeline is clear and present. Unbundling can be undertaken in phases, functional, structural and eventually, legal.

(f) **Monitoring and enforcement** of licence conditions by the regulator is weak. Besides, locating licensing, enforcing and monitoring responsibilities in the same regulator creates a conflict of interest, because admitting to non-performance by the licensee might be construed as the failure of regulatory due diligence while awarding licences. There is scope for hiving off implementation monitoring to a separate agency reporting to the regulator.

(g) **Regulatory capacity:** This is also a major problem in the case of the PNGRB, as it might be in the context of other developing countries. The PNGRB had to rely on professional staff borrowed from the same entities it regulated, indicating a blatant conflict of interest. The regulator should have the freedom to hire competent professionals at market rates of remuneration. The practice of borrowing staff from the regulated entities must cease.

(h) **Transparency on data:** Information asymmetry, common to all regulators, is an acute problem in developed countries, but has worse consequences for developing country regulators who have to deal with a government monopoly shielded by the government. Where the regulator is called upon to fix tariffs for a pipeline already constructed, the PNGRB has no way of ascertaining whether the costs claimed in the tariff proposal were necessary or commensurate. The regulator is always at a disadvantage because of information asymmetry. Benchmarking international standards with the flexibility to adapt to local context could alleviate the problem to some extent.

Assessing free capacity for use by third-party shippers is a persistent regulatory challenge. Setting up independent systems operators (ISOs) could take care of this to some extent.

(i) Time-bound mandate: The PNGRB must be entrusted with a time-bound mandate to introduce a gas market within the country. However, an ISO would be required to notify, and enforce rules of trading and monitor the same. In the electricity sector, Power System Operation Corporation (POSOCO), a subsidiary of Power Grid Corporation of India Ltd (PGCIL), is an autonomous body in charge of load dispatch and settlements. A similar ISO for gas will have to be set up.

There is a case for bringing the gas ISO under the overall remit of the PNGRB as is the case in the electricity sector, where POSOCO functions under the regulatory purview of the Central Electricity Regulatory Commission (CERC). However, since the ISO would be a professional organization, any regulatory oversight has to be light-handed. The PNGRB can act as the arbiter in any disputes between the ISO and other stakeholders.

Transmission tariffs (zonal or entry-exit or postage) will be determined by the PNGRB under the provisions of the PNGRB Act, 2006. In June 2020, the petroleum minister announced that the current tariff policy would be reviewed, possibly to introduce uniform tariffs so that consumers away from source/LNG terminals do not have to pay steep tariffs resulting from locational disadvantage.

(j) Advent of LNG terminals on both coasts: The presence of LNG terminals on two coasts of our long coastline has lent urgency to domestic pipeline infrastructure. At present, India has six operational LNG regasification terminals operational with a capacity of about 42.5 MMtpa. Four more with a cumulative capacity of 19 MMtpa are under construction while another 10 MMtpa is in the planning stages. This opens up the possibility of multiple sources of gas to be supplied across the country which will require infrastructure creation at a fast pace.

(k) Freight transport sector: LNG transport, currently at an incipient stage in India, is set to take off because of the advantages it offers in this sector. This would involve setting up LNG dispensing stations along the highways. While the price of LNG dispensed through these stations will be linked to the import price of LNG, additional costs such as that of the cost of transporting LNG, the cost of dispensing, marketing margins and taxes will have to be regulated by some agency. Also, since multiple LNG cargoes might be imported at different prices, there needs to be some transparency in the pricing of LNG to freight consumers. All these tasks will have to be entrusted to the same regulator. LNG has multiple uses—bulk consumers in industries and commerce, as well as the emerging freight users. A separate and dedicated regulator for the LNG transport sector is bound to introduce complications, not limited to jurisdiction alone. Regulation of LNG transport is best entrusted to the PNGRB. However, this may require an amendment to the PNGRB Act, 2006, apart from strengthening the capacity of the PNGRB. A separate division within the PNGRB might be worth considering.

Notes

1. Ministry of Petroleum and Natural Gas, 'Policy of Natural Gas Pipelines', *Gazette of India* Part 1 Section 1, New Delhi: MoP&NG, Government of India, 20 December 2006, accessed 15 June 2020, http://petroleum.nic.in/sites/default/files/Policy%20of%20 Natural%20Gas%20pipelines%202006.pdf

2. Petroleum and Natural Gas Regulatory Board Act, 2006.

3. Ibid.

4. Ibid.

5. Jon Stern and Stuart Holder, 'Regulatory Governance: Criteria for assessing the performance of regulatory systems – An application to

infrastructure industries in the developing countries of Asia', *Utilities Policy*, Vol. 8 No. 1 (1999), pp, 33–50.

6. Compiled from data available on www.pngrb.gov.in

7. Shine Jacob, 'PNGRB likely to extend deadline by at least 3 months for city gas players', *Business Standard*, 18 April 2020, https://www.business-standard.com/article/companies/pngrb-likely-to-extend-deadline-by-at-least-3-months-for-city-gas-players-120041800061_1.html

8. Compiled from data available www.pngrb.gov.in

9. PNGRB Notifications, https://pngrb.gov.in/NG-pipeline-govt_authorization.html

10. Ibid.

11. Ibid.

12. PNGRB, Cause List, https://pngrb.gov.in/causelist.html

13. Press Trust of India, 'Government gives power to oil regulator to issue gas distribution licenses', 15 July 2010, *The Hindu*, https://www.thehindu.com/business/Economy/Government-gives-power-to-oil-regulator-to-issue-gas-distribution-licences/article16196397.ece

14. The bid document envisaged the highest weightage for the number of household connections proposed to be extended by the bidder, followed by network tariff to be charged, the length of pipelines proposed to be constructed and compression charge for CNG, respectively.

15. PNGRB, Notification, https://pngrb.gov.in/pdf/public-notice/commt05102017.pdf

16. Revised guidelines for supply of natural gas to CGD entities, GOI Notification # L16013/3/2012-GP-12, dated 20 August 2014.

17. http://petroleum.nic.in/natural-gas/new-initiatives, accessed 16 June 2020.

18. PNGRB, Gazette Amendments, https://www.pngrb.gov.in/OurRegulation/pdf/Gazette-Amendments/GSR604(E).pdf

23

CLEAN FUELS: MANAGING THE TRANSITION [1]

ROBERT VAN DER GEEST

Senior Gas Specialist, The World Bank

SIMON STOLP

Practice Leader-Infrastructure, India, The World Bank Group

FRANK VAN OORDT

Global Head, TCF Energy & Metals, Rabobank;
member of the TCF global management team

MICHAEL STANLEY

Global Leader, Energy Transition in Coal Regions,
The World Bank Group

BACKGROUND

TRANSITION CAN BE HARD, AS people need to change their behaviour. An energy transition can be even harder, because of the complexity of the energy value-chain and the many stakeholders involved—such as upstream fuel suppliers, midstream fuel transport companies, downstream traders and fuel distribution companies, as well as upstream, midstream and downstream regulatory authorities. Furthermore, as India is currently in the middle of massive economic and social changes, it is particularly hard to achieve a transition to cleaner fuel. Moreover, such a transition requires a lot of capital. This could be a challenge to attract, as Indian enterprises may not have built up a mature enough credit rating, while the financial system in the country is itself still under development.

Coal and oil products (in a large industry), micro, small, and medium-sized enterprises, (MSMEs), and heavy-duty vehicles (HDVs) dominate the current fuel mix in India. Recognizing this, the World Bank commissioned a study in 2018—with support from the Energy Sector Management Assistance Programme (ESMAP) Trust Fund—to identify the potential role that natural gas could play to improve air quality and to understand what it was that was keeping consumers in these sectors from switching to natural gas.

This paper presents insights from this 2018 study and addresses the challenges of financing the transition to cleaner fuel in the context of air pollution in India, focusing on switching from primitive solid and liquid fuels to natural gas in sectors that are difficult to electrify.

According to the World Health Organization (WHO), nine out of the ten cities with the worst ambient air quality in the world are in India. These include the Delhi, Faridabad and Gurugram in the National Capital Region (NCR).[2] Estimates for 2017, revealed that around 1.2 million people died as a result of air pollution in India—that accounts for one in eight deaths in the country.[3] On the other hand, cleaner air could potentially increase life expectancy across the country by five years and even up to twelve years, in certain districts in the NCR.[4] These numbers are astounding, but they still fall short of describing how millions struggle every day as they walk to school and/or work, or simply walk to the market or go for a walk.

India's fuel mix is currently dominated by coal (44 per cent) and oil (25 per cent), both of which are recognized as major sources of particulate matter (PM). Natural gas, which hardly produces any PM, has always had a small market share in India, which currently stands at around 6 per cent.[5] Coal is more popular than natural gas for power generation, mainly because most coal is produced domestically, whereas gas mostly needs to be imported. Furthermore, liquid fuel is more popular than natural gas in industry, mainly because the gas transmission and distribution network across the country is still in the early stages of its development. The transport sector, notably heavy-duty transport, is also still dominated by oil products (in particular, diesel), simply because most HDVs in India are equipped with diesel engines.

Under Prime Minister Narendra Modi, the Government of India has set an ambitious target of more than doubling the share of natural gas in the fuel mix by 2030.[6] This seems particularly challenging as the share of gas in India's fuel mix actually dropped from around 8 per cent in 2009 to around 6 per cent today. In order to reach the target set for 2030, gas would have to play a much bigger role in all sectors of the Indian economy. This requires the government to implement significant policy, regulatory and fiscal reforms, and to play an active role in the further development of gas infrastructure.

Ever since 2009, the Petroleum and Natural Gas Regulatory Board (PNGRB) has been making a key contribution to the development of the gas transmission and distribution networks of India, by organizing licence bidding rounds for the construction of city gas distribution (CGD) across the country. According to PNGRB's roadmap, 70 per cent of the population should have access to natural gas by 2030, up from just 20 per cent today. This would be a major achievement and cross one of the main hurdles to increasing the role of natural gas in the country's fuel mix.

It remains to be seen whether India will manage to reach this impressive target, but access to capital does not seem to be a big obstacle in the expansion of the country's gas infrastructure. So far, the different bidding rounds for CGD licences have been oversubscribed and the development of different CGD systems is well on track, which may be due to that fact that a winning contestant gains exclusive access to a certain geographical market area for a number of years. Gas distribution companies typically manage to build their business cases for investment into new gas pipelines and facilities, based on estimated and latent market demand for natural gas in their respective geographical areas. In particular, this demand focuses on CNG as motor fuel, a premium niche of the gas market in which India has already made an impressive head start.

Case Study 1: Transition of Public Transport in Delhi to CNG

India has a commendable legacy of fuel-switching—from diesel and petrol to natural gas—to improve air quality, particularly in Delhi, which is often quoted as an example of a best practice of introducing gas in the transport sector.

Back in the 1990s, Delhi had earned the sad distinction of being the third most polluted city in the world. This resulted in a petition (a Public Interest Litigation) being filed with the Supreme Court of India calling for measures to improve air quality. On 28 July 1998, the court ruled that all public transport in Delhi—all buses, three-wheelers, and taxis—would have to be replaced or converted to CNG by April 2001, and that sufficient CNG filling stations would have to be made available. The court also ordered financial incentives, be made available to vehicle owners for conversion to CNG.

In April 2001, CNG was about 70 per cent cheaper than petrol per unit of energy (₹12.20 or $0.17 per kilogramme (kg) of CNG, versus ₹28.75 or $0.41 per litre of petrol). This was a big financial incentive for investing in vehicle replacement, at least for large and financially strong vehicle and fleet owners. At the same time, the Delhi government, through the Delhi Financial Corporation (DFC), made concessional loans available to small and financially not-so-strong entrepreneurs—

such as individual auto-rickshaw owners—in order to bring conversion within reach for them too. Note that these loans did not indebt the government commensurately, as they were subsequently paid back from savings on fuel cost.

This story of the conversion of public transport to CNG in Delhi is a good example of an intervention, whereby the government uses a classical combination of policy instruments known as the 'carrot and the stick'—in this case, making concessional loans available while enforcing a court order. This is also a good example of how a new and tailored financial product, in this case, concessional loans to financially constrained entrepreneurs can be instrumental in implementing change.

POTENTIAL ROLE OF NATURAL GAS TO IMPROVE AIR QUALITY

Despite Delhi's success story of converting buses, auto-rickshaws and taxis to CNG, the transport sector is still a significant source of PM emissions in the city. In a recent study by the Automotive Research Association of India (ARAI) together with The Energy and Resources Institute (TERI),[7] motor fuel is estimated to be responsible for 39 per cent of all PM2.5 emissions and 19 per cent of all PM10 emissions in Delhi. In fact, road dust kicked up by vehicles adds another 18 per cent of all PM2.5 emissions and a further 35 per cent of all PM10 emissions in the city, which means that the transport sector as a whole is the source of more than half of all PM2.5 and PM10 emissions in Delhi.

There are other sources of air pollution (other than the transport sector), in Delhi. Most notably the construction sector and power generation—together these two sectors contribute an additional 30 per cent of all PM2.5 emissions and a further 20 per cent of all PM10 emissions in the city. Beyond the city limits of Delhi, in the NCR, the transport sector is still a large source of pollution, but the dominant PM sources turn out to be the industrial sector, in particular, small enterprises burning coal and fuel oil, the residential use of primitive solid fuel and the agricultural sector, notably via the burning of crop residue. According to the ARAI/TERI study,[8] industry is responsible for 24 per cent of all PM2.5 emissions and 28 per cent of all PM10 emissions in the NCR.[9]

The results of this study on the potential role of gas across different industrial sectors and in transportation, shows that there are a variety of different reasons why gas is not more popular today. The representatives of large industrial enterprises, who were interviewed, explained that gas would not be competitive versus coal but would be competitive versus oil—if their facilities were connected to the gas grid. At the same time, they have concerns about the long duration, inflexible minimum offtake requirements and price uncertainty and volatility in typical gas contracts being offered to industrial customers, and complaints about the pancaking of different taxes.

India's ambitious programme of 'gasification', driven by the Petroleum and Natural Gas Regulatory Board (PNGRB), is expected to address the issue of connectivity between industrial enterprises. However, the World Bank recommends that the PNGRB develop standard terms and conditions so as to guarantee a certain level of flexibility in gas-supply agreements (GSAs), and that the Government of India consider the pros and cons of bringing gas under the new Goods and Services Tax (GST).

For MSMEs, the decision to convert from fuel oil to natural gas would also be driven by lower fuel prices. However, small enterprises would have the additional challenge of making capital available and attracting financing for upfront investment in gas connection and gas-fired equipment and for making a security deposit to the local gas distribution company. This would be particularly challenging for many small businesses that have not been registered as formal enterprises. It is believed that energy service companies (ESCOs) could play a key role in fuel switching projects, similar to the role that they play in energy efficiency initiatives. The ESCOs could help raise awareness and educate small enterprises in understanding what their technical options are and comprehending the business case for switching to gas. In fact, the business process of converting an industrial facility to gas is very similar to implementing an energy-efficiency project, which is typically highly sector- and technology-specific.

Transition of HDVs to Cleaner Fuel

A particularly interesting case for switching to cleaner fuel is the HDV. It makes up a segment that runs almost exclusively on diesel today. However, switching to CNG may not be an option even though Delhi has a well-developed network of CNG filling stations. This is because CNG has 75 per cent lower energy density than diesel, which means that it is not a suitable fuel for heavy-duty transport. Similarly, the amount of energy that HDVs need to operate makes them unsuitable candidates for conversion to electric vehicles (EVs), at least with the current battery technology.

Liquefied natural gas has a much higher energy density than CNG, albeit still 40 per cent lower than diesel. Nevertheless, recent important advances in the use of LNG as motor fuel for HDVs have increased its acceptance, especially in China which has hundreds of thousands of LNG-fuelled HDVs on the road.[10] India can readily adopt the best practices and lessons learnt from China in terms of LNG filling stations and vehicle technology and apply them to the National Capital Region (NCR).

The transition of HDVs to LNG would involve a wide spectrum of stakeholders, including LNG suppliers, designated CGD companies, tax, transport and environmental authorities, truck manufacturers and dealerships, truck repair and maintenance service companies, commercial vehicle loan providers and, last but not least, transport companies, that is, the owners and operators of the trucks.

In order to assess the potential of switching HDVs from diesel to LNG in the NCR and on the Delhi–Mumbai Industrial Corridor (DMIC), ICF International has interviewed the entire range of stakeholders identified above, to better understand the current business environment of each of the parties involved, and to understand what needs to be done to unlock the potential for heavy-duty transport to switch from diesel to LNG. The main findings of this survey are as follows.

- Current fiscal, commercial, technical (safety) and environmental regulations allow the use of LNG as motor fuel in India today.

- LNG is readily available at existing regasification terminals and can easily be made available at filling stations around the country, either by trucking it from the point of entry to the filling stations, or by producing LNG in small-scale liquefaction plants at filling stations that are already connected to the CGD network. Over time, the LNG supply will become available over expanding geographical areas, as the gas transmission and distribution network is gradually built across India.

- Gas suppliers, both wholesale suppliers and licensed CGD monopolies are interested in supplying LNG to HDVs as they consider this an extension of their highly lucrative business models supplying CNG as motor fuel to light-duty vehicles (LDVs). In fact, the business case for building the CGD network in many cities is typically anchored to the estimated demand from natural-gas vehicles (NGVs).

- Indian car manufacturers have developed trucks running on LNG, but are not producing such vehicles, as there is insufficient demand as yet. However, LNG trucks could be imported, at least during an initial pilot phase, for instance from China where the use of LNG for HDVs is a proven technology. In the long run though, high import tariffs on Chinese HDVs would render an imported LNG truck uncompetitive, versus a diesel truck made in India. This catalytic progression from early imported HDVs to a sustained flow of Indian manufactured HDVs aligns with the Government of India's Make in India policy.

- Truck and fleet owners are not unwilling to invest in LNG trucks, but they also require targeted learning to better understand the operational and maintenance implications of using LNG as motor fuel. They recognize the business case of using LNG as fuel, as it would be approximately 25 per cent cheaper per kilometre (km) than diesel, but they would have difficulties raising additional upfront capital required to buy an LNG truck, which would be approximately 30 per cent more expensive than a diesel truck. The main reason is that most transport companies in India are small and financially limited enterprises, with just one or two trucks. This makes it more challenging for them to qualify for a loan from a commercial bank. Moreover, the transport sector in India is currently going through difficult times due to overcapacity, which means that it is even harder for transport companies to obtain a loan at this time.[11]

There is a strong similarity between the business case for LNG as motor fuel for HDVs and the business case for CNG as motor fuel for public transport (back in 2001) in Delhi. In both cases, the difference in fuel prices makes it attractive to switch to natural gas, but at the same time, it is difficult for small entrepreneurs to raise the upfront capital required to invest in a natural-gas vehicle. This implies that the government and industry alike could learn from the CNG case study in Delhi—if presented in a targeted format, designed as a tailored financial product available to a large number of small enterprises and the resulting positive outcome of switching to gas as a primary fuel. Given the large number of customers involved, it would be more appropriate to talk about *prêt-a-porter*, that is, a standard product designed with a specific purpose for a large number of customers in this segment, rather than a *tailored* financial product, which suggests that it was created for a single player.

Interestingly, India has recently been going through a very successful energy transition of a large-scale switch to energy-efficient light-emitting diodes (LEDs) in public buildings and for street lighting.

Case Study 2: Unnat Joyti by Affordable Leds for All (Ujala)

The use of LED lighting offers significant energy savings, which means that the lifetime cost is considerably cheaper than that of regular incandescent lighting. But capturing these cost benefits requires an upfront capital investment that is beyond the scope of most household consumers in India. India's publicly owned super-ESCO, Energy Efficiency Services Ltd (EESL), was asked to address this challenge and roll-out LED light replacements across India. To do so, EESL brought two innovative approaches to the LED market which drove down costs and supported consumers in financing the capital investment required to transition to more efficient lighting.

First, EESL engaged in a series of bulk-procurement rounds—giving manufacturers of LED lighting orders far in excess of what they would have otherwise received in the wholesale lighting market in India. This incentivized LED manufacturing India, increasing the number of manufacturers from two to twenty in a matter of years. This rise also introduced economies of scale to the LED market. As a result, the prices of LED bulbs, both through EESL's bulk procurement rounds and in the broader Indian market have fallen dramatically—from over ₹600 ($8.5) to around ₹160 ($2.2) per unit—over the past two years.

Even at ₹160 ($2.2) per bulb, the upfront cost of LED lighting is still sometimes difficult to afford for a large number of India's household consumers. This issue was solved by EESL by allying with India's electricity distribution companies and offering consumers 'on-bill financing'. A household that wants to make the switch to an LED bulb, now only has to pay the first 10 per cent of the cost. Its electricity utility provides the LED bulb and receives the balance of payment for its cost over monthly instalments through the consumer's electricity bill. The consumer, who is now saving more on his electricity bill, hardly notices the additional payment he is making for his investment in LED lighting.

By financing the upfront procurement of large quantities of LED bulbs, taking on immediate ownership risk of this 'asset', and then distributing LED bulbs to consumers at affordable pricing, with payments made on an instalment basis—EESL has built a role as a successful market intermediary. By recruiting electricity distribution companies to distribute and collect payment for LED bulbs, it has also leveraged an expansive distribution network across India. This hasn't just created a market for EESL, it has changed the market for LED lighting in India fundamentally—raising awareness among consumers, increasing domestic manufacture tenfold, and reducing prices across the market on a sustainable basis.

In order to finance its upfront investment in LED lighting, EESL had approached a number of multilateral development banks, including the World Bank. These banks were willing to finance the business model that EESL had developed, which allowed it to considerably scale-up the UJALA programme. This financing also allowed EESL to adopt similar approaches to scaling up investment in energy-efficient streetlights, ceiling fans and tube lights. It has now supported the transformation of these markets also.

The benefits of EESL's market intervention have been impressive. To date, 360 million LED bulbs have been delivered through EESL's programme. This has resulted in energy savings of almost 50 teraWatt hours (TWh) per year and a reduction in carbon dioxide (CO_2) emissions of 40 million tons per year.

This success story presents a number of positive outcomes in the case of fuel switching for HDVs. First of all, it addresses the challenge faced by those with limited financial means, to raise upfront capital. It offers them the option to invest in a technology that pays itself back on the basis of lower operational costs. With regard to HDV owners switching from diesel to LNG as fuel handholding—in a similar way as EESL helped end users of light bulbs adopt new technology—could be envisaged. Finally, the model of bulk procurement could also be used to incentivize Indian car makers to develop and produce natural-gas-run HDV on a large-scale, which would bring unit prices down.

The EESL's model of interventionist bulk procurement and on-bill financing provides an example of several mechanisms which could be used to design financing for the high upfront costs of transition to LNG for heavy-duty trucking. Similar to the case of LED lighting, LNG-fuelled HDVs are relatively well-defined standardized products. However, early on in such a transition, we would expect financing costs to still be high, due to the small size of the market, and a lack of familiarity among investors. The story of rooftop solar power in India would be another example that could provide further solutions to the issues that the LNG HDV market would face in its early years.

Case Study 3: Creating a Market for Rooftop Solar

In accordance with the United Nations Climate Change Convention's Conference of Parties 21 (COP21) Nationally Determined Contributions, the Government of India approved a revision of cumulative domestic targets for solar photovoltaic (PV) installation from 20,000 MW to 100,000 MW by 2022. This includes an official target of 40,000 MW of Grid Connected Rooftop Solar PV (GRPV).

However, despite a clear commercial case for rooftop solar power in the commercial and industrial sector, the rooftop solar sector in 2016 remained stagnant—financing costs sat at almost double the official Indian base rates and only 500 MW of rooftop solar was developed. In this context, the Ministry of New and Renewable Energy

(MNRE) suggested that the World Bank and several other multilateral development banks focus on the development of this market, seek to increase volumes of affordable financing to the market, introduce best practices and create market awareness through programmes founded on the provision of catalytic financing and broad and deep capacity development.

In response, the World Bank Group, in partnership with State Bank of India, arranged a $650 million line of discounted financing for rooftop solar, alongside a $23 million capacity development programme that helped structure the market for commercial and industrial rooftop solar at several levels. This programme has contributed to the uptake of rooftop solar PV across India.

As of March 2019, the total installed rooftop solar power capacity stood at 4,375 MW—an eightfold increase in installed capacity since 2016. Since the launch of the World Bank programme, several other development financial institutions have introduced their credit lines, replicating the World Bank model, leveraging over ₹279.68 billion ($4 billion) in private sector finance to date.

Since 2016, the weighted average tariff for utility-scale, grid-connected solar projects declined from around 7.1 cents/kWh to around 4.2 cents/kWh. In addition, there now exists a more favourable policy environment for rooftop solar power, with net-metering regulations designed under the programme now notified in most states.

Despite the obvious commercial potential, the market for rooftop solar power faced very high initial financing costs, and was originally starved of investment due to the lack of awareness and perceived high risks. By working with multilateral development banks to make discount financing available to customers and by providing deep and broad capacity development among consumers, the Government of India has now realized an eightfold increase in market size over the past two years, such that the market has now become self-sustaining. By using a combination of regulatory development and catalytic financing to increase early volumes of investment, the market for LNG in HDVs could be stimulated in a similar manner.

CONCLUSION

This chapter has considered the challenge of financing the transition to cleaner fuel in the context of air pollution in India. Research shows that the transport sector followed by the construction and power generation sectors are significant sources of PM emissions in Delhi. Across the NCR, the transport sector is still a large source of pollution, alongside the industrial sector where small enterprises burn coal and fuel oil. The residential use of primitive solid fuel and the burning of crop residues in agriculture, add to the pollution problem. Given this blend of sources, a transition to cleaner fuel will require substantial capital, targeting a diversity of end users.

While gas could potentially play a significant role in improving the air quality in India's cities—and access to capital for the expansion of the country's gas infrastructure does not appear to be a barrier—a competitive price alone does not lead to gas conversions. Many smaller Indian enterprises lack the credit necessary to capitalize a conversion within a financial system that does not have the appropriate tools to cater to these needs, nor the readily available capital. This chapter proposes a package of financing of upfront investments into gas connections and gas-fired equipment, combined with covering security deposits required by local gas distribution companies.

Moreover, education will be needed, as many smaller enterprises lack the basic understanding of technical conversion options available to them and how switching to gas would be a sound business decision that would serve to enhance their bottom line. We propose that ESCOs need to play a key role in fuel-switching projects, similar to the role that they play in energy-efficiency initiatives in terms of education and advocacy and improving access to capital. Doing so would address a persistent gap that sustains some of the world's worst air pollution.

Besides industry, this chapter has also examined switching to cleaner fuel in HDVs that use more polluting diesel. The important advances in the use of LNG as motor fuel for HDVs in China could also be adopted within India. Here we see a catch: while regulations permit the use of LNG in HDVs and LNG is readily available in many urban locations, Indian manufacturers are not producing LNG trucks as there is insufficient initial demand. Again, both education and advocacy are needed to catalyse the initial conversion to LNG used in HDVs, for which India may have to draw upon its own prior experiences. The CNG conversion for public transport in Delhi back in 2001, EESL's market intervention for LED bulbs, and the increased volumes of affordable financing for rooftop solar power, all provide good practices for creating market awareness and improving access to capital.

What remains is to modify and adopt these success stories to design a process that kick-starts the conversion to natural gas, a process that provides solutions and benefits for consumers. The natural gas value chain in India is complex, spanning multiple policy regimes and regulatory authorities and crossing state and municipal boundaries. A first step might be to implement a pilot project within one strategic sub-sector (MSMEs or HDVs) and in one or more geographic region. The pilot financial product would be deployed to test improved access to capital, underpinned by an education and advocacy campaign for enterprises to better understand their options and realize the benefits. Market feedback and monitoring of key performance indicators would be used to further refine the product and improve upon the advocacy programme and capacity-building with enterprises, so that it can be deployed again at larger scales. Finally, it could expand into areas where the programme would be carried by ESCOs by adapting to local conditions and different enterprise needs. The goal would be a mutually shared one: to displace 'dirty' fuels and bring cleaner air to Indian cities.

Notes

1. The authors would like to acknowledge the work that ICF International Inc. and the Energy and Resources Institute have carried out for the World Bank, on the potential role of natural gas to improve air quality, as well as the financial support for this work from the Energy Sector Management Assistance Programme (ESMAP) trust fund.

2. World Health Organization, 'Ambient Air Quality Database', https://whoairquality.shinyapps.io/AmbientAirQualityDatabase/, accessed December 2019.

3. Kalpana Balakrishnan et al., 'The impact of air pollution on deaths, disease burden and life expectancy across the states of India: the Global Burden of Disease Study 2017', *Lancet Planet Health*, Vol. 3, Issue 1 (2019): E26–E39, doi:10.1016/S2542-5196(18)30261-4

4. 'How many years do we lose to the air we breathe?', *The Washington Post*, 19 November 2018, https://www.washingtonpost.com/graphics/2018/national/health-science/lost-years/

5. International Energy Agency, 'India 2020: Energy Policy Review', (Paris: OECD/IEA, 2020), https://www.iea.org/reports/india-2020

6. Industry Group, 'Vision 2030: Natural Gas Infrastructure in India', Report by the Industry Group for the Petroleum & Natural Gas Regulatory Board, 2013, https://www.pngrb.gov.in/Hindi-Website/pdf/vision-NGPV-2030-06092013.pdf

7. ARAI and TERI, 'Apportionment of PM2.5 & PM10 of Delhi NCR for Identification of Major Sources', Report No. ARAI/16-17/DHI-SA-NCR for the Department of Heavy Industry, Ministry of Heavy Industries and Public Enterprises, Government of India, Pune: The Automotive Research Association of India; New Delhi: The Energy Resources Institute, August 2018, https://www.teriin.org/sites/default/files/2018-08/Report_SA_AQM-Delhi-NCR_0.pdf

8. Ibid.

9. Note that the numbers quoted here include both the direct and the indirect (secondary) contribution of the different sources to PM2.5 and

PM10. In terms of the direct contribution to PM2.5 emissions in the NCR only, transport accounts for between 18 per cent (summer) and 23 per cent (winter); dust accounts for between 34 per cent (summer) and 15 per cent (winter); biomass accounts for between 15 per cent (summer) and 22 per cent (winter); and industry accounts for between 5 per cent (summer) and 10 per cent (winter).

10. Zhen Xin, 'Natural Gas Truck Demand to Rise', 6 July 2018, *China Daily*, http://www.chinadaily.com.cn/a/201807/06/WS5b3eeefca3103349141e1268.html

11. T.E. Raja Simhan, 'Economic slowdown adds to truckers' woes', *The Hindu Business Line*, 6 September 2018, https://www.thehindubusinessline.com/economy/logistics/economic-slowdown-adds-to-truckers-woes/article29349348.ece

24

DECARBONIZATION: MODELS FOR SHARPENING THE TRAJECTORY

AJAY MATHUR

Director-General, The Energy and Resources Institute (TERI)

SOUVIK BHATTACHARJYA

Associate Director, Resource Efficiency and Governance Division, TERI

KARAN MANGOTRA

Associate Director, Earth Science and Climate Change Division, TERI

NITIN BAJPAI

Project Associate, Resource Efficiency and Governance Division, TERI

INTRODUCTION

WHEN LIMITED RESOURCES ARE ALLOCATED in a way that no one is better off without someone being worse off, it is said to be a Pareto efficient or Pareto optimal solution. This is the concept of 'efficiency' in economic systems. However, in the real world, market imperfections arise due to exchange or allocative inefficiencies, leading to 'market failures' or deviations from Pareto optimality.

Several conditions lead to market failures, 'externalities' being a major one among them. This chapter's central theme is climate and pollution externalities, which are an imminent threat to local and global government. Over centuries, anthropogenic activities have pushed up the consumption of cheap fossil fuels like coal and crude oil in an inefficient manner, leading to worsening climate change and air pollution.

Article 5 of the Intergovernmental Panel on Climate Change (IPCC) states, 'nearly all the non-CO_2 (carbon dioxide) climate-altering pollutants are health damaging, either directly or by contributing to secondary pollutants in the atmosphere.'[1] Air pollution and climate change also have the potential to derail future economic growth, particularly in developing countries. At least four of the seventeen SDGs adopted by the United Nations member states in 2015, acknowledge the challenges posed by air pollution and climate change to sustainable development (SDGs 3, 7, 12, and 13).[2]

THE ECONOMICS OF NEGATIVE EXTERNALITY

Negative externalities lead to market failures because market prices often fail to account for the hidden costs associated with producing or consuming marketable goods and services. The solution to negative externalities classified into two major categories—private solutions and public solutions. Ronald Coase argued[3] that externalities can be dealt with by appropriately assigning property rights. But this is difficult to coordinate, and leads to high transactional costs.

The public approach is based on the premise that the government will help the private sector achieve a socially efficient level of production, by *internalizing* the negative externalities. Three forms of market-based solutions have been presented in literature: taxes or fines; incentives or subsidies for pollution abatement or the augmentation of cleaner fuels; and marketable permits. The subsequent sections provide a detailed analysis of these choices.

MARKET-BASED SOLUTIONS AND INTERNATIONAL DEVELOPMENTS

Taxes and Incentives

The concept of pricing externalities through taxes or fines was introduced by Arthur Cecil Pigou and was published in his book titled, *The Economics of Welfare*.[4] According to Pigou, the absolute difference between private costs and total costs borne by society is called the external cost or marginal damages from pollution. Today, a carbon tax is often used in various countries. Since greenhouse gases (GHGs) and local air pollutants (such as particulate matter PM2.5) are released from the same sources, reducing GHGs also reduces air-pollutant emissions.

Another mechanism of taxing GHG emissions is to tax conventional fuel producers, including importers, distributors and consumers. This creates incentives for economic actors to turn to lower carbon alternatives, such as from coal to renewable energy.

However, the taxes have often been too low to reflect true environmental costs or achieve the objectives of the Paris Agreement. An analysis of forty-two member countries of the Organization for Cooperation and Development, that account for 80 per cent of global emissions, reveals that the gap between prevailing carbon prices and actual climate costs is around $30 per metric tonne of carbon dioxide equivalent (tCO2e).[5] Further, equity issues on account of the increased taxes fall disproportionately on the poor, who spend a higher share of their income on consumption.[6]

Nevertheless, carbon pricing is becoming a popular means to mobilize climate action. There are fifty-seven existing or planned carbon pricing initiatives around the world, out of which twenty-nine carbon taxes have already been implemented at the national level. The total revenue proceeds through carbon pricing were estimated at $44 billion in 2018, with more than half generated by carbon taxes.[7] Sweden has one of the highest carbon prices in the world at nearly €114/tCO2e which is imposed over and above the already existing energy tax.

Canada also has a very ambitious carbon pricing programme. In 2019, Canada introduced a comprehensive nationwide tax on coal, gas and oil with $15/tCO2e, rising to $38/tCO2e by 2022.[8] In 2019, the carbon tax rate in British Columbia rose from $35 to $40 per tCO2e, and was expected to reach $50 by 2021. The tax revenues are used for redistributive purposes, maintenance of industrial competitiveness and promotion of new green initiatives.

Norwegian pension funds have decided to double investments in renewables from $7 billion to $14 billion. The British carbon tax of $25/tCO2e has stimulated electricity to switch rapidly from coal to cleaner energy sources, particularly natural gas.[9]

In the United States, a bipartisan carbon tax bill, titled the 'Energy Innovation and Carbon Dividend Act' of 2019, proposes $40/tCO2e tax on refineries, mines wells and ports.[10] The bill has been designed for redistributive purposes—an average family of four would receive about $2,000 from the programme in the first year.[11]

In the developing world, Mexico has mentioned carbon pricing as an explicit strategy in its Nationally Determined Contributions (NDCs). The Mexican Congress (in 2014) legislated a carbon tax to be imposed on fossil-fuel use, at $3.50 per tonne of emissions making Mexico the first non-developed country to adopt a carbon tax.

The way forward to strengthen carbon pricing includes a progressive increase in prices, as well as a broadened emission coverage. While increased pricing is indeed welcome, there also is a clear need to reflect on the true social costs in the legislated carbon prices.

Emission Trading

More recently, emission trading has emerged as a popular market-based solution, which involves marketable (tradeable) permits under a cap and trade system.

International experience with the emission trading system (ETS) offers practical lessons about implementation and evidence about their impact. The European Union's (EU) ETS is the world's largest trading system, covering half of the EU's CO_2 emissions. The EU ETS has had a genuine impact in reducing emissions and maintaining industrial competitiveness through enhanced efficiencies, even during periods of recession.

Australia has been using tradable allowances extensively since the 1990s, to reduce water pollution and consumption.[12] The UK introduced its first GHG trading scheme in 2002, auctioning subsidies on mitigation, but this approach attracted only limited participation. In California (US) and Québec (Canada), the Regional Greenhouse Gas Initiative (RGGI) has performed well, with (nearly) full auctioning benchmarked sector-wise.[13] In 2017, China announced its own national carbon market, as part of its pledge in the Paris Agreement.

The attractiveness of the ETS is its flexibility in allowing participants to decide when and where to invest in abatement. Cap-and-trade mechanisms also lead to better emission data collection and sharing regimes. However, such systems have their weaknesses in practice, such as low emissions caps, price volatility and allocative uncertainties or arbitrariness.[14]

Carbon tax offers a more transparent system, lowering the scope for speculation or corruption. Further, a tax-based system also has lower administrative and compliance costs.

Internal Carbon Pricing (ICP)

Many corporations have voluntarily been adopting ICP to manage climate-related business risks and to prepare for low-carbon transitions. It also helps companies prepare for financial impacts from possible national/global carbon taxes and increasing energy prices. Therefore, ICP helps to create revenues to develop innovative business solutions to climate-change-related issues.

An example of ICP is a 'carbon fee' which motivates employees to meet emission reduction targets, while a shadow price approach can help in long-term investment decisions to effect early investment in low-emission technologies. For example, Badische Anilin und Soda Fabrik (BASF) use two types of ICP—a regionally differentiated shadow price and a global social cost of carbon (SCC). The former helps in efficiency assessments across its facilities, whereas the latter assesses the risks across the value chain.

CLEAN DEVELOPMENT MECHANISM

Under the Kyoto Protocol, the clean development mechanism (CDM) was successful in initiating a global market to reduce carbon emissions and mobilizing finance towards climate action in developing countries.[15] By March 2019, 8,000 projects in about eighty countries led to the issuance of more than 1.9 billion certificates of emission reduction (CERs) since 2004.[16] India is the second-largest issuer of credits (253 million) after China (1.08 billion).

The CDM has vetted and approved about 260 methodologies for measuring baseline emissions and monitoring emission reductions (including projects in industrial gases, solar and wind, and clean cook stoves and water filters).[17] Therefore, CDM has successfully created strong infrastructural forward linkages for any new market mechanism to build on.[18]

The Paris Agreement is the successor to the Kyoto Protocol and has provisions of a market-based mechanism embedded under Article 6.4 of the Agreement. Its focus remains similar to that of the CDM, i.e., 'to contribute to the reduction of emission levels in the host Party ... that can also be used by another Party to fulfil its nationally determined contribution' (Paris Agreement, 2015). Therefore, experience with CDM methodologies and projects will be helpful to the participating countries, especially India.

MARKET-BASED INNOVATIONS IN INDIA

India is reported to house seven of the world's ten most polluted cities. As per 2017 estimates, ambient air pollution (exposure to PM2.5) is responsible for up to 67 million deaths in India.[19] Factors such as industrialization, rapid urbanization and increased demand for mobility are primarily responsible for the deterioration in air quality. In 2016, the World Bank [20] put the costs of air pollution in India as 8 per cent of its GDP. India is also the world's fourth-highest GHG-emitter, accounting for 7 per cent of global emissions in 2017.

India launched the National Clean Air Programme (NCAP) in 2019 as a comprehensive strategy to address air pollution. It aims to reduce PM2.5 and PM10 concentration by 20–30 per cent in 2024. Suggested actions include reducing public transport's reliance on diesel, encouraging industry to switch to cleaner energy and cutting road traffic by the imposition of fuel taxes and congestion charges. Such a transition is only possible when there are appropriate pricing signals that nudge human behaviour.

India has so far used a combination of regulations, as well as market-based instruments to address these issues. On 7 December 2015, the Ministry of Environment, Forest and Climate Change brought out new norms for coal-based power stations to cut down emissions of PM10, SO2, and NOx. Steps are already being taken to upgrade to Bharat Stage (BS VI) fuel from BS IV, which came into effect after 1 April 2020.

The Indian Clean Environment Cess levied on coal since 2010 has been frequently referred to as 'India's carbon tax'. The proceeds of this were used to create the National Clean Environment Fund (NCEF). The cess has successively been revised from ₹50/tonne ($0.71/tonne) coal in 2010, to ₹400/tonne ($5.72/tonne) coal in 2016.

By 2017, more than ₹860 billion ($12.29 billion) funds were generated, of which ₹160 billion ($2.28 billion) went into promoting clean energy. However, with the introduction of the Goods and Services

Tax (GST) in 2017, the cess has been renamed as GST Compensation Cess, leading to the diversion of the resources.[21] Further, concerns have been raised by environment policy experts about whether the current cess is reflective of the true environmental costs.[22]

Perform Achieve Trade (PAT) Mechanism

PAT is a market-based mechanism developed in 2012 to achieve energy efficiency in key sectors and is currently running its third cycle (2017–18 to 2019–20) in India. Under PAT, specific energy-saving targets are assigned to designated consumers (DCs) belonging to energy-intensive industries. The energy savings by DCs undergo verification by the empanelled auditors of India's Bureau of Energy Efficiency (BEE). Upon verification, they are awarded tradeable energy saving certificates (ESCerts).

Thereafter, the ESCerts are traded among over and underachievers, such that each DC is able to meet its assigned targets. These can be traded at the Indian Energy Exchange (IEX) and Power Exchange India Limited (PXIL), or bought directly by other units under PAT to meet their compliance requirements.[23] PAT has been adding DCs with every subsequent cycle. However, the over-achievement of targets under Cycle I can be attributed to low target setting, inadequacy of non-compliance penalties and enforcement mechanisms.

Other ETS Schemes

In 2011, India unveiled its two-year pilot ETS mechanism in Gujarat, Tamil Nadu and Maharashtra. In 2019, the Gujarat government launched the pilot of one of the world's first ETS for PM emissions, which is a departure from the traditional command and control approach of environmental regulations. This is similar to the US Acid Rain Program of the 1990s for controlling SO_2 and NO_x emissions.

Renewable Purchase Obligations (RPOs)

RPOs are designed to promote renewables and drive the renewable energy certificate (REC) markets. These specify a target share of renewables in electricity usage by the state commission to a group of distribution companies, open access users, and large commercial and industrial users, collectively referred to as obligated entities.

However, experience in the initial years shows that the accredited certificates issued were less than 2.5 per cent of the technical potential, indicating underutilization.[24] The IEX and PXIL saw a 10 per cent decline in REC trades in 2019.[25]

Enforcement is the key to successfully functioning markets. There are strict penalties in many countries (the US, Belgium, Italy, etc.) if obligated entities fall short of their targets. In Sweden, the penalty is 150 per cent of the average certificate price. In the UK, a buyout price of £30/MWh is imposed as penalty. However, the Indian market operates at a forbearance price since specific guidelines for enforcement are still not in place.

CDM in India

India signed the Kyoto Protocol in 1997 and subsequently ratified the CDM in 2002. Globally, India's share in CDM project activities is around 20 per cent, against that of China's 50 per cent. Its issuance share of its CERs is 13 per cent against that of China's 60 per cent. Because of a larger share of small-scale CDM projects, India has generated a lower number of CERs in comparison with China, which usually has had large CDM projects.[26] India has particularly faced difficulties in monitoring, reporting and verification (MRV) of projects, which raises transaction costs.

India has also been a victim of CDM fatigue, caused by low market prices. Due to a crisis in CER prices, more than fifty developers in India (and also in China) plan to decrease investments in CDM projects.[27] The major barrier to implementing new CDM projects came after a 2012 EU directive of restricting the use of CERs from developing nations.

WAY FORWARD

India's adoption of market-based approaches has been encouraging. However, there has not been substantial analysis to understand how these approaches have helped to decouple emissions from economic growth. Further development in pricing mechanisms must take into account the failures of market instruments in other countries.[28]

India should explore market-based options in newer regions and sectors and build penal mechanisms that capture the cost of inaction. Criticisms regarding acceptability and constraints for low-carbon transformations must be addressed proactively. Significant efforts must be made to better capture the true environmental costs. Questions of equity and clean energy access to the underprivileged must be also addressed. A framework for meeting these prescriptions is presented in Figure 1.

Harnessing demand to drive mitigation projects: Priority must be given to regulate high-mitigation projects with substantial sustainable benefits. On this basis, low-carbon technologies facing significant barriers can be supported by existing or future market mechanisms. Authorities should work towards easing the process to reduce transaction costs. India should also support projects through the better utilization of the GST Clean Environment Cess.

Developing synergies between different mechanisms: Different mechanisms such as ETS and carbon tax have resulted in prosperity in their regional provinces. Learning from international experiences, India should work towards building a proactive framework of new market mechanisms, and implement more pilot projects for better learning.

Enhancing industry participation: Capacity-building for various market mechanisms, such as transparent reporting, should progressively

Figure 1: The way forward for pricing externalities

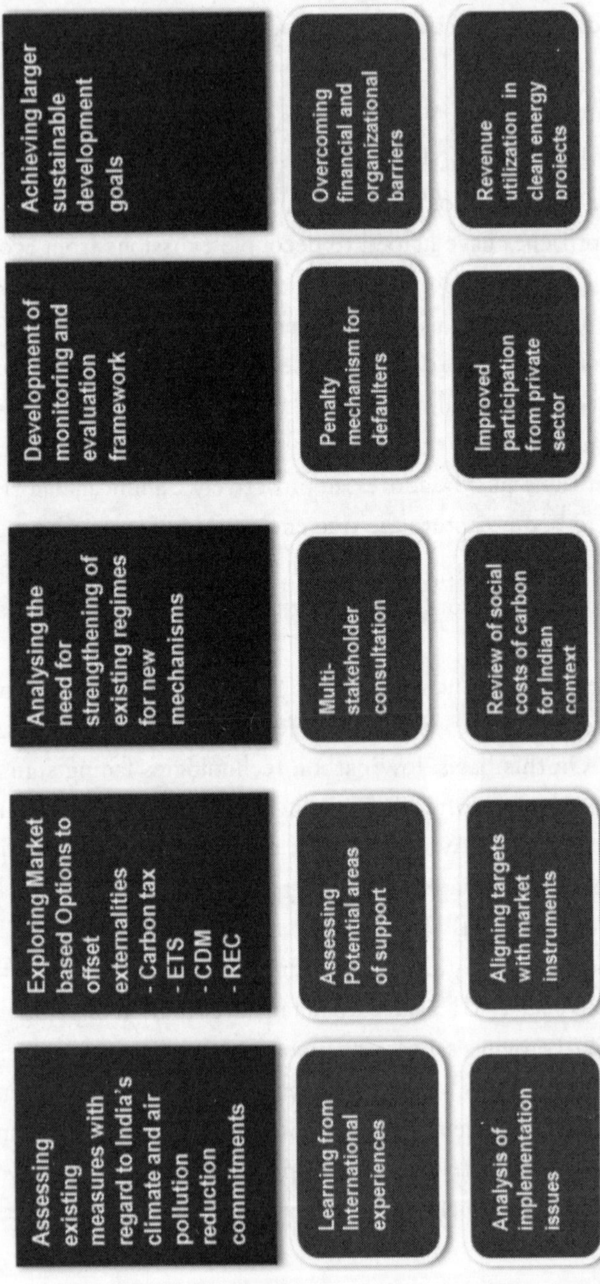

Source: TERI Compilation

be made mandatory. Through enhanced private participation, an attitude towards sustainability should be cultivated.

Constituting a multi-stakeholder advisory group: The government needs to incorporate social costs over private prices, using specified market instruments. It must also understand stakeholders' concerns and priorities and make the regulatory mechanisms more acceptable to them.

Utilization of revenues from different mechanisms: Revenues from carbon pricing should sponsor a wide array of low-carbon technologies, like augmenting natural-gas production and distribution. Revenue utilization is a key determinant of the success of carbon-pricing initiatives.[29]

Review of social cost estimates: The estimation of social costs suffers from inherent subjectivity. There is a need for a better analysis of social costs for Indian conditions, which may drive the decision-making process for tools like carbon tax.

The recent Covid-19 pandemic has posed an unprecedented crisis to public health. As the world grapples with the alarming spread of the virus, it presents policymakers around the world with a critical trade-off between securing lives or livelihoods. Interestingly, it also offers the opportunity to reset the existing economic regime and formulate a greener structure to achieve climate goals.

With the severely high contagion rate of Covid-19, continued economic activity leads to infections multiplying rapidly, causing a further threat to public health and, in turn, to domestic and global economies. In such a case, negative externalities arise when basic economic interactions are allowed to continue. On the other hand, a complete lockdown of economic activity halts sources of livelihoods which—in the absence of a strong social system—creates an indirect threat to lives.

In many ways, the impact of the pandemic offers a glimpse of the negative externalities that climate change will cause in the not-too-distant future. The pandemic, therefore, offers an opportunity to make structural changes ensuring that the economic systems recover in a greener manner for the development to be more resilient and longer lasting. To this effect, on 22 April 2020, UNFCCC executive secretary Patricia Espinosa said, 'With this restart, a window of hope and opportunity opens ... an opportunity for nations to green their recovery packages and shape the twenty-first-century economy in ways that are clean, green, healthy, safe and more resilient.'[30]

In India, most economic activity came to a standstill after the government imposed a twenty-one-day nationwide lockdown beginning on 25 March 2020. The lockdown was extended thrice through 31 May 2020, with some relaxations to allow the resumption of economic activity. On 13 May 2020 Prime Minister Narendra Modi laid out his vision for an 'Atmanirbhar Bharat' or Self-Reliant India. His vision rests on five pillars—bringing a quantum, not incremental, jump in the economy; creating a modern infrastructure; setting up a technology-based system of governance; leveraging our young demographic and harnessing India's huge domestic demand. He also mentioned that India's Covid-19 relief package should focus on land, labour, liquidity and laws to revive the economy that has come to a standstill due to the lockdown.

The current crisis has posed a threat to global economies that is as severe as some of the previous economic recessions. In hindsight, economic crises are short-term shocks to an otherwise long-term growth trajectory. They recur every one or two decades on average and are likely to remain so in the long run. While the nature of crises may not be known, well-structured economic systems, in harmony with the ecological and social systems, help minimize the impact, reduce negative externalities on livelihoods and hasten the pace of recovery. Therefore, it is imperative that global economies recover in a manner such that the economies are increasingly resilient to subsequent shocks.

Notes

1. Kirk R. Smith et al., 'Human Health: Impacts, Adaptation, and Co-benefits', in C.B. Field et al. (eds), *Climate Change 2014: Impacts, Adaptation, and Vulnerability. Part A: Global and Sectoral Aspects. Contribution of Working Group II to the Fifth Assessment Report* of the Intergovernmental Panel on Climate Change, New York and Cambridge: Cambridge University Press, 2014, pp. 709–54, https://www.ipcc.ch/site/assets/uploads/2018/02/WGIIAR5-Chap11_FINAL.pdf

2. UN Department of Economic and Social Affairs, 'Sustainable Development Goals', knowledge platform (n.d.), *United Nations*, https://sustainabledevelopment.un.org/?menu=1300

3. R.H. Coase, 'The Problem of Social Cost', *The Journal of Law & Economics*, Vol. III, October 1960.

4. Arthur C. Pigou, *The Economics of Welfare*, London: Macmillan and Co., 1920.

5. OECD, 'Effective Carbon Rates 2018: Pricing Carbon Emissions Through Taxes and Emissions Trading', Paris: OECD Publishing, Organization for Co-operation and Development, 2018, https://doi.org/10.1787/9789264305304-en

6. Rohit Azad and Shouvik Chakraborty, 'The "Right to Energy" and carbon tax: A game changer in India', *Ideas for India*, 22 April 2019, https://www.ideasforindia.in/topics/environment/the-right-to-energy-and-carbon-tax-a-game-changer-in-india.html

7. Celine Ramstein et al., 'State and Trends of Carbon Pricing 2019', Washington DC: World Bank, 13 June 2019, doi:10.1596/978-1-4648-1435-8.

8. Brad Plumer and Nadja Popovich, 'These Countries Have Prices on Carbon. Are they Working?', 2 April 2019, *New York Times*, https://

www.nytimes.com/interactive/2019/04/02/climate/pricing-carbon-emissions.html

9. Ibid.

10. Joseph Robertson, 'Bipartisan carbon fee and dividend bill now before U.S. Congress', 4 February 2019, *Carbon Pricing Leadership Coalition*, https://www.carbonpricingleadership.org/blogs/2019/2/3/bipartisan-carbon-fee-and-dividend-bill-now-before-us-congress

11. Kate Yoder, 'Republicans are backing a "carbon dividend". What the heck is that?', 21 June 2018, *Grist*, https://grist.org/article/republicans-are-backing-a-carbon-dividend-what-the-heck-is-that/

12. Simone Borghesi, 'Water tradable permits: a review of theoretical and case studies', *Journal of Environmental Planning and Management*, Vol. 57, No. 9 (2014): pp. 1305–32, doi:10.1080/09640568.2013.820175

13. RGGI is a cooperative effort among the states of Connecticut, Delaware, Maine, Maryland, Massachusetts, New Hampshire, New Jersey, New York, Rhode Island, and Vermont, to cap and reduce CO_2 emissions from the power sector.

14. M. Wråke et al., 'What have we learnt from the European Union's Emissions Trading System', *Ambio* 41 (2012), pp. 12–22, doi:10.1007/s13280-011-0237-2

15. Axel Michaelowa, 'Strengths and weaknesses of the CDM in comparison with new and emerging market mechanism', Paper No. 2 for the CDM Policy Dialogue, Zurich: Centre for Comparative and International Studies, Political Economy of Development, Institute of Political Science, University of Zurich, 2012, cdmpolicydialogue.org/research/1030_strengths.pdf

16. UNFCCC, 'CDM Insights', 31 May 2019, https://cdm.unfccc.int/Statistics/Public/CDMinsights/index.html#ptimes

17. UNFCCC, 'CDM Can Inspire, Inform, Outfit Any New Mechanism under Paris Agreement,' 3 May 2018, https://unfccc.int/news/cdm-can-inspire-inform-outfit-any-new-mechanism-under-paris-agreement

18. David Held and Charles Roger, 'Three Models of Global Climate Governance: From Kyoto to Paris and Beyond', *Global Policy*, Vol. 9, Issue 4 (2018), pp. 527–37, https://doi.org/10.1111/1758-5899.12617

19. Kalpana Balakrishnan et al., 'The impact of air pollution on deaths, disease burden, and life expectancy across the states of India: the Global Burden of Disease Study 2017', *Lancet Planet Health*, Vol. 3, Issue 1 (2019): E26–E39, doi:10.1016/S2542-5196(18)30261-4

20. World Bank and Institute for Health Metrics and Evaluation, 'The Cost of Air Pollution: Strengthening the Economic Case for Action', Washington DC: World Bank; Seattle: IHME, University of Washington, http://documents.worldbank.org/curated/en/781521473177013155/pdf/108141-REVISED-Cost-of-PollutionWebCORRECTEDfile.pdf

21. M. Ramesh, 'GST: A Big Blow to Clean Energy Financing', *Hindu Business Line*, 12 April 2017, https://www.thehindubusinessline.com/economy/gst-a-big-blow-to-clean-energy-financing/article9634391.ece

22. Ian Parry, 'Why a Carbon Tax Makes Sense: Putting A Price on Pollution', *Finance and Development*, Vol. 56, No. 4 (2019), https://www.imf.org/external/pubs/ft/fandd/2019/12/pdf/the-case-for-carbon-taxation-and-putting-a-price-on-pollution-parry.pdf

23. Bureau of Energy Efficiency, 'PAT Cycle', New Delhi: BEE, Ministry of Power, Government of India, 2015, https://beeindia.gov.in/content/pat-cycle

24. Gireesh Shrimali and Sumala Tirumalachetty, 'Renewable energy certificate markets in India—A review', Renewable & Sustainable Energy Reviews, 26 (2013), pp. 702–16, http://wgbis.ces.iisc.ernet.in/biodiversity/sahyadri_enews/newsletter/issue45/bibliography/Renewable%20energy%20certificate%20markets%20in%20India.pdf

25. Press Trust of India, 'Renewable energy certificate sales down 10 per cent to 5.04 lakh in December', *The Economic Times*, 30 December 2019,

https://economictimes.indiatimes.com/small-biz/productline/power-generation/renewable-energy-certificate-sales-down-10-per-cent-to-5-04-lakh-in-december/articleshow/73027104.cms?from=mdr

26. Dr B. Mahananda Chittawadagi, 'CDM Projects and Sustainable Development: A Study of Sustainability Claims of Select CDM Projects in Karnataka', *International Journal of Innovative Science, Engineering & Technology*, Vol. 2, Issue 9 (2015), http://ijiset.com/vol2/v2s9/IJISET_V2_I9_122.pdf

27. Ibid.

28. GIZ, 'Carbon Market Roadmap for India: Looking Back on CDM and Looking Ahead', New Delhi: Deutsche Gesellschaft für Internationale Zusammenarbeit (GIZ) GmbH; Ministry of Environment and Forests, Government of India, n.d., http://ncdmaindia.gov.in/ViewPDF.aspx?&pub=2.pdf

29. David Klenert et al., 'Making Carbon Pricing Work for Citizens', *Nature Climate Change*, Vol. 8 (2018), pp. 669–77, https://www.nature.com/articles/s41558-018-0201-2?WT.feed_name=subjects_economics

30. Video Statement from executive secretary on Earth Day, https://unfccc.int/news/in-earth-day-address-un-climate-chief-points-to-window-of-hope

CONVERSION FACTORS

Table 1: Weight to Volume Conversion

Product	Weight (Mt)	Volume (kl)	Barrel (Bbl)	To convert Volume at 29.5° C to Volume at 15° C multiply by
Petrol	1	1.4110	8.50	0.9832
Diesel	1	1.2100	7.45	0.9879
Kerosene	1	1.2850	7.90	0.9864
Aviation turbine fuel (ATF)	1	1.2880	8.10	0.9862
Light diesel oil	1	1.1720	7.37	0.9877
Furnace oil	1	1.0710	6.74	0.9899
Crude oil	1	1.1700	7.33	
Calculations for Petrol and Diesel have been made on BS IV norms				
Source: Indian Petroleum & Natural Gas Statistics, Ministry of Petroleum and Natural Gas				

Table 2: Volume Conversion

1 US barrel (Bbl)	159 litres
1 US gallon	3.78 litres
1 kilo litre (kl)	6.29 Bbl
1 US barrel (Bbl)	42 gallons
1 Mbd (million barrels per day)	50 MMtpa

Table 3: Contents

Natural gas	Contains 60–95 per cent methane			
Liquefied petroleum gas (LPG)	Contains propane (40 per cent) and butane (60 per cent)			

Table 4: Natural Gas Conversions

1 scm (standard cubic metre)	= 1 cubic metre @ 1 atmosphere pressure and 15.56 ° C	
1 cubic metre (m³)	= 35.31 cubic feet	
1 Bcm (Billion cubic metre)/ Year of gas (consumption or production)	= 2.74 MMscm/d	365 days a year
1 Tcf (Trillion cubic feet) of gas reserve	= 3.88 MMscm/d	100 per cent Recoverable for 20 years @ 365 days/annum)
1 MMtpa of LNG	= 3.60 MMscm/d	Molecular weight of 18 @ 365 days/annum)
1 Mt of LNG	= 1314 scm	Molecular weight of 18

Gross calorific value (GCV)	10,000 kcal/scm	
Net calorific value (NCV)	90% of GCV	
1 Million Btu (MMBtu)	= 25.2 SCM	@10,000 kcal/scm; 1 MMBtu= 252,000 kcal)
Specific gravity of gas	0.62	Molecular weight of dry air=28.964 gm/mole)
Density of gas	= 0.76 kg/scm	Molecular weight of gas 18 gm/mol

₹69.92 = $1 as given by Reserve Bank of India 2018–19 average exchange rate value, unless otherwise stated by the authors

LIST OF CONTRIBUTORS

Ajay Mathur
Director-General, Energy & Resources Institute (TERI)

Akos Losz
Energy Analyst-Gas, Coal and Power Markets Division, International Energy Agency

Akshaya Koshy
Commercial Manager; ExxonMobil in Angola

Amit Mehta
Head-Gases, Reliance Industries Limited
Director, IGS and Reliance Gas Pipeline Limited

Anita Odedra
Independent Non-Executive Independent Director, Euronav

Anupama Sen
Executive Director, Electricity Programme
Senior Research Fellow at the Oxford Institute for Energy Studies

Ashok Gulati
Infosys Chair Professor for Agriculture, Indian Council for Research on International Economic Relations (ICRIER)

Ashu Singhal
Chief GM (Corp. Strategy, Planning & Advocacy); Director, OPAL

David G. Victor
PhD, Professor of Innovation and Public Policy; School of Global Policy and Strategy; UC San Diego and Adjunct Senior Fellow at The Brookings Institution

Frank van Oordt
Global Head TCF Energy & Metals, Rabobank; member of the TCF global management team

Gautham Babu Dasari
India Gas Advocacy and Regulations Lead, Shell Energy

Gurpreet Chugh
Managing Director, ICF India

Hiten Premji Sutar
Director, Ernst & Young LLP

Ian Cronshaw
Consultant; Former Division Head, International Energy Agency (2005 to 2011)

Jean Baptiste Dubreuil
Senior Natural Gas Analyst, International Energy Agency

Karan Mangotra
Associate Director, Centre for Global Environment Research

Kishore Kumar Hota
Additional General Manager, NTPC Limited

Martin J. Houston
Vice-Chairman and co-founder, Tellurian Inc
Chairman, EnQuest PLC
Non-executive director of BUPA Arabia and CC Energy

Michael Stanley
Global Leader, Energy Transition in Coal Regions, The World Bank Group

Neetu Vinayek
Chartered Accountant

Mike Fulwood
Senior Research Fellow, Oxford Institute for Energy Studies
Fellow, Center on Global Energy Policy, Columbia University

Nitin Bajpai
Research Associate at The Energy and Resources Institute

Prabhat Singh
CEO, Petronet LNG

Pritha Banerjee
Consultant, Indian Council for Research on International Economic
Relations (ICRIER)

Rajeev Kumar
Vice President, Business Development and Integration, bp India

Rajeev Mathur
Executive Director, GAIL (India) Limited

Rahul Tongia
Senior Fellow, Centre for Social and Economic Progress (CSEP)

Renee Pirrong
Head of Research, Tellurian

Robert van der Geest,
Senior Gas Specialist, The World Bank

Samantha Gross
Director, Energy Security and Climate Initiative, Brookings Fellow

Santosh Sonar
Executive Director, B S R & Associates LLP, Mumbai

Sarah Khoo
Asia Head – Market Advocacy and Regulations, Shell Energy

Seema Phatnani
Commercial Advisor, bp India

Simon J. Stolp
Practice Leader-Infrastructure, India, The World Bank Group

Souvik Bhattacharjya
Associate Director, Centre for Resource Efficiency and Governance Division; TERI, New Delhi

Sudha Mahalingam
Raja Ramanna Chair Professor, National Institute of Advanced Studies, Bengaluru

Talmiz Ahmad
Former Indian Ambassador to Saudi Arabia, Oman and the United Arab Emirates, and Ram Sathe Chair Professor for International Studies, Symbiosis International University, Pune, India

Tim Boersma
Fellow, Center on Global Energy Policy, Columbia University

Vikram Singh Mehta
Chairman and Distinguished Fellow, Centre for Social and Economic Progress (CSEP)

ACKNOWLEDGEMENTS

THIS VOLUME STARTED UNDER THE umbrella of Brookings India. It came to completion under the Centre for Social and Economic Progress (CSEP), the successor entity to Brookings India, in the midst of the Covid-19 pandemic. It would have been difficult to bring this project across the finishing line without the support of a number of people, several of whom worked long hours to overcome the pressures of managing the transition from Brookings to CSEP and 'work from home'.

My thanks, first and foremost, are to the authors who have contributed to this book. I thank them for their initial positive response to my request to bring together a compendium on natural gas. A lot has been written on this subject, but few publications have looked at it through an integrated lens. I was gratified at the readiness of the contributors to help fill this lacuna and to draw up a policy road map to increase the usage of natural gas in the energy basket, as India journeys to a clean energy system. I thank them for the time they spent in discussions with me and my colleagues on their respective chapters and for their patience.

In equal measure, my thanks are to the Mitsubishi Corporation, British Petroleum and the Australian Government for their financial support to Brookings India's Energy, Natural Resources and

Sustainability vertical. As a think-tank without a revenue model, but which has built its reputation on the pillar of independence, the institution could not have accepted such support if it were encumbered or conditional. I am grateful to the above donors for respecting this core value.

Swati D'Souza was consultant to the project. She brought her knowledge of the industry to help refine the details and scope of the project; she was the focal point of contact for liaison with the authors; and she was responsible for managing the multiple administrative and operational issues that inevitably arise in a project involving so many people from so many different locations. This project owes a great deal to her hard work, efficiency, knowledge and commitment. I am most appreciative of her effort and contribution. I thank her for it.

At an early stage of the project, I drew on a number of people for ideas. Vivek Rae, my friend and former Secretary, Petroleum was most generous with his time. He attended all of the initial meetings held to decide the nature and scope of the project. His advice was most helpful. Ajay Sriram, Chairman and Senior Managing Director, DCM Shriram Ltd., also a long-standing and close friend helped me understand better the issues related to gas as a feedstock for fertilisers. The Chairman of NTPC, Gurdeep Singh was forthcoming with his support and agreed to contribute to the project through his colleagues; Dr Nand Singh of the Fertiliser Association of India; D.K. Sarraf, Chairman, Petroleum and Natural Gas Regulatory Board; and Mr R.P. Gupta, at the time the Senior Adviser, Energy, NITI Aayog provided wise counsel and encouragement. I am most grateful to all of them.

In the latter stages of the project, I drew on the support of a number of my colleagues. Zehra Kazmi, the head of Communications for CSEP, provided advice on the design and layout of the volume. More than that, despite the pressures of creating a new website and brand for CSEP, she took on the responsibility of liaising with the authors and the publisher after Swati had left the organization. Her diligence helped me meet the deadlines set by the publisher. In the final stages of this book, Ganesh Sivamani joined me to review and fact check the draft. He too had another full-time job and yet he dived into the project. He must have worked long into the night to correct my errors. He offered excellent suggestions for improving the draft. Rishita Sachdeva who joined CSEP as an intern was assigned to this book for a few weeks. She was most helpful in tying up many loose ends. I thank each of them for their help and support.

Siddhesh Inamdar, our point person at HarperCollins, was consistently supportive. I thank him for overseeing this publication.

Finally, my thanks to Brookings India/CSEP for providing me with a platform. I deem it an honour to be part of an organization that so values independence of thought and quality of result. I cannot hold CSEP responsible for the contents of this book, but my hope is CSEP will appreciate the product.

INDEX

ABOUT THE EDITOR

VIKRAM SINGH MEHTA is the Chairman of the Centre for Social and Economic Progress (formerly Brookings India) in New Delhi. He started his career with the IAS and later worked with a number of energy companies in India and abroad, serving as chairman of the Shell Group of Companies in India from 1994 to 2012. He was the recipient of Asia House's 'Businessman of the Year' Award in 2010 and Asia Centre for Corporate Governance and Sustainability's Award for 'Best Independent Director' in India for 2016. He is on the board of several companies and writes a regular column for the *Financial Express* and *The Indian Express*.